Harden's

London Restaurants 2016

"Gastronomes' bible"
Evening Standard

Survey driven reviews of over 1,600 restaurants

Put us in your client's pocket!

Branded gift books and editions for iPhone
call to discuss the options on 020 7839 4763.

© Harden's Limited 2015

ISBN 978-0-9929408-6-7

British Library Cataloguing-in-Publication data:
a catalogue record for this book is available from
the British Library.

Printed in Italy by Legoprint

Research and editorial assistants: Sarah Ashpole, Clare Burnage, Jamie Cairns, George Reeves, Wayne Tuckfield, Saffy Ellison

Assistant editor: Karen Moss

Harden's Limited
The Brew, Victoria House, 64 Paul Street, London, EC2A 4NA

Would restaurateurs (and PRs) please address communications to 'Editorial' at the above address, or ideally by email to: editorial@hardens.com

The contents of this book are believed correct at the time of printing. Nevertheless, the publisher can accept no responsibility for errors or changes in or omissions from the details given.

No part of this publication may be reproduced or transmitted in any form or by any means, electronically or mechanically, including photocopying, recording or any information storage or retrieval system, without prior permission in writing from the publisher.

CONTENTS

RATINGS & PRICES

Ratings

Our rating system does not tell you – as most guides do – that expensive restaurants are often better than cheap ones! What we do is compare each restaurant's performance – as judged by the average ratings awarded by reporters in the survey – with other similarly-priced restaurants. This approach has the advantage that it helps you find – whatever your budget for any particular meal – where you will get the best 'bang for your buck'.

The following qualities are assessed:

F — Food
S — Service
A — Ambience

The rating indicates that, ***in comparison with other restaurants in the same price-bracket***, performance is...

5 — Exceptional
4 — Very good
3 — Good
2 — Average
1 — Poor

NEW SINCE LAST YEAR!
Regular readers remember we've turned our marking system on its head.
5 is the new 0!

Prices

The price shown for each restaurant is the cost for one (1) person of an average three-course dinner with half a bottle of house wine and coffee, any cover charge, service and VAT. Lunch is often cheaper. With BYO restaurants, we have assumed that two people share a £7 bottle of off-licence wine.

Telephone number – *all numbers are '020' numbers.*

Map reference – *shown immediately after the telephone number.*

Full postcodes – *for non-group restaurants, the first entry in the 'small print' at the end of each listing, so you can set your sat-nav.*

Website and Twitter – *shown in the small print, where applicable.*

Last orders time – *listed after the website (if applicable); Sunday may be up to 90 minutes earlier.*

Opening hours – *unless otherwise stated, restaurants are open for lunch and dinner seven days a week.*

Credit and debit cards – *unless otherwise stated, Mastercard, Visa, Amex and Maestro are accepted.*

Dress – *where appropriate, the management's preferences concerning patrons' dress are given.*

Special menus – *if we know of a particularly good-value set menu we note this (e.g. "set weekday L"), together with its formula price (FP), calculated exactly as in 'Prices' above. Details change, so always check ahead.*

'Rated on Editors' visit' – *indicates ratings have been determined by the Editors personally, based on their visit, rather than derived from the survey.*

SRA Star Rating – *the sustainability index, as calculated by the Sustainable Restaurant Association – see page 8 for more information.*

HOW THIS GUIDE IS WRITTEN

A quarter century of the Harden's survey

This guide is based on our 25th annual survey of what 'ordinary' diners-out think of London's restaurants. In 1998, we extended the survey to cover restaurants across the rest of the UK; it is by far the most detailed annual survey of its type. Out-of-town results are published in our UK guide.

This year, the total number of reporters in our combined London/UK survey, conducted mainly online, exceeded 6,700, and, between them, they contributed over 60,000 individual reports.

How we determine the ratings

In the great majority of cases, ratings are arrived at statistically. This essentially involves 'ranking' the average survey rating each restaurant achieves in the survey – for food, service and ambience – against the average ratings of the other establishments which fall in the same price-bracket.

(This is essentially like football leagues, with the most expensive restaurants going in the top league and the cheaper ones in lower leagues. The restaurant's ranking *within its own particular league* determines its ratings.)

How we write the reviews

The tone of each review and the ratings are largely determined by the ranking of the establishment concerned, which we derive as described above.

At the margin, we may also pay some regard to the proportion of positive nominations (such as for 'favourite restaurant') compared to negative nominations (such as for 'most overpriced').

To explain why a restaurant has been rated as it has, we extract snippets from survey comments ("enclosed in double quotes"). On well-known restaurants, we receive several hundred reports, and a short summary cannot possibly do individual justice to all of them.

What we seek to do – *without any regard to our own personal opinions* – is to illustrate the key themes which have emerged in our analysis of the collective view.

The only exception to this is the newest restaurants, where survey views are either few or non-existent, and where we may be obliged to rely on our own opinion. Unless the review carries the small print note "Rated on Editors' visit", however, the ratings awarded are still our best analysis of the survey view, not our own impression.

We Brits are dining out more than ever before – eating an incredible eight billion meals out. Alongside our passion for food we've developed a thirst for knowledge, about where our food is from and how it's been produced, so that we can enjoy our meal safe in the knowledge that it isn't at the expense of others.

It's easy to make those choices when shopping for food for home; just look for the labels. You can ensure your basket only contains free-range eggs and Fairtrade coffee. But it's not quite so simple when you go out to eat and quizzing the waiter doesn't make for a relaxing night out...

Food Made Good is here to help all food lovers indulge their passion for dining out without having to check their principles in at the cloakroom. Just look for our gold stars on menus, windows and websites. It's the simple and easy way to be reassured that wherever you choose to eat sources its food fabulously, watches its environmental footprint and cares about its local community.

All of the restaurants in the guide with **Food Made Good** stars have completed the sustainability rating in the last 12 months. **Food Made Good** is run by the Sustainable Restaurant Association to give people the chance to turn their passion for food into action.

Sustainability levels:

One Star	***Good***
Two Stars	***Excellent***
Three Stars	***Exceptional***

Sustainable Restaurant Awards 2015

Daylesford | Captain's Galley	*Joint Sustainable Restaurant of the Year*
The Truscott Arms	*Sustainable Pub of the Year*
Lussmanns	*Sustainable Small Group of the Year*
Arbor, The Green House	*Award for Environment*
River Cottage | ODE-dining	*Award for Sourcing.*

To find out more visit **www.foodmadegood.org.**

SURVEY FAQs

Q. How do you find your reporters?

A. Anyone can take part. Simply register at www.hardens.com. Actually, we find that many people who complete our survey each year have taken part before. So it's really more a question of a very large and ever-evolving panel, or jury, than a random 'poll'.

Q. Wouldn't a random sample be better?

A. That's really a theoretical question, as there is no obvious way, still less a cost-efficient one, by which one could identify a random sample of the guests at each of, say, 5,000 establishments across the UK, and get them to take part in any sort of survey. And anyway, which is likely to be more useful: a sample of the views of everyone who's been to a particular place, or the views of people who are interested enough in eating-out to have volunteered their feedback?

Q. What sort of people take part?

A. A roughly 60/40 male/female split, from all adult age-groups. As you might expect – as eating out is not the cheapest activity – reporters tend to have white collar jobs (some at very senior levels). By no means, however, is that always the case.

Q. Do people ever try to stuff the ballot?

A. Of course they do! A rising number of efforts are weeded out every year. But stuffing the ballot is not as trivial a task as some people seem to think: the survey results throw up clear natural voting patterns against which 'campaigns' tend to stand out.

Q. Aren't inspections the best way to run a guide?

A. It is often assumed – even by commentators who ought to know better – that inspections are some sort of 'gold standard'. There is no doubt that the inspection model clearly has potential strengths, but one of its prime weaknesses is that it is incredibly expensive. Take the most famous practitioner of the 'inspection model', Michelin. It doesn't claim to visit each and every entry listed in its guide annually. Even once! And who are the inspectors? Often they are catering professionals, whose likes and dislikes may be very different from the establishment's natural customer base. On any restaurant of note, however, Harden's typically has somewhere between dozens and hundreds of reports each and every year from exactly the type of people the restaurant relies upon to stay in business. We believe that such feedback, carefully analysed, is far more revealing and accurate than an occasional 'professional' inspection.

SURVEY MOST MENTIONED

These are the restaurants which were most frequently mentioned by reporters. (Last year's position is given in brackets.) An asterisk* indicates the first appearance in the list of a recently opened restaurant.

1 J Sheekey (1)
2 Clos Maggiore (4)
3 Le Gavroche (3)
4 The Ledbury (5)
5 Chez Bruce (7)
6 Scott's (2)
7 Gymkhana (12)
8 The Delaunay (6)
9 Fera at Claridge's (-)
10 The Wolseley (10)

11 Brasserie Zédel (11)
12 Dinner (9)
13 The Cinnamon Club (13)
14 Pollen Street Social (8)
15 Galvin La Chapelle (14)
16 La Trompette (19)
17 The Square (15)
18 The River Café (17)
19 La Poule au Pot (22)
20= Gordon Ramsay (33)

20= The Chiltern Firehouse (-)
22 Gauthier Soho (28)
23 Le Caprice (30)
24 The Palomar (-)
25 Pied à Terre (20)
26= Benares (24)
26= Galvin Bistrot de Luxe (26)
28 Medlar (21)
29 Amaya (40)
30 Zuma (32)

31 Bleeding Heart Restaurant (16)
32 Marcus (22)
33 Andrew Edmunds (35)
34 City Social (-)
35= Moro (-)
35= Bar Boulud (-)
37 Grain Store (30)
38= Spring (-)
38= Terroirs (38)
40 Zucca (27)

SURVEY NOMINATIONS

Top gastronomic experience

1 Le Gavroche (2)
2 The Ledbury (1)
3 Chez Bruce (4)
4 Fera at Claridge's (-)
5 Dinner (3)
6 Gordon Ramsay (7)
7 Pied à Terre (6)
8 Pollen Street Social (5)
9 Story (-)
10 Hedone (-)

Favourite

1 Chez Bruce (1)
2 Clos Maggiore (3)
3 The Wolseley (10)
4 Le Gavroche (5)
5 J Sheekey (2)
6 Gauthier Soho (-)
7 Le Caprice (8)
8 La Trompette (-)
9 The Ledbury (4)
10 Moro (-)

Best for business

1 The Wolseley (1)
2 The Delaunay (2)
3 The Square (3)
4 City Social (-)
5 Galvin La Chapelle (4)
6 L'Anima (9)
7 Coq d'Argent (7)
8 The Don (6)
9 Scott's (8)
10 Bleeding Heart Restaurant (5)

Best for romance

1 Clos Maggiore (1)
2 La Poule au Pot (2)
3 Andrew Edmunds (3)
4 Bleeding Heart Restaurant (4)
5 Chez Bruce (6)
6 Le Gavroche (5)
7 Galvin La Chapelle (8)
8 Fera at Claridge's (-)
9 Le Caprice (-)
10 Gauthier Soho (10))

Best breakfast/brunch

1 The Wolseley (1)
2 The Delaunay (2)
3 Duck & Waffle (3)
4 Riding House Café (4)
5 Roast (5)
6 The Grazing Goat (-)
7 Cecconi's (7)
8 Colbert (6)
9 Dean Street Townhouse (-)
10 Balthazar (10)

Best bar/pub food

1 The Anchor & Hope (1)
2 Harwood Arms (3)
3 Bull & Last (2)
4 The Ladbroke Arms (7)
5 The Jugged Hare (4)
6 The Truscott Arms (9)
7 Princess Victoria (-)
8 Pig & Butcher (8)
9 The Camberwell Arms (-)
10 The Eagle (-)

Most disappointing cooking

1 The Chiltern Firehouse (-)
2 Oxo Tower (Rest') (1)
3 Pollen Street Social (-)
4 Colbert (3)
5 Grain Store (-)
6 Dinner (2)
7 Gordon Ramsay (5)
8 Alain Ducasse at The Dorchester (9)
9 Dabbous (10)
10 The Wolseley (-)

Most overpriced restaurant

1 The River Café (1)
2 Oxo Tower (Rest') (2)
3 The Chiltern Firehouse (-)
4 Dinner (3)
5 Gordon Ramsay (4)
6 Marcus (5)
7 Alain Ducasse at The Dorchester (6)
8 Pollen Street Social (10)
9 Aqua Shard (-)
10 Savoy Grill (-)

SURVEY HIGHEST RATINGS

FOOD		SERVICE	
£95+			
1	The Ledbury	1	Pied à Terre
2	Story	2	Le Gavroche
3	One-O-One	3	Marianne
4	Pied à Terre	4	The Ledbury
5	Le Gavroche	5	Fera at Claridge's
£70-£94			
1	The Five Fields	1	The Five Fields
2	Yashin	2	The Goring Hotel
3	HKK	3	Alyn Williams
4	Ametsa	4	Koffmann's
5	Hunan	5	L'Autre Pied
£54-£69			
1	Sushi Tetsu	1	Sushi Tetsu
2	Dinings	2	Chez Bruce
3	Chez Bruce	3	Trinity
4	Gauthier Soho	4	Bellamy's
5	Trinity	5	Gauthier Soho
£40-£54			
1	Sushi-Say	1	Caraffini
2	Babur	2	Quantus
3	José	3	Il Portico
4	Jin Kichi	4	Yming
5	Honey & Co	5	Roots at N1
£39 or less			
1	Bao	1	Paradise Hampstead
2	Silk Road	2	Carob Tree
3	Ragam	3	Andina
4	Santa Maria	4	Meza SW17
5	A Wong	5	Golden Hind

SURVEY HIGHEST RATINGS

	AMBIENCE		OVERALL
1	Sketch (Lecture Rm)	1	The Ledbury
2	The Ritz Restaurant	2	Le Gavroche
3	The Ledbury	3	Marianne
4	Le Gavroche	4	Pied à Terre
5	The Greenhouse	5	Kitchen Table at Bubbledogs

1	Min Jiang	1	The Five Fields
2	The Goring Hotel	2	The Goring Hotel
3	Galvin La Chapelle	3	J Sheekey
4	City Social	4	Scott's
5	Sushisamba	5	Launceston Place

1	Clos Maggiore	1	Sushi Tetsu
2	La Poule au Pot	2	Chez Bruce
3	Wallace	3	Clos Maggiore
4	Bob Bob Ricard	4	Trinity
5	The Grazing Goat	5	The Grazing Goat

1	Andrew Edmunds	1	José
2	Brasserie Zédel	2	Babur
3	Tate Britain (Rex Whistler)	3	Andrew Edmunds
4	José	4	Roots at N1
5	Shampers	5	Il Portico

1	Churchill Arms	1	Andina
2	Andina	2	Carob Tree
3	The Eagle	3	Paradise Hampstead
4	Blanchette	4	Blanchette
5	Princi	5	Bao

SURVEY BEST BY CUISINE

These are the restaurants which received the best average food ratings (excluding establishments with a small or notably local following).

Where the most common types of cuisine are concerned, we present the results in two price-brackets. For less common cuisines, we list the top three, regardless of price.

For further information about restaurants which are particularly notable for their food, see the cuisine lists starting on page 244. These indicate, using an asterisk*, restaurants which offer exceptional or very good food.

British, Modern

£55 and over		Under £55	
1	The Ledbury	1	The Dairy
2	The Five Fields	2	Rabbit
3	Story	3	Shoe Shop
4	Marianne	4	Lamberts
5	The Clove Club	5	The Ladbroke Arms

French

£55 and over		Under £55	
1	Le Gavroche	1	Brawn
2	Pied à Terre	2	Casse-Croute
3	Hibiscus	3	Blanchette
4	Gauthier Soho	4	Charlotte's W4
5	Koffmann's	5	Cigalon

Italian/Mediterranean

£55 and over		Under £55	
1	Bocca di Lupo	1	L'Amorosa
2	L'Anima	2	Querce
3	The River Café	3	Pentolina
4	Zucca	4	Bibo
5	Enoteca Turi	5	Café Murano

Indian & Pakistani

£55 and over		Under £55	
1	Amaya	1	Babur
2	Gymkhana	2	Ragam
3	Rasoi	3	Roots at N1
4	Trishna	4	Tayyabs
5	Cinnamon Kitchen	5	Ganapati

Chinese

£55 and over

1 HKK
2 Yauatcha W1
3 Hunan
4 Hakkasan W1
5 Min Jiang

Under £55

1 Silk Road
2 A Wong
3 Pearl Liang
4 Barshu
5 Taiwan Village

Japanese

£55 and over

1 The Araki
2 Sushi Tetsu
3 Dinings
4 Yashin
5 Zuma

Under £55

1 Sushi-Say
2 Kanada-Ya
3 Tsunami
4 Pham Sushi
5 Jin Kichi

British, Traditional

1 St John
2 Scott's
3 St John Bread & Wine

Vegetarian

1 Gate W6
2 Vanilla Black
3 Ethos

Burgers, etc

1 Patty & Bun
2 Honest Burgers
3 Bleecker St Burger

Pizza

1 Homeslice
2 Franco Manca
3 Oak W11

Fish & Chips

1 Nautilus
2 Golden Hind
3 Toff's

Thai

1 Sukho Fine Thai Cuisine
2 Addie's Thai Café
3 Isarn

Steaks & Grills

1 Rib Room
2 Goodman
3 Flat Iron

Fish & Seafood

1 One-O-One
2 J Sheekey
3 Bentley's

Fusion

1 Bubbledogs (Kitchen T)
2 E&O
3 Eight Over Eight

Spanish

1 José
2 Ametsa
3 Moro

Turkish

1 Fez Mangal
2 Mangal 1
3 Best Mangal

Lebanese

1 Meza Trinity Road
2 Chez Abir
3 Fairuz

TOP SPECIAL DEALS

The following menus allow you to eat in the restaurants concerned at a significant discount when compared to their evening à la carte prices.

The prices used are calculated in accordance with our usual formula (i.e. three courses with house wine, coffee and tip).

Special menus are by their nature susceptible to change – please check that they are still available.

Weekday lunch

£85+ Alain Ducasse at The Dorchester
Le Gavroche

£80+ Gordon Ramsay
The Ledbury
Marcus

£70+ Hedone

£65+ Fera at Claridge's
Pétrus
Rib Room
Roux at the Landau
Sketch (Lecture Rm)
The Square

£60+ The Clove Club
Dorchester Grill
Pied à Terre
Pollen Street Social
Story

£55+ Alyn Williams
L'Atelier de Joel Robuchon
Dabbous
Galvin at Windows
Hibiscus
Hunan
Launceston Place
Massimo
Murano
Nobu
Nobu Berkeley
Novikov (Asian restaurant)
One-O-One
Oxo Tower (Rest')
Rasoi
Savoy Grill
Seven Park Place
Theo Randall

£50+ Babbo
China Tang
Gilbert Scott
The Glasshouse
Koffmann's
Medlar
Orrery
Outlaw's Seafood and Grill
Oxo Tower (Brass')
Quilon
J Sheekey
J Sheekey Oyster Bar
Skylon
Social Eating House
Sotheby's Café
Spring
Texture
La Trompette
Typing Room
Zafferano

£45+ The Cavendish
Daphne's
Harwood Arms
The Ivy
Kensington Place
Little Social
Otto's
Plateau
La Poule au Pot
Quaglino's
Sumosan
Tamarind
Trinity

£40+ The Abingdon
Amaya
The Bingham
The Dysart Petersham
L'Etranger
Galvin Bistrot de Luxe
Garnier
Kitchen W8
Lima
Plum + Spilt Milk
Quirinale
Quo Vadis
Rivea
The Terrace
Le Vacherin
Vasco & Piero's Pavilion

£35+ Bistro Aix
Café des Amis
Cecconi's
Il Convivio
The Enterprise
Essenza
Frederick's
The Ivy Market Grill
Lucio
Magdalen
Merchants Tavern
Quattro Passi
Red Fort
Royal Exchange Grand Café
Sartoria
Sukho Fine Thai Cuisine
Sushi Tetsu
Tredwell's
Trishna

Twist At Crawford
Village East
The White Onion

£30+ The Anchor & Hope
Bistrò by Shot
The Brackenbury
Chapters
Eelbrook
Hereford Road
Joe Allen
Linnea
Market
Mazi
Mele e Pere
Mon Plaisir
Suksan
The Tommy Tucker

£25+ Alquimia
La Bodega Negra
Cornish Tiger
Ishtar
Lemonia
The Lucky Pig Fulham
The Orange Tree
Trangallan
The Wet Fish Café

£20+ Cellar Gascon
Gem
Le Sacré-Coeur
Yming

£15+ Kolossi Grill
Olympus Fish
Sichuan Folk
Two Brothers
Yoshi Sushi

Pre/post-theatre (and early evening)

£60+ Pied à Terre

£55+ L'Atelier de Joel Robuchon
The Goring Hotel
The Northall
Savoy Grill
Skylon

£50+ Asia de Cuba
Bentley's
Gilbert Scott
Koffmann's
Oxo Tower (Brass')
Spring

£45+ Green's
The Ivy
Yashin Ocean House

£40+ Boulestin
Chiswell Street Dining Rms
Christopher's
The Keeper's House
Kitchen W8
Kopapa
The Swan at the Globe
Le Vacherin

£35+ Bistro Aix
Dean Street Townhouse
Gay Hussar
One Canada Square
Quo Vadis
Red Fort
Tredwell's
Trishna

£30+ Mon Plaisir

£20+ Yming

Sunday lunch

£70+ Dorchester Grill
Galvin at Windows

£65+ The Goring Hotel

£60+ Launceston Place
Roast

£55+ Bibendum
Medlar
Orrery
Petersham Hotel
Skylon
Trinity

£50+ Galvin La Chapelle
The Glasshouse
Kitchen W8
Le Pont de la Tour
Tate Britain
La Trompette
Veeraswamy
Wild Honey

£45+ Dean Street Townhouse

£40+ Brawn
Café Bohème
Charlotte's Place
Merchants Tavern
Sonny's Kitchen
Le Vacherin

£35+ Bradley's
Brasserie Gustave

£30+ Grumbles

THE RESTAURANT SCENE

Off-the-charts good

This year we list a record 179 newcomers – the largest ever in the 25-year history of the guide, easily overtaking the pre-crash level of 158 seen in 2008.

Closings – up a tad on last year – remain relatively low at 56: a very similar level to that seen for the last three years.

Combining the two factors, the level of net openings this year (openings minus closings) has again set a new peak: at 123, the figure comfortably exceeds last year's total – itself a record – of 101.

It is tempting to think that this is the 'new normal'. But the ratio of openings to closings remains at incredibly strong, 'bull market' levels – at 3.2:1, only one year (1996) has been higher since we started keeping this score, and only five of the last 25 years have exceeded a rate of 2.4:1.

It is tempting to prognosticate a downwards turning point based on these figures. For how much longer can London continue to boom?. But with the continued, seemingly unstoppable growth of the capital unsurprisingly comes the demand for more grub!

We are also, by the year, very aware of the much greater ease of collecting this information. Until recent times, this guide might be the only media coverage many outlying neighbourhood restaurants would receive in a year. But now every detail of every eatery is recorded in such micro-detail by review sites, blogs, social media (not to mention the big data vendors tracking mobile phone movements), that almost certainly to some degree the guide is noting more restaurants than once it did simply because it is so much easier to "clock" them as they arrive.

Still, it is hard to escape the feeling that the London restaurant scene is on the most massive roll, akin to some new form of life created by a mad (or inspired!) out-of-control scientist in a SciFi B movie. Every day the email in-box brings news of some new hybrid cuisine, some new specialist, or the rapid roll out of an existing concept.

With such vitality, however, comes a dilemma. Restaurants which once would have seemed outstanding nowadays seem commonplace. The bar is higher and higher, the challenge to stand out from the crowd tougher and tougher.

Every year, we choose what to us seem to be the most significant openings of the year. This year, our selection is as follows:

The Araki
Bonhams
Ivy Chelsea Garden
Paradise Garage
Smith & Wollenskys
Bao
Duck & Rice
Kitty Fisher's
Portland
Smoking Goat

Turning Japanese?

If there has been one constant trend in the last 25 years, it has been the enduring popularity of Italian cuisine. And it is rather uninteresting to report that this trend continues uninterrupted this year, accounting for about 10% of newcomers.

More eye-catching is the continuing rise-and-rise of Japanese cuisine, which was the classification for practically as many newcomers as Italians this year. It's a phenomenon that's easily overlooked, perhaps because of the quiet cultural style of Nipponese imports.

Americanisation is another significant trend, but its significance may be over-stated because US-inspired brands and imports generally shout so loud about what they have to offer! No doubting, however, that the US-style craze for steaks, BBQs and other meatylicious fare continues unabated. Millennials, it seems, prefer munching burgers to saving the planet…

The other most popular cuisines this year were Spanish concepts, and 'fusion' – our catch-all for a multitude of novel ideas.

London's restaurant compass continues to shift, drawn by the new magnetic poles of Shoreditch, Hackney and Haggerston. Although central London is still where we record most new openings, it is now closely followed by East London, and then South London, in terms of popularity for new sites. West London accounted for exactly half the openings out East this year, transforming the situation that prevailed when we started the guide (in which we recorded just six restaurants in an "E" postcode).

West London activity still exceeds that of North London however, which – despite the odd sign of life – still maintains a surprisingly tame restaurant scene.

If London is following Tokyo's path at all, it is perhaps evident in two areas. One (incredibly welcome) trend is restaurant-goers' increasing focus on the quality of ingredients. Another is the focus on restaurants pursuing a single activity or dish. So this year, we've seen newcomers focussed solely on egg dishes, porridge, cheese toasties… even now just chips!

Prices

The average price of dinner for one at establishments listed in this guide is £50.51 (compared to £49.46 last year). Prices have risen by 2.1% in the past 12 months: a lower rate than in the preceding 12 months. While this continues a downward trend also evident last year, this rate significantly exceeds the current very low rate of inflation (effectively zero). Thus this year's real level of restaurant price rises is higher than last year's (which broadly tracked inflation).

OPENINGS AND CLOSURES

Openings (179)

Amaru
Anima e Cuore
The Araki
Babaji Pide
Bad Egg
Balls & Company
Bandol
Bao
Bar Termini
Barbecoa WI
Barrafina WC2
Beer and Buns
Bellanger
Berber & Q
Bird N7
Bistrò by Shot
Blacklock
Bleecker Street Burger
Blixen
Bó Drake
Bone Daddies W8, ECI
Bonhams Restaurant
Boom Burger SW9
Botanist EC2
Bouillabaisse
Café Murano WC2
Carousel
Casa Cruz
Cau SE3, SW19, EI
The Cavendish
Ceru
Ceviche Old St
Charlotte's W5
Chez Antoinette
Chick 'n' Sours
Chicken Town
Chifafa
Chiswick Smokehouse
Counter
Craft London
Crosstown Doughnuts
The Culpepper
Darwin Brasserie
Delancey & Co.
DF/Mexico WI
Dip & Flip SW19
The Duck & Rice
Dumplings' Legend
Ellory
Engawa
Enoteca Rabezzana
Ethos
Fields
Flat Iron WC2
Flat Three
Flotsam and Jetsam
Foxlow N16
45 Jermyn St
Friends of Ours
Gatti's EC2
German Gymnasium
Gourmets des Ternes SWI
The Greek Larder
The Green Room
Gremio de Brixton
Habanera
Hood
Hoppers
Homeslice WI
House of Ho WI
House Restaurant
Hungry Donkey
Iddu
Ippudo London E14
The Italian Job
The Ivy Café
The Ivy Chelsea Garden
The Ivy Kensington Brasserie
The Ivy Market Grill
Jago
Jar Kitchen
Jinjuu
John Doe
Joint Marylebone WI
Jones & Sons
José Pizarro
K10 EC3
Kanada-Ya SWI
Kateh Knightsbridge SWI
Kitchen
Kitty Fisher's
Kricket
Kurobuta Harvey Nics SWI
Lantana Café NWI
Lardo Bebè E8
The Lucky Pig Fulham
Luppolo
Lurra

Openings (continued)

M Restaurant Victoria Street
Mamma Dough SE23, SW9
The Marksman
Masala Grill
Max's Sandwich Shop
Mayfair Pizza Company
maze Grill SW10
The Melt Room
Meza SW17
Mission
Modern Pantry EC2
MOMMI
Morada Brindisa Asador
Morden & Lea
Morelli's Gelato
Murakami
Naughty Piglets
Oka
Old Tom & English
Oldroyd
On The Bab W1, WC2
One Sixty Smokehouse E1
Les 110 de Taillevent
Paradise Garage
Patron
Pedler
Pennethorne's Cafe Bar
Percy & Founders
The Petite Coree
Piquet
Portland
Pulia
Queenswood
The Refinery
Resident of Paradise Row
Restaurant de Paul EC2
The Richmond
Ristorante Frescobaldi
Rox Burger
Sackville's
Salmontini
The Salon
Le Salon Privé
Salt & Honey
Salvation In Noodles N4
Señor Ceviche
Sesame
Sexy Fish
Shackfuyu
Shake Shack WC1, E20
Shikumen
Shoe Shop
Shotgun
Smith & Wollensky
Smoking Goat
Snaps & Rye
Social Wine & Tapas
Som Saa
Sosharu
Taberna Do Mercado
Tem Tép
The Tommy Tucker
Tonic & Remedy
Tonkotsu E8
The Truscott Cellar
Tulse Hill Hotel
Twist At Crawford
Verdi's
Vico
Villa Di Geggiano
Vintage Salt EC2
West Thirty Six
The White Onion
Wimsey's
The Woodstock
Workshop Coffee W1, EC1
Wormwood
Yama Momo
Yasmeen
Yauatcha City

Closures (56)

Alloro
Assaggi
Bam-Bou
Bistrot Bruno Loubet
Bouchée
Brula
Cadogan Arms
Café Anglais
Café des Amis
Cantina Vinopolis
Chabrot Bistrot d'Amis
Criterion
Deuxième
Entrée
Ergon
Eriki
Fino
Fitou's Thai Restaurant
Food for Thought
Fountain
Foxtrot Oscar
GB Pizza
Gilak
Green Man & French Horn
Hole in the Wall
Juniper Dining
Kentish Canteen
Koya
Lawn Bistro
LMNT
Marani
Made in Italy W1
New Angel
New Tom's
Noodle House
One Kensington
Orchard
Ozer
Pavilion
Penkul & Banks
Portal
Racine
Sakura
Sam's Brasserie
1701
64 Degrees
Shiori
Shrimpy's
Solly's
T.E.D
Trois Garçons
21 Bateman Street
Union Café
Upstairs
Whits
Wishbone

25 YEARS – WHAT'S CHANGED?

Most industries change a fair amount in 25 years, and pundits talk up the "step changes" they observe. But even the most ardent cynic would agree that the restaurant industry today has risen to new heights in the last quarter-century.

In the early '90s, the joke went that in heaven, the lovers were Italian, the chefs French, the mechanics German, and the police British. In hell, the police were Italian, the mechanics French, the lovers German, and guess which nationality the chefs were…

Twenty five years ago:

• it was taken as read that the UK was in the culinary Dark Ages, especially by visiting Americans.

• the idea that our TV chefs would be household names in France and the US would have been hilarious.

• the experience of half-decent food in a pub was a rarity, and pretty disgusting fare the norm.

• an interest in eating out, food and wine was seen as middle-aged and fuddy-duddy.

• MasterChef (first episode July 2, 1990) was scarcely a year old, and the idea that kids would take interest in Junior MasterChef would have seemed pie-in-the-sky.

So what changed?

The new rock 'n' roll

When we started our guide in 1991, one of the biggest objections to a new title from bookshop buyers was that eating out was too highbrow ("only for posh bastards").

The chef oft-cited with changing all that, Marco Pierre White, featured in our first guide as head chef at Harvey's in Wandsworth. His cookbook, White Heat, had just been published, and – on its re-release this year to celebrate its 25th anniversary – was described in a recent *Caterer & Hotelkeeper* as "the book that showed, warts and all, that the kitchen was a cool place to be".

It was MPW's PR man of that time, Alan Crompton-Batt, who is sometimes credited with having observed that cooking was "the new rock 'n' roll". Perhaps he should have known, as he was an ex-music-promoter himself (for the late '70s band, The Pyschedelic Furs). With another of his clients, Nico Ladenis (then with three Michelin stars) the cultivation of the 'bad boy' chef had begun (although we had to wait a few more years for all the effing).

The launch of other new restaurants, however, played just as significant a role in popularising the idea that eating out is for all. In early 1993, Sir Terence Conran moved into restaurants bringing all the money and expertise he'd acquired in running his huge retail empire, Storehouse plc.

With the opening of Quaglino's, with its Q-shaped ashtrays and cigarette girl (now there's something else you wouldn't see nowadays) Sir Tel spun a compelling narrative of bringing the *fraternité* of Parisian brasseries to London.

More-or-less simultaneously, Planet Hollywood launched scarcely five minutes' walk away, with Arnold Schwarzenegger, Sylvester Stallone and Bruce Willis at the opening. The two debuts in short succession channelled a previously unknown amount of professionalism, capital and hype to catalyse a major shift towards democratising the idea of eating out, particularly in the London media.

Chefs trade 'the stainless steel box' for TV

By the late '90s, the Harden's office started to field fairly regular calls from TV production companies. It wasn't us they wanted to make famous, unfortunately. The question they wanted answered: "Do you know any chefs who you think would make good TV? To be honest it doesn't really matter if they can cook – what we need is a big personality: somebody who looks good on camera."

With Gordon Ramsay, the first London restaurant chef to become a global TV personality, the producers sure got that (and also someone who could cook). The rise of the Ramsay phenomenon globally was a terrific emblem of the newly discovered, insatiable desire for food-led programming.

All the glamour transformed middle-class attitudes to the kitchen. Tom Jaine, editor of the *Good Food Guide* 25 years ago, commented in a November 2014 interview for *Radio 4's Food Programme* that, in those days "respectable was owning not doing." He went on to draw the contrast with today, where many recipients of an expensive education from the country's top schools are drawn to a vocational path that a generation ago was on no-one's radar.

A proper food culture

Hand-in-hand with a growing interest in chefs has come a growing interest in, and respect for, ingredients and cooking.

The now-ubiquitous (then largely unknown) interest in local sourcing is part of a much foodier interest in food, that has helped spawn many more creative eating formats. Twenty five years ago, the 2-course or 3-course meal was the staple of the trade. Nowadays, the expectation has shifted completely, and it is de rigeur that anywhere with ambition will focus on tapas, sharing plates and tasting menus.

From glam to gastropubs

Away from the glamour of the TV studios, some more prosaic changes were about to transform eating out.

In 1989, the Secretary of State for Trade and Industry passed The Beer Orders. In terms of succeeding in their aims – which was to drive down the price of beer – the legislation was an abject flop. But by restricting the number of tied pubs, a new tidal wave of entrepreneurialism flourished in the pub industry which continues to this day.

Other factors have also significantly changed access by the trade to prime sites. Twenty five years ago, the City of London and top landlords thought restaurants were non-U and prevented them opening. Nowadays, any new development works hard to secure a name chef to PR.

Demographics of dining out

Five years prior to the launch of this guide, in 1986, London hit its lowest population level in the 20th Century at 6.8m. Fast forward to this year, and London's population hit a new peak, breaking through its previous 1939 high of 8.6m. That's growth of a quarter in just over a quarter of a century, and all those people need feeding.

But it's not just more people who have inspired more restaurants. The people themselves are going out more. In part that's because London is richer than it was 25 years ago, but also it's because its residents have changed.

Mass immigration has driven down the average age of Londoners, and provided lots of willing customers (as well as motivated, skilled manpower for restaurants).

And then there's the change in our nesting habits over the last quarter century. When we started our guide, the average age of UK women when they first gave birth was under 27. Nowadays it's over 30, and in London older still. In parallel, the average age for purchasing a first home for 'Generation Rent' has gone up from mid-20s to early-30s. All that energy and disposable income that would have been soaked up by nesting in an earlier generation, nowadays is available for gadding about the town for a few years more.

Private what?

The shake-up of gastropubs detailed above was largely driven by a growing industry with a new name at that time unknown to most people outside of the City: Private Equity.

The Punch Taverns deal – part of the sell-off by the brewers of the pubs – was one of the first to start to whet the appetite of the investment trade for the restaurant business.

For a trade that historically has generally been funded from savings, friends-and-family and business 'angels', the arrival of serious money on the scene nowadays provides the prospect of a bonanza exit for anyone with a hot idea apt for a 'roll out'. This promise is reflected today in the never-ending stream of new ventures – from pop-ups to proto-chains – with slick graphic design and a lucrative end in mind.

Tweet, tweet, tweet... pop!

Restaurateurs are natural self-promoters, and have taken to social media like a duck to water.

And for first-time restaurateurs, the arrival of Twitter and Facebook has helped overcome one of the biggest hurdles to them entering the business – premises. With the ability to advertise a stall, a house party, or a residency in some crumbling quarter of the East End, this prime barrier to entry has been significantly lowered.

The explosion of the technology has further boosted the emergence of younger diners at the heart of the most fashionable eating out trends. Twenty and 30-somethings by and large own the street food phenomenon further overturning all the old stereotypes about discernment about food being a fogey-ish concern.

And then there was one...

As well as changes in the restaurant trade, the lifetime of this guide has also seen more change in the publishing industry than in most of its 500-year history.

The rise of digital has been particularly disruptive to publishers of local information, and restaurant guides are no exception. Although there is some satisfaction in being the 'last man still standing', it is sobering (for us anyway!) that this publication is now the only annual guide dedicated exclusively to London restaurants still widely sold in bookshops, when in recent memory our competitors included *Time Out*, *Zagat*, and *Rough Guides* (and going further back, *Nicholson* and *The Evening Standard*).

Google, Yelp! and TripAdvisor have all targeted the local listings business, and, when it comes to "share of eyeballs", dominate the market nowadays. User Generated Reviews are now a common currency of the internet, and have revolutionised the way consumers learn about even the most humble of products, not just restaurants.

However, we like to think – and our readers and website users seem to agree – that Harden's has long been part of that progress, and there is still a lot of value in the carefully curated user feedback that has always been at the heart of the Harden's survey.

Anyone can contribute a review to the survey, and feed it into the mix. We look carefully for cheats, and we throw out many bogus reports. We follow restaurants carefully year-on-year and watch for patterns. We know the market in depth, and provide a critical overview and summary, rather than a lucky dip of random commentary. Supporters still find the system produces a handy, pithy, objective perspective to help them get the best bang for their buck.

Please help us in our endeavours by signing up to, and participating in, the survey at **www.hardens.com**. With your help, perhaps we can report to you all the changes that we see take place over the next 25 years…

DIRECTORY

Comments in "double quotation marks" were made by reporters.

Establishments which we judge to be particularly notable have their NAME IN CAPITALS.

A Cena TW1 **£50** 4 4 4

418 Richmond Rd 8288 0108 1–4A

St Margaret's locals are mightily satisfied with this neighbourhood Italian, just south of Richmond Bridge – "the interesting food is of high quality", the wine is "very good", and staff are "absolutely charming". / TW1 2EB; www.acena.co.uk; @acenarestaurant; 10 pm; closed Mon L & Sun D; booking: max 6, Fri & Sat.

A Wong SW1 **£35** 5 4 3

70-71 Wilton Rd 7828 8931 2–4B

"Beats Chinatown any day!"; "stunningly good" cooking (not least "fabulous dim sum") and "helpful, non-hassling" service have helped win a huge fan club for this canteen-style Chinese two-year-old – "part of Pimlico's improving food scene". / SW1 1DE; www.awong.co.uk; @awongSW1; 10.15 pm; closed Mon L & Sun.

Abbeville Kitchen SW4 **£52** 3 3 3

47 Abbeville Rd 8772 1110 10–2D

"It never disappoints", say local fans of this "noisy and bustling" Clapham "gem"; its "interesting" menu incorporates "great sharing plates" – "nothing earthshaking but sound and consistent cooking". / SW4 9JX; www.abbevillekitchen.com; @abbevillek; 10.30 pm, Sun 9.30 pm; Mon-Thu D only, Fri-Sun open L & D.

Abeno **£42** 3 4 1

47 Museum St, WC1 7405 3211 2–1C

17-18 Great Newport St, WC2 7379 1160 4–3B

Okonomi-yaki (fancy Japanese omelettes "cooked in front of you") is "good fun", and "done well" at these "comfy" but rather "tired-looking" West End fixtures. / www.abeno.co.uk; 10 pm - 11 pm; no Amex; WC2 no booking.

Abi Ruchi N16 **£28** 4 4 2

42 Stoke Newington Church St 7923 4564 1–1C

Even on Stoke Newington's Church Street, an area not short of choice for good Indian cuisine, this family-run Keralan shines thanks to "warm and friendly staff", "authentic thalis" and "great prices" – "it deserves to be much better known". / N16 0LU; www.abiruchi.com; 11 pm, Fri & Sat 11.30 pm, Sun 10 pm.

The Abingdon W8 **£63** 3 4 4

54 Abingdon Rd 7937 3339 5–2A

"Top end gastropub" in the chichi backstreets of Kensington, which combines "a well-run bar" with a comfy, "buzzing" dining room (the best seats are in booths); it's "a bit pricey" but has been a "dependable local" for over 20 years. / W8 6AP; www.theabingdon.co.uk; 10.30 pm, Fri & Sat 11 pm, Sun 10 pm; set weekday L £42 (FP).

About Thyme SW1 **£51** 3 4 4

82 Wilton Rd 7821 7504 2–4B

"Delighting locals and those from further afield" – a stalwart local in west Pimlico, lauded for its "unusual cuisine" ("Spanish with a twist") and in particular for staff who are "polite, solicitous, but not over-bearing"; if there's a quibble it's that the odd dish "lacks oomph". / SW1V 1DL; www.aboutthyme.co.uk; 10.30 pm; closed Sun.

L'Absinthe NW1 £46 2 3 3
40 Chalcot Rd 7483 4848 8–3B
"The owner JC makes the place!" – even if "better food can be found elsewhere", his "warmth of welcome at all times" ensures this Primrose Hill corner bistro is "always crowded". / NW1 8LS; www.labsinthe.co.uk; @absinthe07jc; 10 pm; closed Mon, Tue L, Wed L & Thu L.

Abu Zaad W12 £23 3 3 2
29 Uxbridge Rd 8749 5107 7–1C
Near the top of Shepherd's Bush Market, a "hospitable" Syrian café, serving "appealing and filling" mezze and kebabs at "fantastic" prices; no alcohol, but "lovely fresh juices" and "nice complimentary extras like tea and baklava". / W12 8LH; www.abuzaad.co.uk; @abuzaaduk; 11 pm; no Amex.

Adam Handling at Caxton
Caxton Grill SW1 £74 3 3 2
2 Caxton St 7227 7773 2–4C
Is it "a bad case of MasterChef-itis"? – some "tortured" or "pretentious" dishes disappoint quite a few reporters at Adam Handling's "very hotel-like" dining room, tucked away in Westminster. A majority, though, say his ambitious cuisine can be "really outstanding", service is "eager" and – in this thin area – it's still "a good addition". / SW1H 0QW; www.caxtongrill.co.uk/caxton/adam-handling; @AH_Caxton; 10.30 pm.

Adams Café W12 £32 3 5 3
77 Askew Rd 8743 0572 7–1B
"A stunning little traditional Shepherd's Bush caff that turns North African at night"; "friendly management" create "a really local feel" and its "great tagines" make it a firm cheap 'n' cheerful favourite. Licensed nowadays, but you can still BYO (wine only), at £4 corkage. / W12 9AH; www.adamscafe.co.uk; 10 pm; closed Sun.

Addie's Thai Café SW5 £34 4 4 2
121 Earl's Court Rd 7259 2620 5–2A
"Dishes taste as if they were fresh off the streets of Bangkok", at this "fantastic, cheap 'n' cheerful" café, which is "worth a detour" to the "insalubrious environs, at the top of Earl's Court Road". / SW5 9RL; www.addiesthai.co.uk; 11 pm, Sun 10.30 pm; no Amex.

The Admiral Codrington SW3 £50 2 2 4
17 Mossop St 7581 0005 5–2C
Long one of Chelsea's more popular watering holes – an animated backstreet boozer that "still feels like a pub", and serves "decent" nosh in its sizeable dining room (with a roof that retracts in summer). / SW3 2LY; www.theadmiralcodrington.co.uk; @TheAdCod; 10 pm, Thu-Sat 11 pm, Sun 9.30 pm.

Afghan Kitchen N1 £27 4 2 1
35 Islington Grn 7359 8019 8–3D
"Delicious dishes" can be chosen from a small menu at this tiny, "spartan" café of decades' standing, by Islington Green; it's "a bit of a tight squeeze", to put it mildly. / N1 8DU; 11 pm; closed Mon & Sun; no credit cards.

Aglio e Olio SW10 **£43** 3 3 2
194 Fulham Rd 7351 0070 5–3B
"Go early – the noise level rises over the evening", at this "chaotic, cramped but fun Italian", near the Chelsea & Westminster Hospital – a "cheap 'n' cheerful" classic for "authentic and fresh-tasting mainstream dishes" (notably pasta). / SW10 9PN; 11.30 pm.

Al Duca SW1 **£46** 3 3 2
4-5 Duke of York St 7839 3090 3–3D
"I thought it would be incredibly expensive given its looks and location!" – but this low-key St James's Italian "gives good value in an area bereft of such options", and, in particular, "for a central working lunch", it's ideal. / SW1Y 6LA; www.alduca-restaurant.co.uk; 11 pm; closed Sun.

Al Forno **£34** 2 4 4
349 Upper Richmond Rd, SW15 8878 7522 10–2A
2a King's Rd, SW19 8540 5710 10–2B
"They cater to all-comers, at these bustling, fun and down-to-earth" local Italians; the "solid" food is "very acceptable" ("huge pizzas" in particular), but it's the "smiling service" and "hugely welcoming family friendliness" that stand out. / 10 pm - 11 pm.

Alain Ducasse at The Dorchester W1 **£126** 2 2 2
53 Park Ln 7629 8866 3–3A
"Never a three-star!" – the Gallic über-chef's foodie temple in Mayfair is just "not up to par"; OK, a minority of fans are duly wowed, but for a sizeable majority its "Michelin-by-numbers" cuisine, "characterless" style and ferocious prices create a "distinctly average" experience. / W1K 1QA; www.alainducasse-dorchester.com; @Chefalainducasse; 9.30 pm; closed Mon, Sat L & Sun; jacket required; set weekday L £87 (FP).

Albertine W12 **£36** 2 3 4
1 Wood Ln 8743 9593 7–1C
"How different from Westfield just across the street" – a "genuine, worn, old wine bar", with a "charming" and "reassuring" atmosphere and "a long and varied wine list"; the simple fare may avoid fireworks, but is "light and appetising". / W12 7DP; www.albertinewinebar.co.uk; @AlbertineWine; 10.30 pm; closed Sat L & Sun; no Amex.

Albion **£50** 1 2 2
NEO Bankside, Holland St, SE1 3764 5550 9–3B
2-4 Boundary St, E2 7729 1051 12–1B
Whether you need "a weekend breakfast fill-up before a walk around trendy Shoreditch", or a stop-off "handy for Tate Modern", Sir Terence Conran's café duo can serve a purpose, although nothing about them excels, and the food in particular is "very average". / www.albioncaff.com; 11 pm.

The Albion N1 **£45** 2 1 3
10 Thornhill Rd 7607 7450 8–3D
"Atmospheric", tucked-away old inn, with a "great outside space" that's long been "an Islington institution"; however despite "decent pub grub", it's too often "totally let down by its lacklustre service" – maybe "go for a drink, but not to eat". / N1 1HW; www.the-albion.co.uk; @thealbionpub; 10 pm, Sun 9 pm.

Ali Baba NW1 £23 323
32 Ivor Pl 7723 5805 2–1A
"The ambience of a genuine Egyptian café" permeates this "basic" BYO (behind a Marylebone take-away), where you eat in a living room, complete with TV (typically on, with the sound turned down), and enjoy "home-cooked" fare at very "modest" prices. / NW1 6DA; www.alibabarestaurant.co.uk; midnight; no credit cards.

The Almeida N1 £62 222
30 Almeida St 7354 4777 8–3D
There's been an air of "transition" at this "spacious" D&D London fixture, opposite the eponymous Islington Theatre, which has ditched its charcuterie trolley, and modernised the cuisine; there's a sense of 'plus ça change' though with accusations that it's still "rather ordinary all round". / N1 1AD; www.almeida-restaurant.co.uk; @Almeida_N1; 10.30 pm; closed Mon L & Sun D.

Alounak £33 323
10 Russell Gdns, W14 7603 1130 7–1D
44 Westbourne Grove, W2 7229 0416 6–1B
"Incredibly cheap, good, authentic and reliable Persian BYO cafés" in Bayswater and Olympia, attracting "a great mix of diners"; service is "rushed but pleasant". / 11.30 pm; no Amex.

Alquimia SW15 £50 342
30 Brewhouse Ln 8785 0508 10–2B
"It's lovely to sit outdoors close to the Thames in fine weather", at this tapas-joint in the (otherwise "rather soulless") Putney Wharf development, where service is "friendly and efficient", and the food's of high quality. / SW15 2JX; www.alquimiarestaurant.co.uk; @AlquimiaRestUK; 11.30 pm, Sun 10.30 pm; set weekday L £28 (FP).

Alyn Williams
Westbury Hotel W1 £82 453
37 Conduit St 7183 6426 3–2C
Alyn Williams's "stunning" cuisine, along with notably "solicitous" service helps create a mightily "civilised" experience at this sleek – if slightly "muted" – hotel dining room, just off Bond Street. Top Menu Tip – "very good-value set lunch menu". / W1S 2YF; www.alynwilliams.com; @Alyn_Williams; 10.30 pm; closed Mon & Sun; jacket required; set weekday L £58 (FP).

Amaru
Ivory House E1 NEW £37
St Katharine Docks, East Smithfield 7702 4765 9–3D
New Japanese-Peruvian fusion outlet that's dropped anchor in St Katharine Docks, with backing from the owners of Spanish tapas joint Bravas; survey feedback was limited (hence no rating), but encouraging. / E1W 1AT; www.amaru.london; @Amaru_SKD; 9 pm.

Amaya SW1 £78 534
Halkin Arc, 19 Motcomb St 7823 1166 5–1D
"Mind-blowing"... "mouth-watering"... "memorable" – the Indian 'tapas' cooked on-view in the open kitchen of this sleek Belgravian, make it arguably London's best 'nouvelle Indian'; any quibbles? – service can be "inconsistent". / SW1X 8JT; www.amaya.biz; 11.30 pm, Sun 10.30 pm; set weekday L £43 (FP).

Ametsa with Arzak Instruction Halkin Hotel SW1 £86 442
5 Halkin St 7333 1234 2–3A
"We'd heard bad things, but it was stunningly good!" – star Spanish chef, Juan Mari Arzak's "stark" Belgravian can still seem "underwhelming" to some, but (after some rocky early years) it won much more consistent adulation this year for its "passionate" service, and "fascinating, semi-molecular Basque cuisine". / SW1X 7DJ; www.comohotels.com/thehalkin/dining/ametsa; @AmetsaArzak; 10 pm; closed Mon L & Sun.

Amico Bio £38 232
43 New Oxford St, WC1 7836 7509 4–1C
43-44 Cloth Fair, EC1 7600 7778 9–2B
An "interesting Italian–vegetarian concept" in Bloomsbury and Smithfield – fans extol its "delicious, and ethically-minded" fare, but to critics "it's a great idea, but the realisation is pretty average". / www.amicobio.co.uk; EC1 10.30 pm; EC1 closed Sat L & Sun; no booking.

L'Amorosa W6 £43 543
278 King St 8563 0300 7–2B
"A great addition to west London" – Andy Needham is "showing his Zafferano pedigree" at his "small" and "friendly" neighbourhood yearling near Ravenscourt Park; the cooking is "the real deal" ("sublime" pasta in particular) and there's "interesting and manageably priced wine". / W6 0SP; www.lamorosa.co.uk; @LamorosaLondon; 9.30 pm, Fri & Sat 10 pm; closed Mon & Sun D; set always available £33 (FP).

Anarkali W6 £36 342
303-305 King St 8748 1760 7–2B
Veteran Hammersmith Indian which "is always very welcoming" and "highly recommended" for its "freshly cooked" fare; even those who say it's "nothing spectacular" note "I always end up meeting friends there for a curry". / W6 9NH; www.anarkalifinedining.com; @AnarkaliDining; midnight; closed Mon L & Sun L; no Amex.

The Anchor & Hope SE1 £50 433
36 The Cut 7928 9898 9–4A
"London's best gastropub" (for the 10th year running) – this "rammed" but "engaging" South Bank fixture is "still an exciting and exhilarating food experience" which "incorporates unusual ingredients (including game and offal) much superior to the norm". "I just wish you could book" (though you can for Sunday lunch). / SE1 8LP; www.anchorandhopepub.co.uk; @AnchorHopeCut; 10.30 pm; closed Mon L & Sun D; no Amex; no booking; set weekday L £31 (FP).

Andina E2 £35 344
1 Redchurch St 7920 6499 12–1B
"Not only is the atmosphere buzzing" – the "fabulous ceviche packs a punch", as do the other "fresh and delicate" dishes, at this trendy Shoreditch Peruvian yearling. / E2 7DJ; www.andinalondon.com; 11 pm; SRA-3.*

The Andover Arms W6 £46 344

57 Aldensey Rd 8748 2155 7–1B

"Everything you could want from a local" – this "cosy" backstreet Brackenbury Village boozer is a "rare" unspoilt pub, "energetically managed", with "proper pub grub"; (that's not why it's perpetually "jammed" however – "that TripAdvisor made it their No. 3 restaurant in London is a case study of all the flaws of its system"). / W6 0DL; www.andoverarms.com; @theandoverarms; 11.30 pm; no Amex.

Andrew Edmunds W1 £46 445

46 Lexington St 7437 5708 3–2D

"For the perfect first date", this "magical" (if "cramped"), candle-lit Soho townhouse is second to none – a "shabby-chic treasure" that's "barely changed in three decades" (although actually, behind the scenes, they put in a big new kitchen this year). The "simple, daily changing fare" is unfailingly good value, but the star turn is the "incredible wines at stunning prices". / W1F 0LW; www.andrewedmunds.com; 10.45 pm, Sun 10.30 pm; no Amex; booking: max 6.

Angels & Gypsies
Church Street Hotel SE5 £45 333

29-33 Camberwell Church St 7703 5984 1–3C

It's not quite 'on the map' as once it was, but this casual bar in Camberwell still wins praise for its "unusual and amazing tapas". / SE5 8TR; www.angelsandgypsies.com; @angelsngypsies; 10.30 pm, Fri & Sat 11 pm.

Angelus W2 £70 353

4 Bathurst St 7402 0083 6–2D

"Sommelier-turned-restaurateur Thierry Tomassin offers a stunning, heavily French-accented wine list" and superb, "cosseting" service at his "romantic" converted pub, near Lancaster Gate; fans applaud its "high-class" Gallic cuisine too, although in comparison with the vino it can seem "nice, but a bit 'so what?'" / W2 2SD; www.angelusrestaurant.co.uk; 11 pm, Sun 10 pm.

Angler
South Place Hotel EC2 £77 444

3 South Pl 3215 1260 12–2A

"A surprise find in the City, especially on top of a hotel" – the D&D London's rooftop venture is a superb all-rounder, complete with "great views" and an outside terrace; the fish-heavy menu is "elegantly realised", and the set-up is "super for business – calm, smart and efficient". / EC2M 2AF; www.anglerrestaurant.com; @southplacehotel; 10 pm; closed Sat L; booking: max 14.

The Anglesea Arms W6 £50 334

35 Wingate Rd 8749 1291 7–1B

"It's back, thank goodness!", say fans of this "true gastropub" near Ravenscourt Park (which re-opened in new hands last year) – a "lovely", if plain, old inn, long known as one of London's very best, with "way-above-average" seasonal cooking; not absolutely everyone's still smitten though – refuseniks say it's "good that it's returned, but it's lacking something nowadays". / W6 0UR; www.angleseaarmspub.co.uk; @_AngleseaArmsW6; 10 pm, Sun 9 pm; closed weekday L.

L'Anima EC2 £70 333

1 Snowden St 7422 7000 12–2B

"It's a bit of a noisy goldfish bowl, ambience-wise", but the "buzz of City high-flyers" continues to attest to the business-friendly appeal of this "pricey-but-worth-it" Italian; founding chef Francesco Mazzei moved on in March 2015 – fingers crossed Antonio Favuzzi maintains an even keel. / EC2A 2DQ; www.lanima.co.uk; 11 pm, Sat 11.30 pm; closed Sat L & Sun.

L'Anima Café EC2 £46 444

10 Appold St 7422 7080 12–2B

The "less formal (and more keenly priced) sister restaurant of L'Anima" occupies "spacious and inviting" premises around the corner from its sibling, and serves "highly authentic" Italian grub, including pizza. / EC2A 2AP; www.lanimacafe.co.uk; @LAnimacafe; 10 pm; closed Sun.

Anima e Cuore NW1 NEW £44 432

129 Kentish Town Rd 7267 2410 8–2B

Forget the "unprepossessing frontage" – this "tiny" and "low key" Kentish Town newcomer is a "lovely and quirky" trattoria, with "personal, if erratic" service, and an ever-changing menu of "divine pasta" and homemade gelato. / NW1 8PB; 9 pm, Sun 2.30 pm.

Annie's £46 235

162 Thames Rd, W4 8994 9080 1–3A

36-38 White Hart Ln, SW13 8878 2020 10–1A

"Beautiful Boho decor" ("mismatched chairs, rickety tables") and "delightful staff" create "a lovely vibe" at these "romantic" neighbourhood favourites, in Barnes and Strand-on-the-Green; the food's not amazing, but it's "consistent", and brunch is a big hit. / www.anniesrestaurant.co.uk; 10 pm, Sat 10.30 pm, Sun 9.30 pm.

The Anthologist EC2 £45 223

58 Gresham St 0845 468 0101 9–2C

"A vast space, but always a very busy one" – this bar/restaurant, near the Guildhall, is hardly a foodie hotspot, and can be "too noisy", but makes a very versatile City rendezvous. / EC2V 7BB; www.theanthologistbar.co.uk; @theanthologist; 11 pm, Thu & Fri 1 am; closed Sat & Sun; SRA-3.*

L'Antica Pizzeria NW3 £37 433

66 Heath St 7431 8516 8–1A

"Amazing pizza, with an unusually soft and fluffy base" is the product of the "proper, red-hot, wood-fired oven" in use at this "bustling", brick-walled, "café-style" outfit – "a cosy and welcoming little slice of Naples" in central Hampstead. / NW3 1DN; www.anticapizzeria.co.uk; 10.30 pm; Mon-Thu D only, Fri-Sun open L & D.

Antico SE1 £47 343

214 Bermondsey St 7407 4682 9–4D

"It's not as trendy as some nearby rivals", but this three-year-old Bermondsey Italian is still "a favourite haunt of many locals" providing "good, authentic" flavours, and a "lively" ("noisy at peak times") atmosphere. / SE1 3TQ; www.antico-london.co.uk; @AnticoLondon; 10.30 pm; closed Mon.

Antidote W1 **£62** 4 3 3
12a Newburgh St 7287 8488 3–2C
"Tucked away off Carnaby Street", this "wine bar gem" – with "a lovely, small upstairs dining room" – serves some "truly superb" dishes alongside a "fantastic biodynamic wine list". (However, if you seek it out mindful of the kitchen's connection to Hedone's Mikael Jonsson, aside from the marvellous bread, you may leave "a bit disappointed"). / W1F 7RR; www.antidotewinebar.com; @AntidoteWineBar; 10.30 pm; closed Sun; booking: max 8.

Apollo Banana Leaf SW17 **£20** 4 2 1
190 Tooting High St 8696 1423 10–2C
"Ignore the decor and occasionally rushed service" if you visit this "unprepossessing little BYO" ("an old travel agent's shop" in Tooting); "who cares" when the South Indian/Sri Lankan dishes are "fantastic" and "unbelievably cheap"? / SW17 0SF; www.apollobananaleaf.com; 10.30 pm; no Amex.

Applebee's Café SE1 **£45** 4 4 3
5 Stoney St 7407 5777 9–4C
"What could be better?" – "fresh fish straight off the ice" and "simply cooked" is served at this "enjoyably busy" Borough Market café (attached to a fishmongers) and at "sensible prices" too; in a hurry? – grab "a freshly grilled seafood wrap". / SE1 9AA; www.applebeesfish.com; @applebeesfish; 10 pm, Fri 10.30 pm; closed Sun; no Amex.

Apulia EC1 **£39** 3 3 2
50 Long Ln 7600 8107 9–2B
"Informal Italian standby" whose "authentic short menu" makes it "a good bet for a quick bite or working lunch near the Barbican". / EC1A 9EJ; www.apuliarestaurant.co.uk; 10 pm, Sun 3.30 pm; closed Sun D.

aqua kyoto W1 **£75** 2 2 3
240 Regent St (entrance 30 Argyll St) 7478 0540 3–2C
"Great views over rooftops onto Regent Street" are a highpoint of this "noisy and dark" nightclub-esque operation, six floors above the West End; but although its cocktails and Asian-inspired food is well-rated, even fans can find it "very expensive". / W1B 3BR; www.aqua-london.com; @aqualondon; 10.30 pm; closed Sun D; booking: max 6.

aqua nueva W1 **£66** 3 3 4
240 Regent St (entrance 30 Argyll St) 7478 0540 3–2C
Serving northern Spanish food in opulent rooftop surroundings, this nightclubby venue near Oxford Circus provides a restaurant, terrace, Cava bar and two private dining rooms no less! – it was much more consistently highly rated this year. / W1B 3BR; www.aqua-london.com; @aqualondon; 10.30 pm; closed Sun.

Aqua Shard SE1 **£85** 1 1 4
Level 31, 31 St Thomas St 3011 1256 9–4C
"The views and the loos are amazing… the rest's not worth it" – that's the often-damning verdict on the "wondrously designed" but shamelessly "overpriced" vantage point on the Shard's 31st-floor. / SE1 9RY; www.aquashard.co.uk; @aquashard; 10.30 pm.

Arabica Bar and Kitchen SE1 £49 3 2 3
3 Rochester Walk 3011 5151 9–4C
Fans of this "casual" (unusually stylish) Borough Market Lebanese acclaim its "fabulous food at reasonable prices"; sceptics however feel it's "fine but nothing special" – "pretty standard, and while pleasant, no more than that". / SE1 9AF; www.arabicabarandkitchen.com; @ArabicaLondon; 10.30 pm, Thu 11 pm, Fri & Sat 11.30 pm, S; closed Sun D.

The Araki W1 NEW £366 5 4 4
Unit 4 12 New Burlington St 7287 2481 3–3D
"The sushi is out-of-this-universe, but the prices are too" at this tiny Mayfair newcomer – by quite a margin the UK's most expensive dining experience – where "as one of only 9 customers, the skill of Mitsuhiro Araki is fully on display for your personal benefit"; is it worth the mind-boggling cost? – to most of our reporters the answer is yes! / W1S 3BH; www.the-araki.com; 8.30 pm; D only, closed Mon.

Arbutus W1 £54 3 3 2
63-64 Frith St 7734 4545 4–2A
"Seasonal" cuisine (from "an interesting menu, with lots of unusual cuts and offal") twinned with "excellent and affordable" wine (by the glass and carafe) have won foodie renown for this "unpretentious" ("cramped") Soho spot; of late, however, its performance has been more "middle-of-the-road". / W1D 3JW; www.arbutusrestaurant.co.uk; @arbutus; 10.45 pm, Fri & Sat 11.15 pm, Sun 10.30 pm.

Archduke Wine Bar SE1 £52 2 2 2
153 Concert Hall Approach, South Bank 7928 9370 2–3D
These characterful railway arches "have offered food for decades in various guises" (currently, as an outpost of the 'Black & Blue' chain); "for a quick bite pre-Festival Hall" it's mightily convenient, but otherwise "you wouldn't rush back". / SE1 8XU; www.blackandbluerestaurants.com; 10.30 pm, Sun 10 pm.

Ariana II NW6 £30 4 3 2
241 Kilburn High Rd 3490 6709 1–2B
"Small and basic, but it's the food you come for" – that's the trade-off at this "busy local Afghan BYO" in Kilburn, serving "excellent" scoff ("impeccable stews") at "throwaway prices". / NW6 7JN; www.ariana2restaurant.co.uk; @Ariana2kilburn; midnight.

Ark Fish E18 £43 4 4 2
142 Hermon Hill 8989 5345 1–1D
"Efficient" staff who "look like they're enjoying themselves" add to the appeal of this South Woodford fish 'n' chip restaurant, hailed by some as "the best in East London". / E18 1QH; www.arkfishrestaurant.co.uk; 9.45 pm, Fri & Sat 10.15 pm, Sun 8.45 pm; closed Mon; no Amex.

Artigiano NW3 £48 3 3 3
12a Belsize Ter 7794 4288 8–2A
"For what it is, where it is, excellent!" – a "very decent" and "friendly" Italian in the "quietish backwater" of Belsize Park, whose harshest critic says "it's middle of the road, but there's certainly no reason to complain". / NW3 4AX; www.etruscarestaurants.com; @artigianoesp; 10 pm; closed Mon L.

F S A

L'Artista NW11 £34 2 4 4

917 Finchley Rd 8731 7501 1–1B

Archetypal "cheap 'n' cheerful Italian family spot" that's long inhabited the railway arches near Golders Green tube; aside from the "huge pizzas", the food's only "tolerable", but its "friendly waiters" and buoyant atmosphere carry the day, and it's "always busy". / NW11 7PE; www.lartistapizzeria.com; 11.30 pm.

L'Artiste Musclé W1 £49 2 2 4

1 Shepherd Mkt 7493 6150 3–4B

"You feel like you're in France", at this cute, "cramped", little corner-bistro in Shepherd Market, where even fans admit that the "straightforward" fare is "not really the point". / W1J 7PA; @lartistemuscle; 10 pm, Fri-Sun 10.30 pm.

Artusi SE15 £46 4 3 2

161 Bellenden Rd 3302 8200 1–4D

The "simple confidence of the Italian cooking" helps inspire rave reviews for this neighbourhood yearling, hailed by fans as "a perfect culinary experience"; the odd critic though – while acknowledging "it's fairly decent" – feels "the trendy Peckham effect means prices are drifting up". / SE15 4DH; www.artusi.co.uk; @artusipeckham; 10 pm.

Asakusa NW1 £36 5 3 2

265 Eversholt St 7388 8533 8–3C

"Extraordinary value given its top quality and rock-bottom prices" – this "rare Japanese", near Mornington Crescent, serves a wide menu majoring in "amazing sushi", and its "friendly" service softens the "very cramped, mock Tudor interior". / NW1 1BA; 11.30 pm, Sat 11 pm; D only, closed Sun.

Asia de Cuba
St Martin's Lane Hotel WC2 £89 2 2 2

45 St Martin's Ln 7300 5588 4–4C

Glossily glam' (and "so, so loud") boutique-hotel hang-out, where accusations of style over substance are deafening nowadays; even fans concede its "massive" sharing plates are "very, very, very expensive" and to doubters it's just "a disaster". / WC2N 4HX; www.morganshotelgroup.com; @asiadecuba; midnight, Thu-Sat 12.30 am, Sun 10.30 pm; set pre theatre £51 (FP).

Assunta Madre W1 £104 3 3 2

9-10 Blenheim St 3230 3032 3–2B

With fish flown in fresh from Italy every day this Mayfair spin-off from a Roman original gets a thumbs-up for its seafood; most diners however feel the yearling's "excellent" food is overshadowed by "exorbitant prices" – the plonk is particularly expensive. / W1S 1LJ; www.assuntamadre.com; @assuntamadre; midnight.

Atari-Ya £30 532

20 James St, W1 7491 1178 3–1A
7 Station Pde, W3 8896 1552 1–2A
1 Station Pde, W5 8896 3175 1–3A
595 High Rd, N12 8446 6669 8–1B
31 Vivian Ave, NW4 8202 2789 1–1B
75 Fairfax Road, NW6 7328 5338 8–2A

"The best sushi" – "the quality of the fish is second to none" – rewards a visit to these "un-glamorous" caffs (run by Japanese food importers); there are only a few tables ("always heaving with folks from Japan"). / www.atariya.co.uk; W1 8 pm, NW4 & NW6 9.30 pm, W9 9 pm; NW4, NW6 closed Mon.

L'Atelier de Joel Robuchon WC2 £95 333

13-15 West St 7010 8600 4–2B

"Exquisite presentation" and "stratospheric" prices are long-running talking points at the Parisian über-chef's "dark and sexy" Covent Garden outpost (where "the top seats are at the chef's counter in the ground-floor dining room"). For most reporters it's still "simply out-of-this-world", but sliding ratings support those who say "the wow-factor has decreased compared to previous years". Swish penthouse bar, with roof terrace. / WC2H 9NE; www.joelrobuchon.co.uk; @latelierlondon; midnight, Sun 10 pm; no trainers; set weekday L & pre-theatre £59 (FP).

Athenaeum
Athenaeum Hotel W1 £67 333

116 Piccadilly 7499 3464 3–4B

"It aspires to no great heights", but this "pleasant" and well-located dining room (facing Green Park) wins consistent praise for its "lovely afternoon teas" ("the sandwiches kept coming…") and "good value set lunches". / W1J 7BJ; www.athenaeumhotel.com; @TheAthenaeum; 11 pm.

The Atlas SW6 £45 444

16 Seagrave Rd 7385 9129 5–3A

In the backstreets, near Earl's Court 2 (currently being demolished), a characterful hostelry that's very much "still a pub", but with a kitchen that "goes well above-and-beyond expectations", serving "often creative", "Italian-influenced" fare; cute side patio. / SW6 1RX; www.theatlaspub.co.uk; @theatlasfulham; 10 pm.

Augustine Kitchen SW11 £46 341

63 Battersea Bridge Rd 7978 7085 5–4C

"It suffers from a dreadful location", but this bistro yearling in Battersea is establishing itself on the back of its "interesting selection of dishes from Savoie", all at a very "bon prix" ("better value than you'd get north of the river"). / SW11 3AU; www.augustine-kitchen.co.uk; @augustinekitchen; 10.30 pm; closed Mon & Sun D.

Aurora W1 £52 345

49 Lexington St 7494 0514 3–2D

"A fantastic little find" in Soho (rather eclipsed by Andrew Edmunds across the road); staff are "very friendly and helpful", it has a "charming" vibe, the "regularly changing, seasonal cooking" is "dependably good", and "its cute courtyard is lovely in warm weather". / W1F 9AP; www.aurorasoho.co.uk; 10 pm, Wed-Sat 10.30 pm, Sun 9 pm.

L'Autre Pied W1 **£81** **4 4 3**
5-7 Blandford St 7486 9696 2–1A
"Tremendous", "high-quality" cuisine (including "bargain tasting menus with excellent wine flights") ensures that Pied à Terre's "first-class" Marylebone spin-off continues to "punch above the weight" of its small ("slightly dull and cafe-like") premises. / W1U 3DB; www.lautrepied.co.uk; 10 pm; closed Sun D.

L'Aventure NW8 **£60** **4 5 5**
3 Blenheim Ter 7624 6232 8–3A
Catherine Parisot's "little piece of France" is a treasured St John's Wood "institution", and its "gorgeous" style has "survived its recent revamp" unscathed; service is "fantastically kind" (except when La Patronne is having an off day) and its "old-school" cuisine bourgeoise is "superb" (if from a rather "unchanging" menu). / NW8 0EH; 11 pm; closed Sat L & Sun.

The Avenue SW1 **£56** **2 3 3**
7-9 St James's St 7321 2111 3–4D
It's "a good venue for a business lunch or dinner", but this large, echoey, rather '90s St James's brasserie – nowadays with an American spin to its menu – "needs a tweak" food-wise to become more of a destination. / SW1A 1EE; www.avenue-restaurant.co.uk; @avenuestjames; 10.30 pm; closed Sat L & Sun.

Awesome Thai SW13 **£28** **3 4 2**
68 Church Rd 8563 7027 10–1A
According to Barnes locals, this long-running Thai is "as the name says", but "what really sets it apart is the family atmosphere, with very attentive service", plus "reasonable prices". / SW13 0DQ; www.awesomethai.co.uk; @AwesomeThai1; 10.30 pm, Sun 10 pm; Mon-Thu D only, Fri-Sun open L & D.

Azou W6 **£44** **3 3 3**
375 King St 8563 7266 7–2B
"For something a bit different" up Hammersmith way, fans tip this sweet North African café on the main drag, and its "tasty" tagines; others though feel it's "overrated". / W6 9NJ; www.azou.co.uk; @azourestaurant; 11 pm.

Babaji Pide W1 NEW **£39** **3 4 3**
73 Shaftesbury Ave 3327 3888 4–3A
"Queues are already forming", at Alan Yau's ambitious new Turkish concept, in the heart of the West End; tables may be "cramped", but there's a "bustling atmosphere" around the open kitchen, and the pizza (pide)-based scoff is, on early feedback, well-rated. / W1D 6EX; www.babaji.com.tr; 11 pm, Fri & Sat 11.30 pm, Sun 10 pm.

Babbo W1 **£80** **3 3 3**
39 Albermarle St 3205 1099 3–3C
Near The Ritz, fans hail this "romantic" Mayfair Italian as "a truly delightful operation" with "really lovely food"; to its least enthusiastic followers it's "all right, but nothing special". / W1S 4JQ; www.babborestaurant.co.uk; @BabboRestaurant; 11 pm, Sun 10.30 pm; closed Sat L & Sun L; set weekday L £51 (FP).

Babur SE23 £52 554
119 Brockley Rise 8291 2400 1–4D
"Long live Babur!" – this "stand-out" stalwart remains one of SE London's most notable stars, with an "ever-evolving" menu of "cracking Indian fusion dishes" served by "lovely, friendly and personal" staff in an "understated" and "lively" setting. / SE23 1JP; www.babur.info; @BaburRestaurant; 11.30 pm.

Babylon
Kensington Roof Gardens W8 £72 234
99 Kensington High St 7368 3993 5–1A
"You are transported to a far-away place, and yet you are in the centre of Kensington", when you visit this "spectacular" venue, overlooking the famous, lush rooftop gardens below ("arrive early and take a stroll around"); at the price "the cooking lacks a little polish" (so look out for lunch deals). / W8 5SA; www.virgin.com/roofgardens; 10.30 pm; closed Sun D; SRA-3.*

Bacco TW9 £49 343
39 Kew Rd 8332 0348 1–4A
"So much better than the chains!" – this "lovely, easy-going Italian", with its "thoughtful" staff, is well-located opposite Richmond station (and "very handy for either the Orange Tree or Richmond Theatres"); menu-wise "the fresh pasta's always a good choice". / TW9 2NQ; www.bacco-restaurant.co.uk; @BaccoRichmond; 11 pm; closed Sun D.

Il Bacio £36 333
61 Stoke Newington Church St, N16 7249 3833 1–1C
178-184 Blackstock Rd, N5 7226 3339 8–1D
"Always my first choice for a cheap, reliably good local" – these Stoke Newington and Highbury "stalwarts" are a safe bet for "excellent pizza and pasta". / www.ilbaciohighbury.co.uk; 10 pm - 11 pm; no Amex.

Bad Egg
City Point EC2 NEW £40 433
Unit 1b, 1 Ropemaker St 3006 6222 12–2A
The moniker gives it away – Neil Rankin's (of Smokehouse Islington) new Moorgate diner is all about "cheeky, naughty and delicious" yolky dishes, that early reports say are "great value". Top Menu Tip: £32 per person boozy brunch which offers unlimited drinks refills. / EC2Y 9AW; www.badegg.london; @badoeuf; Mon-Fri 10 pm, Sat 8 pm, Sun 6 pm; closed Sun D.

Bageriet WC2 £14 444
24 Rose St 7240 0000 4–3C
"Tiny (only 8 seats), but not to be missed" – this bakery and coffee shop is an "authentic corner of Sweden in Covent Garden", with "excellent coffee and divinely decadent cakes"; superb Scandi sarnies too. / WC2E 9EA; www.bageriet.co.uk; @BagerietLondon; 7 pm; closed Sun.

Balans £48 2 3 3

60-62 Old Compton St, W1 7439 2183 4–2A
Westfield, Ariel Way, W12 8600 3320 7–1C
214 Chiswick High Rd, W4 8742 1435 7–2A
187 Kensington High St, W8 7376 0115 5–1A
Westfield Stratford, E20 8555 5478 1–1D

The Soho original has all the "charm", but other branches of this late-night chain are "capable" and "well located", and remain a "go-to choice" for breakfast served with a little "vibe and edge", plus "the guaranty of interesting fellow diners at the shared tables". / www.balans.co.uk; midnight-2 am; 34 Old Compton St 24 hrs, E20 11pm; some booking restrictions apply.

The Balcon
Sofitel St James SW1 £59 2 3 2

8 Pall Mall 7968 2900 2–3C

"A perfect location for people coming from different areas" and "pretty consistent" cooking can make this "pleasant" hotel brasserie, off Trafalgar Square, an "ideal venue" for business or pre-theatre; on the downside, it can seem rather "empty". / SW1Y 5NG; www.thebalconlondon.com; 10.45 pm, Sun 9.45 pm.

Bald Faced Stag N2 £48 3 3 3

69 High Rd 8442 1201 1–1B

"Great name… even better food!" – an East Finchley gastropub that makes a "fantastic local" thanks to its "consistently good" cooking. / N2 8AB; www.thebaldfacedstagn2.co.uk; @thebaldfacestagn2; 10.30 pm, Sun 9.30 pm.

Balls & Company W1 NEW £37

58 Greek St 7851 6688 4–2A

The first restaurant from Aussie 'MasterChef: The Professionals' finalist, Bonny Porter, opened in the heart of Soho just as our survey closed this year, so a pronouncement on her 'meatballs with an elegant twist' will have to wait. / W1D 3DY; www.ballsandcompany.london; @BallsandCompany; 11 pm; closed Sun.

Balthazar WC2 £63 2 2 3

4-6 Russell St 3301 1155 4–3D

NYC supremo, Keith McNally's "pricey and flash" Grand Café in Covent Garden is "a disappointing replica" of the Manhattan original; still, even some who concede it's "a definite case of style over substance" say "the buzzy ambience is compensation", or tip it "for a girlie brunch". / WC2E 7BN; www.balthazarlondon.com; @balthazarlondon; 11.30 pm, Fri & Sat 11.45 pm, Sun 10.30 pm.

Baltic SE1 £53 3 3 3

74 Blackfriars Rd 7928 1111 9–4A

"There's more hiding behind the facade than you'd expect", at this warehouse-conversion in Borough – a "light and airy" (slightly "cavernous") space; the eastern European fodder can be "surprisingly good", but it's the "amazing list of vodkas" which ensures a visit's "loads of fun". / SE1 8HA; www.balticrestaurant.co.uk; @BalticLondon; 11.15 pm, Sun 10.30 pm; closed Mon L.

The Banana Tree Canteen £35 2 2 2

103 Wardour St, W1 7437 1351 3–2D
21-23 Westbourne Grove, W2 7221 4085 6–1C
166 Randolph Ave, W9 7286 3869 8–3A
237-239 West End Ln, NW6 7431 7808 1–1B
75-79 Battersea Rise, SW11 7228 2828 10–2C
412-416 St John St, EC1 7278 7565 8–3D

For "good-value fast food", these Asian-fusion canteens provide an "interesting" selection of dishes, and some "delicious cocktails" too; they're "uncomfortable" though, and strike sceptics as "inauthentic" and "underwhelming". / @bananatree247; Sun-Tue 10.30 pm, Wed-Sat 11 pm; booking: min 6.

Bandol SW10 NEW

6 Hollywood Rd awaiting tel 5–3B

From the owners of Earl's Court yearling, Margaux, a new, more ambitious Gallic venture in Chelsea, set to open in autumn 2015, dishing up sharing plates of Provençal and Niçoise cuisine. / SW10 9HY; @margaux_bandol.

Bangkok SW7 £42 3 3 2

9 Bute St 7584 8529 5–2B

To its (largely silver-haired) devotees, this "old school" South Kensington Thai is "always a winner", even after over 40 years in business; its cooking style is, though, arguably a tad "monolithic". / SW7 3EY; www.thebankokrestaurant.co.uk; 10.45 pm; no Amex.

Bank Westminster
St James Court Hotel SW1 £62 2 2 2

45 Buckingham Gate 7630 6644 2–4B

A "lovely conservatory" is an undisputed highlight of this "very professional brasserie", near Buckingham Palace; other aspects are mixed – what is a "good business restaurant" to fans, is to foes "overpriced, with standards equivalent to Garfunkel's or Café Rouge". / SW1E 6BS; www.bankrestaurants.com; @bank_westmin; 11 pm; closed Sat L & Sun.

Banners N8 £42 3 4 5

21 Park Rd 8348 2930 1–1C

"Make sure you're hungry" if you visit this "beloved" Crouch End stalwart, where the Caribbean-influenced scran comes in "huge portions"; brunch is a massive deal here – "you won't get a table unless you're early". / N8 8TE; www.bannersrestaurant.com; 11.30 pm, Fri & Sat midnight, Sun 11 pm; no Amex.

Bao W1 NEW £28 5 4 2

53 Lexington St no tel 3–2D

"A Soho legend in the making!"; this Taiwanese phenomenon has (with backing from the Sethi family, of Gymkhana fame) "successfully made the transition from Hackney street stall to tiny restaurant"; the pay-off for the legendary queues? – "heavenly soft buns filled with tasty, slow-cooked meat", and "the best, crunchy fried chicken in London". / W1F 9AS; www.baolondon.com; @bao_london; 10 pm; closed Sun.

Baozi Inn WC2 £24 4 3 2

25 Newport Ct 7287 6877 4–3B

"I don't mind the lack of space (even the lack of a place to put my coat)" – this Chinatown caff "isn't cheerful, but it is cheap and very good", serving "top Sichuan street food" ("succulent baozi buns… delicious noodles…"). / WC2H 7JS; www.baoziinnlondon.com; 10 pm, Fri & Sat 10.30 pm; no credit cards; no booking.

Bar Boulud
Mandarin Oriental SW1 £70 3 3 3

66 Knightsbridge 7201 3899 5–1D

"How can you not love their burgers?" – they're "the best in town" according to the armies of fans of this NYC super-chef's "stylish" and "always buzzing" brasserie in the basement of a grand Knightsbridge hotel; its ratings are slipping though, perhaps because it's just "not cheap". / SW1X 7LA; www.barboulud.com; @barbouludlondon; 10.45 pm, Sun 9.45 pm.

Bar Esteban N8 £39 5 3 4

29 Park Rd 8340 3090 1–1C

Crouch End locals "can't recommend this place heartily enough" – from the "almost perfect" tapas to the "bustling" atmosphere – a "wonderful" neighbourhood restaurant. / N8 8TE; www.baresteban.com; Mon-Sat 10.30 pm, Sun 9 pm; closed weekday L.

Bar Italia W1 £28 3 4 5

22 Frith St 7437 4520 4–2A

"Bringing a little bit of Italia to our streets since time immemorial" – a tiny Soho legend serving up "the best coffee in London and great people-watching", 24/7. / W1D 4RT; www.baritaliasoho.co.uk; @TheBaristas; open 24 hours, Sun 4 am; no Amex; no booking.

Bar Termini W1 NEW £35 4 4 4

7 Old Compton St 07860 945018 4–2B

"Small, cosy, and perfect for pre- or post-dinner drinks", Tony Conigliaro's (of Zetter Townhouse fame) new Soho cicchetti and cocktail bar attracts nothing but raves – from the "faultless" service to the "unbeatable" Italian coffee. / W1D 5JE; www.bar-termini.com; @Bar_Termini; Mon-Thu 11.30 pm, Fri & Sat midnight, Sun 10.30 pm.

Barbecoa £65 1 2 1

194-196 Piccadilly, W1 awaiting tel 3–3D NEW

20 New Change Pas, EC4 3005 8555 9–2B

"Stunning views over the rooftop of St Paul's Cathedral" at the City original is the "saving grace" at Jamie O's temple for meat-lovers, where prices are "shocking" for what's basically a BBQ – "I've had better on street markets". A massive 300-cover new Piccadilly sibling is set to open in December 2015. / www.barbecoa.com; @Barbecoa_london.

La Barca SE1 £73 2 3 2

80-81 Lower Marsh 7928 2226 9–4A

"In the gastronomic desert of Waterloo", it's worth knowing of this "definitely old-style, but popular" Italian "time-warp"; its prices are a little "through the roof", but "you end up getting drawn back" by its "tasty" cooking and "excellent" service. / SE1 7AB; www.labarca-ristorante.com; @labarca1976; 11.30 pm; closed Sat L & Sun.

FSA

Il Baretto W1 £63 3 2 2

43 Blandford St 7486 7340 2–1A

"Expensive but easy-going Italian, in a very noisy Marylebone basement"; fans love its "fun" and "always buzzing" style and "quality" pizza and pasta – to critics "the food's good, but not good value, and it's not the most relaxed place". / W1U 7HF; www.ilbaretto.co.uk; @IlBarettoLondon; 10.15 pm, Sun 9.45 pm.

Barnyard W1 £44 2 2 2

18 Charlotte St 7580 3842 2–1C

"More thought to making the food good, rather than the look trendy" would go down well at Ollie Dabbous's conscientiously "casual", and rather "gimmicky" Fitzrovia diner ("decked out to look like the inside of a barn"); it's at its best for "a lively brunch". / W1T 2LZ; www.barnyard-london.com; Mon-Wed 10 pm, Thu-Sat 10.30 pm, Sun 8.30 pm.

Barrafina £42 5 5 5

54 Frith St, W1 7813 8016 4–2A

10 Adelaide St, WC2 7440 1456 4–4C

43 Drury Ln, WC2 7440 1456 4–2D NEW

"I'm never happier than perched on a stool here, watching the incredible food being prepared!" – The Hart Bros have fully captured the zeitgeist with their "thrilling" small foodie meccas in Soho and Covent Garden – "truly exciting, vibrant London experiences" founded in "some of the best tapas outside Barcelona" (and in particular "peerlessly fresh fish"), "fabulous" wines and sherries, and "empathetic" service. "You wait over an hour for a seat, but it really is THAT good!" Incredibly, the second branch is rated just as highly as the Frith Street original, and to sound in-the-know, remark on how the Josper Oven makes the fish taste even better at Adelaide Street. Can they pull it off again with Branch No. 3? / www.barrafina.co.uk; 11 pm, Sun 10 pm; no booking.

Barrica W1 £45 3 3 3

62 Goodge St 7436 9448 2–1B

"Like being transported to Madrid" – a "surprisingly genuine" Fitzrovia tapas bar, well-acclaimed for its "substantial, scrumptious plates", "fab wine list" and "decent value". / W1T 4NE; www.barrica.co.uk; 10.30 pm; closed Sun.

Barshu W1 £54 4 1 2

28 Frith St 7287 8822 4–3A

It's "not for the faint-hearted", but for a "fragrant chilli fix", the "uncompromisingly" fiery Sichuan cuisine at this Soho café makes it "one of the best Chinese options in town"; you don't go for the ambience however, and service is "curt". / W1D 5LF; www.barshurestaurant.co.uk; @BarshuLondon; 10.30 pm, Fri & Sat 11 pm.

Basilico £39 4 4 1

Branches throughout London

"The champions of pizza delivery" – this small chain provides "top quality, with fantastic ingredients", if you're prepared to "splash out a bit" price-wise. / www.basilico.co.uk; @basilicopizzas; 11 pm; no booking.

Bea's Of Bloomsbury WC1 £39 4 3 3
44 Theobalds Rd 7242 8330 2–1D
"An absolute must if you're in the area at tea-time" – a "very cosy café near the Holborn Library", serving "great coffee and the best cupcakes this side of the Atlantic"; (there are also small spin-offs near St Paul's and near Farringdon Station). / WC1X 8NW; www.beasofbloomsbury.com; @beas_bloomsbury; 7 pm; L only.

Beach Blanket Babylon £65 1 1 3
45 Ledbury Rd, W11 7229 2907 6–1B
19-23 Bethnal Green Rd, E1 7749 3540 12–1C
Atmospheric Gaudi-esque decor underpins the surprisingly enduring appeal of these hip haunts, in Notting Hill and Shoreditch – it sure ain't the clueless service, nor the inept and pricey food. / www.beachblanket.co.uk; 10.30 pm; W11 booking advisable Fri-Sat.

Beagle E2 £47 4 3 3
397-399 7613 2967 12–1B
Occupying two Hoxton railway arches, a big, "cool but approachable" brasserie with open kitchen from a former Rochelle's Canteen chef that's typically "packed and buzzing" (and can be very noisy), and serves "reasonably priced" fare. / E2 8HZ; www.beaglelondon.co.uk; @beaglelondon; 10.30 pm, Sun 5 pm; closed Sun D.

Beast W1 £113 2 2 2
3 Chapel Pl 7495 1816 3–1B
"Theatrics far outweigh the food", at this "utterly mad" Goodman-group yearling, where "huge" quantities of top-quality surf 'n' turf are served in a low-lit communal space, "evoking the spirit of a medieval banquet"; to converts it's "obscenely delicious", but to those appalled by the "US-style portion excess" and "maniac pricing", "it's just gross". / W1G 0BG; www.beastrestaurant.co.uk; @beastrestaurant; 10 pm; closed Mon & Sun.

Beer and Buns EC2 NEW £36
3 Appold St 7539 9209 12–2B
Billing itself as the Square Mile's only pop-up (although now in permanent residence above K10 Appold Street) this newcomer offering Japanese beers, buns and "hot-n-spicy" wings pleases a few early days reporters, albeit in "a noisy environment". / EC2A 2AF; www.beerandbuns.co.uk; Mon-Fri 11 pm.

The Begging Bowl SE15 £37 3 3 3
168 Bellenden Rd 7635 2627 1–4D
"A real Thai", say fans of this "tiny" and "tightly packed", no-bookings Peckham hotspot, extolling its "superb", authentic flavours; doubters though say it's "by numbers for the middle class locals slumming it… oooh such adventure!" / SE15 4BW; www.thebeggingbowl.co.uk; @thebeggingbowl; Mon-Sat 9.45 pm, Sun 9.15 pm.

Bel Canto
Corus Hotel Hyde Park W2 £52 2 4 4
1 Lancaster Gate 7262 1678 6–2C
An entertaining night out; considering you go to have your dinner punctuated by professionally-sung operatic arias, the food at this fun Bayswater basement dining room can be rather better than you might expect. / W2 3LG; www.belcantolondon.co.uk; 9.15 pm; D only, closed Mon & Sun.

Belgo £42 222

29-31 Old Compton St, W1 7437 7284 4–2A NEW
50 Earlham St, WC2 7813 2233 4–2C
67 Kingsway, WC2 7242 7469 2–2D
72 Chalk Farm Rd, NW1 7267 0718 8–2B

"Cavernous" Belgian moules-frites halls complete with waiters dressed as monks; critics say they've "lost their novelty", but the opening of the first new branch in years – in Soho – shows there's plenty of life in the old dog yet? Top Tips – the "brilliant Continental beer selection", and early evening 'Beat the Clock' deal.
/ www.belgo-restaurants.co.uk; 10 pm - 11 pm, WC2 Thu midnight, Fri & Sat 1am.

Bellamy's W1 £60 344

18-18a Bruton Pl 7491 2727 3–2B

"A refined atmosphere not found in many restaurants" helps make Gavin Rankin's "clubby" and "luxurious" brasserie – tucked away in a tranquil Mayfair mews – a particular "winner for a business lunch"; its straightforward, often "rich" cuisine is "expensive but worth it".
/ W1J 6LY; www.bellamysrestaurant.co.uk; 10.30 pm; closed Sat L & Sun.

Bellanger N1 NEW

9 Islington Grn awaiting tel 8–3D

Corbin & King head outside of the West End as they take over the site some still recall as Browns (long RIP), near Islington Green; the naming strategy for the duo's latest European grand café continues the vintage car riff of the Wolseley and Delaunay – this time the marque was Bellanger Frères (1912–1925). / N1 2XH; www.bellanger.co.uk; 10.30pm, Sun 10 pm.

Bellevue Rendez-Vous SW17 £46 333

218 Trinity Rd 8767 5810 10–2C

"Old-school French menu" and "very solid cooking" in a "lovely local" near Wandsworth Common; it was good under its previous owners, but fans say both "venue and service has improved" since the Gazette group took it over. / SW17 7HP; www.bellevuerendezvous.com; 10.30 pm; closed Mon L; no Amex.

Belvedere W8 £68 224

Holland Pk, off Abbotsbury Rd 7602 1238 7–1D

"A delightful walk through the park" sets the scene at this "elegant" Art Deco feature in Holland Park (and when it's warm, you can sit on the terrace); its pricey and "unadventurous" cooking has never been a highlight, but seemed even more "disappointing" this year.
/ W8 6LU; www.belvedererestaurant.co.uk; 10.30 pm; closed Sun D; set always available £43 (FP).

Benares W1 £95 322

12a Berkeley Square Hs, Berkeley Sq 7629 8886 3–3B

"Beautifully thought out" and "adventurous" 'nouvelle Indian' cuisine continues to make Atul Kochar's slick-looking (but "windowless") Mayfair operation one of the Capital's best-known dining destinations; slipping ratings, though, accompany fears that it risks becoming for "expense accounters only". / W1J 6BS; www.benaresrestaurant.co.uk; @benaresofficial; 10.45 pm.

Bengal Clipper SE1 £42 322

Shad Thames 7357 9001 9–4D

"Solid, upmarket Indian" near Butler's Wharf, sometimes let down by "variable service", though "the food is usually to a high standard". / SE1 2YR; www.bengalclipper.co.uk; @bengalclipper; 11.30 pm, Sun 11 pm.

Bentley's W1 £82 4 4 3

11-15 Swallow St 7734 4756 3–3D

"Always fun, especially in the downstairs oyster bar" – Richard Corrigan's "classy" fish veteran, near Piccadilly Circus, won vigorous praise this year for its "amazing" oysters and other "bang-on" fish and seafood; there's a "pleasingly traditional" upstairs restaurant too. / W1B 4DG; www.bentleys.org; @bentleys_london; 10.30 pm; no jeans; booking: max 8; set pre-theatre £52 (FP).

Berber & Q E8 NEW £42 4 3 4

Arch 338 Acton Mews no tel 1–2D

If you can hack the "thumping house music" at this "über-hip Haggerston railway arch renovation" you'll be dealt metal trays of "smoky, sticky, melt-in-the-mouth BBQ'd meats", surprisingly "sublime veg dishes" and "excellent" cocktails; be prepared to queue though (no ressies – natch!). / E8 4EA; www.berberandq.com; @BerberAndQ; 10.30 pm, Sun 9.30 pm; D only, closed Mon; no booking.

The Berners Tavern London EDITION W1 £72 2 2 4

10 Berners St 7908 7979 3–1D

"You feel like a movie star" in this "opulent" and "dramatic" room – one of London's "most gorgeous" – which offers the scope for "fabulous people watching"; prices are "inflated" however, and the food (under Jason Atherton, no less) is no better than "competent". / W1T 3NP; www.bernerstavern.com; 11.45 pm, Sun 10.15 pm.

Best Mangal £36 4 3 2

619 Fulham Rd, SW6 7610 0009 5–4A

104 North End Rd, W14 7610 1050 7–2D

66 North End Rd, W14 7602 0212 7–2D

"Fantastic grilled meats", "all cooked over a mammoth charcoal grill", are supplemented by "super-fresh salads" at these "cheerful and cheap" Turks, in west London. / www.bestmangal.com; midnight, Sat 1 am; no Amex.

Bianco43 £43 3 2 2

7 Northumberland Ave, WC2 7321 2915 2–3C

43 Greenwich Church St, SE10 8858 2668 1–3D

1-3 Lee Rd, SE3 8318 2700 1–4D

"Excellent pizzas" (from a Neapolitan wood-fired oven), plus other well-rated fare, win praise for this Italian trio, which have expanded from their original bases in Greenwich and Blackheath, with a recent opening near Trafalgar Square. / www.bianco43.com.

Bibendum SW3 £75 2 3 3

81 Fulham Rd 7581 5817 5–2C

"On a fine day, one of the loveliest rooms in London" – this "civilised" stalwart in the old Michelin Building is a landmark of Brompton Cross; its "stonking" wine list is nowadays a more reliable attraction than its "variable" cuisine, however, and "you'll need deep pockets to enjoy it". / SW3 6RD; www.bibendum.co.uk; 11 pm, Sun 10.30 pm; booking: max 10; set Sun L £55 (FP).

Bibendum Oyster Bar SW3 £52 2 4 2

81 Fulham Rd 7589 1480 5–2C

A cute spot for a luxurious light bite – the chic café off the foyer of Chelsea's Conran Shop is "great for shellfish" ("and has been serving hot food for a few years now" too). / SW3 6RD; www.bibendum.co.uk; @bibendumrestaurant; 10 pm; no booking.

Bibimbap Soho £29 322

10 Charlotte St, W1 7323 6890 2–1C
11 Greek St, W1 7287 3434 4–2A
39 Leadenhall Mkt, EC3 7283 9165 9–2D

"The Korean experience is intensified by the K-Pop posters and Polaroids of happy punters" at these "fast, fun and creative" outfits in Soho, Fitzrovia and Leadenhall Market, whose signature dish – "basically a big stone bowl filled with rice, veg, and meat or seafood" – is "excellent value".

Bibo SW15 £50 443

146 Upper Richmond Rd 8780 0592 10–2B

The interior is "simple and quite stark", but this Putney sibling to Barnes's Sonny's wins an all-round thumbs-up for its "casual" style, "knowledgeable and professional" service, and "superb and authentic" modern Italian cooking. / SW15 2SW; www.biborestaurant.com; @biborestaurant; 10.45 pm.

Big Easy £50 223

12 Maiden Ln, WC2 3728 4888 4–3D
332-334 King's Rd, SW3 7352 4071 5–3C
Crossrail Pl, E14 awaiting tel 11–1C

"Chaotic" service can add to the "buzzy" sense of "mania" at these fun (and kid-friendly) crab shacks, where the lobster, shrimp and other fare come in "massive portions"; there's quite a feeling, though, that the less established Covent Garden branch "isn't a patch on Chelsea". / www.bigeasy.co.uk; @bigeasytweet; Mon-Thu 11 pm, Fri-Sat 11.30, Sun 10.30 pm.

Bilbao Berria SW1 £52 223

2 Regent St 7930 8408 3–3D

There are plusses and minuses at this Theatreland spot (with restaurant below); positives include "plush" decor and "unusual, delicious" tapas – negatives "Fawlty Towers service" and stiff prices. / SW1Y 4LR; www.bilbaoberria.co.uk; Mon-Wed 10.30 pm, Thu-Sat 11 pm; closed Sun.

Bill's £39 123

Branches throughout London

Explosive growth has "lost the identity and special character" of this easygoing chain, whose cooking is too often "barely average" nowadays; the rustic interiors are "still fun and appealing" however, and – for family-friendliness and "a large variety of breakfast options" it still wins many nominations. / most branches 11 pm; no booking.

The Bingham TW10 £65 324

61-63 Petersham Rd 8940 0902 1–4A

"A picturesque setting, with wonderful views over the Thames" makes this "romantic" Richmond boutique hotel dining room "an ideal spot for a long summer lunch", even if "the food can vary from lovely to blah". Top Tip – "the phenomenal value market lunch menu". / TW10 6UT; www.thebingham.co.uk; @thebingham; 10 pm; closed Sun D; no trainers; set weekday L £41 (FP).

Bird £38 332

81 Holloway Rd, N7 3195 8788 8–2D
42-44 Kingsland Rd, E2 7613 5168 12–1B

You can choose anything, so long as it's fried chicken, if you visit this hip, year-old Shoreditch canteen – on most accounts a "simple and brilliant" formula.

Bird in Hand W14 £46 333
Brook Green 7371 2721 7–1C
"The pizzas are the best" at this "good local hang-out" – an attractively converted ex-pub in Brook Green; the rest of the menu is now modern tapas, which some locals judge "less impressive". / W14 0LR; www.thebirdinhandlondon.com; @TBIHLondon; 10 pm, Sun 9.15 pm.

Bird of Smithfield EC1 £63 223
26 Smithfield St 7559 5100 9–2B
Fans of this five-story old Georgian townhouse in Smithfield (with summer roof terrace) love its "classy, tranquil and smooth" style, and "funky" cooking; its ratings are dragged down though by refuseniks who say "it's not as good as expected, and too expensive". / EC1A 9LB; www.birdofsmithfield.com; @BirdoSmithfield; 10 pm; closed Sun; cancellation charge for larger bookings; set always available £36 (FP).

Bistro 1 £28 232
27 Frith St, W1 7734 6204 4–3A
33 Southampton St, WC2 7379 7585 4–3D
"Excellent prices for central london" found the appeal of these popular budget West End bistros; are they getting a bit complacent though? – "I go about 15 times a year, and while it's still great value, quality is slipping". / www.bistro1.co.uk; @bistro1_london; midnight.

Bistro Aix N8 £53 442
54 Topsfield Pde, Tottenham Ln 8340 6346 8–1C
"They say it's in Crouch End, but it feels like rural France" – so say fans of this "small", "closely packed" and rather "romantic" fixture, which serves "traditional" bistro fare that's "well-executed and presented". / N8 8PT; www.bistroaix.co.uk; @bistroaixlondon; 10 pm, Fri & Sat 11 pm; Mon-Thu D only, Fri-Sun open L & D; no Amex; set weekday L & pre-theatre £39 (FP).

Bistrò by Shot SW6 NEW £48 343
28 Parsons Green Ln 7371 7533 10–1B
A "cosy", all-day, café-cum-bistro near Parsons Green, with an evening menu featuring 'proper' cooking; initial reports suggest it's a cut-above (and that goes for the coffee too). / SW6 4HS; www.bistrobyshot.com; @Bistrobyshot; 10 pm, Sun 6 pm; closed Sun D; set weekday L £31 (FP).

Bistro Union SW4 £46 343
40 Abbeville Rd 7042 6400 10–2D
"Great quality and great value" inspire most who report on Adam (Trinity) Byatt's "bustly" Clapham bistro; no denying the few critics, though, for whom it "doesn't quite make it", "sacrificing taste and quality for trendiness and novelty factor". / SW4 9NG; www.bistrounion.co.uk; @BistroUnion; 10 pm, Sun 8 pm.

Blackfoot Bar & Backroom Dining EC1 £45 333
46 Exmouth Mkt 7837 4384 9–1A
"Pork in all forms of delicious-ness" and the "genuine character" of its setting (a reclaimed pie 'n' mash shop) win consistent (if not quite universal) praise for Allegra McEvedy's Farringdon yearling. / EC1R 4QL; www.blackfootrestaurant.co.uk; @blackfootEC1; 10.15 pm; closed Sun.

Blacklock W1 NEW **£35** 4 4 3

25 Great Windmill St 3441 6996 3–2D

"Chops, chops and more chops" is the promise at this "buzzy", new "industrial-style" Soho basement; it certainly does "exactly what it says on the tin", and "it's hard to go wrong with large piles of meat at a decent price". / W1D 7LH; www.theblacklock.com; @blacklocksoho; 11.30 pm; closed Sun.

Blanchette W1 **£39** 3 4 5

9 D'Arblay St 7439 8100 3–1D

"What a find!"; this "lovely and romantic" (if "cramped") Soho yearling is "a gem" – superb "buzzy" atmosphere, "knowledgeable" service, and "delightful" Gallic take on 'tapas' too. / W1F 8DS; www.blanchettesoho.co.uk; @blanchettesoho; 11 pm, Sun 9 pm.

Bleecker Street Burger E1 NEW **£16** 4 3 2

Unit B Pavilion Building, Spitalfields Mkt 07712 540501 12–2B

"Patties cooked to perfection with drooling cheese" is the promise of New Yorker, Zan Kaufman's popular pop-up, whose permanent Spitalfields Market perch is starting to supplant her roving matt-black van. / E1 6AA; www.bleeckerburger.co.uk; @bleeckerburger; 9 pm.

Bleeding Heart Restaurant EC1 **£63** 3 3 5

Bleeding Heart Yd, Greville St 7242 8238 9–2A

"Tucked away in a quiet corner of Hatton Garden", this "old-fashioned" warren – comprising a restaurant, tavern and bistro – is equally superb for "business bonding", or "seductive romance". The Gallic cuisine is "a safe bet", but it's the "epic" wine list and marvellously "cosy and intimate" style that are the real clinchers. / EC1N 8SJ; www.bleedingheart.co.uk; @bleedingheartyd; 10.30 pm; closed Sat & Sun.

Blixen E1 NEW **£51** 3 2 3

65a Brushfield St 7101 0093 12–2B

"Filling a gap in the market near Spitalfields" – this "light and airy" new brasserie is a "good all-dayer" occupying an attractively converted former bank (and with a "beautiful outside terrace"); service, however, is not always "up to speed". / E1 6AA; www.blixen.co.uk; @BlixenLondon; 11 pm, Sun 8 pm.

Blue Elephant SW6 **£54** 2 2 3

The Boulevard 7751 3111 10–1B

On the plus-side, this "out-on-a-limb" Imperial Wharf Thai has "romantic" lush jungle decor, and nice waterside views; there are significant negatives too though – "it's not a patch on the old one in Fulham Broadway", and prices are OTT ("you could find better value in Mayfair without trekking to Chelsea Harbour!)" / SW6 2UB; www.blueelephant.com; @BlueElephantLon; 10.30 pm, Fri & Sat 11.30 pm; closed weekday L.

Bluebird SW3 **£63** 1 2 3

350 King's Rd 7559 1000 5–3C

Airy, potentially stylish bar/restaurant, on the first floor of the well-known Chelsea landmark, which shows "no great love for guests or cooking" and is "so expensive"; come on D&D London, it's time to sort this one out… / SW3 5UU; www.bluebird-restaurant.co.uk; @bluebirdchelsea; 10.30 pm, Sun 9.30 pm; set always available £32 (FP).

Blueprint Café
Design Museum SE1 £48 235
28 Shad Thames, Butler's Wharf 7378 7031 9–4D
"If you can't get romantic with the amazing views of the Thames and Tower Bridge here, best settle down to the single life!"; predictably though "it's the venue that impresses" – even fans say the food "won't blow your socks off", and to critics it's plain "lazy". / SE1 2YD; www.blueprintcafe.co.uk; @BlueprintCafe; 10.30 pm.

Bó Drake W1 NEW £44 223
6 Greek St no tel 4–2A
A "very cool, young vibe" infuses this "small and stylish" new addition to Soho, whose combination of East Asian cuisine and BBQ (plus cocktails) "is in high demand"; not everyone is wowed though, with a couple of reports of "a totally underwhelming experience". / W1D 4DE; www.bodrake.co.uk; @bodrakesoho; 10.30 pm; closed Sun.

Bob Bob Ricard W1 £65 345
1 Upper James St 3145 1000 3–2D
"Love the 'press for champagne' button on every table!" – this "wacky" Soho diner is "perfect for an intimate meal" or "girls' lunch" thanks to its fun, boothed seating, "OTT" decor and "charming" service; on the downside, the cooking is no more than "high-end comfort food" and "prices are silly for what you get". Top Menu Tip – "excellent beef Wellington". / W1F 9DF; www.bobbobricard.com; @BobBobRicard; Sun-Fri 11.15 pm, Sat midnight; closed Sat L; jacket required.

The Bobbin SW4 £46 343
1-3 Lillieshall Rd 7738 8953 10–1D
"A cosy little gem in a side street off the Pavement in Clapham", with "an airy conservatory and adorable garden out back", providing "excellent" service, and "a great range" of pub grub. / SW4 0LN; www.thebobbinclapham.com; @bobbinsw4; 10 pm, Sun 9 pm.

Bobo Social W1 £45 443
95 Charlotte St 7636 9310 2–1C
"Outstanding" rare-breed burgers are improbably served on "chintzy crockery" at this "tiny, simple, town-house, front room conversion" at the northerly end of Fitzrovia's restaurant row; it's all "a welcome departure from the typical, ranch-style approach" – nice cocktails too. / W1T 4PZ; www.bobosocial.com; @BoboSocial; 10.30 pm; closed Sun.

BOCCA DI LUPO W1 £58 544
12 Archer St 7734 2223 3–2D
"Phenomenal" Italian tapas – "really unusual" dishes from all over the country, including lots of game and offal – help inspire mass adulation for Jacob Kennedy and Victor Hugo's "wildly popular" venture, near Piccadilly Circus. It has a "wonderful", "casual" atmosphere too – if an "incredibly noisy" one – with many reports tipping the bar-side perches as the best seats in the house. Desserts are "particularly original" too (or "skip pud, and go to Gelupo, their 'sister' ice cream shop opposite"). See also Vico. / W1D 7BB; www.boccadilupo.com; @boccadilupo; 11 pm, Sun 9.30 pm; booking: max 10.

Al Boccon di'vino TW9 **£67** 4 4 5

14 Red Lion St 8940 9060 1–4A

"Holy moly!"; "a mind-boggling parade of Italian dishes" from a "never-ending, no-choice tasting menu" rewards the trip to this "mad one-off" in central Richmond; "you never know quite what you're going to get", and "it's a little overwhelming, but certainly an experience!" / TW9 1RW; www.nonsolovinoltd.co.uk; 8 pm; closed Mon, Tue L & Wed L.

Bodean's **£44** 2 2 3

10 Poland St, W1 7287 7575 3–1D
4 Broadway Chambers, SW6 7610 0440 5–4A
169 Clapham High St, SW4 7622 4248 10–2D
201 City Rd, EC1 7608 7230 12–1A NEW
16 Byward St, EC3 7488 3883 9–3D

These "very casual" US-style BBQ haunts "have some real competition" nowadays, and – though "reliable" – their meaty-licious mix of ribs, pulled pork, steaks, burgers and dogs needs to "up its game" to stand out as once it did. / www.bodeansbbq.com; 11 pm, Sun 10.30 pm; booking: min 8.

La Bodega Negra W1 **£50** 2 2 4

16 Moor St 7758 4100 4–2B

Fans say there's a "fun" (if "so noisy") time to be had at this dim-lit Mexican basement in Soho – the food's "quite good" too ("if overpriced for what it is") but the service can be "appalling". / W1D 5NH; www.labodeganegra.com; 1 am, Sun midnight; set weekday L £28 (FP).

Boisdale SW1 **£63** 2 2 3

13-15 Eccleston St 7730 6922 2–4B

"Plush jock-inese decor"... "spectacular cigar terrace and whisky selection"... "amazing wine list"... "traditional, meaty Scottish fare"... live jazz – this Belgravia bastion is well-known as a "clubbable" redoubt of male revelry; its ratings were hit this year though by some reports of "terrible" service and "unexciting" meals. / SW1W 9LX; www.boisdale.co.uk; @boisdale; midnight; closed Sat L & Sun.

Boisdale of Bishopsgate EC2 **£66** 2 2 2

202 Bishopsgate, Swedeland Ct 7283 1763 9–2D

"A Dickensian alley" leads to this City offshoot of the Victoria original "with an old world club-like feel to it"; fans applaud its meaty Caledonian fare and appeal as a business venue – critics though find the cooking merely "acceptable". / EC2M 4NR; www.boisdale.co.uk; @Boisdale; 11 pm, Sat midnight; closed Sat L & Sun.

Boisdale of Canary Wharf E14 **£63** 3 3 3

Cabot Pl 7715 5818 11–1C

Canary Wharf spin-off from the famous Belgravia Caledonian that's "a little on the expensive side", but often tipped especially for business, thanks to its "excellent" steaks and seafood bar, "great range of drinks" and "spacious" interior; "cigars outside a bonus" (if you like that sort of thing). / E14 4QT; www.boisdale.co.uk; @boisdaleCW; 11 pm; closed Sun D.

Bombay Brasserie SW7 £59 333

Courtfield Close, Gloucester Rd 7370 4040 5–2B

This "posh" South Kensington stalwart wins praise for its "refined" cooking and "elegant" decor (particularly in the conservatory); even fans can find it "pricey" however, and its ratings slipped a tad this year – perhaps the challenges caused by its ongoing refurbishment programme. / SW7 4QH; www.bombaybrasserielondon.com; @bbsw7; 11.30 pm, Sun 10.30 pm; closed Mon L.

Bombay Palace W2 £49 542

50 Connaught St 7723 8855 6–1D

"All the ambience of Terminal 3, but quality is sky high!" – this grand but "drab" Bayswater Indian is "not the most exciting venue", but "that does nothing to disguise the fabulous flavours" of its "exemplary" cooking, which has been "consistent over many years"; it closed unexpectedly in summer 2015, but was set to re-open in mid-autumn. / W2 2AA; www.bombay-palace.co.uk; @bombaypalacew2; 11 pm.

Bone Daddies £34 444

30-31 Peter St, W1 7287 8581 3–2D

Whole Foods, Kensington High St, W8 7287 8581 5–1A NEW

The Bower, Baldwin St, EC1 7439 9299 12–1A NEW

"Go early to avoid the crazy queues, and being rammed next to loads of self-adoring 20-somethings", if you grab a bite at this "rock 'n' roll ramen house" in Soho, which doesn't only offer "silky, rich noodle dishes", but lots of other "enormously tasty" snacks. (Top Menu Tips include the "incredible miso aubergine" and "ever-so nice green tea ice cream".) It has an OK spin-off over Kensington's Whole Foods too, and – coming soon – a branch in its spiritual home – Shoreditch (and see also Shackfuyu).

Bonhams Restaurant
Bonhams Auction House W1 NEW £68 433

101 New Bond St 7468 5868 3–2B

Especially for a business lunch, consider this very smart if low key new dining room, set at the back of the famous Mayfair auction house (but also with its own entrance) – Tom Kemble's cooking is notably "accomplished", and "there are some genuine bargains lurking within the wine list". / W1S 1SR; www.bonhams.com/locations/RES; 8.30 pm; closed Sat & Sun.

Bonnie Gull W1 £58 443

21a Foley St 7436 0921 2–1B

"Like a weekend to the Cornish coast without the traffic!" – this "cute" Fitzrovia "seafood shack" may be "cramped" and "noisy" but it has won a wide reputation with its "simply prepared and beautifully cooked fish". See also Bonnie Gull Seafood Bar in Exmouth Market. / W1W 6DS; www.bonniegull.com; @BonnieGull; 9.45 pm, Sun 8.45 pm.

Bonnie Gull Seafood Bar EC1 £55 332

55-57 Exmouth Mkt 3122 0047 9–1A

"Little portions of deliciousness" from a menu of "simple", but "different" fishy small plates mostly win a very good rep for this Exmouth Market café, although there is also a school of thought that it's "fine but not outstanding". / EC1R 4QE; www.bonniegullseafoodbar.com; @BonnieGull; 9.30 pm; closed Sun.

The Booking Office
St Pancras Renaissance Hotel NW1 **£66** 2 2 4
Euston Rd 7841 3566 8–3C
All agree the "unique" setting – the conversion of St Pancras's old ticket office – is "glorious" and "very atmospheric" at what's nowadays an adjunct to a swish hotel; too often of late however, it's been "a shame" about its "poor cooking", and "prices are very salty". / NW1 2AR; www.bookingofficerestaurant.com; 11 pm.

Boom Burger **£20** 3 3 2
272 Portobello Rd, W10 8960 3533 6–1A
1 Brixton Station Rd, SW9 awaiting tel 10–2D NEW
"Jamaican patties are all the rage at this different Portobello venue" (which now has a new Brixton spin off). / www.boomburger.co.uk; @BOOMburgerLDN.

Boopshis W1 **£40** 3 3 3
31 Windmill St 3205 0072 2–1C
"The owners found their Austrian grandmother's recipe book and copied well!" – a "cheap 'n' cheerful" corner café in Fitzrovia, majoring in "excellent schnitzels"; a downside? – "it can get a bit boring after a few visits!" / W1T 2JN; www.boopshis.com; @boopshis; 10 pm; closed Sun.

Boqueria SW2 **£34** 3 4 4
192 Acre Ln 7733 4408 10–2D
"It's easy to over-order" at this "vibrant" and extremely popular little outfit, between Clapham and Brixton – the "terrific tapas" is "inexpensive", and there's "a really warm welcome" too. / SW2 5UL; www.boqueriatapas.com; @BoqueriaTapas; 11 pm, Fri & Sat 12 am, Sun 10 pm; closed weekday L.

Il Bordello E1 **£50** 3 5 4
81 Wapping High St 7481 9950 11–1A
"Exemplary service" – "full of Italian warmth" – helps win this "closely packed" and "noisy" Wapping local "gem" a hugely devoted following, and its atmosphere's "terrific"; as for the "proper, homely Italian cooking", portions are "enormous" (with "brilliant pizza" a highlight). / E1W 2YN; www.ilbordello.com; 11 pm, Sun 10.30 pm; closed Sat L.

Boro Bistro SE1 **£42** 3 3 3
Montague Cl, 6-10 Borough High St 7378 0788 9–3C
Limited feedback this year on this small bistro (with outside terrace), cutely nestled against picturesque Southwark Cathedral – it's well-rated though, and praised for its good value tapas-y fare. / SE1 9QQ; www.borobistro.co.uk; @borobistro; 10.30 pm; closed Mon & Sun.

La Bota N8 **£35** 3 3 4
31 Broadway Pde 8340 3082 1–1C
"Wonderful cooking at hard-to-beat prices" ensures that this long-established Crouch End tapas haunt is "always busy". / N8 9DB; www.labota.co.uk; 11 pm, Sun 10.30 pm; closed Mon L; no Amex.

The Botanist £63 2 2 3

7 Sloane Sq, SW1 7730 0077 5–2D

Broadgate Circle, EC2 awaiting tel 12–2B NEW

The hugely convenient location of this "very buzzy" Sloane Square rendezvous, "probably explains why it's overpriced"; it has a new Broadgate sibling, which is "good for a quick business lunch", but likewise only "averagely good" in most respects.
/ www.thebotanistlondon.com.

Boudin Blanc W1 £58 2 2 4

5 Trebeck St 7499 3292 3–4B

"A beautiful Mayfair setting" (with many al fresco tables) and "festive" atmosphere ensures this Shepherd Market bistro remains "absolutely packed"; its menu of Gallic staples is "not cheap" though, and sceptics feel it's now "trading on its location". / W1J 7LT; www.boudinblanc.co.uk; 11 pm.

Bouillabaisse W1 NEW £84

4 Mill St 3794 8448 3–2C

Kurt Zdesar's seafood specialist on the former site of Alvin Leung's Bo London (RIP) in Mayfair opened in June 2015, too late for our survey; at £60 a portion, let's hope they do a good job with the signature dish. / W1S 2AX; www.bouillabaisse.co.uk; @BouillabaisseW1; 10.30 pm.

Boulestin SW1 £70 2 3 2

5 St James's St 7930 2030 3–4D

"Reviving the name of the very famous Boulestin", Joel Kissin's ambitious yearling occupies "elegant" premises "tucked away in St James's", and is "brilliant in warm weather" thanks to its "delightful private courtyard"; it's "not cheap" though, and while the food is "trying hard", critics feel it's "lost its way". / SW1A 1EF; www.boulestin.co.uk; @BoulestinLondon; 10.30 pm; closed Sun; set pre theatre £42 (FP).

The Boundary E2 £63 3 3 5

2-4 Boundary St 7729 1051 12–1B

The "stunning rooftop terrace", and "impressive basement dining room" both win praise for Sir Terence Conran's "chilled" Shoreditch operation; its "professional" cuisine is well-rated too, although "tiny" portions are a bugbear. / E2 7DD; www.theboundary.co.uk; @BoundaryLDN; 10.30 pm; D only, ex Sun L only.

The Brackenbury W6 £52 3 4 3

129-131 Brackenbury Rd 8741 4928 7–1C

"It's so nice to have this neighbourhood pearl back in business"; Ossie Gray's year-old regime at this convivial, if higgledy-piggledy, Hammersmith favourite is working well, and "you have to admire doing proper cooking in a small backstreet spot"; "strong wine list too". / W6 0BQ; www.brackenburyrestaurant.co.uk; @BrackenburyRest; 10 pm; closed Mon; set weekday L £33 (FP).

Bradley's NW3 £59 3 3 2

25 Winchester Rd 7722 3457 8–2A

"Close by Hampstead Theatre" – this Swiss Cottage backstreet fixture is "always full before a show"; for other occasions, it inspires limited feedback, but it's quite a classy spot in an "area that's not well-endowed" – "fish is particularly reliable". / NW3 3NR; www.bradleysnw3.co.uk; 10 pm; closed Sun D; set Sun L £37 (FP).

Brady's SW18 **£34** 3 3 3

Dolphin Hs, Smugglers Way 8877 9599 10–2B

"Upmarket", "quirky" fish 'n' chip restaurant, run by the Brady family, whose longstanding success allowed it to expand to a Battersea riverside site a year ago; one or two regulars feel it has "no ambience" now, but ratings support those who say it's "still an excellent, unpretentious local". / SW18 1DG; www.bradysfish.co.uk; @Bradyfish; 10 pm; closed Mon, Tue L, Wed L, Thu L & Sun; no Amex; no booking.

La Brasserie SW3 **£55** 2 2 4

272 Brompton Rd 7581 3089 5–2C

"Truly French in feel" – this "slick and buzzy" old-favourite is, say fans, "always a safe bet", particularly for a languid breakfast with the papers; it's not cheap however, and harsher critics jibe that its "Chelsea clientele is obviously easily pleased…" / SW3 2AW; www.labrasserielondon.co.uk; @labrasserie; Mon-Sat 11.30 pm, Sun 11 pm; no booking, S & Sun L; set always available £35 (FP).

Brasserie Blanc **£51** 2 2 2

Branches throughout London

Raymond B's brasserie chain "looks more attractive than most" (especially its wonderfully situated Covent Garden branch above the piazza); even many fans describe its performance as "nothing outstanding" though, and some reports were "terrible" this year ("Maman Blanc would be appalled…") / www.brasserieblanc.com; most branches close between 10 pm & 11 pm; SE1 closed Sun D, most City branches closed Sat & Sun.

Brasserie Chavot W1 **£71** 3 4 4

41 Conduit St 7183 6425 3–2C

Eric Chavot's "classy and delightful" Mayfair chamber "just gets better and better", winning very solid praise this year for its "spacious" setting, "consistently excellent" service and for its "high-quality", "upmarket brasserie fare". / W1S 2YQ; www.brasseriechavot.com; @brasseriechavot; 10.30 pm, Sun 9 pm.

Brasserie Gustave SW3 **£49** 4 5 3

4 Sydney St 7352 1712 5–2C

A charming host of the "bon-bibeur variety", along with "definitively French" cooking have made a big hit of this brasserie yearling, on the Chelsea site that was formerly MPW's Sydney Street Grill (RIP); named for Gustave Eiffel (designer of a Parisian landmark) – its amiably clichéd style is "one of dated reminisces through-and-through". / SW3 6PP; www.brasserie-gustave.com; @brassergustave; 10.30 pm, Fri & Sat 11 pm; closed Mon & Tue L; set Sun L £39 (FP).

Brasserie Toulouse-Lautrec SE11 **£45** 3 3 3

140 Newington Butts 7582 6800 1–3C

"A good bolt hole" in the unlovely environs of Elephant & Castle, this Gallic venture provides "dependable bistro-ish food in large portions, plus friendly service, all at a decent price". / SE11 4RN; www.btlrestaurant.co.uk; @btlrestaurant; 10.30 pm, Sat & Sun 11 pm.

BRASSERIE ZÉDEL W1 **£40** 2 4 5

20 Sherwood St 7734 4888 3–2D

"Sumptuous and gilded", Corbin & King's "amazing" (listed) Art Deco basement is reminiscent of the grandest Parisian brasseries, and in three short years has become a West End landmark. OK, the realisation of the huge Gallic menu is extremely "pedestrian", but compensation is provided by the "really efficient" service and – mindful of all the grandeur – prices that are "astonishing value" for somewhere a stone's throw from Piccadilly Circus. / W1F 7ED; www.brasseriezedel.com; @brasseriezedel; 11.45 pm; set always available £29 (FP).

Bravas E1 **£44** 3 3 3

St Katharine Docks 7481 1464 9–3D

"A nice surprise in lovely St Katharine Docks" – this "buzzy" yearling provides an "attractive" vantage-point from which to envy the marina's yacht-owners, and "genuine" tapas that's "slightly out-of-the-ordinary". / E1W 1AT; www.bravastapas.co.uk; @Bravas_Tapas; 10 pm.

Brawn E2 **£50** 5 4 4

49 Columbia Rd 7729 5692 12–1C

"Quirky" but "outstanding" dishes from Ed Wilson, twinned with "adventurous wines, with advice from passionate staff" make for a "fascinating foodie experience", at this "rustic" East End bistro, which remains Caves de Pyrène's top property. / E2 7RG; www.brawn.co; @brawn49; 11 pm; closed Mon L & Sun D; no Amex; set Sun L £41 (FP).

Bread Street Kitchen EC4 **£67** 1 1 1

10 Bread St 3030 4050 9–2B

As a business option, Gordon Ramsay's "enormous" venue in a City shopping mall does have a few fans; for non-expense-accounters though, it's "a Kitchen Nightmare", given its "thoroughly impersonal" style, "thinly stretched" service, and food that's very "run-of-the-mill". / EC4M 9AJ; www.breadstreetkitchen.com; @breadstkitchen; 11 pm, Sun 8 pm.

Brew **£38** 2 2 3

45 Northcote Rd, SW11 7585 2198 10–2C NEW
Lower Richmond Rd, SW15 8789 8287 10–2A
342 Old York Rd, SW18 8871 0713 10–2B
21 High St, SW19 8947 4034 10–2B

"A great brunch range" and "top quality coffee" help win praise for these "easygoing" hang-outs in Clapham, Putney, Wandsworth and Wimbledon; they often miss their mark too though – even many who say the food is "fine" say it's "extortionately pricey for what it is", and service-wise can evoke the spirit of "compu'er says no"! / www.brew-cafe.com.

Briciole W1 **£40** 3 4 3

20 Homer St 7723 0040 6–1D

Fans of Latium's "buzzy" little brother in the backwoods of Marylebone say it "continues to delight" with its "very attentive" service and "simple, high-quality deli food" from an open kitchen; "don't go when it's busy though", when it can seem more "average". / W1H 4NA; www.briciole.co.uk; @briciolelondon; 10.15 pm.

Brick Lane Beigel Bake E1 £6 4 2 1

159 Brick Ln 7729 0616 12–1C

"Unbeatable for fending off the munchies 24/7!"; a treasured "defiantly no frills" East Ender, serving "the best take-away salt beef beigel in London" – "how long can it hold out against gentrification?" / E1 6SB; open 24 hours; no credit cards; no booking.

Brigade
The Fire Station SE1 £54 2 3 3

139 Tooley St 0844 346 1225 9–4D

Former fire station, near London Bridge – nowadays a bistro providing employment for the homeless; most (if not quite all) reporters are satisfied by the provisions, and all agree it's "a worthwhile social enterprise". / SE1 2HZ; www.thebrigade.co.uk; @brigadeSE1; 10 pm; closed Sun.

The Bright Courtyard W1 £59 4 3 4

43-45 Baker St 7486 6998 2–1A

There's "major competition nearby" (from the Royal Chinas), but this "upmarket Chinese" is – for its smaller following – "by far the best", with "modern and superior surroundings" (indeed with a bright courtyard), and dim sum that's "excellent" and "sophisticated". / W1U 8EW; www.lifefashiongroup.com; @BrightCourtyard; 10.45 pm, Thu-Sat 11.15 pm.

Brilliant UB2 £38 4 4 3

72-76 Western Rd 8574 1928 1–3A

"The name says it all!", say fans of this Southall legend, lost in a tangle of suburban streets – "it's busy and vaguely chaotic" but serves "authentic Punjabi food" that's "excellent value". / UB2 5DZ; www.brilliantrestaurant.com; @BrilliantRST; 11 pm, Fri & Sat 11.30 pm; closed Mon, Sat L & Sun L.

Brinkley's SW10 £54 2 2 4

47 Hollywood Rd 7351 1683 5–3B

"A really fun, local haunt" for the (older) Chelsea set – John Brinkley's buzzy bar/restaurant is an "old favourite" hereabouts, although its "fantastic value wines" are the big draw, not its "very average food"; (sadly its lovely garden is now an extension to the main restaurant). / SW10 9HX; www.brinkleys.com; @BrinkleysR; 11 pm, Sun 10.30 pm; closed weekday L.

The Brown Cow SW6 £43 3 3 3

676 Fulham Rd 7384 9559 10–1B

"Nearly as good as its sibling the Sand's End" – a heart-of-Fulham gastropub (on the site that was Manson, RIP) with quality cooking and an atmosphere that's "part pub, part French brasserie". / SW6 5SA; www.thebrowncowpub.co.uk; @TheBrownCowPub; 10 pm.

The Brown Dog SW13 £50 3 3 4

28 Cross St 8392 2200 10–1A

"A perfect country-style pub, tucked away in a super-cute terraced Barnes backstreet, and a great oasis for a quiet, relaxing meal from the short menu of simple, fresh dishes"; "being able to take the dog along is a bonus". / SW13 0AP; www.thebrowndog.co.uk; @browndogbarnes; 10 pm, Sun 9 pm.

(Hix at Albemarle)
Brown's Hotel W1 **£73** 2 2 2
Albemarle St 7518 4004 3–3C
Fans of this "discreet and quiet" Mayfair "oasis" approve of its "classy", business-friendly grandeur, including for a "civilised breakfast"; "despite being well-appointed, it feels somewhat soulless" however, and even with Mark Hix's involvement, the cooking is "very mainstream" and "very expensive". / W1S 4BP; www.thealbemarlerestaurant.com; @HIXMayfair; 11 pm, Sun 10.30 pm.

Brunswick House Café SW8 **£48** 2 2 5
30 Wandsworth Rd 7720 2926 10–1D
The "surreal" set up – "an eccentric but charming dining room full of reclaimed objects from the adjacent architectural salvage operation" – is the special draw to this vast Georgian house, at Vauxhall Cross; on the downside, service can be "shoddy", and "you pay a lot" nowadays for food that arguably "tries too hard". / SW8 2LG; www.brunswickhousecafe.co.uk; 10 pm; closed Sun D.

Bubbledogs W1 **£30** 1 2 3
70 Charlotte St 7637 7770 2–1C
"A glass of fizz and a huge variety of hot dogs… great!", so say fans of this Fitzrovia two-year-old, for whom it's "delightfully fun"; "once is enough" for many reporters though, who either find the concept no more than "faintly amusing", or who "just don't get it". / W1T 4QG; www.bubbledogs.co.uk; @bubbledogsUK; 9 pm; closed Sun.

(Kitchen Table)
Bubbledogs W1 **£102** 4 4 4
70 Charlotte St 7637 7770 2–1C
"What a concept!" – you discover this "haven of gastronomy arranged around an open chef's table" by walking through a curtain from the adjoining hot dog place; it's a "unique" and "fascinating" experience – "great fun talking to the chef", with cuisine that's "imaginative, well-balanced, amusing, exciting… absolutely superb". / W1T 4QG; www.kitchentablelondon.co.uk; @bubbledogsKT; 9.30 pm (6 pm & 7.30 pm seatings only); D only, closed Mon & Sun.

Buddha-Bar London SW1 **£69** 3 3 3
145 Knightsbridge 3667 5222 5–1D
"Lacking the caché of its international counterparts", this nightclubby operation generates little feedback for a large haunt in the heart of Knightsbridge; still, even if it's "not cheap", its Pan-Asian fare is worth a try. / SW1X 7PA; www.buddhabarlondon.com; @BuddhaBarLondon; 10 pm.

Buen Ayre E8 **£52** 5 3 3
50 Broadway Mkt 7275 9900 1–2D
A carnivore's delight, this "bare" and "noisy" Argentine 'parrilla' in Hackney provides a "fantastic informal atmosphere" – "tremendous steak (cooked just the way it should be)" and "a great choice of Malbec" help make it "impossible to get a table". / E8 4QJ; www.buenayre.co.uk; 10.30 pm; no Amex.

Buenos Aires Cafe £51 343
86 Royal Hill, SE10 8488 6764 1–*3D*
17 Royal Pde, SE3 8318 5333 1–*4D*
"Excellent steaks, pizza and decent wine" are highlights of this popular Blackheath Argentinian (run by a retired tango dancer!); no feedback this year on its café-like Greenwich offshoot. / www.buenosairesltd.com; SE3 10.30 pm, SE10 7 pm, Sat & Sun 6 pm; no Amex.

The Builders Arms SW3 £48 234
13 Britten St 7349 9040 5–*2C*
Some feel "it rests on its lovely location", but this modernised backstreet boozer is nevertheless one of Chelsea's better watering holes, with an "excellent" ambience and reasonable scran. / SW3 3TY; www.geronimo-inns.co.uk; @BuildersChelsea; 10 pm, Thu-Sat 11 pm, Sun 9 pm; no booking.

The Bull N6 £46 234
13 North Hill 8341 0510 1–*1C*
"A real gem" that's "widely popular among Highgate residents" – a "most comfortable" pub with its own microbrewery, serving "a fantastic selection of beers and ales", plus food that's "successful enough". / N6 4AB; thebullhighgate.co.uk; @Bull_Highgate; 10 pm.

The Bull & Gate NW5 £49 323
389 Kentish Town Rd 3437 0905 8–*2B*
It took Young's two years to restore this old Kentish Town boozer, but by all accounts it's a huge improvement – "great food, so different from how it was". / NW5 2TJ; www.bullandgatenw5.co.uk; @BullandGateNW5; 10 pm, Sun 9 pm.

Bull & Last NW5 £60 433
168 Highgate Rd 7267 3641 8–*1B*
"Just what a gastropub should be" – North London's top boozer is an "always enjoyable" Kentish Town destination, with "hearty food that gives a nice nod to the seasons". / NW5 1QS; www.thebullandlast.co.uk; @thebullandlast; 10 pm, Sun 9 pm.

Bumpkin £52 222
119 Sydney St, SW3 3730 9344 5–*2B*
102 Old Brompton Rd, SW7 7341 0802 5–*2B*
209 Westbourne Park Rd, W11 7243 9818 6–*1B*
Westfield Stratford City, The Street, E20 8221 9900 1–*1D*
"The success is mystifying" of these "casual" faux-rustic diners, that make much of their local sourcing and seasonality; aside from being "patient with kids", service can be "atrocious" and the food "distinctly average". / www.bumpkinuk.com; 11 pm; closed Mon.

Bunnychow W1 £11 322
74 Wardour St 3697 7762 3–*2D*
South African former street-food pop-up that now has a permanent Soho base, serving "cheap, bountiful and tasty" scoff; in case you're wondering, a bunnychow is a stuffed loaf. / W1F 0TE; www.bunnychow.com; @thebunnychow.

Buona Sera £40 333
289a King's Rd, SW3 7352 8827 5–3C
22 Northcote Rd, SW11 7228 9925 10–2C
"I've been going for 26 years: same staff, same menu, same ambience – what's not to like?"; the "happy but loud" Battersea original of this Italian duo is perpetually "crammed with yelling locals of all ages" drawn by its "cheap, simple and tasty" pizza and pasta; (no-one much mentions SW3, with its funny double-decker seating). / midnight; SW3 11.30 pm, Sun 10 pm; SW3 closed Mon L.

Burger & Lobster £45 323
29 Clarges St, W1 7409 1699 3–4B
36 Dean St, W1 7432 4800 4–2A
6 Little Portland St, W1 7907 7760 3–1C
40 St John St, EC1 7490 9230 9–1B
Bow Bells Hs, 1 Bread St, EC4 7248 1789 9–2B
"For a simple, no-nonsense meal" with "a real buzz", armies of fans still heartily recommend these "relaxed" surf 'n' turf diners, lauding the "succulent lobsters" and "amazing" burgers. Ratings continue to slide south however, and for a few cynics it's turning into "McDonald's, but with better lighting". / www.burgerandlobster.com; @Londonlobster; 10.30 pm; Clarges St closed Sun D, Bread St & St John St closed Sun.

Busaba Eathai £39 224
Branches throughout London
"Just that bit more interesting than Wagamama" (same founder) – these highly popular, communal Thai canteens make a "dependable" option, even if their stylish interiors "have greater wow factor than the food"; "favourite dish? – the calamari". / www.busaba.co.uk; 11 pm, Fri & Sat 11.30 pm, Sun 10 pm; W1 no booking; WC1 booking: min 10.

Bush Dining Hall W12 £45 222
304 Uxbridge Rd 8749 0731 7–1B
For a "homely brunch" or "simple" bite, fans recommend this Boho café next to the music venue; the menu is "limited" however, and critics see its distressed, vintage style as a case of "Shepherd's Bush mutton dressed as Chiswick lamb!" / W12 7LJ; www.bushhalldining.co.uk; @BushHallDining; 10.30 pm, Fri & Sat 10 pm; closed Sun D.

Butcher & Grill SW11 £42 223
39-41 Parkgate Rd 7924 3999 5–4C
Battersea restaurant, deli and attached butcher shop; for a steak or brunch it has its fans, but service is "not always up to scratch", and "the food has a way to go to be more than average". Top Menu Tip – on 'Happy Mondays' get 50% off steaks. / SW11 4NP; www.thebutcherandgrill.com; @ButcherGrill; 11 pm, Sun 4 pm; closed Sun D.

The Butcher's Hook SW6 £48 343
477 Fulham Rd 7385 4654 5–4A
"It's brilliant!", say fans of this attractive boozer, just down the road from Stamford Bridge, applauded for its "always great cooking and friendly staff". / SW6 1HL; www.thebutchershook.co.uk; @thebutchershook; 10.30 pm; no Amex.

Butlers Wharf Chop House SE1 **£59** 2 3 3
36e Shad Thames 7403 3403 *9–4D*
The main reason to seek out this Thames-side business-standby is for "great views of Tower Bridge" – the food can be hit-and-miss ("better to eat that which hasn't been cooked") and the place feels "in need of a refurb". / SE1 2YE; www.chophouse-restaurant.co.uk; @BWChophouse; 11 pm, Sun 10 pm.

La Buvette TW9 **£42** 3 3 4
6 Church Walk 8940 6264 *1–4A*
"Tucked away" in "a lovely old courtyard beside a church", right in the heart of Richmond, this "sweet and secluded" bistro feels rather "special", and serves "dependable" and "good value", traditional French cuisine (if from a "limited" menu). / TW9 1SN; www.labuvette.co.uk; @labuvettebistro; 10 pm.

Byron **£38** 2 3 3
Branches throughout London
"In spite of the Five Guys and Shake Shacks of the world, this takes some beating!"; its attractive, "individually designed" branches "come in all shapes and sizes", staff are "very cheery and efficient" and "you always get a delicious burger". / www.byronhamburgers.com; -most branches 11 pm.

C London W1 **£100** 1 2 3
25 Davies St 7399 0500 *3–2B*
"Full of wannabes!"; this "extortionately expensive" Mayfair eurotrash-magnet too often provides "amateur" service and "terrible" Italian food – "thank god we were taken!" / W1K 3DE; www.crestaurant.co.uk; 11.45 pm.

C&R Cafe **£35** 4 2 2
3-4 Rupert Ct, W1 7434 1128 *4–3A*
52 Westbourne Grove, W2 7221 7979 *6–1B*
"A stand-out in Chinatown" – the original West End branch of this Malaysian duo, serving "excellent", "cheap" food that's "a great approximation of the real thing" (high marks for the lesser known Bayswater outlet too). Top Menu Tip – "the best laksa in the UK!" / www.cnrrestaurant.com; 10.30pm; W2 closed Tue.

Caboose
The Old Truman Brewery E1 **£31**
Ely's Yd, Brick Ln 07437 209 275 *12–2C*
For a "small get-together with family and friends", this custom-built railway cabin outside Brick Lane's Old Truman Brewery is an "amazing" place, according to its tiny fan club (too few reports for a rating); complementing the keenly priced private hire experience is a street food offering of slow smoked meats and burgers. / E1 6QR; www.wearecaboose.com; @WeAreCaboose; 11 pm.

Café 209 SW6 **£26** 2 3 3
209 Munster Rd 7385 3625 *10–1B*
"Joy is hilarious" – long may she reign over her tiny BYO caff in deepest Fulham, where "cheap" Thai chow is part of a visit that's "very good fun". / SW6 6BX; 10.30 pm; D only, closed Sun, closed Dec; no Amex.

Café Below EC2 £40 334

St Mary-le-Bow, Cheapside 7329 0789 9–2B

"Hard to believe such a quiet haven exists just off Cheapside" as this "atmospheric crypt" under Bow Bells church, where service is "friendly and fast", and the "simple", "distinctive", "daily-changing" cooking is "delicious" and "decently priced". Top Menu Tip – "the set, 3-course Friday dinner is a bargain". / EC2 6AU; www.cafebelow.co.uk; @cafebelow ; 9 pm; closed Mon D, Tue D, Sat & Sun.

Café Bohème W1 £48 244

13 Old Compton St 7734 0623 4–2A

"Perennially jam-packed", all-hours French-style bar/café/restaurant in the heart of Soho, where everyone loves the "lively" vibe; it "can deliver some very good dishes" too, but some non-drinkers find it "so crowded you don't really want to eat". / W1 5JQ; www.cafeboheme.co.uk; @CafeBoheme1; 2.45 am, Sun midnight; no booking; set Sun L £41 (FP).

Café del Parc N19 £43 543

167 Junction Road 7281 5684 8–1C

"There's no menu" – you eat the chef's selection of "magical", "Moorish-influenced" tapas at this "terrific", if "tiny" neighbourhood "sparkler" in Tuffnell Park, and service is "brilliant" too. / N19 5PZ; www.delparc.com; @delParc; 10.30 pm; open D only, Wed-Sun; no Amex.

Café du Marché EC1 £55 334

22 Charterhouse Sq 7608 1609 9–1B

"Well hidden down an alleyway in Smithfield", this "delightfully tucked-away" stalwart imports the ambience of a rustic French farmhouse to EC1, serving a "solidly Gallic" menu of "classic bistro fare". By day it's a business lunch favourite, at night live jazz adds to its "cosy, candlelit and romantic" appeal. / EC1M 6DX; www.cafedumarche.co.uk; @lecafedumarche; 10 pm; closed Sat L & Sun.

Café East SE16 £23 422

100 Redriff Rd 7252 1212 11–2B

"Tremendous value at negligible cost" is provided by this "fast-paced", "basic" and "noisy" canteen in Bermondsey, "which sticks faithfully to its Vietnamese roots" (in particular the "satisfying and delicious pho"). / SE16 7LH; www.cafeeast.foodkingdom.com; @cafeeastpho; 10.30 pm, Sun 10 pm; closed Tue.

Cafe Football
Westfield Stratford E20 NEW £46 233

The St 8702 2590 1–1D

Themed around 'the beautiful game', this large and glossy Stratford venue doesn't aim for foodie fireworks, but is "great for kids, or to watch a game with the lads". / E20 1EN; www.cafe-football.com; @cafefootballuk; 11.30 pm.

Café in the Crypt
St Martin's in the Fields WC2 £33 223

Duncannon St 7766 1158 2–2C

"If you want a quick bite" near Trafalgar Square, St Martin-in-the-Fields "bustling" self-service crypt is just the job – the food (soup, sarnies, a few hot dishes) is only "average", but the characterful setting is "delightful", portions are "generous", and prices low. / WC2N 4JJ; stmartin-in-the-fields.org/cafe-in-the-crypt; 8 pm, Thu-Sat 9 pm, Sun 6 pm; no Amex; no booking.

Café Murano £53 444
33 St James's St, SW1 3371 5559 3–3C
34-36 Tavistock St, WC2 3371 5559 4–3D NEW
"Satisfying on every level" – Angela Hartnett's "cosmopolitan and delightful" year-old spin off in St James's has shot to fame thanks to its "disciplined" service and "well-pitched", "reasonably priced" Italian fare; post-survey, a 140-cover Covent Garden sibling opened in late June 2015. / www.cafemurano.co.uk.

Café Pistou EC1 £46 323
8-10 Exmouth Mkt 7278 5333 9–1A
"Bustling and characterful little bistro" that on most accounts is a welcome addition to Exmouth Market; the small plates are possibly a bit "too small" though, and loud music contributes to a "noisy" atmosphere. / EC1R 4QA; www.cafepistou.co.uk; @CafePistou; 10.30 pm.

Café Spice Namaste E1 £56 443
16 Prescot St 7488 9242 11–1A
Cyrus Todiwala's "vibrantly decorated" Indian is a longstanding bright spark in the "culinary desert" south of Whitechapel; service is "jolly" and his "original" and "delicate" Parsi cooking remains a distinct "cut above" ("the specials are always worth a try"). / E1 8AZ; www.cafespice.co.uk; @cafespicenamast; 10.30 pm; closed Sat L & Sun.

Caffè Caldesi W1 £60 343
118 Marylebone Ln 7487 0754 2–1A
A "comfortable" and "pleasant all-rounder" that's long been a fixture of Marylebone; the "robust, regional food is utterly reliable" and "served with friendliness and care". / W1U 2QF; www.caldesi.com; 10.30 pm, Sun 9.30 pm.

Caffé Vergnano £39 223
Staple Inn, 337-338 High Holborn, WC1 7242 7119 9–2A
62 Charing Cross Rd, WC2 7240 3512 4–3B
Royal Festival Hall, SE1 7921 9339 2–3D
2 New Street Sq, EC4 7936 3404 9–2A
Smaller outlets can still be "a delightful sanctuary with excellent coffee", but the best-known and biggest SE1 branch ("convenient for the Festival Hall", and serving light Italian dishes) put in a mixed showing this year, with too many reports of cooking that was "tired" and "tasteless". / www.caffevergnano1882.co.uk; EC4 11 pm, SE1 midnight; WC2 8 pm, Fri & Sat midnight; EC4 Sat & Sun; no Amex.

La Cage Imaginaire NW3 £49 344
16 Flask Walk 7794 6674 8–1A
"A smashing little French restaurant in a cute corner of Hampstead Village", this "hidden gem" is "very cosy" indeed; however, food-wise it's "variable (you suspect when the chef is off, they're not as clued up)". / NW3 1HE; www.la-cage-imaginaire.co.uk; @CageImaginaire; 11 pm.

Cah-Chi £37 332
394 Garratt Ln, SW18 8946 8811 10–2B
34 Durham Rd, SW20 8947 1081 10–2B
"Numerous well-dressed Korean diners are testament to the freshness and quality of the cooking" (some of it BBQ-ed at the table) at these "simple" venues, in Earlsfield and Raynes Park; BYO. / www.cahchi.com; SW20 11 pm; SW18 11 pm, Sat & Sun 11.30 pm; SW20 closed Mon; cash only.

The Camberwell Arms SE5 £55 4 3 3

65 Camberwell Church St 7358 4364 1–3C

"Unusual and utterly delicious" British fare – "strong cooking geared towards offal" – helps make this "confident" yearling "a great addition to SE5"; it's from the same stable as Anchor & Hope – "at least the wait here is shorter". / SE5 8TR; www.thecamberwellarms.co.uk; @camberwellarms; closed Mon L & Sun D.

Cambio de Tercio SW5 £69 3 3 3

161-163 Old Brompton Rd 7244 8970 5–2B

"Expert" cooking (in particular "innovative" tapas) and a "spectacular selection of Spanish wines" has carved a major culinary reputation for Abel Lusa's "colourful" Earl's Court Spaniard; one or two "average" experiences, however, dented ratings this year. / SW5 0LJ; www.cambiodetercio.co.uk; @CambiodTercio; 11.15 pm, Sun 11 pm.

Camino £47 3 3 3

3 Varnishers Yd, Regent Quarter, N1 7841 7331 8–3C

The Blue Fin Building, 5 Canvey St, SE1 3617 3169 9–4A NEW

15 Mincing Ln, EC3 7841 7335 9–3D

33 Blackfriars Ln, EC4 7125 0930 9–2A

The "buzzy" King's Cross original of this emerging chain now has a popular (if "terribly noisy") spin off, near the Old Bailey, and a new outlet in Bankside too; all win praise for "helpful" service and "tasty" tapas. / www.camino.uk.com; EC3 & EC4 closed Sat & Sun.

(Hotel du Vin)
Cannizaro House SW19 £60 2 3 3

West Side, Wimbledon Common 0871 943 0345 10–2A

"Delightfully positioned" by Wimbledon Common, this "romantic" small property is nowadays part of the Hotel du Vin group; you can eat in either the 'bistro' or garden-side Orangerie – reports are few, but suggest that since it changed hands the food is somewhat "improved". / SW19 4UE; www.hotelduvin.com/locations/wimbledon/; @HotelduVinBrand; 10 pm.

Canta Napoli £37 3 3 2

9 Devonshire Rd, W4 8994 5225 7–2A

136 High St, TW11 8977 3344 1–4A

"Terrific, half-metre pizzas" and service that "tries to please" are highlights of these Chiswick and Teddington Italians. / 10.30 pm; no Amex.

Canteen £42 2 2 1

Royal Festival Hall, SE1 0845 686 1122 2–3D

Park Pavilion, 40 Canada Sq, E14 0845 686 1122 11–1C

Crispin Pl, Old Spitalf'ds Mkt, E1 0845 686 1122 12–2B

The promise is of British "comfort food" efficiently delivered at these spartan canteens (whose handily located South Bank branch can be "great for a business lunch"); its ratings are perennially hamstrung though by incidents of "sloppy" service, and "the worst cooking ever". / www.canteen.co.uk; 11 pm, E14 & W1 Sun 7 pm; no booking weekend L.

Cantina Laredo WC2 £52 4 4 4

10 Upper St Martin's Ln 7420 0630 4–3C

"It's great how they make the guacamole at the table" – that's just part of the array of "fresh", "clean-flavoured" Mexican food at this "polished" and "buzzy" Covent Garden operation. / WC2H 9FB; www.cantinalaredo.co.uk; @CantinaLaredoUK; 11.30 pm, Fri & Sat midnight, Sun 10.30 pm.

Canton Arms SW8 £48 3 2 4

177 South Lambeth Rd 7582 8710 10–1D

"In a drab bit of Stockwell", this well-reputed Anchor & Hope sibling is extolled by its fans for its "unfussy, brilliant dishes with huge flavours and no messing about"; it's rated lower than its stablemate though, and sceptics – experiencing average meals – say "it gets good reviews, but we've been unlucky". / SW8 1XP; www.cantonarms.com; 10.30 pm; closed Mon L & Sun D; no Amex; no booking.

Canvas SW1 £70

1 Wilbraham Pl 7823 4463 5–2D

It's all change at this ambitious venture, which in 2014 relocated to Chelsea (to the home of Le Cercle, RIP), and in spring 2015 lost both chef Michael Riemenschneider, and his 'design-your-own-menu' concept; feedback is limited and divided (hence the ongoing lack of a rating) – to fans its "a wondrous experience", but to critics has "no redeeming features". / SW1X 9AE; www.canvaschelsea.com; @CanvasbyMR; 9.30 pm, Fri & Sat 10 pm; D only, closed Mon.

Capote Y Toros SW5 £49 3 4 4

157 Old Brompton Rd 7373 0567 5–2B

"Straight out of Andalucía" – Cambio de Tercio's neighbouring bar "isn't a cheap night out", but is, on most accounts, "a real gem", with "extremely good tapas", plus a quaffable selection of wines, sherries and gins. / SW5 0LJ; www.cambiodetercio.co.uk; @CambiodTercio; 11.30 pm; D only, closed Mon & Sun.

LE CAPRICE SW1 £74 3 4 4

Arlington Hs, Arlington St 7629 2239 3–4C

"Sooooo smooth, soooo suave" – this "effortless" '80s brasserie tucked away behind the Ritz has always "eschewed culinary heights", and even if its "classy comfort food" is a tad less excellent under Richard Caring's ownership, it's "the front of house staff and overall buzz which make it so special". / SW1A 1RJ; www.le-caprice.co.uk; @CapriceHoldings; 11.30 pm Mon-Sat, Sun 10.30 pm.

Caraffini SW1 £53 3 5 4

61-63 Lower Sloane St 7259 0235 5–2D

"There's always a wonderful, sincere welcome" at this "traditional" Chelsea stalwart, near Sloane Square, whose "white-haired clientele" would find it "a sad day if anything changed"; prices are "fair" for the "always dependable" Italian fare. / SW1W 8DH; www.caraffini.co.uk; Mon-Fri 11.30 pm, Sat 11 pm; closed Sun.

Caravaggio EC3 £62 3 3 2

107-112 Leadenhall St 7626 6206 9–2D

To impress a business associate, this "busy" City Italian provides "spacious tables" and "very responsive service", plus cooking that's consistently well rated. / EC3A 4DP; www.etruscarestaurants.com; 10 pm; closed Sat & Sun.

Caravan £45 323

1 Granary Sq, N1 7101 7661 8–3C
11-13 Exmouth Mkt, EC1 7833 8115 9–1A
"Big on bizarre-sounding breakfast dishes" – and with "top expertise in the art of coffee-making" – these "hip and trendy" fusion-haunts get "very busy", particularly as major brunch destinations; nowadays the "cavernous, coolly industrial" King's Cross branch overshadows the Exmouth Market original. / www.caravanonexmouth.co.uk; EC1 10.30 pm, Sun 4 pm; closed Sun.

Carob Tree NW5 £35 454

15 Highgate Rd 7267 9880 8–1B
"The manager gives the best service ever" at this "always bustling" ("loud") Dartmouth Park favourite; the menu is "mainly Greek", and the big draw is the fish – "a top selection, simply and beautifully cooked". / NW5 1QX; no web; 10.30 pm, Sun 9 pm; closed Mon; no Amex.

Carom at Meza W1 £35 233

100 Wardour St 7314 4002 3–2D
Closed by fire in May 2015, D&D London's "buzzy" ("loud") Soho Indian has been popping up all over London ahead of a 2016 relaunch; the food takes a back seat, but the cavernous room, complete with bar and DJ, is "great for socialising" and "appeals to any kind of party". / W1F 0TN; www.meza-soho.co.uk; @CaromSoho; 11 pm; closed Sat L & Sun.

Carousel W1 NEW £53 433

71 Blandford St 7487 5564 3–1A
"I can't stop going back!" – the "inspired rotating chef programme" creates "a wonderful diversity of menus", at this Marylebone merry-go-round, which hosts an ever-changing roster of guest chefs; it's a bit of a Russian Roulette job though – the odd meal turns out "too experimental". / W1U 8AB; www.carousel-london.com; @Carousel_LDN; 11.30 pm.

The Carpenter's Arms W6 £46 333

91 Black Lion Ln 8741 8386 7–2B
A tucked-away Hammersmith location helps set up a "relaxed" atmosphere at this backstreet pub, praised for its "great value" cooking; cute garden too. / W6 9BG; www.carpentersarmsw6.co.uk; 10 pm, Sun 9 pm.

Casa Brindisa SW7 £46 232

7-9 Exhibition Rd 7590 0008 5–2C
Fans may "love everything" about this "hugger mugger" Brindisa-outpost near South Kensington tube (best on the "chilled" terrace), but tapas-wise, "it's not cutting edge", in fact arguably "a bit formulaic". / SW7 2HE; www.casabrindisa.com; @TapasKitchens; 11 pm, Sun 10 pm.

Casa Cruz W11 NEW £48

123 Clarendon Rd 3321 5400 6–2A
A luxurious new addition to the borders of Notting Hill and Holland Park, from South American restaurateur Juan Santa Cruz, set over two floors, and complete with first-floor roof terrace; early days press reports have focused more on the steep pricing than the Argentinian-inspired European food. / W11 4JG; www.casacruz.london; @CasaCruzrest; 12.30 am, Sun 5 pm; closed Mon.

F S A

Casa Malevo W2 £56 3 2 3
23 Connaught St 7402 1988 6–1D
"Great steaks" and "other delicious Latino delicacies" are the pay-off for truffling out this "cosy", "dimly-lit" Argentinian, in a "slightly out-of-the-way" corner of Bayswater. / W2 2AY; www.casamalevo.com; @casamalevo; 10.30 pm, Sun 10 pm.

Casse-Croute SE1 £45 4 4 4
109 Bermondsey St 7407 2140 9–4D
"Take all the best bits of a tiny Parisian bistro, put it in SE1, et voilà!" – this "bustling, chaotic and cramped" little two-year-old is a stroke of "genius", serving "the classic bistro fare you rarely find in France nowadays" in "fun", if "basic" conditions. / SE1 3XB; www.cassecroute.co.uk; @CasseCroute109; Mon-Sat 10 pm, Sun 4 pm; closed Sun D.

Cau £49 4 3 3
10-12 Royal Pde, SE3 8318 4200 1–4D NEW
33 High St, SW19 8318 4200 10–2B NEW
1 Commodity Quay, E1 7702 0341 9–3D NEW
"A good addition to Wimbledon" – this new Argentinean offers "an eclectic mix of original small and large plates", "smiley" service, and "stylish" surroundings, all "without devastating your wallet!". There are branches in Blackheath and St Katharine Docks too.

The Cavendish W1 NEW £75 3 4 4
35 New Cavendish St 7487 3030 2–1A
There's a "gentleman's club" vibe to the design of this ambitious, all-day Marylebone newcomer, which has inspired promising early reports on its straightforward but comprehensive selection of dishes (incorporating a raw bar, with an array of ceviches, and caviars). / W1G 9TR; 35newcavendish.co.uk; @35newcavendish; 10.30 pm, Sun 6 pm; set weekday L £45 (FP).

Cây Tre £36 3 2 3
42-43 Dean St, W1 7317 9118 4–2A
301 Old St, EC1 7729 8662 12–1B
"Some of the best pho ever" is a highlight of the "honestly priced, simple, tasty fare" at this "busy and buzzy" (if totally "unpretentious") Vietnamese duo, in Soho and Shoreditch. / www.vietnamesekitchen.co.uk; 11 pm, Fri & Sat 11.30 pm, Sun 10.30 pm; booking: min 8.

Cecconi's W1 £77 3 3 5
5a Burlington Gdns 7434 1500 3–3C
"The central bar is a great focal point" at this "slick" and "sophisticated" brasserie, whose long opening hours (from breakfast on) and flexible Italian tapas menu help make it "a great Mayfair meeting place" (although it can feel a bit like "Hedge Fund Central"). / W1S 3EP; www.cecconis.co.uk; @SohoHouse; 11.30 pm, Sun 10.30 pm; set weekday L £35 (FP).

Cellar Gascon EC1 £33 3 3 3
59 West Smithfield Rd 7600 7561 9–2B
"Tasty and innovative" little appetisers and "interesting" wines by the glass make for a gastronomic treat at this small wine bar spin-off, from Smithfield's Club Gascon (next door). / EC1A 9DS; www.clubgascon.com; midnight; closed Sat & Sun; set always available £17 (FP), set weekday L £20 (FP).

Les 110 de Taillevent W1 NEW
16 Cavendish Sq awaiting tel 3–1B
In autumn 2015 (as we were going to press) the first London outpost of the fabled Parisian brasserie's spin-off brand was due to open on the former site of a branch of Her Majesty's banker Coutts & Co, just north of Oxford Street; wine and pairing menus are set to be a major feature of what should be an interesting opening (the 'cent dix' of the title refers to the number of wine bins). / W1G 9DD; www.taillevent.com; @LeTaillevent.

Ceru SE1 NEW **£36** 333
More London Riverside, London Rivieria 3195 3001 9–4D
A "little gem" – this pop-up looking for a permanent home is currently rooted by Tower Bridge (with a smattering of outside seats); as one would expect from restaurateur Barry Hilton (Yalla Yalla) it wins praise for its "fresh tastes of the Levant". / SE1 2DB; www.cerurestaurants.com; @cerulondon; 10 pm.

Ceviche **£46** 344
17 Frith St, W1 7292 2040 4–2A
Alexandra Trust, Baldwin St, EC1 3327 9463 12–1A NEW
"Intriguing" Peruvian fare – in particular "fantastic ceviche" washed down with "wonderful" Pisco Sours – still wins praise for this atmospheric Soho South American, whose "bustling" new EC1 sibling is also off to a good start; "pushy" service and "noisy" conditions can grate though. / www.cevicheuk.com; @cevicheuk; SRA-3.*

Chakra W11 **£55** 312
157-159 Notting Hill Gate 7229 2115 6–2B
"Brilliant" food can be found at this "posh", but slightly "weird" ("white leather and chandeliers") Notting Hill Indian, but the overall effect is too often spoiled by "shambolic service" and top end prices – "we had to ask three times for our rather substantial bill!" / W11 3LF; www.chakralondon.com; @ChakraLondon; 11 pm, Sun 10.30 pm.

Chamberlain's EC3 **£63** 343
23-25 Leadenhall Mkt 7648 8690 9–2D
"In the fascinating heart of Leadenhall Market", this well-established fish restaurant majors in "mainstream" favourites (grilled Dover sole, lobster, and so on); lunch prices can seem "forbidding", but "for the well-off who like their fish" it's well-rated. / EC3V 1LR; www.chamberlains.org; @chamberlainsldn; 9.30 pm, Sun 4 pm; closed Sat & Sun D.

Champor-Champor SE1 **£51** 334
62 Weston St 7403 4600 9–4C
Hidden away in Borough, this "quirky" Thai-Malay fusion outfit is just as known for its "unique" decor as it is for its "flavoursome" food – a "varied and lively crowd" provides a further boost to the atmosphere too. / SE1 3QJ; www.champor-champor.com; @ChamporChampor; 10 pm; D only.

The Chancery EC4 **£66** 443
9 Cursitor St 7831 4000 9–2A
Graham Long's "thoughtful" and "beautifully executed" cuisine wins high praise for this "smart and fairly formal" 10-year-old, near Chancery Lane, not only recommended as a "very professional" business option, but also as a foodie destination in its own right. / EC4A 1LL; www.thechancery.co.uk; @chancerylondon; 10.30 pm; closed Sat L & Sun.

Chapters SE3 £50 332
43-45 Montpelier Vale 8333 2666 1–4D
"The best all-rounder in Blackheath" (by the Common) – open all day, with "always friendly service", and "reliable brasserie fare"; however, while of a "perfectly creditable standard, it's not very individual". / SE3 0TJ; www.chaptersrestaurants.com; @chaptersvillage; 11 pm, Sun 9 pm; set weekday L £30 (FP), set dinner £33 (FP).

Charlotte's £51 344
6 Turnham Green Ter, W4 8742 3590 7–2A
Dickens Yard, 2 New Broadway, W5 awaiting tel 1–3A NEW
"Staff give just the right amount of attention" at this ("slightly cramped and noisy") "neighbourhood gem" in Chiswick, where an evening often kicks off in the tiny bar, with its "enticing selection of wonderful gins". In autumn 2015 it is to get this new Ealing sibling in addition to the existing grander W5 operation (see also). / www.charlottes.co.uk.

Charlotte's Place W5 £52 343
16 St Matthew's Rd 8567 7541 1–3A
"It's great to have quality cooking in W5!" – this "homely" neighbourhood favourite, on the Common, delivers "well-presented, seasonal food" in a "warm and friendly manner". / W5 3JT; www.charlottes.co.uk; @Charlottes1984; 10.30 pm, Fri & Sat 11 pm, Sun 9 pm; set Sun L £43 (FP).

Chettinad W1 £38 433
16 Percy St 3556 1229 2–1C
"Delicious and authentic South Indian food" (from the state of Tamil Nadu), with "consistently superior spicing" wins very high praise for this café-style Fitzrovian. Top Tip – "amazing value lunchtime thalis". / W1T 1DT; www.chettinadrestaurant.com; @chettinadlondon; Mon-Sat 11 pm, Sun 10 pm; no Amex.

Cheyne Walk Brasserie SW3 £70 333
50 Cheyne Walk 7376 8787 5–3C
"Full of beautiful people", a stylish Gallic brasserie near the Thames in Chelsea; the "straightforward" menu is "pricey", but on most accounts "the quality of the food is matched by the scents and theatre of the central wood-grill" (where most of the cooking takes place). / SW3 5LR; www.cheynewalkbrasserie.com; 10.30 pm, Sun 9.30 pm; closed Mon L; set always available £55 (FP).

Chez Abir W14 £38 432
34 Blythe Rd 7603 3241 7–1D
Previously known as Chez Marcelle (till she retired), this "little gem" in the backstreets behind Olympia may be only "modest and functional", but "remains an excellent source of authentic Lebanese food". / W14 0HA; 11 pm; closed Mon.

Chez Antoinette WC2 NEW £44
Unit 30 The Market Building 7240 9072 4–3D
Forget on-trend pizzas and burgers; this cute, new 'Tartinerie' in the heart of Covent Garden Market is giving the one-dish restaurant craze a touch of Gallic class, with a menu devoted to the classic French tartine. / WC2E 8RD; www.chezantoinette.co.uk; Mon-Thu 7 pm, Fri & Sat 11 pm, Sun 8 pm.

CHEZ BRUCE SW17 £66 554

2 Bellevue Rd 8672 0114 10–2C

"Still at the top of its game after all these years" – Bruce Poole's "unpretentious" yet "consistently excellent" neighbourhood restaurant is yet again the survey's No. 1 favourite, and "well worth the schlep to Wandsworth Common". "There are no fads – just classic, interesting, perfectly executed cooking", matched with service that "while impeccable, is completely devoid of airs and graces". All this plus "stellar" wine and a "cheeseboard probably visible from space". And price-wise, it's "so reasonable for something so good!" / SW17 7EG; www.chezbruce.co.uk; @ChezBruce; 10 pm, Fri & Sat 10.30 pm, Sun 9 pm.

Chez Patrick W8 £50 353

7 Stratford Rd 7937 6388 5–2A

"A side-order of French cheekiness" is the order of the day at this stalwart spot in a Kensington backwater, where "charming owner" Patrick "seems to be on first name terms with all his customers"; fish and seafood are the highlight of the "simple", "well-prepared" Gallic fare. / W8 6RF; www.chez-patrick.co.uk; 10.30 pm; closed Sun D.

Chick 'n' Sours E8 NEW £32 424

390 Kingsland Rd 3620 8728 1–1D

On Dalston's main drag, a "fun and buzzy" little fried chicken specialist from pop-up maestro Carl Clarke, where poultry is given an oriental twist and accompanied by sour cocktails – it's an "excellent" combo. / E8 2AA; www.chicknsours.co.uk; @chicknsours; 10 pm, Fri & Sat 10.30 pm, Sun 09.30 pm.

Chicken Shop £32 344

199-206 High Holborn, WC1 7661 3040 2–1D NEW
79 Highgate Rd, NW5 3310 2020 8–1B
Soho House, Chestnut Grove, SW12 8102 9300 10–2C NEW
141 Tooting High St, SW17 8767 5200 10–2B
27a Mile End Rd, E1 3310 2010 12–2D

"They do one thing and do it well" at these "posh Nando's" – "succulent free range chicken cooked on a spit, great chips, salad and little else apart from some puds" (notably "delicious apple pie"); they look "quirky" and "fun" too, "if only you could book…" / www.chickenshop.com; Mon - Sun 10.30 pm ; WC1V closed Sun.

Chicken Shop & Dirty Burger E1 £32 332

27a Mile End Rd 3310 2010 12–2D

"It's greasy, it's dirty, but it tastes so good" – a Whitechapel two-in-one, where you can opt for either of Soho House's casual, "comfort food" brands. / E1 4TP; www.chickenshop.com; @chickenshop; 11 pm, Sun 10 pm; closed weekday L.

Chicken Town N15 NEW

Tottenham Grn 3310 2020 1–1C

A new, healthy – part crowd-funded – twist on London's ubiquitous chicken shop was slated to open in the badlands of Tottenham as this guide went to press, founded by Create and supported by the Mayor, no less. / N15 4JA; @Chickentown; 11 pm, Sun 10 pm.

Chifafa EC1 NEW £11 4 3 3

45-47 Clerkenwell Rd no tel 9–1A

'To save the reputation of the kebab' is the bold mission statement of this posh, new, little Clerkenwell pit stop; for once the marketing doesn't lie, with high marks for its healthy nosh ('no doners, no chips, no foam, no neon'), and "speedy service". / EC1M 5RS; www.chifafa.com; @chifafakebabs; 11.30 pm, Sat 9 pm.

Chilango £16 3 3 2

76 Chancery Ln, WC2 7430 1323 2–1D
27 Upper St, N1 7704 2123 8–3D
32 Brushfield St, E1 3246 0086 12–2B
64 London Wall, EC2 7628 7663 9–2C
142 Fleet St, EC4 7353 6761 9–2A

"You can't go wrong with a big burrito" from these US imports, and you get a "fast turnaround" too; they've not made the same waves here as they have Stateside however. / www.chilango.co.uk; @Chilango_uk; EC4, EC2, EC1 9 pm, N1 10 pm, Fri & Sat midnight; EC4, EC2, E1 closed Sat & Sun; no booking.

Chilli Cool WC1 £33 3 1 1

15 Leigh St 7383 3135 2–1D

"The really interesting, Sichuan 'nose to tail' food will take your breath away (literally!)", at this Bloomsbury dive, and "makes it worth enduring the very offhand service"; ("order less than you think, as portions are huge"!) / WC1H 9EW; www.chillicool.com; 10.15 pm; no Amex.

The Chiltern Firehouse W1 £82 1 2 4

1 Chiltern St 7073 7676 2–1A

"Full of Z-listers, models and wannabe movers-and-shakers", this achingly hip Marylebone yearling is "so overhyped" it's hilarious. It's undoubtedly a "gorgeous-looking" place and "fun" too (especially if you like people-watching), but you pay "silly money" for service that's "confused" (going on "obnoxious"), and food for which "mediocre would be a flattering description". / W1U 7PA; www.chilternfirehouse.com; 10.30 pm.

China Tang
Dorchester Hotel W1 £72 2 1 3

53 Park Ln 7629 9988 3–3A

"Bog-standard" Chinese fare ("no better than Chinatown but double the cost") is served by "indifferent" staff at Sir David Tang's "opulent and buzzy" Mayfair basement (whose top feature is its gorgeous, '30s-Shanghai-style cocktail bar). / W1K 1QA; www.chinatanglondon.co.uk; @ChinaTangLondon; 11.45 pm; booking: max 14; set weekday L £50 (FP).

Chinese Cricket Club EC4 £63 4 3 1

19 New Bridge St 7438 8051 9–3A

Shame about the "cold and formulaic" atmosphere at this hotel dining room, near Blackfriars Bridge – even those who say it "lacks heart" and is "unjustifiably pricey" concede the food is "good and ambitious". / EC4V 6DB; www.chinesecricketclub.com; @chinesecclub; 10 pm; closed Sat & Sun L.

Chisou £51 442

4 Princes St, W1 7629 3931 3–1C
31 Beauchamp Pl, SW3 3155 0005 5–2D

"Always-outstanding sashimi and sushi" and "some unusual izakaya-style dishes" are washed down with a "mind-blowing sake selection" at the low-key Mayfair original of this small group; SW3 is little-known but also well-rated, but the W4 branch is no more. / www.chisourestaurant.com; Mon-Sat 10.30 pm, Sun 9.30 pm.

Chiswell Street Dining Rooms EC1 £62 222

56 Chiswell St 7614 0177 12–2A

Near the Barbican, this "slightly faceless, but perfectly decent" operation serves a need for its City clientele – it's "pricey" but "a good venue for a business lunch", and loosens up a little in the evenings. / EC1Y 4SA; www.chiswellstreetdining.com; @chiswelldining; 11 pm; closed Sat & Sun; set pre theatre £41 (FP).

Chor Bizarre W1 £63 323

16 Albemarle St 7629 9802 3–3C

Trinkets and ornaments festoon this antique-laden Mayfair Indian (named for one of Mumbai's biggest flea markets); despite the odd gripe that it's "pricey", most reporters applaud its cooking. / W1S 4HW; www.chorbizarre.com; @ChorBizarreUK; 11.30 pm, Sun 10.30 pm.

Chotto Matte W1 £55 434

11-13 Frith St 7042 7171 4–2A

"Loving this Peruvian/Japanese fusion!" – this "large and absolutely buzzing" Soho yearling "ticks all the boxes" with its "wild" cooking and "really cool" atmosphere. / W1D 4RB; www.chotto-matte.com; @ChottoMatteSoho; Mon-Sat 1 am, Sun 11 pm.

Chriskitch N10 £27 442

7 Tetherdown 8411 0051 1–1C

"Muswell Hill locals queue around the block" for this "brave but wonderful venture", in "a converted front room with awkward seating"; "there's no menu – it's whatever the chef cooks on the day", but its salads, cakes and so on have "brilliant flavours", and "the mismatched furniture and rickety tables add to the charm". / N10 1ND; www.chriskitch.com; @chriskitch_; Mon-Fri 6 pm, Sat & Sun 5 pm.

Christopher's WC2 £72 223

18 Wellington St 7240 4222 4–3D

A "beautiful" interior is the only surefire plus-point of this well-established, grand American restaurant in a spacious Covent Garden townhouse; "they seem to be trying hard", and it's a favourite for a number of reporters, but standards are inconsistent and its surf 'n' turf cuisine can appear "dull and overpriced". / WC2E 7DD; www.christophersgrill.com; @christopherswc2; 11.30 pm, Sun 10.30 pm; booking: max 12; set pre theatre £40 (FP).

Churchill Arms W8 £36 345

119 Kensington Church St 7792 1246 6–2B

"The brilliant jungle atmosphere" is "something else" at this slightly "bonkers" pub, off Notting Hill Gate, where Thai food is served in a conservatory filled with "dried butterflies and hanging flowers"; the scoff's "always delicious" too, and "super cheap" – "eat yourself to a standstill for little more than a tenner!" / W8 7LN; www.churchillarmskensington.co.uk; @ChurchillArmsW8; 10 pm, Sun 9.30 pm.

F S A

Chutney Mary SW1 £58 444

73 St James's St 7351 3113 3–4D

Moved this year from its long-standing Chelsea home to a "wonderfully decorated" new site in St James's, this renowned Indian seems to have transported well – the new location is "lovely", as is the "superb, fragrant and subtle" cooking, and all-in-all it's "expensive but worth it". / SW1A 1PH; www.chutneymary.com; @RealindianFood; 10.30 pm; closed Sat L & Sun.

Chutneys NW1 £31 222

124 Drummond St 7388 0604 8–4C

"I've been going for over 20 years and it never disappoints"; a mainstay of Euston's 'Little India' scene, this "friendly" Keralan won't "blow you away", but the lunchtime and Sunday evening buffet is "ridiculously good value"; BYO too. / NW1 2PA; www.chutneyseuston.co.uk; 11 pm; no Amex; need 5+ to book.

Ciao Bella WC1 £42 244

86-90 Lamb's Conduit St 7242 4119 2–1D

"Pictures of the golden age of Italian cinema lining the walls and a white piano" set the tone at this "buzzing" trattoria veteran (a favourite of Boris Johnson, apparently); the "classic cheap 'n' cheerful scran is lifted by the ambiente" – it's "so friendly, so happy, (and ideal with kids too)". / WC1N 3LZ; www.ciaobellarestaurant.co.uk; 11.30 pm, Sun 10.30 pm.

Cibo W14 £54 454

3 Russell Gdns 7371 6271 7–1D

Lost in a side-street on the Kensington/Olympia border, Michael Winner's favourite Italian (or it was) is rather forgotten nowadays, but fans still cross town for its "delightful" approach, not least "simple, flavoursome and unfussy" cooking that's "always fantastic". Top Menu Tip – "very successful" fish and seafood dishes. / W14 8EZ; www.ciborestaurant.net; 10.30 pm; closed Sat L & Sun D.

Cigala WC1 £50 222

54 Lamb's Conduit St 7405 1717 2–1D

"Homely" Bloomsbury Hispanic long known as "a charming" neighbourhood "gem", with "simple and tasty" tapas; quite a number of reporters found it "most unremarkable" this year however, citing "mediocre" cooking and a "pretty poor" ambience. / WC1N 3LW; www.cigala.co.uk; 10.45 pm, Sun 9.45 pm.

Cigalon WC2 £52 332

115 Chancery Ln 7242 8373 2–2D

The "beautiful" and "airy" room (in days of yore, an auctioneers' premises) is the "special", feature of this Club Gascon sibling ("very handily located for legal types"), but its Provençal cooking is "usually excellent" too. / WC2A 1PP; www.cigalon.co.uk; @Cigalon_London; 10 pm; closed Sat & Sun.

THE CINNAMON CLUB SW1 £72 334

Old Westminster Library, Great Smith St 7222 2555 2–4C

London's most "impressive"-looking Indian occupies Westminster's "soaring" former library, near the Abbey (and looks even more dashing after its recent £1m refit). Nearly fifteen years old, it's still one of the capital's most noteworthy culinary destinations, thanks not least to Vivek Singh's "seriously brilliantly spiced" (if "expensive") cuisine. / SW1P 3BU; www.cinnamonclub.com; @CinnamonClub; 10.30 pm; closed Sun; no trainers; set always available £47 (FP); SRA-3.*

Cinnamon Kitchen EC2 £58 4 2 2
9 Devonshire Sq 7626 5000 9–2D
"Delicious food with superb flavours" makes this Indian-fusion venture in the City a worthy cousin to the Cinnamon Club; however – aside from the "beautiful terrace" within an impressive atrium – the setting can seem "bland" and "noisy", and service can be "muddled".
/ EC2M 4YL; www.cinnamon-kitchen.com; @cinnamonkitchen; 11 pm; closed Sat L & Sun; set always available £26 (FP).

Cinnamon Soho W1 £45 4 2 2
5 Kingly St 7437 1664 3–2D
"The less well-known, more basic sibling of the Cinnamon Club family" lives just off Regent Street; "it's not a big place", the ambience is "about average" and service can falter, but its "wonderful Indian-fusion fare" is "superior" and "good value".
/ W1B 5PE; www.cinnamon-kitchen.com/soho-home; @cinnamonsoho; 11 pm, Sun 4.30 pm; closed Sun D.

City Barge W4 £47 3 3 3
27 Strand-on-the-Green 8994 2148 1–3A
"It's high time Strand-on-the-Green had a decent pub!" – this refurbished boozer enjoys "a great setting by the Thames" and cooking that's "very promising". / W4 3PH; www.citybargechiswick.com; @citybargew4; Mon-Thu 11 pm, Fri & Sat midnight, Sun 10.30 pm.

City Càphê EC2 £18 5 2 2
17 Ironmonger St no tel 9–2C
"Closest to the streets of Ho Chi Minh I've tasted in London!" – an "astonishingly good" Vietnamese café, near Bank, with "wonderful" salads, báhn mi and pho; "be prepared to brave a queue down the street". / EC2V 8EY; www.citycaphe.com; 3 pm; L only, closed Sat & Sun.

City Miyama EC4 £52 3 4 2
17 Godliman St 7489 1937 9–3B
"A typical, old-style Japanese near St Paul's that hasn't changed in 30 years"; there's a character-free basement, but "it's best eating at the ground floor sushi counter… delicious!" / EC4B 5BD; www.miyama-restaurant.co.uk; 10 pm; closed Sat & Sun.

City Social EC2 £76 3 3 5
Tower 42 25 Old Broad St 7877 7703 9–2C
"Stunning views" help create a "fabulous" and business-friendly setting for Jason Atherton's year-old City eyrie, on the 24th floor of Tower 42; but – after its magnificent debut – ratings slipped this year, and though fans still say its cuisine is "superb", critics say it "lacks x-factor". / EC2N 1HQ; www.citysociallondon.com; 9 pm; closed Sat & Sun.

Clarke's W8 £69 4 4 3
124 Kensington Church St 7221 9225 6–2B
Sally Clarke's "fabulous", "honest", "incredibly fresh", seasonal cuisine is "re-establishing itself" after a few rocky years at her long-serving Kensington HQ; service is "charming and sensitive", and the refurb and expansion a year or two ago has "enhanced the ambience".
/ W8 4BH; www.sallyclarke.com; @SallyClarkeLtd; 10 pm; closed Sun; booking: max 14.

Claude's Kitchen
Amuse Bouche SW6 £50 444

51 Parsons Green Ln 7371 8517 10–1B

"Lucky Parsons Green locals" to have this "special little marvel" opposite the tube, with a ground floor bar and cosy upstairs dining room – its "interesting small menu" is "always a treat". / SW6 4JA; www.claudeskitchen.co.uk; @AmuseBoucheLDN; 10 pm; closed weekday L.

Clockjack Oven W1 £32 333

14 Denman St 7287 5111 3–3D

"Fun and funky" rotisserie yearling in Soho, whose "great chicken and amazing chicken bites" make for "reliable, cheap, cheerful, tasty" central nosh. / W1D 7HJ; www.clockjackoven.com; @ClockjackOven; 10 pm, Fri & Sat 11 pm, Sun 9 pm.

CLOS MAGGIORE WC2 £65 455

33 King St 7379 9696 4–3C

"A girl knows she's being spoilt" at this Covent Garden "haven" – the survey's No. 1 romantic choice – where for full effect you must sit in the "magical back conservatory, which is second-to-none for a date". Service is "charming and courteous" and the cooking "delicious", if arguably eclipsed by the "massive tome" of a wine list. / WC2E 8JD; www.closmaggiore.com; @ClosMaggioreWC2; 11 pm, Sun 10 pm; booking: max 7.

The Clove Club EC1 £95 433

Shoreditch Town Hall, 380 Old St 7729 6496 12–1B

"Deserving its many awards" – this groovy pop-up-turned-permanent in Shoreditch's fine old town hall wins kudos for its "incredibly interesting" cuisine, "perfectly matched" wines and "casual" approach. The setting can seem "spartan" though, service is a little "earnest" and to some diners "the new ticketing system for reservations smacks of hubris". / EC1V 9LT; www.thecloveclub.com; @thecloveclub; 9.30 pm; closed Mon L & Sun; set weekday L £60 (FP).

Club Gascon EC1 £75 333

57 West Smithfield 7600 6144 9–2B

"Brilliantly executed flavour combinations from SW France" – featuring "foie gras in every imaginable form" – and "a wine list with some unusual gems" have won a huge following for this Gallic, City-fringe business stalwart; but has its performance been slightly "tired" of late? / EC1A 9DS; www.clubgascon.com; @club_gascon; 10 pm, Fri & Sat 10.30 pm; closed Sat L & Sun.

Coco Di Mama EC4 £12 342

Branches throughout the City

"Truly Italian coffee" – "the best in the city" – plus "excellent" pastries and some good pasta win praise for this small Square Mile chain. / www.cocodimama.co.uk; 5 pm; L only.

Cocochan W1 £50 333

38-40 James St 7486 1000 3–1A

"An imaginative fusion of Eastern cuisines", helps win consistent praise for this café-style St James's venture; "tables are quite close together, but that makes for interesting conversations with your neighbours!" / W1U 1EU; www.cocochan.co.uk.

Colbert SW1 £58 123

51 Sloane Sq 7730 2804 5–2D

"How did Corbin and King get things so wrong?" – this "buzzing" Sloane Square two-year-old looks "elegant", but service can be "appalling" and the brasserie fare is "seriously underwhelming" – "it's like an expensive Café Rouge!" / SW1W 8AX; www.colbertchelsea.com; @ColbertChelsea; Sun 10.30 pm, Mon-Thu 11 pm, Fri & Sat 11.30 pm; booking: max 6.

La Collina NW1 £56 322

17 Princess Rd 7483 0192 8–3B

At its best in summer, when you can sit in its "attractive garden", this "small" Primrose Hill local impresses (nearly) all its (older) fan club with its "interesting" Piedmontese cooking "subtly prepared from fresh ingredients". / NW1 8JR; www.lacollinarestaurant.co.uk; @LacollinaR; 10.15 pm, Sun & Mon 9.15 pm; closed Mon L.

Le Colombier SW3 £60 334

145 Dovehouse St 7351 1155 5–2C

"A little bit of France in Chelsea" – Didier Garnier's "delightful", "old-fashioned" stalwart is a treasured (if rather pricey) backstreet favourite, especially for an older Francophile crowd; it's "not known for its originality" – expect "classic" dishes delivered to a "consistent" standard. / SW3 6LB; www.le-colombier-restaurant.co.uk; 10.30 pm, Sun 10 pm.

Colony Grill Room Beaumont Hotel W1 £59 322

Brown Hart Gdns 7499 1001 3–2A

"A new favourite" for many reporters; Corbin & King have made a strong debut with this "club-like" Mayfair yearling – a "beautiful" (if "noisy") room that "feels like it's been here for years"; true to their DNA, the American-inspired menu is "good but a bit too much on the side of comfort food". / W1K 6TF; www.thebeaumont.com; @ColonyGrillRoom; midnight, Sun 11 pm.

Como Lario SW1 £48 244

18-22 Holbein Pl 7730 2954 5–2D

"A huge regular following of well-heeled locals" sustains this "old-school" Italian, "tucked away in a side street close to Sloane Square"; "the cooking's a little variable, but if you know the right dishes it's great". / SW1W 8NL; www.comolario.co.uk; 11.30 pm, Sun 10 pm.

Compagnie des Vins Surnaturels WC2 £52 334

8-10 Neals Yd 7344 7737 4–2C

"Try to guess the mystery wine!" – one of an "intriguing selection by the glass", served at this Covent Garden yearling – a "great place" for a drink, and with "good" small plates too. / WC2H 9DP; www.cvssevendials.com; @CVS7Dials; midnight.

Comptoir Gascon EC1 £45 333

63 Charterhouse St 7608 0851 9–1A

"Splendidly earthy dishes from SW France" – "the deluxe duck burger is a treat" – and "esoteric" wines to match are "knowledgeably" served at this "cute" Club Gascon spin-off, near Smithfield; it can seem "expensive for what it is" though, especially given the "wee portions". / EC1M 6HJ; www.comptoirgascon.com; @ComptoirGascon; 10 pm, Thu & Fri 10.30 pm; closed Mon & Sun.

F S A

Comptoir Libanais £34 443

Branches throughout London

A "cleverly conceived" Lebanese chain, with "characterful" branches; critics say their food is "nothing special", but most reports praise its "really lovely soft drinks" and "value-for-money mezze". / www.lecomptoir.co.uk; W12 9 pm, Thu & Fri 10 pm, Sun 6 pm; W1 9.30 pm; W12 closed Sun D; no bookings.

Il Convivio SW1 £58 333

143 Ebury St 7730 4099 2–4A

With its "smooth" service, and "spacious" interior, this "stylish" Belgravian "old favourite" is, say fans, always "under-rated"; there is the occasional report of "uninspiring" cooking, but on most accounts it's "beautifully judged". / SW1W 9QN; www.ilconvivio.co.uk; 10.45 pm; closed Sun; set weekday L £39 (FP).

Coopers Restaurant & Bar WC2 £50 223

49a Lincoln's Inn Fields 7831 6211 2–2D

A Lincoln's Inn Fields "staple" – "very popular amongst the Bar and the Judiciary, but that's not necessarily a recommendation for the food!"; fans do applaud its "informal" style and solid value, but other "struggle to find something appealing on the menu". / WC2A 3PF; www.coopers-restaurant.com; @coopers_bistro; 11 pm; closed Sat & Sun.

Copita Del Mercado E1 £39 432

60 Wentworth St 7426 0218 12–2C

"A beacon in the culinary wasteland around Petticoat Lane Market" (from the team behind Soho's Copita) serving "fresh, tasty and innovative tapas" that's "in a different league to its nearest rivals"; on the downside, it's "a bit soulless". / E1 7TF; www.copitadelmercado.com; @copitamercado; 10.30 pm.

Le Coq N1 £42 232

292-294 St Paul's Rd 7359 5055 8–2D

Fans hail "a winning formula" for this Islington yearling, offering "tasty rôtisserie chicken, with a good selection of sides" (from a limited set menu incorporating two starters and desserts); it also has its critics though, who judge it "disappointing". / N1 2LH; www.le-coq.co.uk; @LeCOQrestaurant; 10.15 pm.

Coq d'Argent EC2 £74 233

1 Poultry 7395 5000 9–2C

With its "stunning rooftop garden", this well-known D&D London venue is "perfect for business entertaining" and – especially in summer – something of "a City boy power-lunch extravaganza"; the food is "acceptable but dull" – "if they really sorted it out, it would be one of London's top spots". / EC2R 8EJ; www.coqdargent.co.uk; 9.45 pm; closed Sun D.

Cork & Bottle WC2 £48 235

44-46 Cranbourn St 7734 7807 4–3B

"Somehow sheltered from the worst ravages of the tourist hell that is Leicester Square", this "proper, independent wine bar" is a treasured "haven in the West End"; "you don't go for the food, but it's perfectly tolerable to accompany the exceptional wine list, and lovely, old-school cellar ambience". / WC2H 7AN; www.thecorkandbottle.co.uk; @corkbottle1971; 11.30 pm, Sun 10.30 pm; no booking at D.

Corner Room E2 £48 344
Patriot Sq 7871 0461 1–2D
"Hidden away at the back of the hotel", this "tiny", "sparse" chamber shares a kitchen with the better-known Typing Room; for fans, it's "a wonderful fashionista inside secret" and a "splendid gastronomic delight", but for sceptics "the food doesn't taste quite as good as hoped". / E2 9NF; www.viajante.co.uk/corner-room/; @townhallhotel; 10.30 pm.

Cornish Tiger SW11 £51 333
1 Battersea Rise 7223 7719 10–1C
All agree this ambitious modern British yearling is "a lovely variation to the normal Battersea Rise opening"; but while some acclaim its "affordable, most interesting and piquant seasonal cuisine", others feel "it's not bad but a bit ordinary". / SW11 1GH; www.cornishtiger.com; @cornishtiger; 11 pm, Sun 6 pm; closed Mon; set weekday L £25 (FP).

Corrigan's Mayfair W1 £90 344
28 Upper Grosvenor St 7499 9943 3–3A
Richard Corrigan's "spacious" and dignified Mayfair dining room has long been a business favourite, and – although it's undeniably pricey – won very solid praise this year for its "top quality" cuisine and service that's "attentive yet unobtrusive". / W1K 7EH; www.corrigansmayfair.com; @CorriganMayfair; 10.45 pm, Sun 9.30 pm; closed Sat L; booking: max 10.

Côte £44 222
Branches throughout London
"A step up from Café Rouge" – these useful "modern, all-day French brasseries" are nowadays the survey's most talked-about chain; the cooking will "never win awards" but is "solid", "affordable" and "pleasant enough". / www.cote-restaurants.co.uk; 11 pm.

Counter SW8 NEW £48 222
Arch 50, 7-11 South Lambeth Pl 3693 9600 10–1D
"A much needed addition to Vauxhall", say fans of this "unlikely debut in the railway arches" praised for its brasserie fare (including an "excellent value brunch"); it's pricey though, the space can feel "confined", and service in particular is a "work in progress". (NB – if you do go, "just make sure go into the right arch and not one of the fetish clubs by mistake!") / SW8 1SP; www.counterrestaurants.com; @eatatcounter; 12.30 am, Fri & Sat 1.30 am.

The Cow W2 £54 444
89 Westbourne Park Rd 7221 0021 6–1B
"Fab fresh shellfish" makes the packed bar of Tom Conran's Irish boozer in Bayswater "heaven" for lovers of Guinness and oysters, and other seafood treats; more limited, but positive feedback too on its quirky, first floor dining room. / W2 5QH; www.thecowlondon.co.uk; 10 pm, Sun 10 pm; no Amex.

Coya W1 £76 323
118 Piccadilly 7042 7118 3–4B
"Sexy and dark" Peruvian haunt in Mayfair extolled by fans for its "incredibly buzzy" (ie "very noisy") vibe, and its "zingy" fare (not least "wonderful ceviche"); it's arguably "too expensive" though, and to some reporters the whole set-up is "just the wrong side of euro-trashy". / W1J 7NW; www.coyarestaurant.com; @coyarestaurant; Sun-Wed 10.30 pm, Thu-Sat 11 pm; booking: max 12.

FSA

Craft London SE10 NEW £64 224

Peninsula Sq 8465 5910 1–3D

"Great to have a proper restaurant at the Dome!" – under-served locals laud the arrival of foodie luvvie Stevie Parle at this "spacious", 3-floor venue, with "fantastic" river views from the rooftop bar; but his 6-course meals in the dining room are "very expensive" (maybe grab pizza in the café), and service "needs to up its game". / SE10 0SQ; www.craft-london.co.uk; @CraftLDN; Café 6 pm, Rest 10.30 pm, Sun 4 pm.

Crazy Bear W1 £64 334

26-28 Whitfield St 7631 0088 2–1C

A "quirky hidden gem", "tucked away off Tottenham Court Road", with a glam, if slightly faded cellar bar ("very unusual WCs"), and stylish, ground floor dining room; it's not the destination it once was, but still "great fun" and with "good Thai food" too. / W1T 2RG; www.crazybeargroup.co.uk; @CrazyBearGroup; 10.30 pm; closed Mon L & Sun; no shorts.

Crocker's Folly NW8 £55 223

23-24 Aberdeen Pl 7289 9898 8–4A

Praise for this monumental St John's Wood gin palace – "lavishly restored" by the Lebanese Maroush group, but with a British menu – is primarily aimed at its "extraordinarily beautiful" Victorian setting; the food is "unexciting" though and service "needs to improve" – perhaps the curse of Crocker strikes again? (Frank Crocker went bust in 1898 when he built this as a railway hotel… but they moved the station.) / NW8 8JR; www.crockersfolly.com; @Crockers_Folly; 10.30 pm.

The Crooked Well SE5 £49 344

16 Grove Ln 7252 7798 1–3C

This sizeable, stylish Camberwell gastropub is "simple" in its aims – a "pleasant neighbourhood place" with good all-round standards. / SE5 8SY; www.thecrookedwell.com; @crookedwell; 10.30 pm; closed Mon L; no Amex.

The Cross Keys SW3 £54 334

1 Lawrence St 7351 0686 5–3C

"Back with a bang!"; it's not a hotspot for culinary fireworks, but Chelsea's oldest boozer (recently re-opened) has a brilliant atmosphere, and generally wins the thumbs-up for its "friendly and attentive" service and "honest" pub tucker. / SW3 5NB; www.thexkeys.co.uk; @CrossKeys_PH; midnight.

Crosstown Doughnuts W1 NEW £5 342

4 Broadwick St 7734 8873 3–2D

First permanent site for this purveyor of designer doughnuts – "the best 'nuts in town", with great fillings. / W1F 8HJ; www.crosstowndoughnuts.com; @CrosstownDough; 10 pm.

The Culpepper E1 NEW £43 434

40 Commercial St 7247 5371 12–2C

"A superb new addition to Spitalfields" – this old gin-palace underwent a "cool and comfy refurb" this year, and combines a busy bar with a more "chilled upstairs dining room"; prices are not bargain basement, but the best dishes from its "inventive" menu are "exceptional". / E1 6LP; www.theculpepper.com; @TheCulpeper; Mon-Thu midnight, Fri & Sat 2 am, Sun 11 pm.

Cumberland Arms W14 **£44** 4 4 3

29 North End Rd 7371 6806 7–2D

An unexpected find, in the still un-lovely area at the top of the North End Road, near Olympia – an "unpretentious" but "wonderful" pub, with "delicious" food, "well-kept beers" and "lots of affordable wines". / W14 8SZ; www.thecumberlandarmspub.co.uk; @thecumberland; 10 pm, Sun 9.30 pm.

Cut
45 Park Lane W1 **£117** 2 2 2

45 Park Ln 7493 4545 3–4A

What is it about Americans and their pricing strategies? – US über-chef Wolfgang Puck's "strangely proportioned" Mayfair dining room offers "steaks of the highest quality", and yet it is "insanely overpriced". / W1K 1PN; www.45parklane.com; @the_cut_bar; 10.30 pm.

Da Mario SW7 **£42** 2 3 3

15 Gloucester Rd 7584 9078 5–1B

"Still thriving" – a "long-time favourite Italian", near the Royal Albert Hall, where "excellent pizza" is a highlight; "it's a bit cramped but always lively", and very "family friendly". / SW7 4PP; www.damario.co.uk; 11.30 pm.

Da Mario WC2 **£42** 3 4 4

63 Endell St 7240 3632 4–1C

"To be treasured amongst all the chains of Covent Garden" – a "small and noisy" traditional Italian, "packed with regulars" drawn by its "reliable" fare at "fair prices". / WC2H 9AJ; www.da-mario.co.uk; 11.15 pm; closed Sun.

Dabbous W1 **£82** 3 3 2

39 Whitfield St 7323 1544 2–1C

Aficionados of Ollie Dabbous's foodie legend still extol the "inventive and refreshing" cuisine at his "chilled" Fitzrovia HQ. However, ever-more sceptics "don't understand the hype", given the grungy, "industrial" decor and food that increasingly seems "strange", "gimmicky" and "none-too-thrilling". / W1T 2SF; www.dabbous.co.uk; @dabbous; 9.30 pm (bar open until 11.30 pm); closed Sun; set weekday L £57 (FP).

Daddy Donkey EC1 **£15** 4 3 2

100 Leather Ln 07950 448448 9–2A

"Truly the daddy!"; punters still flock to this legendary Clerkenwell food truck to experience its "amazing burritos" – "even when there's a queue, the anticipation just makes you want it more!" / EC1N 7TE; www.daddydonkey.co.uk; @daddydonkey; Mon-Fri 4 pm; L only, closed Sat & Sun.

The Dairy SW4 **£40** 5 4 3

15 The Pavement 7622 4165 10–2D

"Well worth the trip to Clapham!" – this notable "Brooklyn-vibe" two-year-old provides an "endlessly interesting" selection of "unbelievable" tapas-style dishes "explained in detail by the waiting team". Top Tip – "one of London's best-value tasting menus". / SW4 0HY; www.the-dairy.co.uk; 9.45 pm; closed Mon, Tue L & Sun D; SRA-2.*

Dalchini SW19 £36 342

147 Arthur Rd 8947 5966 10–2B

"Interesting Indo-Chinese cooking" helps win a regular following for this well-established 'Hakka' haunt, opposite Wimbledon Park tube. / SW19 8AB; www.dalchini.co.uk; 10.30 pm, Fri & Sat 11 pm, Sun 10 pm; no Amex; set always available £24 (FP).

Daphne's SW3 £72 232

112 Draycott Ave 7589 4257 5–2C

This "very, very Chelsea" haunt – once famously Princess Di's fave – is "taking time to settle in after a major makeover" in 2014; some fans – "not crazy about the new decor" – still applaud its "classic" Italian cuisine, but others feel it's become "a little disappointing". / SW3 3AE; www.daphnes-restaurant.co.uk; @CapriceHoldings; 11 pm, Sun 10 pm; set weekday L £47 (FP).

Daquise SW7 £49 222

20 Thurloe St 7589 6117 5–2C

Advocates of this South Ken survivor (est 1947) say it "deserves better ratings" for its "semi-Polish" fodder (more contemporary nowadays than in times past); it's sometimes accused, though, of "tired" results. / SW7 2LT; www.daquise.co.uk; @GesslerDaquise; 11 pm; no Amex.

The Dartmouth Castle W6 £47 344

26 Glenthorne Rd 8748 3614 7–2C

Whether it's as "a perfect spot for a business lunch in Hammersmith", or "a great place for an evening pint", this "buzzy" little gastropub is "always reliable and good value". / W6 0LS; www.thedartmouthcastle.co.uk; @DartmouthCastle; 10 pm, Sun 9.30 pm; closed Sat L.

Darwin Brasserie
Sky Garden EC3 NEW £64 223

20 Fenchurch St 033 3772 0020 9–3D

Inevitably, "the magnificence of the view over the Thames and Tower of London isn't matched by the food" at this new "barn of a place" at the top of the Walkie Talkie, plus it's "absurdly overpriced", and service "needs work"; even so, by the standards of such places "it's fine". / EC3M 3BY; www.skygarden.london/darwin; @SG_Darwin; 10.30 pm, Sun 8.30 pm.

Daylesford Organic £42 213

44b Pimlico Rd, SW1 7881 8060 5–2D
Selfridges & Co, 400 Oxford St, W1 0800 123 400 3–1A
6-8 Blandford St, W1 3696 6500 2–1A NEW
208-212 Westbourne Grove, W11 7313 8050 6–1B

Lady Bamford's painstakingly stylish organic cafés – now also in Marylebone – are most often tipped for brunch; more generally they are "decent enough but too expensive for what they are", and service "lacks focus". / www.daylesfordorganic.com; SW1 & W11 7 pm, Sun 4 pm – W1 9 pm, Sun 6.15 pm; W11 no booking L.

Dean Street Townhouse W1 £56 234

69-71 Dean St 7434 1775 4–2A

"Spillover from the bar helps fuel the really buzzing atmosphere" at the Soho House group's clubby Soho brasserie, which is "a little noisy but great fun"; its "comfort food" cooking is best for brunch – otherwise "there's not much actively bad about it, it's just a bit 'meh'!" / W1D 3SE; www.deanstreettownhouse.com; @deanstreettownhouse; 11.30 pm, Fri & Sat midnight, Sun 10.30 pm; set pre-theatre £38 (FP).

Defune W1 £67 4 3 2
34 George St 7935 8311 3–1A
"Like Tokyo... but you might be able to fly there for these prices!" – so "bring a fat wallet" if you visit this long-established Marylebone Japanese, where there's "no atmosphere" but "outstanding teppanyaki" and top sushi. / W1U 7DP; www.defune.com; 10.45 pm, Sun 10.30 pm.

Dehesa W1 £50 3 3 4
25 Ganton St 7494 4170 3–2C
For a "casual" occasion, this "busy and buzzing" corner-site, just off Carnaby Street, is an "intimate and very friendly" choice (if a "cramped" one); its "interesting" Italian/Spanish tapas can be "excellent" too, but doesn't excel as once it did. / W1F 9BP; www.dehesa.co.uk; @SaltYardGroup; 10.45 pm; SRA-2.*

Delancey & Co. W1 NEW £15 4 3 3
34 Goodge St 7637 8070 3–1D
"I can't tear myself away from the salt beef!" – this new, NYC-style 'Grab n' Go & Grab n' Sit Deli' delivers a slice of the Lower East Side to Fitzrovia. / W1T 2PR; www.delanceyandco.co.uk; @DelanceyandCo; 9 pm.

THE DELAUNAY WC2 £58 3 4 5
55 Aldwych 7499 8558 2–2D
"Less hectic than the Wolseley but with all the good bits" – Corbin & King's "so-very-civilised" three-year-old, on the fringe of Covent Garden, is a less showy, more "luxurious" alternative to its bigger stablemate (and likewise "pitch perfect" for business). The Mittel-European cooking "isn't really the point", but it's usually highly "satisfactory" (in particular the "utterly fab" breakfasts and "most delicious afternoon teas"). / WC2B 4BB; www.thedelaunay.com; @TheDelaunayRest; midnight, Sun 11 pm.

Delfino W1 £49 3 2 2
121A Mount St 7499 1256 3–3B
"Surprisingly good pizza, in the middle of Mayfair, at reasonable prices" – that's the USP at this straightforward spot, by the Connaught. / W1K 3NW; www.finos.co.uk; 10.45 pm; closed Sun.

Delhi Grill N1 £35 4 4 3
21 Chapel Mkt 7278 8100 8–3D
Styling itself an Indian 'dhabas' (an informal canteen), this "delightful" curry shop on Chapel Market provides "terrific", "fresh" street food "that's much more interesting than usual", all at "very cheap prices". / N1 9EZ; www.delhigrill.com; 10.30 pm; no credit cards.

La Delizia Limbara SW3 £40 3 2 3
63-65 Chelsea Manor St 7376 4111 5–3C
"Proper", "no-frills" pizza – amongst "the best in town" – justifies the discovery of this "cheerful" and crowded "hole in the wall", in a quiet backstreet, off the King's Road. / SW3 5RZ; www.ladelizia.org.uk; @ladelizia; 11 pm, Sun 10.30 pm; no Amex.

Department of Coffee EC1 £15 4 4 5
14-16 Leather Ln 7419 6906 9–2A
"Faultless coffee" helps this City hang out live up to its name, but it has "friendly" service and consistently well-rated snacks too. / EC1N 7SU; www.departmentofcoffee.co.uk; 6 pm, Sat & Sun 4 pm; L only.

The Depot SW14 £44 2 2 5

Tideway Yd, Mortlake High St 8878 9462 10–1A

"If you're lucky enough to nab a window table, it's magical gazing over the Thames" at this long-established spot, near Barnes Bridge; "food and service have never matched the location", but are "good enough", and it's "really recommended for a multi-generation lunch". / SW14 8SN; www.depotbrasserie.co.uk; @TheDepotBarnes; 10 pm, Sun 9.30 pm; set always available £32 (FP).

Les Deux Salons WC2 £54

40-42 William IV St 7420 2050 4–4C

New owner Sir Terence Conran has taken on this big, two-floor site, just off Trafalgar Square, and given a re-tread to its faux-Parisian brasserie style; it re-opened in June 2015, too late for survey feedback – early press reports suggest it's now more the handy Theatreland amenity it was originally meant to be. / WC2N 4DD; www.lesdeuxsalons.co.uk; @lesdeuxsalons; 10.45 pm, Sun 5.45 pm; closed Sun D; set always available £37 (FP).

DF Mexico £31 4 3 3

28-29 Tottenham Court Rd, W1 no tel 2–1C NEW

Old Truman Brewery, 15 Hanbury St, E1 3617 6639 12–2C

"Fabulous Mexican street food" wins high praise for this year-old diner in Brick Lane's Old Truman Brewery, from the founders of Wahaca – "a great concept, which should be all over London". A new branch opened on Tottenham Court Road in September 2015. / www.dfmexico.co.uk.

Diner £34 2 3 3

Branches throughout London

Though one or two critics do write them off, these "hip" (perhaps "slightly cheesy") US-style diners also garner a fair amount of praise too for "some of the most calorific shakes ever", "burgers to die for" and "real, kosher style hot-dogs just like back home in NYC!" / www.goodlifediner.com; most branches 11 or 11.30 pmMidnight Fri - Sat; booking: max 10.

Dinings W1 £56 5 4 1

22 Harcourt St 7723 0666 8–4A

"The best sushi this side of Tokyo Fish Market" is to be had at Tomonari Chiba's "worn out looking" den in Marylebone (either sit at the ground-floor counter or in the "bizarre" basement); take care though – "you can really blow a big hole in your wallet here!" / W1H 4HH; www.dinings.co.uk; @diningslondon; 10.30 pm; closed Sun.

DINNER
MANDARIN ORIENTAL SW1 £100 3 3 3

66 Knightsbridge 7201 3833 5–1D

"I love a bit of history with my meal!" – Heston's "self-consciously creative" menu of rediscovered Olde Worlde English dishes is "pure foodie heaven" for fans of this park-side chamber ("lovely views if you get a window table"). Esteem for the place continues to wane year-on-year, however, and to a growing band of refuseniks "what first seemed novel and exciting now seems boring" and "oh-so overpriced". Top Menu Tips for first-timers – the Meat Fruit ("to die for") and Tipsy Cake ("divine"). / SW1X 7LA; www.mandarinoriental.com; 10.30 pm.

Dip & Flip £25 422

87 Battersea Rise, SW11 no tel 10–2C
62 The Broadway, SW19 no tel 10–2B NEW

"Awesome burger 'n' chips, made even better with a rich succulent gravy!" – that's the deal at this Battersea joint where "no knives and forks, just a roll of kitchen roll" makes a visit "a great big, messy, indulgence"; now also in Wimbledon too. / www.dipandflip.co.uk.

Dirty Burger £14 322

78 Highgate Rd, NW5 3310 2010 8–2B
Arch 54, 6 South Lambeth Rd, SW8 7074 1444 2–4D
13 Bethnal Green Rd, E1 7749 4525 12–1C

"A dirty indulgence after a late night" – these self-consciously "rustic" shacks make a "handy pitstop" for their "heavenly", "sticky, gooey fistfuls of flavour", "amazing fries" and "fabulous shakes". / www.eatdirtyburger.com; Mon-Thu 11 pm - midnight, Fri & Sat 1 am - 2 am, Sun 8 pm - 11 pm.

Dishoom £40 434

12 Upper St Martins Ln, WC2 7420 9320 4–3B
Kingly St, W1 awaiting tel 3–2D NEW
Stable St, Granary Sq, N1 7420 9321 8–3C
7 Boundary St, E2 7420 9324 12–1B

A "brilliant vibe" has been captured by this "energetic" and impressively executed concept – a growing chain of Mumbai-inspired Parsi cafés; "vibrant street-food" (including a great "brunch Bombay-style") is served in its "stunningly designed" outlets; "shame you can't book". In autumn 2015, a new branch is slated to open off Carnaby Street. / www.dishoom.com; @Dishoom; 11 pm, Sun 10 pm.

Diwana Bhel-Poori House NW1 £26 321

121-123 Drummond St 7387 5556 8–4C

"Forget service, forget ambience!"; it's the grub – in particular the "delicious and incredible-value lunchtime buffet" – that makes this "scruffy" canteen both a Little India institution, and "a vegetarian's dream"; "I've been enjoying deluxe dosas here for 30 years and they haven't changed… in a good way"; BYO. / NW1 2HL; www.diwanabhelpoori.com; 11.45 pm, Sun 11 pm; no Amex; need 10+ to book.

The Dock Kitchen Portobello Dock W10 £60 345

342-344 Ladbroke Grove, Portobello Dock 8962 1610 1–2B

"The magical canal-side setting at night" is a huge plus-point at Stevie Parle's "designer-style" venture, in deepest Notting Hill; its "unique, ever-changing menu pays homage to all four corners of the globe" – fans applaud its "mastery, in spite of its breadth", but to sceptics it's "a little bit too eclectic at times". / W10 5BU; www.dockkitchen.co.uk; @TheDockKitchen; 9.30 pm; closed Sun D.

The Don EC4 £65 333

20 St Swithin's Ln 7626 2606 9–3C

This well-established venue near Bank combines a "civilised" ground floor, with a more atmospheric cellar bistro; critics feel its cooking has become more "complacent" in recent times, but it remains a top City entertaining spot. / EC4N 8AD; www.thedonrestaurant.com; @thedonlondon; 10 pm; closed Sat & Sun; no shorts.

Donna Margherita SW11 £44 4 3 3

183 Lavender Hill 7228 2660 10–2C

For a "friendly Italian meal" in south London this "always busy" Battersea Neapolitan exudes an "excited buzz", and its pizza and other fare is generally a safe bet. / SW11 5TE; www.donna-margherita.com; @DMargheritaUK; 10.30 pm, Fri & Sat 11 pm; Mon-Thu D only, Fri-Sun open L & D.

Donostia W1 £49 5 4 4

10 Seymour Pl 3620 1845 2–2A

"Simply amazing" and "authentic" Basque tapa/pintxos are dished up by "really helpful" and "knowledgeable" staff at this "stylish yet informal" fixture, "in a quiet corner, north of Marble Arch". See also Lurra. / W1H 7ND; www.donostia.co.uk; @DonostiaW1; 11 pm; closed Mon L.

Dorchester Grill
Dorchester Hotel W1 £102 2 3 2

53 Park Ln 7629 8888 3–3A

"New decor's a big improvement", as this famous chamber has at long last ditched its vile, faux-Scottish theme; ratings remain lacklustre across the board though – the whole operation still needs a major kick up the backside to avoid being just-another-overpriced-Mayfair-dining-room. / W1K 1QA; www.thedorchester.com; @TheDorchester; 10.15 pm, Sat 10.45 pm, Sun 10.15 pm; no trainers; set weekday L £64 (FP), set Sun L £74 (FP).

Dotori N4 £28 4 3 2

3a Stroud Green Rd 7263 3562 8–1D

"The secret of this excellent-value, tiny, cramped Korean near Finsbury Park station is well-and-truly out, and you have to book well in advance, even mid week"; "if you don't know what to order, staff will talk you through it". / N4 2DQ; www.dotorirestaurant.wix.com/dotorirestaurant; 10.30 pm; closed Mon; no Amex.

The Dove W6 £46 2 2 5

19 Upper Mall 8748 5405 7–2B

A "quintessential", small 18th-century pub, "beautifully located" on the Thames in Hammersmith, which is supremely "cosy in winter", and has "a sunny terrace in summer" – just the job for a Sunday roast. / W6 9TA; www.fullers.co.uk; 11 pm; closed Sun D; no booking.

Dragon Castle SE17 £36 3 3 2

100 Walworth Rd 7277 3388 1–3C

"In the most unlikely of locations", near Elephant & Castle, this "cavernous" Cantonese is "worth a trip"; it may look a little "tired", but its dim sum is "amazing value, and comes in great abundance". / SE17 1JL; www.dragon-castle.com; @Dragoncastle100; Mon-Sat 11 pm, Sun 10 pm.

Drakes Tabanco W1 £49 3 2 3

3 Windmill St 7637 9388 2–1C

"An educational selection of wonderful sherries on tap" beefs up the attractions of this "authentic" Andalucían-inspired Fitzrovian ("off the hustle and bustle of Charlotte Street"), but its "yummy" tapas is also "very well done". / W1T 2HY; www.drakestabanco.com; 10 pm.

The Drapers Arms N1 £50 223
44 Barnsbury St 7619 0348 8–3D
"Sociable" Islington gastropub, which remains a big hit locally; service is "inconsistent" however, and the food can turn out "mediocre" – "go for the excellent, knowledgeably-selected wines". / N1 1ER; www.thedrapersarms.com; @DrapersArms; 10.30 pm; no Amex.

Dub Jam WC2 £24 443
20 Bedford St 7836 5876 4–3C
"Come for the potent rum punch, stay for the awesome Caribbean BBQ" – so say fans of this "laid-back, cheap 'n' cheerful" shack, in Covent Garden. / WC2E 9HP; www.dubjam.co.uk; @dubjambbq; 11.30 pm, Fri & Sat midnight, Sun 10.30 pm.

The Duck & Rice W1 NEW £58 235
90 Berwick St 3327 7888 3–2D
There's real "whoa factor" to the "striking" fit-out and "great vibe" of Wagamama-creator, Alan Yau's much-anticipated "Chinese gastropub concept", in the heart of sleazy Soho (formerly, The Endurance, RIP). No surprise that some find it "over-hyped" considering food that's arguably only "good-to-average", but beer and dim sum in the downstairs bar is a particularly "winning combination". / W1F 0QB; www.theduckandrice.com; @theduckandrice; Mon -11.30 pm, midnight, Sun 10.30 pm.

Duck & Waffle EC2 £68 225
110 Bishopsgate, Heron Tower 3640 7310 9–2D
"Go mainly for the extraordinary views" to this 24/7, 40th-floor hang-out; "the signature dish (confit duck with a fried egg, waffle and syrup) is better than it sounds", but opinions are mixed on the "mainly meaty, high-cholesterol" fare and you pay "City boys' drinks prices". Maybe try breakfast or coffee. / EC2N 4AY; www.duckandwaffle.com; @DuckandWaffle; open 24 hours.

Ducksoup W1 £54 344
41 Dean St 7287 4599 4–2A
"A dark, intimate, welcoming den in Soho"; the "beautiful" Mediterranean small plates are "creative" and "served with real charm". / W1D 4PY; www.ducksoupsoho.co.uk; @ducksoup; 10.30 pm; closed Sun D; need 6+ to book at certain times.

Duke of Sussex W4 £46 334
75 South Pde 8742 8801 7–1A
A "dramatic" interior, and "lovely rear dining room and garden" score points for this traditional Victorian tavern by Acton Green Common, as does its very dependable "Spanish-inspired" tapas, and more substantial fare. / W4 5LF; www.metropolitanpubcompany.com; @thedukew4; 10.30 pm, Sun 9.30 pm.

Duke's Brew & Que N1 £54 323
33 Downham Rd 3006 0795 1–2D
"Hipster heaven" is to be found at this "laid back" US-style Dalston hang-out in the form of "proper, Texan-style BBQ (ribs to die for)" and "brilliant" home-brewed beer; even fans however can find it "massively too expensive". / N1 5AA; www.dukesbrewandque.com; @DukesJoint; 10.30 pm, Sun 9.30 pm.

Dumplings' Legend W1 NEW £35 4 2 3
16 Gerrard St 7494 1200 4–3A
"Don't let the modern, white exterior fool you" – this Chinatown newcomer's dim sum is "of very high quality"; as is often the case in these parts though, service "can be a bit off-hand". / W1D 6JE; www.dumplingslegend.com; midnight, Fri & Sat 3 am, Sun 11 pm.

Durum Ocakbasi N3 £30 3 2 2
119 Ballards Ln 8346 8977 1–1B
"Good, marinated meaty kebabs" at "cheap prices", plus "fast service" means there's "always a queue" at this "consistently reliable" Finchley Turk. / N3 1LJ; durumrestaurant.co.uk; midnight.

The Dysart Petersham TW10 £69 4 4 3
135 Petersham Rd 8940 8005 1–4A
Kenneth Culhane's "super" cooking can come as a "real surprise" at this leafily located pub – a large Arts & Crafts house overlooking Richmond Common; despite its "leaded windows, log fires, and twinkly lights in the trees outside", at lunch it can "lack atmosphere". / TW10 7AA; www.thedysartarms.co.uk; @dysartpetersham; 9.30 pm; closed Sun D; set weekday L £42 (FP).

E&O W11 £60 3 3 4
14 Blenheim Cr 7229 5454 6–1A
"Still exciting and vibrant" – this "intimate and buzzing" (if slightly "arrogant") Notting Hill hang-out is "not quite as outstanding as it was half a dozen years ago", but "still the place to go" for many, thanks to its "amazing Pan-Asian tapas and cocktails". / W11 1NN; www.rickerrestaurants.com; 11 pm, Sun 10.30 pm; booking: max 6.

The Eagle EC1 £34 4 3 5
159 Farringdon Rd 7837 1353 9–1A
Even after all these years, there's still "rarely a false note" at "the original and best gastropub" – an engagingly "grungy" and "low-key" hang-out, near Exmouth Market; the "rustic" Mediterranean cooking is "reasonably priced", and "there's always something new and interesting on the menu". / EC1R 3AL; www.theeaglefarringdon.co.uk; @eaglefarringdon; 10.30 pm; closed Sun D; no Amex; no booking.

Ealing Park Tavern W5 £44 3 3 4
222 South Ealing Rd 8758 1879 1–3A
South Ealing locals are divided on the new regime at this "huge" neighbourhood gastropub; but while some are disappointed, most say it's "much improved", with "smarter" decor and "thoroughly enjoyable" cooking. / W5 4RL; www.ealingparktavern.com; @ealingtavern; 10 pm, Sun 9 pm.

Earl Spencer SW18 £45 4 2 3
260-262 Merton Rd 8870 9244 10–2B
Despite its trafficky Wandsworth location, this sizeable road house is "a wonderful local" with cooking that's "consistently a cut-above on the pub food scale"; "the beer's always excellent too :-)". / SW18 5JL; www.theearlspencer.co.uk; @TheEarlSpencer; 11 pm; Mon-Thu D only, Fri-Sun open L & D; no booking, Sun.

Eat 17 **£39** 342
28-30 Orford Rd, E17 8521 5279 1–1D
64-66 Brooksbys Walk, E9 8986 6242 1–1D
"A real find!" in Walthamstow – a "fun and friendly" spot with "interesting" food that's "very well priced"; also with an offshoot in Hackney. / www.eat17.co.uk.

Eat Tokyo **£24** 422
50 Red Lion St, WC1 7242 3490 2–1D
15 Whitcomb St, WC2 7930 6117 4–4B
169 King St, W6 8741 7916 7–2B
18 Hillgate St, W8 7792 9313 6–2B
14 North End Rd, NW11 8209 0079 1–1B
"High end it isn't", but for "authentic" Japanese fare that "doesn't cost the earth" – "amazingly fresh sushi" and "very good bento boxes" – these "deservedly busy" staples are just the job. / Mon - Sat 11.30pm, Sun 11 pm.

Ebury Restaurant & Wine Bar SW1 **£53** 233
139 Ebury St 7730 5447 2–4A
A great, "old-school" wine bar, not far from Victoria; the cooking is only "standard", but the atmosphere is "charming" and there's an "excellent wine list". / SW1W 9QU; www.eburyrestaurant.co.uk; 10.15 pm.

Eco SW4 **£36** 224
162 Clapham High St 7978 1108 10–2D
Owned by one of the co-founders of Franco Manca, this perennially "lively" Clapham institution (now 20 years old) has long been the home of some "great pizza". / SW4 7UG; www.ecorestaurants.com; @ecopizzaLDN; 11 pm, Fri & Sat 11.30 pm.

Edera W11 **£61** 353
148 Holland Park Ave 7221 6090 6–2A
"A little pricey" but "very solid and reliable" – that's the universal view on this low-key, quite "stylish" Holland Park Sardinian (also "a dependable spot for business"). Top Menu Tip – "truffles a speciality". / W11 4UE; www.atozrestaurants.com; 11 pm, Sun 10 pm.

Edwins SE1 **£48** 333
202-206 Borough High St 7403 9913 9–4B
"At a safe distance from the City expense-accounters and Borough Market crowds", this year-old bistro above a pub is well rated all-round (especially for its "good-value" set menu). / SE1 1JX; www.edwinsborough.co.uk; @edwinsborough; 11.30 pm, Sat midnight, Sun 4 pm; closed Sun D.

Eelbrook SW6 **£56** 343
Eel Brook Common, New King's Rd 3417 0287 10–1B
"A relaxing park-side location" adds to the appeal of this year-old venture, by Fulham's Eel Brook Common; weekend brunch is a highlight, but the menu of small plates is well-rated generally. / SW6 4SE; @EelbrookTweets; 10.30 pm, Sun 5.30 pm ; set weekday L £32 (FP).

8 Hoxton Square N1 £49 4 4 3
8-9 Hoxton Sq 7729 4232 12–1B
"Ticking all the boxes for a relaxing evening with friends" – a "lovely and intimate" spin-off from 10 Greek Street that "would be good, even without its secret weapon of a wine list"; the cooking's "low key, but accomplished, and extremely well-prepared". / N1 6NU; www.8hoxtonsquare.com; @8HoxtonSquare; 10 pm; closed Sun D.

Eight Over Eight SW3 £56 3 2 4
392 King's Rd 7349 9934 5–3B
"It looks a bit like a '90s nightclub", but Will Ricker's "very popular" Chelsea haunt makes "a good poor man's Nobu" – the Pan-Asian tapas is "consistently high quality", and it's still quite the "buzzing scene". / SW3 5UZ; www.rickerrestaurants.com; 11 pm, Sun 10.30 pm.

Electric Diner W11 £44 2 4 4
191 Portobello Rd 7908 9696 6–1A
"Busy and bustling" diner, where you battle with Notting Hill's trustafarians for a "fun" brunch, featuring "top burgers", or "a welcome twist on a Full English"; however even some who think it's great concede that "you don't go for the pretty average food". / W11 2ED; www.electricdiner.com; @ElectricDiner; 11 pm, Sun 10 pm.

Elena's L'Etoile W1 £52 1 1 1
30 Charlotte St 7636 7189 2–1C
"What was once a shining star, is now just very tired…" – this ancient Gallic Fitzrovian (est 1896) "used to be remarkable when it was presided over by Elena", but "continues its lurch downwards", and is nowadays well "past its sell-by". / W1T 2NG; www.elenasletoile.co.uk; @elenasletoile; 10.30 pm; closed Sat L & Sun.

Elliot's Café SE1 £50 2 2 3
12 Stoney St 7403 7436 9–4C
An "ever-changing" menu ("mainly small plates") and interesting wines inspire devotees of Brett Redman's "buzzy" bare-brick café, in Borough Market; "standards seem to have dropped this year" though – staff can be "uninterested" and a few meals were "a great disappointment" – the pressure of opening The Richmond E8? / SE1 9AD; www.elliotscafe.com; @elliotscafe; 9.30 pm; closed Sun; booking: max 8.

Ellory
Netil House E8 NEW
Westgate St awaiting tel 1–2D
A collaboration between ex-Mayfields chef, Matthew Young and sommelier, Jack Lewens (Spring and River Café) that's got foodies excited; it's expected to open in Hackney's über-hip Netil House in October 2015. / E8 3RL.

Ember Yard W1 £49 3 3 3
60 Berwick St 7439 8057 3–1D
"I love the use of charcoal!" – this Salt Yard group yearling serves "deep-flavoured" tapas from its char grill, which can be "wonderful"; it's a stylish spot too, although it can get "too squashed", and one or two doubters feel the food is "OK, but could be better". / W1F 8SU; www.emberyard.co.uk; @SaltYardGroup; midnight; SRA-2.*

Emile's SW15 £48 342

96-98 Felsham Rd 8789 3323 10–2B

"Emile adds that personal touch" to his longstanding Putney backstreet "stalwart", where the "well-priced, French bistro-esque" cooking and "well-selected" wines "continue to offer good value". / SW15 1DQ; www.emilesrestaurant.co.uk; 11 pm; D only, closed Sun; no Amex.

The Empress E9 £45 444

130 Lauriston Rd 8533 5123 1–2D

"A favourite stop-off after a bracing walk in Victoria Park" – this popular East End gastropub "always hits the mark" with its "different" cooking, "spot-on" service, and "great vibes". / E9 7LH; www.empresse9.co.uk; @elliottlidstone; 10 pm, Sun 9.30 pm; closed Mon L; no Amex.

Engawa W1 NEW £86 343

2 Ham Yd 7287 5724 3–2D

Just off Shaftesbury Avenue, a small and "tightly packed" new temple to Japan's outrageously expensive Kobe and Wagyu beef (plus sake bar); many reporters do laud "exquisite food" and "stunning presentation", but – at the vertiginous prices – even some fans "expected better quality cuts of the meat". / W1D 7DT; www.engawa.uk; 11.15 pm.

Enoteca Rabezzana EC1 NEW £48 223

62-63 Long Ln 7600 0266 9–2B

The Italian grub is not the star attraction at this "fun" if "chaotic" new City wine bar – it's the massive selection of wines by the glass ("over 100 of them") that make it worth seeking out. / EC1A 9EJ; www.rabezzana.co.uk; @RabezzanaLondon; midnight, Sat 1 am.

Enoteca Turi SW15 £61 443

28 Putney High St 8785 4449 10–2B

"Don't be put off by the slightly off-piste location, near Putney Bridge!" – Giuseppe and Pamela Turi's "personal" yet "efficient" stalwart offers "a truly memorable" combination of "beautifully cooked, regional Italian cuisine" and one of London's top Italian wine lists ("about the size of the Encyclopaedia Britannica"). "Worryingly, it's under threat from its landlord – long may it survive!" / SW15 1SQ; www.enotecaturi.com; @enoteca_turi; 10.30 pm, Fri & Sat 11 pm; closed Sun.

The Enterprise SW3 £58 233

35 Walton St 7584 3148 5–2C

In a chichi Chelsea enclave, this corner-bar/restaurant is a real "local's hang-out"; "you don't go for the food" (though it's not bad), but the "friendly" service and "fun" ambience. / SW3 2HU; www.theenterprise.co.uk; 10 pm, Sat 10.30 pm; no booking, except weekday L; set weekday L £38 (FP).

Esarn Kheaw W12 £34 441

314 Uxbridge Rd 8743 8930 7–1B

Rather forgotten nowadays, but this stalwart Shepherd's Bush café still wins praise for its "personable service, and very delicious and highly authentic" north Thai cooking; "the shabby mint decor is all part of the charm". / W12 7LJ; www.esarnkheaw.co.uk; @esarn_kheaw; 11 pm; closed Sat L & Sun L; no Amex.

L'Escargot W1 £60 333

48 Greek St 7439 7474 4–2A

Brian Clivaz's datedly glamorous old-timer provides a "cosseting" and "romantic" refuge from Soho, and its slightly "formal and traditional" style would also suit a business occasion; under new owners for a year now, the Gallic cuisine is proving "reliable". / W1D 4EF; lescargotrestaurant.co.uk; @EscargotLondon; midnight; closed Sun D.

Essenza W11 £60 323

210 Kensington Park Rd 7792 1066 6–1A

Notting Hill offers up a "good local Italian" with a "very high standard of Roman-inspired food"; expect to receive "a warm welcome, very generous helpings of well-prepared dishes and a lively atmosphere". / W11 1NR; www.essenza.co.uk; @Essenza_LND; 11.30 pm; set weekday L £38 (FP).

Ethos W1 NEW £38 423

48 Eastcastle St 3581 1538 3–1C

"Bonus points for an interesting concept" – a new, self-service veggie, where you "load up as much as you like and pay-by-weight"; "prices add up pretty quickly", but there's an "excellent selection" of "perky", health-conscious dishes (and "you don't need a hair shirt to enjoy them"). / W1W 8DX; www.ethosfoods.com; @ethosfoods; 10 pm, Sun 5 pm.

L'Etranger SW7 £72 342

36 Gloucester Rd 7584 1118 5–1B

"The wine list's amazing", the "interesting" Asian/French fusion cuisine can be "exceptional", and service is "very professional" too at this lesser-known spot near the Royal Albert Hall; it's "expensive" though, and – "being unpredictably quiet or busy" – the "ambience is patchy". / SW7 4QT; www.etranger.co.uk; 11 pm; set weekday L £44 (FP).

Everest Inn SE3 £35 453

41 Montpelier Vale 8852 7872 1–4D

"Fresh-tasting Gurkha curries" and other "unusual Nepali dishes", together with "smiling and efficient" service win consistent praise for this local Blackheath favourite. / SE3 0TJ; www.everestinnblackheath.co.uk; midnight, Sun 11 pm.

Eyre Brothers EC2 £64 533

70 Leonard St 7613 5346 12–1B

"Terrific Iberian tapas, made with care from well-sourced produce, and a strong wine list" inspire fervent praise for this low-key, but quite swish haunt, near Silicon Roundabout, whose "quiet ambience and big tables" have long established it as a business favourite. / EC2A 4QX; www.eyrebrothers.co.uk; 10 pm; closed Sat L & Sun.

Faanoos £27 223

472 Chiswick High Rd, W4 8994 4217 7–2A

11 Bond St, W5 8810 0505 1–3A

481 Richmond Road, SW14 8878 5738 1–4A

"Simple but tasty Persian fare at very reasonable prices" – that's the formula that wins fans for these "cheap and cheerful" locals in Chiswick and Ealing, where the oven-baked flatbread is a "pleasure"; now with a site in East Sheen too. / SW14 11 pm; W4 11 pm; Fri & Sat midnight.

Fabrizio EC1 £50 442

30 Saint Cross St 7430 1503 9–1A

"Fabrizio is a wonderful host" and injects life into his "basic" Hatton Garden premises, where the "simple and fresh" Sicilian dishes are "authentic", and offer "very good value for money". / EC1N 8UH; www.fabriziorestaurant.co.uk; 10 pm; closed Sat L & Sun.

Fabrizio N19 £35 242

34 Highgate Hill 7561 9073 8–1C

"Ideal for a family outing" – this Highgate Hill trattoria is "a consistent neighbourhood Italian, serving fresh pasta and pizza choices of the day". / N19 5NL; www.fabriziolondon.co.uk; 10 pm; no Amex.

Fairuz W1 £48 343

3 Blandford St 7486 8108 2–1A

"A very consistent performer" – this Lebanese "longstanding favourite", in Marylebone, serves "excellent mezze", and its staff are extremely hospitable too. / W1H 3DA; www.fairuz.uk.com; 11 pm, Sun 10.30 pm.

La Famiglia SW10 £52 222

7 Langton St 7351 0761 5–3B

A '60s, "old-school, family-run Italian" in the heart of Chelsea that's still a "characterful" classic for its loyal fan club, especially for a family occasion (and with "a lovely garden in summer"); even some fans might however concede that to some extent it's "living on its past, and very expensive". / SW10 0JL; www.lafamiglia.co.uk; 11 pm.

FERA AT CLARIDGE'S
CLARIDGE'S HOTEL W1 £144 344

55 Brook St 7107 8888 3–2B

After a dazzling debut, Simon Rogan's second year in this "stunning" Art Deco chamber still inspires adulation for his "wizard" tasting menus and "astonishingly good wine matches". Prices, however, are "breathtaking", and ratings slipped perceptibly across the board this year, with growing gripes about "an absence of fireworks". / W1K 4HR; www.claridges.co.uk/fera; 10 pm; set weekday L £65 (FP); SRA-2.*

Fernandez & Wells £32 224

16a, St Anne's Ct, W1 7494 4242 3–1D
43 Lexington St, W1 7734 1546 3–2D
73 Beak St, W1 7287 8124 3–2D
Somerset Hs, Strand, WC2 7420 9408 2–2D

"Consistently terrific coffee", and "wonderful sarnies, pastries and cakes" distinguish these "quirky, if not comfy" cafés; Somerset House is its most striking outlet, and the tiny Soho ones are good too – South Ken seems more of a "rip-off", with staff who are "too cool to care". / www.fernandezandwells.com; Lexington St & St Anne's court 10 pm, Beak St 6 pm, Somerset House 11 pm; St Anne's Court closed Sun.

Fez Mangal W11 £26 543

104 Ladbroke Grove 7229 3010 6–1A

"Hectic, as it's often jammed with customers" – an "inexpensive Turkish BBQ" in Notting Hill, whose "freshly prepared" food is "first rate"; "BYO too!" / W11 1PY; www.fezmangal.co.uk; @FezMangal; 11.30 pm; no Amex.

Ffiona's W8 **£56** 3 4 4

51 Kensington Church St 7937 4152 5–1A

"Ffiona has become a personal friend" to regulars at her "unique and very intimate" Kensington venue, whom she makes feel "welcome and special"; food-wise it's a case of "well-cooked staples, plus a few more international dishes", and there's a popular weekend brunch. / W8 4BA; www.ffionas.com; @ffionasnotes; 11 pm, Sun 10 pm; closed Mon; no Amex.

Fields SW4 NEW **£30**

2 Rookery Rd 7838 1082 10–2C

The owners of Balham's achingly hip coffee shop Milk bring a second location to SW London with this brunch-tastic revamp of a modest park café in Clapham Common. / SW4 9DD; www.fieldscafe.com; @The5Fields; 5 pm.

Fifteen N1 **£60** 1 2 2

15 Westland Pl 3375 1515 12–1A

"What is all the fuss about?"; Jamie Oliver's Hoxton Italian continues – as it always has done – to provide "a totally overrated experience with terrible food", and at prices that are plain "rude". / N1 7LP; www.fifteen.net; @JamiesFifteen; 10 pm; booking: max 12.

The Fifth Floor Restaurant Harvey Nichols SW1 **£62** 3 3 3

109-125 Knightsbridge 7235 5250 5–1D

Few reports nowadays on this forgotten-about landmark atop the famous Knightsbridge department store – a "light and airy space, with a top-lit glass ceiling and simple but appropriate decor"; for a "classy" lunch though, fans say it's "first rate". / SW1X 7RJ; www.harveynichols.com; 11 pm; closed Sun D; SRA-2.*

Fire & Stone **£42** 2 2 2

31-32 Maiden Ln, WC2 7632 2084 4–3D

Westfield, Ariel Way, W12 7763 2085 7–1C

The cavernous Covent Garden original is the mainstay of this modern pizza chain; but while fans like its trademark weird-and-wonderful array of toppings, sceptics say they're "odd and don't work", or rail at general "chain-style dreariness". / www.fireandstone.com; WC2 11 pm; W12 11.15 pm; E1 11pm, Sun 8 pm.

Fischer's W1 **£58** 3 4 4

50 Marylebone High St 7466 5501 2–1A

Whether it's "another star in the Corbin & King stable" or merely "a useful addition to Marylebone", this "fun pastiche of old Vienna" earnt higher ratings this year; the slightly "kitsch Austrian" interior is "gemütlich", and the Mittel-European victuals – mainly wurst and schnitzels – is "good but pricey". / W1U 5HN; www.fischers.co.uk; @fischers; 11 pm, Sun 10 pm.

Fish Central EC1 **£32** 3 3 2

149-155 Central St 7253 4970 12–1A

For "very crisp" fish 'n' chips at "unbeatable prices" this family-run Clerkenwell chippy is a hit with cabbies and Barbican-goers alike; take a punt on one of the specials – "be it lobster, halibut or Dover sole, it's some of the best". / EC1V 8AP; www.fishcentral.co.uk; 10.30 pm, Fri & Sat 11 pm; closed Sun.

Fish Club £40 422
189 St John's Hill, SW11 7978 7115 10–2C
57 Clapham High St, SW4 7720 5853 10–2D
"Amazing fish 'n' chips" – using "the best range of fresh fish", and with "unbeatable" roast root and sweet potato accompaniments – mean these "slightly cramped" south London chippies are "well worth a few extra quid over the average". / www.thefishclub.com; 10 pm; closed Mon L; no bookings.

Fish in a Tie SW11 £36 243
105 Falcon Rd 7924 1913 10–1C
"Good food in generous portions at unbeatable prices", summarises the appeal of this "most reliable (if predictable)" Clapham Junction bistro, whose menu is "diverse, Italian in feel, with an ever-changing list of specials". / SW11 2PF; www.fishinatie.co.uk; midnight, Sun 11 pm; no Amex.

Fish Market EC2 £49 333
16b New St 3503 0790 9–2D
"An attractive heated courtyard with umbrellas" frames the entrance to this "bright and airy" converted warehouse (a D&D London operation), a stone's throw from the crowds on Bishopsgate; it's somewhat under-the-radar, despite serving dependable "fresh fish, simply cooked". / EC2M 4TR; www.fishmarket-restaurant.co.uk; @FishMarketNS; 10.30 pm; closed Sun.

fish! SE1 £56 322
Cathedral St 7407 3803 9–4C
It's "rather crowded" and "a little expensive", but this glazed shed, by Borough Market, serves a decent array of dishes, including "surprisingly good fish 'n' chips", "excellent mixed grill" and "great fish finger sarnies". / SE1 9AL; www.fishkitchen.com; @fishborough; 10.45 pm, Sun 10.30 pm.

Fishworks £51 322
7-9 Swallow St, W1 7734 5813 3–3D
89 Marylebone High St, W1 7935 9796 2–1A
"Walking through the fish shop to get to the restaurant sets the scene" at these straightforward bistros in Mayfair and Marylebone; "there's a wide range" and results are "consistently good", but the overall experience is a bit "functional". / www.fishworks.co.uk; 10.30 pm.

The Five Fields SW3 £76 555
8-9 Blacklands Ter 7838 1082 5–2D
"It just gets better and better!" – Taylor Bonnyman's "grown-up" and "romantic" two-year-old in the heart of Chelsea is one of London's most deeply impressive all-rounders – service is "impeccable", and the "exciting" cuisine provides "a beautiful blend of original flavours". / SW3 2SP; www.fivefieldsrestaurant.com; @The5Fields; 10 pm; D only, closed Mon & Sun.

Five Guys £13 222
1-3 Long Acre, WC2 7240 2657 4–3C
71 Upper St, N1 7226 7577 8–3D NEW
"An upgrade on McDonald's which hits the spot", say fans of this US-import-chain who dig the "proper dirty burgers", "good salty fries" and "really nice mix of free toppings"; not everyone's wowed though – "you get McD quality at GBK prices!" / www.fiveguys.co.uk.

FSA

500 N19 £48 3 4 2

782 Holloway Rd 7272 3406 8–1C

"An unpromising-looking bit of Holloway hides this Italian treasure which is almost always packed"; the interior is "quite minimal", but it serves "well-thought-out", "seasonal" Sicilian fare, from a "small but unusual menu" (albeit one that "could do with rotating a little more"). / N19 3JH; www.500restaurant.co.uk; @500restaurant; 10.30 pm, Sun 9.30 pm; Mon-Thu D only, Fri-Sun open L & D.

Flat Iron £22 4 4 4

17 Beak St, W1 no tel 3–2D

17 Henrietta St, WC2 no tel 4–4C NEW

9 Denmark St, WC2 no tel 4–1A

"Steak and salad for a tenner – WOW!"; these "simple", "hipster" hang-outs in Soho and by Centrepoint "do what they do very well indeed"; "arrive early, but it's always worth the wait". A second Covent Garden site is set to open in Henrietta Street in October 2015. / www.flatironsteak.co.uk.

Flat Three W11 NEW £75 2 3 3

120-122 Holland Park Ave 7792 8987 6–2A

With its "experimental fusion of Asian and Scandi' inspirations", this "cool", new, Holland Park basement (born of a supper club collaboration) sure is "bringing something new to the 'hood"; but while fans say it's "exciting", or sense "great potential", sceptics say "the menu is incomprehensible", and results plain "poor". / W11 4UA; www.flatthree.london; @FlatThree; Tue-Sat 9.30 pm.

Flesh and Buns WC2 £50 3 3 3

41 Earlham St 7632 9500 4–2C

"Nice buns…"; this "funky" Soho basement (sibling to Bone Daddies) serves "mouthwatering, meat-filled steamed buns" and other "unusual Japanese-influenced dishes" to a "hip" crowd, some of it on communal tables; it's "too loud" though. / WC2H 9LX; www.bonedaddies.com; @FleshandBuns; Mon & Tue 10.30 pm, Wed-Sat 9.30 pm, Sun 9.30 pm.

Flotsam and Jetsam SW17 NEW £14 4 3 4

4 Bellevue Parade 8672 7639 10–2C

"An inviting, new Antipodean-style indie coffee shop and café", by Wandsworth Common; "instantly and deservedly popular", it offers "awesome" brunches, "lovely light lunches" and "top coffee" in a "crowded but fun" setting. / SW17 7EQ; www.flotsamandjetsamcafe.co.uk; 5 pm.

FM Mangal SE5 £28 3 2 2

54 Camberwell Church St 7701 6677 1–4D

With its "hefty grills" and "smoky flatbreads", this "totally unpretentious" Camberwell Turkish grill "never disappoints" – "don't forget the totally addictive charred, marinaded onions". / SE5 8QZ; midnight.

(1707)
Fortnum & Mason W1 **£54** 2 2 3

181 Piccadilly 7734 8040 3–3D

Below the famous food halls, a bar with "reliable" snacks, but which "is really all about the wine" – "a great range of flights", plus the chance to "drink anything from their impressive adjacent wine shop" (with £15 corkage). "Service has dropped off" this year however, and prices seem increasingly "astronomical". / W1A 1ER; www.fortnumandmason.co.uk; @fortnumandmason; 7.45 pm, Sun 5 pm; closed Sun D.

(The Diamond Jubilee Tea Salon)
Fortnum & Mason W1 **£66** 3 3 3

181 Piccadilly 7734 8040 3–3D

"I didn't think posh afternoon tea would be my thing, but I was bowled over!" – Fortnum's "light" and "elegant" third-floor salon is a relatively new addition to the store, with cake trollies and "light and fluffy scones" à gogo; it's pricey though, and critics say "the big hotels do it better". / W1A 1ER; www.fortnumandmason.com; @fortnumandmason; 7 pm, Sun 6 pm; cancellation charge for larger bookings.

(45 Jermyn St)
Fortnum & Mason W1 NEW

181 Piccadilly 7437 3278 3–3D

In autumn 2015, HM's grocer announced that its hallowed (if slightly crusty and expensive) old buttery, The Fountain, would close, to be replaced by an all-day operation with a midnight closing time; 10/10 to F&M for moving with the times, but if they'd run the old one better would they need to revamp? / W1A 1ER; www.fortnumandmason.com.

40 Maltby Street SE1 **£45** 4 3 4

40 Maltby St 7237 9247 9–4D

"30% bistro, 70% wine warehouse under the London Bridge station Arches"; the "very unusual" wine selection is "sensational" and "in the tiny open kitchen Steve Williams and team produce amazing dishes with the freshest seasonal ingredients". / SE1 3PA; www.40maltbystreet.com; @40maltbystreet; 9.30 pm; closed Mon, Tue, Wed L, Thu L, Sat D & Sun; no Amex; no booking.

The Four Seasons **£34** 4 1 1

12 Gerrard St, W1 7494 0870 4–3A
23 Wardour St, W1 7287 9995 4–3A
84 Queensway, W2 7229 4320 6–2C

"Still the benchmark for roast duck" ("it's the best ever") – the claim to fame of this trio of "run down" looking Chinese diners in Bayswater and Chinatown; "don't expect 5-star service though!" – it can be "terrible"! / www.fs-restaurants.co.uk; Queensway 11 pm, Sun 10h45 pm; Gerrard St 1 am; Wardour St 1am, Fri-Sat 3.30 am.

Fox & Grapes SW19 **£55** 2 2 2

9 Camp Rd 8619 1300 10–2A

Right by Wimbledon Common, this "upmarket" gastropub is "ideally located to walk off any over indulgence"; but while fans say its "traditional food with a twist" is "always excellent", for a disgruntled minority it's "shamefully overpriced", and "overall not a great experience". / SW19 4UN; www.foxandgrapeswimbledon.co.uk; @thefoxandgrapes; 9.30 pm, Sun 8.15 pm; no Amex.

The Fox & Hounds SW11 £47 444

66 Latchmere Rd 7924 5483 10–1C

"If only all pubs were like this Battersea gastroboozer" (sibling to Earl's Court's Atlas) – "cracking Med'-inspired food from an open kitchen", "great beer festivals and brewery-led events alongside good wines", and with "a lovely garden". / SW11 2JU; www.thefoxandhoundspub.co.uk; @thefoxbattersea; 10 pm; Mon-Thu D only, Fri-Sun open L & D.

The Fox and Anchor EC1 £49 334

115 Charterhouse St 7250 1300 9–1B

"Stunning" sausage rolls, "excellent pork pies" – not to mention, of course, notorious "blow out breakfasts" ("all washed down with a pint of Guinness") – are the orders of the day at this famous, "very olde worlde" Smithfield tavern. / EC1M 6AA; www.foxandanchor.com; @foxanchor; Mon-Sat 9.30 pm, Sun 6 pm.

Foxlow £50 333

71-73 Stoke Newington Ch' St, N16 7014 8070 1–1C NEW

St John St, EC1 7014 8070 9–2A

"First class" steaks and "cool" styling win fans for these Hawksmoor-lite spin-offs, which now have a Stoke Newington branch as well as the Clerkenwell original; "prices add up quickly" however, results can be "unspectacular", and – while "edgy" – the decor is a tad "functional". / www.foxlow.co.uk.

Franco Manca £20 433

Branches throughout London

"Even my Italian girlfriend rates it!"; "amazingly yummy", sourdough-based pizza ("how do they make it fluffy and crisp simultaneously?") at "very keen" prices wins a ginormous fan club for this fast-expanding, "energetic" ("crowded and noisy") chain; no bookings – "you queue out of the door most days". / www.francomanca.co.uk; SW9 10.30, Mon 5 pm; W4 11 pm; E20 9 pm, Thu-Sat 10 pm, Sun 6 pm; no bookings.

Franco's SW1 £74 343

61 Jermyn St 7499 2211 3–3C

"Attentive" staff know how to treat expense accounters at this St James's Italian, whose dependable cooking and "absence of riff raff" appeal to local pinstripes (including for a working breakfast); it can also seem a tad "boring" and pricey however, and "all those hedgies make a lot of noise". / SW1Y 6LX; www.francoslondon.com; @francoslondon; 10.30 pm; closed Sun.

Franklins SE22 £50 434

157 Lordship Ln 8299 9598 1–4D

"Wonderful seasonal creations at reasonable (Dulwich) prices", win the highest praise for this "really friendly local", which nowadays boasts a neighbouring farm shop on the other side of the road. / SE22 8HX; www.franklinsrestaurant.com; @franklinsse22; 10.30 pm; no Amex.

Frantoio SW10 £56 233

397 King's Rd 7352 4146 5–3B

Expect much "bonhomie" ("you'll be made to feel like a long lost brother!") from the owner of this World's End Italian; the cooking is generally reliable, but primarily it's "always fun" (and "excellent for families"). / SW10 0LR; 11.15 pm, Sun 10.15 pm.

Frederick's N1 **£62** 2 2 4

106 Islington High St 7359 2888 8–3D

"It's been around forever" – this "beautiful" favourite "in the heart of Islington", with its "lovely" and "spacious" interior (especially the conservatory); critics say its pricey, "grown-up" food is "coasting on its longevity" – but it's been like this for as long as we can remember! / N1 8EG; www.fredericks.co.uk; @fredericks_n1; 11 pm; closed Sun; set weekday L £36 (FP).

Friends of Ours N1 NEW **£19** 4 4 2

61 Pitfield St 7686 5525 12–1B

"In the slightly less fashionable bit of Hoxton", this small, sparse new indie café is "a real find"; it dishes up "an interesting range of brunch-type options" and "coffee made with real care". / N1 6BU; www.facebook.com/TheFriendsofOurs; @friends_ofours; 5 pm.

La Fromagerie Café W1 **£39** 3 2 3

2-6 Moxon St 7935 0341 3–1A

"Cheesy heaven on a plate" (along with other "great nibbles") is served in this "buzzing" Marylebone café, adjacent to the famous cheese shop; "perfectly matched" beers and wines too. / W1U 4EW; www.lafromagerie.co.uk; @lafromagerieuk; 6.30 pm, Sat 6 pm, Sun 5 pm; L only; no booking.

The Frontline Club W2 **£52** 3 3 3

13 Norfolk Pl 7479 8960 6–1D

"There always seems to be a journo' or two", at this comfy dining room (part of a club for war reporters), which is particularly "handy for Paddington"; the food's "good value" and eye-catching reportage photography on the walls make for a slightly "different" ambience. / W2 1QJ; www.frontlineclub.com; @frontlineclub; 10.30 pm; closed Sat L & Sun; set always available £33 (FP).

Fulham Wine Rooms SW6 **£55** 3 3 4

871-873 Fulham Rd 7042 9440 10–1B

Bustling Fulham wine bar, where the food offers few pyrotechnics, but is still "a good standard and price in this location" – quality plonk is of course its prime raison d'être, and there's a "great selection by the glass". / SW6 5HP; www.greatwinesbytheglass.com; @winerooms; midnight; closed weekday L.

Gaby's WC2 **£29** 3 3 3

30 Charing Cross Rd 7836 4233 4–3B

"Viva Gaby!"; this small '60s caff by Leicester Square tube (Jeremy Corbyn's favourite!) continues to see off the developers "despite the fact that everything around it is being replaced by faceless chains"; true, service is "perfunctory" and the interior "scruffy", but everyone cherishes its "genuine" style, not to mention "the best falafel" and salt beef. / WC2H 0DE; midnight, Sun 10 pm; no Amex.

Gail's Bread **£27** 3 2 2

Branches throughout London

"Even though it's a chain", these "favourite" bakeries score well for their "amazing cakes", "interesting sarnies", "great coffee" and "excellent bread"; "unless you like being surrounded by yummy mummies and their offspring however, you might want to take-out". / www.gailsbread.co.uk; W11 & WC1 7 pm; NW3 & NW6 8 pm, W1 10 pm, SW7 9 pm, Sun 8 pm; no booking.

Gallery Mess
Saatchi Gallery SW3 **£52** 2 2 3
Duke of Yorks HQ, Kings Rd 7730 8135 5–2D
As "a haunt for ladies-who-lunch" or "a lovely place to meet on business", this "attractive" annex to the galleries housing Charles Saatchi's art collection has its fans, but the "unexciting" cooking is often "underwhelming". / SW3 4RY; www.saatchigallery.com/gallerymess; @gallerymess; 9.30 pm, Sun 6 pm; closed Sun D; set always available £32 (FP).

Gallipoli **£35** 3 4 3
102 Upper St, N1 7359 0630 8–3D
107 Upper St, N1 7226 5333 8–3D
120 Upper St, N1 7226 8099 8–3D
"Buzzy and friendly" (if "cramped and noisy") Turkish bistros – a micro empire with three nearby sites in Islington; their mezze-biased menu includes "all the favourites" at easygoing prices. / www.cafegallipoli.com; 11 pm, Fri & Sat midnight.

Galvin at Windows
Park Lane London Hilton Hotel W1 **£100** 2 2 4
22 Park Ln 7208 4021 3–4A
"For a spectacular business lunch" (or date), this 28th-floor perch – with a "perfect vista" over Buck House and Hyde Park – still has many fans. It has seemed more "machine-like and touristy" of late however, and – at the sky-high prices – can too often seem "decidedly average" nowadays. (Top Tip – skip your meal: head over the hall to the bar, where the view is actually better!) / W1K 1BE; www.galvinatwindows.com; @Galvin_Brothers; 10 pm, Sat & Sun 10.30 pm; closed Sat L & Sun D; no shorts; set weekday L £55 (FP), set Sun L £72 (FP).

Galvin Bistrot de Luxe W1 **£67** 4 4 4
66 Baker St 7935 4007 2–1A
The "bustling" cradle of the Galvin brothers' empire – this "very grown up", slightly "formal" Marylebone bistro is celebrating its tenth birthday, and remains one of the best-liked all-rounders in town, serving a "staunchly Gallic" menu which provides "no pyrotechnics – just solid excellent cooking". / W1U 7DJ; www.galvinrestaurants.com; @galvin_brothers; Mon-Wed 10.30 pm, Thu-Sat 10.45 pm, Sun 9.30 pm; set weekday L £40 (FP), set dinner £42 (FP).

GALVIN LA CHAPELLE E1 **£80** 4 4 5
35 Spital Sq 7299 0400 12–2B
"To impress a client or date", you can't beat the "gorgeous" and "dramatic" setting of the Galvin brothers Spitalfields venture ("like eating in a minor cathedral"); it's a "very slick operation" all round, with "classic, not overly fussy" Gallic cuisine and "top notch" service. / E1 6DY; www.galvinrestaurants.com; @Galvin_Brothers; 10.30 pm, Sun 9.30 pm; set Sun L £53 (FP).

Ganapati SE15 **£43** 5 4 4
38 Holly Grove 7277 2928 1–4C
"The most authentic South Indian outside of Kerala" (well nearly) – this "crowded" but "lovely", tiny "breath-of-fresh-air" makes a "marvellous find" in deepest Peckham; "genial" staff provide "a limited menu" of "crisp dosas" and other "herb-filled, fresh-tasting" fare. / SE15 5DF; www.ganapatirestaurant.com; 10.30 pm, Sun 10 pm; closed Mon; no Amex.

Garnier SW5 £54 4 4 1
314 Earl's Court Rd 7370 4536 5–2A
"Really like the good honest French cooking that goes on here… I just wish they could inject something to make it look less, well, dull"; that's the dilemma at Eric & Didier Garnier's calm "slice of Paris", which makes a surprise find in an "unprepossessing" corner of Earl's Court, with "very sound" traditional cuisine, "keenly priced" wine and notably "excellent and charming" service. / SW5 9BQ; www.garnierestaurant.com; Mon-Sat 10.30 pm, Sun 10 pm; set weekday L £40 (FP).

Le Garrick WC2 £49 2 3 3
10-12 Garrick St 7240 7649 4–3C
This Covent Garden "bolt hole" is a good "safe bet" in this touristy locale; "it's a standard, very French bistro, with no wow factor, but you'll probably go again". / WC2E 9BH; www.frenchrestaurantlondon.co.uk; @le_garrick; 10.30 pm; closed Sun.

The Garrison SE1 £51 3 3 3
99-101 Bermondsey St 7089 9355 9–4D
"The yuppification of Bermondsey" can be partially blamed on this "boisterous" and "cramped", but "very enjoyable, buzzy and busy ex-pub", near the antiques market; all reports found it "worth the trek" this year – hopefully that sentiment will survive its sale in June 2015. / SE1 3XB; www.thegarrison.co.uk; @TheGarrisonSE1; 10 pm, Fri & Sat 10.30 pm, Sun 9.30 pm.

The Gate £43 4 2 3
51 Queen Caroline St, W6 8748 6932 7–2C
370 St John St, EC1 7278 5483 8–3D
"Who needs meat?" – some of London's best vegetarian cooking is to be found at this quite "stylish" duo; the Hammersmith original occupies a "bright" and "airy" hall near the Broadway (recently refurbished), while its "noisy" newer EC1 sibling is "handy for Sadler's Wells". / www.thegaterestaurants.com; @gaterestaurant; EC1 10.30 pm, W6 10.30, Sat 11 pm.

Gatti's £62 3 4 3
1 Finsbury Ave, EC2 7247 1051 12–2B
1 Ropemaker St, EC2 7247 1051 12–2A NEW
A duo of "discreet and efficient" Italianos recommended – especially for business – by all who comment on them; the 20-year-old original is one of Broadgate's oldest denizens, and there's also a larger spin-off near Moorgate. / www.gattisrestaurant.co.uk; closed Sat & Sun.

Gaucho £70 2 2 2
Branches throughout London
"The steaks are great… but value for money it ain't!"; this "plush and glitzy" chain does still win fans for its "succulent" imported Argentinian meat, "excellent" South American wines, and "dramatic" decor, but it has many critics nowadays too, particularly regarding its "ludicrous" prices. / www.gauchorestaurants.co.uk; 11 pm; EC3 & EC1 closed Sat & Sun, WC2 & EC2 closed Sat L & Sun.

GAUTHIER SOHO W1 £65 554

21 Romilly St 7494 3111 4–3A

"Ringing the doorbell adds to the special feel" of a trip to Alexis Gauthier's "beautiful, plush and quiet" Georgian townhouse, in the heart of Soho. But while it "oozes romance and decadence", it's first-and-foremost a gastronomic experience, with "unbelievably slick" service and some of London's best French cooking – "seasonal, classically based, and superb in taste and presentation". Top Menu Tip – leave space for the "always wonderful" signature Louis IV chocolate praline dessert. / W1D 5AF; www.gauthiersoho.co.uk; @GauthierSoho; 10.30 pm; closed Mon L & Sun.

LE GAVROCHE W1 £132 554

43 Upper Brook St 7408 0881 3–2A

Michel Roux's "iconic" Mayfair bastion (est 1967, by his father Albert) provides a "flawless and indulgent" treat, wherein "psychic" staff deliver "elegant" French cuisine and a "wine-lover's" list "full of gems". That the basement setting looks "a little dated" is all part of the traditional charm, and the main man's regular presence helps underpin "a truly magnificent experience". Top Tip – "the best value set lunch ever". / W1K 7QR; www.le-gavroche.co.uk; @legavroche_; 10 pm; closed Sat L & Sun; jacket required; set weekday L £87 (FP).

Gay Hussar W1 £50 225

2 Greek St 7437 0973 4–2A

"Go for the history, not the food", and you'll have a good time at this ancient Soho "institution" (famously "a venue for Socialist political intrigue"); the Hungarian scoff (goulash and so on) "ain't exactly fine dining", but the ambience is "terrific". / W1D 4NB; www.gayhussar.co.uk; @GayhussarsSoho; 10.45 pm; closed Sun; set pre theatre £37 (FP).

Gaylord W1 £58 333

79-81 Mortimer St 7580 3615 2–1B

"Approaching its 50th anniversary", this "'60s throwback" is a "civilised", "old-fashioned" venue, with "quality", "traditional" cuisine (recently jazzed up with a new menu) that fans find "a cut above"; it's "expensive" though, and sceptics feel it's still "in the Dark Ages". / W1W 7SJ; www.gaylordlondon.com; 10.45 pm, Sun 10.30 pm.

Gazette £39 244

79 Sherwood Ct, Chatfield Rd, SW11 7223 0999 10–1C
100 Balham High St, SW12 8772 1232 10–2C
147 Upper Richmond Rd, SW15 8789 6996 10–2B

These "little bits of La Belle France" in Balham, Clapham and Putney win praise for their "chilled" style, "heavily accented" but "friendly" Gallic staff, and "very French" cuisine; the food rating was hit though by one or two "disappointing" reports. / www.gazettebrasserie.co.uk; 11 pm.

Geales £50 233

1 Cale St, SW3 7965 0555 5–2C
2 Farmer St, W8 7727 7528 6–2B

"Delicious" fish 'n' chips wins consistent praise for these posh chippies in Notting Hill and Chelsea, but they come "at a price". / www.geales.com; @geales1; 10.30 pm, Sun 9.30 pm; closed Mon L.

Gelupo W1 £9 433

7 Archer St 7287 5555 3–2D

"Blood orange sorbet… be still my beating heart!" – opposite Bocca di Lupo (same owners) this tiny café has become a key West End pit stop, due to its "fabulous" and "so unusual" ices and granitas ("as good as in Rome!"); now also at Cambridge Circus, within the newly opened Vico. / W1D 7AU; www.gelupo.com; 11 pm, Fri & Sat midnight; no Amex; no booking.

Gem N1 £30 444

265 Upper St 7359 0405 8–2D

"Nothing flashy, but always reliable" – that's the approach at this "satisfying" Turkish/Kurdish spot near Angel, serving "very good mezze and kebabs"; "though it can be hard to hold an audible conversation, it's terrific value". / N1 2UQ; www.gemrestaurant.org.uk; @Gem_restaurant; 11 pm, Fri & Sat midnight, Sun 10.30 pm; no Amex; set weekday L £21 (FP).

La Genova W1 £60 333

32 North Audley St 7629 5916 3–2A

A "lovely old-fashioned" Italian, beloved of an older fan club, whose quiet, central location makes it "a perfect retreat after shopping in the West End"; "the food varies from good to very good". / W1K 6ZG; www.lagenovarestaurant.com; 11 pm; closed Sun.

George & Vulture EC3 £44 225

3 Castle Ct 7626 9710 9–3C

This truly "Dickensian" chop house (Charles was a regular) is a treasured "timeless" period piece, serving "traditional City fare"; lad's business lunches aside though, "it's a disgrace that this wonderful venue has such poor food", and the wine choice isn't so hot either – "'Would you like red or white?' just doesn't cut it anymore!" / EC3V 9DL; 2.15 pm; L only, closed Sat & Sun.

German Gymnasium N1 NEW

26 Pancras Rd 7287 8000 8–3C

In November 2015, D&D London have promised to open the doors to this long-anticipated renovation of a Grade II Victorian landmark by King's Cross, incorporating restaurant, grand café, bars and terrace, with cooking of the Mittel-European school – all sounds a bit Corbin & King? / N1C 4TB; www.germangymnasium.com.

Giacomo's NW2 £37 453

428 Finchley Rd 7794 3603 1–1B

"Everyone is greeted like family" at this "small", "noisy" and "kid-friendly" Child's Hill Italian – a "cosy local" with "fresh, if unsophisticated" cooking. / NW2 2HY; www.giacomos.co.uk; 11 pm.

Gifto's Lahore Karahi UB1 £22 432

162-164 The Broadway 8813 8669 1–3A

"Still buzzy and still producing delicious food!" – a large, Pakistani, Formica-topped canteen that's something of a Southall landmark. / UB1 1NN; www.gifto.com; 11.30 pm, Sat & Sun midnight.

Gilbert Scott
St Pancras Renaissance NW1 **£68** 2 2 3
Euston Rd 7278 3888 8–3C
Undeniably handy for the Eurostar, with a "gorgeous" historic interior, but otherwise Marcus Wareing's St Pancras dining room receives a mixed rep – what, to fans, is "classic British cooking" can also seem "very average for its elevated price", and service often "leaves a lot to be desired". / NW1 2AR; www.thegilbertscott.co.uk; @Thegilbertscott; 10.45 pm; set weekday L & pre-theatre £50 (FP).

Gilgamesh NW1 **£69** 2 2 3
The Stables, Camden Mkt, Chalk Farm Rd 7428 4922 8–3B
"Dauntingly large" Camden Lock venue, with crazy-lavish wood-carved decor; its "pricey", surprisingly ambitious Pan-Asian cuisine has never really lived up, but it's not terrible, and fans say the overall experience is "good fun!!" / NW1 8AH; www.gilgameshbar.com; Sun-Thu 10 pm, Fri & Sat 11 pm.

Gin Joint EC2 **£52** 2 3 3
Barbican Centre, Silk St 7588 3008 12–2A
"Lovely views over the lake" are a highlight at Searcy's "spacious" Barbican Centre brasserie, which despite its trendy name (and gin-based cocktails) is like most of its forebears on this site – the food's "pedestrian", but it's a "top bet if you're going to an event", and "always quiet enough for conversation". / EC2Y 8DS; www.searcys.co.uk/venues/gin-joint; @ginjoint_london; 10 pm.

Ginger & White **£17** 3 3 3
2 England's Ln, NW3 7722 9944 8–2A
4a-5a, Perrins Ct, NW3 7431 9098 8–2A
"Hang out all day" if you're part of the "NW3 in-crowd", at these stylish cafés in Belsize Park and Hampstead – 'go-to' locals for coffee or brunch. / www.gingerandwhite.com; 5.30 pm, W1 6 pm; W1 closed Sun.

Giraffe **£40** 1 1 1
Branches throughout London
"Average in all respects save for the fact that they are great with kids" – these World Food diners (nowadays owned by Tesco!) are "crowded", with "stodgy" fare, but are second only in the survey to PizzaExpress for being impeccably "tolerant of exuberant little ones". / www.giraffe.net; 10.45 pm, Sun 10.30 pm; no booking, Sat & Sun 9 am-5 pm.

The Glasshouse TW9 **£71** 4 4 3
14 Station Pde 8940 6777 1–3A
"From the Chez Bruce stable", this "consistently excellent" neighbourhood spot by Kew Gardens tube continues to win acclaim for its "subtle" and "beautifully judged" cuisine; the interior doesn't suit everyone however, and "though it shares the ambition of CB, it doesn't achieve quite the same level". / TW9 3PZ; www.glasshouserestaurant.co.uk; @The_Glasshouse; 10.15 pm, Sun 9.45 pm; set weekday L £50 (FP), set Sun L £53 (FP).

Gökyüzü N4 **£33** 4 3 3
26-27 Grand Pde, Green Lanes 8211 8406 1–1C
"Deservedly the most popular of all the Turks on Harringay's Grand Parade" – "you cram in" but it's worth it for the "meat feasts" and "exceptionally fresh and zingy salads", all at cheapo prices. / N4 1LG; www.gokyuzurestaurant.co.uk; @Gokyuzulondon; midnight, Fri & Sat 1 am.

Gold Mine W2 £34 521

102 Queensway 7792 8331 6–2C

"I'd travel from Sheffield to London, just for its succulence!" – this Bayswater Chinese competes with its better known local rival, The Four Seasons, as the home of "the Capital's best crispy duck"; likewise it too is "noisy and cramped". / W2 3RR; 11 pm.

Golden Dragon W1 £34 322

28-29 Gerrard St 7734 1073 4–3A

"A better-than-average dim sum option in the heart of Chinatown"; "arrive early to avoid the queue!" / W1 6JW; goldendragonlondon.com; Mon-Thu 11.15 pm, Fri & Sat 11.30 pm, Sun 11 pm.

Golden Hind W1 £26 443

73 Marylebone Ln 7486 3644 2–1A

"A joy for lovers of fish 'n' chips" – this "very basic" Marylebone institution's "unbeatable" scoff and "welcoming" style have only improved since its renovation after a fire in June; "it's also great value as you can BYO". / W1U 2PN; 10 pm; closed Sat L & Sun.

Good Earth £56 332

233 Brompton Rd, SW3 7584 3658 5–2C

143-145 The Broadway, NW7 8959 7011 1–1B

11 Bellevue Rd, SW17 8682 9230 10–2C

"A cut above the usual Chinese" – this quality chain is "always reliable" and its two-year-old Balham branch is proving "a marvellous addition to the area"; never a cheap option, some fans now fear they are "in danger of pricing themselves out of the market". / www.goodearthgroup.co.uk; Mon - Sat 10.30pm, Sun 10 pm.

Goodman £69 443

24-26 Maddox St, W1 7499 3776 3–2C

3 South Quay, E14 7531 0300 11–1C

11 Old Jewry, EC2 7600 8220 9–2C

"Carnivore heaven" – these "macho" haunts are "the best of the upmarket steak chains" (significantly out-gunning Hawksmoor this year), and "superb for old-school business lunches". The steaks of course are "not cheap", but "huge", "cooked to perfection", and served with "great truffle chips". Other attractions include the "interesting specials board with rare cuts", plus "excellent wines at fair mark-ups". / www.goodmanrestaurants.com; 10.30 pm; E14 & EC2 closed Sat & Sun.

GORDON RAMSAY SW3 £128 343

68-69 Royal Hospital Rd 7352 4441 5–3D

Slowly but surely, GR's Chelsea flagship is clawing its way back into London's very top tier. As yet, it still inspires too many gripes about a "boring" experience at "stratospheric" prices, but year-on-year the 'swingometer' is steadily heading in the direction of its admirers who – lauding Clare Smyth's "absolutely impeccable" cuisine – say "the bill is eye-watering, but after such a superb meal, you won't care!" Stop Press – in early October 2015, Clare Smyth announced that she was stepping back, to open her own place in autumn 2016. Her No 2. Matt Abe will succeed her here. / SW3 4HP; www.gordonramsay.com; @GordonRamsey; 10.15 pm; closed Sat & Sun; no jeans or trainers; booking: max 8; set weekday L £82 (FP).

Gordon's Wine Bar WC2 **£33** 2 3 5

47 Villiers St 7930 1408 4–4D

Just about everyone in London has supped a glass of vino at one time or another at this "one-of-a-kind" ancient wine bar, by Embankment tube; the food – cheese, cold cuts, hot dishes, salads – is "nothing special", but the cave-like interior is "amazing", and it has one of the West End's nicest (and biggest) outdoor terraces. / WC2N 6NE; www.gordonswinebar.com; @gordonswinebar; 11 pm; no booking.

The Goring Hotel SW1 **£80** 3 5 5

15 Beeston Pl 7396 9000 2–4B

"Marvellously discreet" bastion near Victoria (complete with royal warrant) – "a fine example of everything old-fashioned and English", not least its "magnificent" staff. "Superb" traditional fare is served in the "beautiful" and "civilised" dining room, with top billing going to the "breakfast fit for a queen" and "quintessential afternoon tea". / SW1W 0JW; www.thegoring.com; @thegoring; 10 pm; closed Sat L; no jeans or trainers; booking: max 8; set pre-theatre £55 (FP).

Gourmet Burger Kitchen **£30** 2 2 2

Branches throughout London

"GBK always delivers what it says on the tin!", say loyalists of this still-popular burger franchise; "it nowadays lags a market it once led" however, and even if it's still "always solid and enjoyable" it's also arguably "nothing to write home about". / www.gbkinfo.com; most branches close 10.30 pm; no booking.

Gourmet Pizza Company
Gabriels Wharf SE1 **£38** 3 3 3

56 Upper Ground 7928 3188 9–3A

"Superb views over the River Thames" and a lovely terrace add to the "fun" of this South Bank spot (run by PizzaExpress); "great toppings as well as the usual ones". / SE1 9PP; www.gourmetpizzacompany.co.uk; 11.30 pm.

Gourmet San E2 **£25** 4 2 1

261 Bethnal Green Rd 7729 8388 12–1D

"Horrible setting, but top notch food" – that's the deal at this well-priced Sichuanese, in Bethnal Green. / E2 6AH; www.oldplace.co.uk; 11 pm; D only.

Les Gourmets des Ternes **£60** 2 2 3

9 Knightsbridge Grn, SW1 3092 1493 5–1D NEW

18 Formosa St, W9 7286 3742 8–4A

This tiny, "very French" Maida Vale spin-off from a Parisan bistro of the same name (now also with a Knightsbridge sibling on the site that was Chabrot d'Amis, RIP) inspires middling feedback – the "standard, simple Gallic fare" can be "delicious", but can also seem "average". / SW1 closed Sun – W9 closed Sun & Mon.

The Gowlett SE15 **£32** 4 3 4

62 Gowlett Rd 7635 7048 1–4D

"Super-thin crust pizzas with delicious toppings" and "the occasional beer festival" help win a thumbs-up for this Peckham pub, now with a trendy small curing and smoke house in the cellar. / SE15 4HY; www.thegowlett.com; @theGowlettArms; 10.30 pm, Sun 9 pm; no credit cards.

Goya SW1 £45 333

34 Lupus St 7976 5309 2–4C

For "easygoing tapas on a sunny corner in Pimlico" this is a useful neighbourhood "staple" – there's a popular bar on the ground floor, so for a quiet dinner "seek a table upstairs". / SW1V 3EB; www.goyarestaurant.co.uk; 11.30 pm, Sun 11 pm.

Grain Store N1 £55 223

1-3 Stable St, Granary Sq 7324 4466 8–3C

Bruno Loubet's "NYC warehouse-y" King's Cross two-year-old divided opinions this year; to its fans this "wonderfully bustling space" remains "an absolute revelation" thanks to "endlessly inventive", "veg-a-centric" cooking, but a few doubters had meals that were "absolutely awful". (Flying from Gatwick? – there's now a branch there too.) / N1C 4AB; www.grainstore.com; @GrainStoreKX; Mon-Wed 11.30 pm, Thu-Sat midnight; closed Sun D; booking: max 14.

The Grand Imperial
Guoman Grosvenor Hotel SW1 £65 332

101 Buckingham Palace Rd 7821 8898 2–4B

"Surprisingly good for this location!"; a "strangely grand, station-hotel dining room" adjacent to Victoria, where – despite "steep" prices – "delicious dim sum" and other "tasty" Cantonese fare make it "worth a visit". / SW1W 0SJ; www.grandimperiallondon.com; @grand_imperial; Thu-Sat 11, Sun-Wed 10.30 pm.

Granger & Co £49 324

175 Westbourne Grove, W11 7229 9111 6–1B

Stanley Building, St Pancras Sq, N1 3058 2567 8–3C NEW

The Buckley Building, 50 Sekforde St, EC1 7251 9032 9–1A

"There's a permanent queue around the corner", at these "laid-back" Antipodean haunts, rammed with "yummy mummies" and "ladies who lunch"; brunch is the massive deal here – "Lo-Cal tasty combos" that "draw inspiration from all over the world". / Mon - Sat 10pm, Sun 5pm.

The Grapes E14 £47 235

76 Narrow St 7987 4396 11–1B

One of the oldest pubs in East London, this "tiny" Thames-side treasure in Limehouse offers a limited menu in the bar (a full roast on Sundays), and "great fish 'n' chips" in the upstairs dining room. Its interesting associations are many – not least that it's currently owned by Gandalf himself (Sir Ian McKellen)! / E14 8BP; www.thegrapes.co.uk; @TheGrapesLondon; 11 pm, Sun 10.30 pm; no Amex.

The Grazing Goat W1 £56 333

6 New Quebec St 7724 7243 2–2A

This "posh pub", quietly located near Marble Arch, is proving "a great addition to Marylebone" with "hearty, satisfying fare" and "a nice if noisy vibe". / W1H 7RQ; www.thegrazinggoat.co.uk; @TheGrazingGoat; 10 pm, Sun 9.30 pm.

Great Nepalese NW1 £36 332

48 Eversholt St 7388 6737 8–3C

"They're such lovely people" at this ancient stalwart, in a grungy Euston side street, where a dedicated fan club hail its "top curries" (incorporating some not-particularly-spicy Nepalese specials). / NW1 1DA; www.great-nepalese.co.uk; 11.30 pm, Sun 10 pm.

Great Queen Street WC2 £49 223
32 Great Queen St 7242 0622 4–1D
Fans still laud it for its "rare assurance" and its "hearty and bold" British fare, but this "buzzy" and "un-flashy" ("cramped and noisy") Covent Garden dining room is increasingly "resting on its laurels" nowadays, producing some meals that are "surprisingly average". / WC2B 5AA; www.greatqueenstreetrestaurant.co.uk; @greatqueenstreet; 10.30 pm; closed Sun D; no Amex.

The Greedy Buddha SW6 £32 322
144 Wandsworth Bridge Rd 7751 3311 10–1B
"Nothing too glamorous, but it does the job!" – a "cramped" curry house, near Parsons Green, where "very good food at low prices" makes it worth enduring service that's "erratic". / SW6 2UH; www.thegreedybuddha.com; @thegreedybudha; 10.30 pm, Fri & Sat 11.30 pm; no Amex.

The Greek Larder Arthouse N1 NEW £50 332
1 York Way 3780 2999 8–3C
A "welcome addition" to King's Cross – this modern Greek newcomer (from the original founder of The Real Greek) is "authentically chaotic", serving "strongly flavoured" small plates at "good prices". / N1C 4AS; www.thegreeklarder.co.uk; @thegreeklarder; 10.30 pm, Sun 5 pm.

Green Cottage NW3 £38 322
9 New College Pde 7722 5305 8–2A
"Long established, popular Chinese" in Swiss Cottage, where "tasty food" comes in "large portions"; ignore the ambience ("not great") and service ("can be abrupt"). / NW3 5EP; 10.30 pm; no Amex.

The Green Room The National Theatre SE1 NEW £42 222
South Bank 7452 3630 2–3D
The NT's new 'neighbourhood diner' and "beautiful" garden is "a very nice addition to the South Bank"; the food is "not particularly inspiring", but it's "good value" and "you can forgive the slightly pretentious presentation, given its emphasis on sustainability and quality". / SE1 9PX; www.nationaltheatre.org.uk; @greenroomSE1; 11 pm, Sun 10.30 pm.

Green's SW1 £75 333
36 Duke St 7930 4566 3–3D
"A choice of booths or tables" adds to the "discreet", "quiet" and business-friendly, clubland-appeal of the Parker Bowles family's St James's "stalwart"; "very classic British food" (majoring in fish) is well-served – "the quality is the highest… and so are the prices". / SW1Y 6DF; www.greens.org.uk; 10.30 pm; closed Sun; no jeans or trainers; set pre theatre £49 (FP).

Greenberry Café NW1 £50 223
101 Regent's Park Rd 7483 3765 8–2B
"Much favoured by locals with laptops and buggies" – this "eating and meeting spot" in Primrose Hill is tipped as a particularly handy option for breakfast, but serves coffee, cakes and light meals throughout the day. / NW1 8UR; greenberrycafe.co.uk; @Greenberry_Cafe; 10 pm, Mon & Sun 4 pm; closed Sun D; no Amex; set always available £29 (FP).

The Greenhouse W1 **£130** 3 4 4

27a Hays Mews 7499 3331 3–3B

Arnaud Bignon's cuisine is "top notch", but it's the "hugely impressive wine list" ("What breadth! What depth!") that draws connoisseurs to Marlon Abela's "spacious", "lovely" and luxurious haunt, "tucked away" in a Mayfair mews; the food can seem "a bit frothy and fancy" though... and "fiendishly expensive". / W1J 5NY; www.greenhouserestaurant.co.uk; 10.15 pm; closed Sat L & Sun; booking: max 8.

Gremio de Brixton St Matthew's Church SW2 NEW **£42** 3 2 4

Effra Rd 7924 0660 10–2D

The "very snug and atmospheric" crypt of St Matthew's Church in Brixton, hosts this new tapas joint, which is consistently well-rated. / SW2 1JF; www.gremiodebrixton.com; 11 pm, Sat 11.30 pm, Sun 9 pm.

Grind Coffee Bar SW15 **£15** 4 2 4

79 Lower Richmond Rd 8789 9073 10–2A

"Better than many of the more central indie coffee houses" – a Putney outfit that does very "tasty" breakfasts in particular; but waiting for the brews themselves can be "painstakingly slow" – "the price of true craftsmanship?" / SW15 1ET; grindcoffeebar.co.uk; 6 pm.

Grumbles SW1 **£43** 2 3 3

35 Churton St 7834 0149 2–4B

"Wonderfully, reassuringly old-fashioned" local bistro in Pimlico, complete with "rustic" interior; expect no fireworks, but "ever-dependable" scran at a "cheap" price. / SW1V 2LT; www.grumblesrestaurant.co.uk; 10.45 pm; set Sun L £32 (FP).

Guglee **£33** 3 3 3

7 New College Pde, NW3 7722 8478 8–2A
279 West End Ln, NW6 7317 8555 1–1B

"Not your average local cuzza" – a duo of "welcoming" West Hampstead and Swiss Cottage Indians serving "light and tasty" street food. / www.guglee.co.uk; 11 pm.

The Guinea Grill W1 **£75** 2 3 3

30 Bruton Pl 7499 1210 3–3B

"In a back mews in the heart of posh London" – an old-fashioned ("cramped") Mayfair stalwart attached to a cute pub, acclaimed for its pies; it's "not so cheap" and sceptics fear "well past its prime" nowadays, but fans still approve its quaint style and "great steaks". / W1J 6NL; www.theguinea.co.uk; @guineagrill; 10.30 pm; closed Sat L & Sun; booking: max 8.

The Gun E14 **£58** 3 2 4

27 Coldharbour 7515 5222 11–1C

This "quaint riverside tavern has so much charm and history" – not to mention a big terrace, and fab river views over to the O2 – and makes "a refreshing escape from Canary Wharf" (a short walk away); "the food's fancy for a pub, if not quite in the upper echelons for a gastropub". / E14 9NS; www.thegundocklands.com; @thegundocklands; 10.30 pm, Sun 9.30 pm.

Gung-Ho NW6 £40 2 3 2
328-332 West End Ln 7794 1444 1–1B
For supporters this West Hampstead stalwart is "still going strong" – "a consistently good and delightful neighbourhood Chinese"; the ambience is more "flat" than once it was however, and quite a few sceptical former fans feel it's "lost its former star quality".
/ NW6 1LN; www.stir-fry.co.uk; 11.30 pm; no Amex.

Gustoso Ristorante & Enoteca SW1 £43 3 5 3
33 Willow Pl 7834 5778 2–4B
"As the word spreads, it's getting harder to get into this super local" in the backstreets of Westminster – "a welcome addition to an area lacking decent places"; service is very "warm", and "there's no need to rely on expenses" to enjoy the "simple and authentic" cooking.
/ SW1P 1JH; ristorantegustoso.co.uk; @GustosoRist; 10.30 pm, Fri & Sat 11 pm, Sun 9.30 pm; set always available £32 (FP).

GYMKHANA W1 £63 5 4 4
42 Albemarle St 3011 5900 3–3C
"Exceeding all my high expectations!" – this "delightfully cosseting" nouvelle Indian, near The Ritz, has quickly become one of London's top destinations; "immensely flavourful", "properly exquisite" dishes (plus "top quality cocktails" and "heroic wine matches") are served, in a "quaint and exotic", "faux-colonial" setting. / W1S 4JH; www.gymkhanalondon.com; @GymkhanaLondon; 10.30 pm; closed Sun.

Habanera W12 NEW £38 3 2 3
280 Uxbridge Rd 8001 4887 7–1C
With its yummy cocktails, "interesting Mexi-vibe" and "decent (if pricey)" tacos and burritos, this new Latino has broken the local W12 ordinance that forbids the opening of half-decent restaurants on the tacky strip running north of Shepherd's Bush Green. / W12 7JA; www.habanera.co.uk; 11 pm, Fri & Sat midnight, Sun 10.30 pm.

Haché £35 3 3 4
329-331 Fulham Rd, SW10 7823 3515 5–3B
24 Inverness St, NW1 7485 9100 8–3B
37 Bedford Hill, SW12 8772 9772 10–2C
153 Clapham High St, SW4 7738 8760 10–2D
147-149 Curtain Rd, EC2 7739 8396 12–1B
"Of the chain burger choices, this is consistently good" – this small group provides excellent "gourmet" options "with some unexpected combinations", and its SW10 branch in particular has an enjoyably "buzzy" atmosphere. / www.hacheburgers.com; 10.30 pm, Fri-Sat 11 pm, Sun 10 pm.

Hakkasan £89 4 3 4
17 Bruton St, W1 7907 1888 3–2C
8 Hanway Pl, W1 7927 7000 4–1A
"Dark", "seductive" and "very sexy" styling – "like a nightclub" (and with "loud" noise levels to match) – provide a "funky" backdrop to a meal at these "dramatic" venues (the cradles of what's a growing global franchise). Though "not cheap", the Chinese cuisine's "top notch" too, especially the "superbly original" dim sum.
/ www.hakkasan.com; midnight, Sun 11 pm.

Ham Yard Restaurant
Ham Yard Hotel W1 £50 1 1 4
1 Ham Yd 3642 2000 3–2D
"The design is super… the courtyard a wonderful addition to Soho", but in other respects the restaurant at this Firmdale hotel is "a shame" – the service can be "dire", and the food is a total "sideshow". / W1D 7DT; www.hamyardhotel.com; @ham_yard; 11.30 pm, Sun 10.30 pm.

The Hampshire Hog W6 £52 2 2 3
227 King St 8748 3391 7–2B
With its "fashionable looks", "eclectic mix of seating" and "delightful garden", this "friendly" large pub has brightened up the grungy environs of Hammersmith Town Hall; quibbles? – service is "charming but can be wayward". / W6 9JT; www.thehampshirehog.com; @TheHampshireHog; 11 pm, Sun 10 pm; closed Sun D.

Harbour City W1 £38 2 1 1
46 Gerrard St 7439 7859 4–3B
"Tasty, fresh, quick, filling" – the wide range of "amazingly cheap" lunchtime dim sum at this "Chinatown stalwart"; otherwise, don't bother. / W1D 5QH; www.harbourcity.com.hk; 11.30 pm, Fri & Sat midnight, Sun 10.30 pm.

Hard Rock Café W1 £59 2 2 4
150 Old Park Ln 7629 0382 3–4B
"You wouldn't go for a quiet or romantic meal", but "if you can bear the volume", the 40-year-old cradle of the Hard Rock brand works "for a noisy, fun, burger with teens". / W1K 1QZ; www.hardrock.com/london; @HardRock; midnight; need 20+ to book.

Hardy's Brasserie W1 £49 2 3 3
53 Dorset St 7935 5929 2–1A
"Largely unchanged since the '80s" – a Marylebone bistro "stalwart" liked for its "welcoming and comforting" style; the food's fairly "reliable" – "excellent weekend brunch" is a relatively recent innovation. / W1U 7NH; www.hardysbrasserie.com; @hardys_W1; 10 pm; closed Sun D.

Hare & Tortoise £32 3 2 3
11-13 The Brunswick, WC1 7278 9799 2–1D
373 Kensington High St, W14 7603 8887 7–1D
156 Chiswick High Rd, W4 8747 5966 7–2A NEW
38 Haven Grn, W5 8810 7066 1–2A
296-298 Upper Richmond Rd, SW15 8394 7666 10–2B
90 New Bridge St, EC4 7651 0266 9–2A
"A definite step-up from Wagamama" – these "always packed" Pan-Asian diners offer "fresh and tasty" snacks (notably "great-value noodles and sushi"), all "at decent prices" and served "hot and quickly". / www.hareandtortoise-restaurants.co.uk; 10.45 pm, Fri & Sat 11.15 pm, EC4 10 pm; W14 no bookings.

Harry Morgan's NW8 £42 2 2 1
31 St John's Wood High St 7722 1869 8–3A
Classic Jewish deli that's long been a feature of St John's Wood's main drag; it's still regularly acclaimed by its devotees for kosher treats "like mum used to make" and "the best salt beef sarnies", but dissenters feel it's "gone way downhill" and is "really awful" nowadays. / NW8 7NH; www.harryms.co.uk; 10.30 pm.

Harwood Arms SW6 £62 5 3 3

Walham Grove 7386 1847 5–3A

The "unassuming frontage" gives no hint of the "gorgeous" British cooking – some of London's best in either a pub or restaurant – at this "marvellous" gastropub "par excellence" in an obscure Fulham backstreet; and at the bar, "you wont find a better Scotch Egg anywhere". / SW6 1QP; www.harwoodarms.com; 9.15 pm, Sun 9 pm; closed Mon L; set weekday L £45 (FP).

Hashi SW20 £36 4 4 3

54 Durham Rd 8944 1888 10–2A

"Already popular with the locals, but should be better-known" – a "cosy little Raynes Park Japanese in an otherwise ordinary suburban road", with "delightful" staff, that's "as good as any West End Japanese". / SW20 0TW; www.hashicooking.co.uk; 10.30 pm; closed Mon; no Amex.

The Havelock Tavern W14 £45 3 2 4

57 Masbro Rd 7603 5374 7–1C

"Classic, always buzzing gastropub" in the backstreets of Olypmia; its culinary ratings don't scale the heights they once did, but it still has a large fan club drawn by its "delicious cooking, from outstanding Sunday roast beef to inventive and daily changing mains". / W14 0LS; www.havelocktavern.com; @HavelockTavern; 10 pm, Sun 9.30 pm; no booking.

The Haven N20 £50 2 2 2

1363 High Rd 8445 7419 1–1B

"A good local choice" in Whetstone, if a "rather noisy" one; "the food is never bad or great", but "reliable". / N20 9LN; www.haven-bistro.co.uk; 11 pm; set always available £31 (FP).

Hawksmoor £64 3 3 3

5a, Air St, W1 7406 3980 3–3D
11 Langley St, WC2 7420 9390 4–2C
3 Yeoman's Row, SW3 7590 9290 5–2C
157 Commercial St, E1 7426 4850 12–2B
10-12 Basinghall St, EC2 7397 8120 9–2C

"Utterly brilliant steaks" and "professional" cocktails have won cult status for Huw Gott and Will Beckett's "lively and clubby" steak houses (a fave rave for "boozy business lunches"); they risk starting to seem "up themselves", however, not helped by increasingly "stupid prices". / www.thehawksmoor.com; all branches between 10 pm & 11 pm; EC2 closed Sat & Sun; SRA-3.*

Haz £37 2 3 2

9 Cutler St, E1 7929 7923 9–2D
34 Foster Ln, EC2 7600 4172 9–2B
112 Houndsditch, EC3 7623 8180 9–2D
6 Mincing Ln, EC3 7929 3173 9–3D

"Always a safe bet" for "an informal business lunch" or "a dinner after work" – these large, "crowded" Turkish operations are "well-priced" and "efficient", and even if the "tasty" sustenance is arguably "without flair", it's also "without offence". / www.hazrestaurant.co.uk; 11.30 pm; EC3 closed Sun.

Heddon Street Kitchen W1 £59 2 3 3

3-9 Heddon St 7592 1212 3–2C

It's hard to get excited for or against Gordon Ramsay's "informal" bar and grill concept, just off Regent Street; its best point is its "fun, laid-back style", but the whole set-up is rather "mid-range", with food that's "OK" but "unmemorable", and service that's "fine but not stand-out". / W1B 4BW; www.gordonramsay.com/heddon-street; @heddonstkitchen; 11 pm, Sun 10 pm.

HEDONE W4 £104 4 3 3

301-303 Chiswick High Rd 8747 0377 7–2A

"The best ingredients in London" and "unique, technical mastery" underpin "staggering", "cutting-edge cuisine at its finest" for most who trek to Mikael Jonsson's open-kitchen HQ, in outer Chiswick. It's an "idiosyncratic" experience however, and sceptics feel there's just "too much fuss and self regard", especially given the "eye-watering expense". Stop Press – In October 2015 the restaurant will close and re-open with half the number of covers, more complicated cooking, and a focus on rare ingredients and wines. Pricing may change too. / W4 4HH; www.hedonerestaurant.com; @HedoneLondon; 9.30 pm; closed Mon, Tue L, Wed L & Sun; set weekday L £70 (FP).

Heirloom N8 £46 3 4 3

35 Park Rd 8348 3565 1–1C

"Field-to-table" is the concept at this Crouch End yearling, where "lots of the produce comes from a farm in rural Bucks"; its "regularly changing" menu and "attentive" service help make it "a good addition to the N8 restaurant-stable". / N8 8TE; heirloomn8.com; @HeirloomN8; 11.30 pm.

Hélène Darroze
The Connaught Hotel W1 £128 2 3 3

Carlos Pl 3147 7200 3–3B

This "elegant", panelled Mayfair dining room (where a "posh brunch" is a recent innovation) continues to inspire mixed feelings; even many hailing "outstanding" cuisine fret at the bills, while those who find the cooking "over-contrived" or "lacking wow" think prices are utterly "gob-smacking". / W1K 2AL; www.the-connaught.co.uk; @TheConnaught; 9.30 pm; closed Mon & Sun; jacket & tie required; SRA-2.*

Hereford Road W2 £49 4 2 3

3 Hereford Rd 7727 1144 6–1B

"Interesting, full-on flavours" from a "simple, high-quality British menu" inspire some foodies to suggest that Tom Pemberton's "stylish" Bayswater fixture is "under-rated". Top Tip – fans say the set lunch deal is "beyond incredible". / W2 4AB; www.herefordroad.org; @3HerefordRoad; 10.30 pm, Sun 10 pm; set weekday L £32 (FP).

The Heron W2 £32 5 2 1

1 Norfolk Cr 7706 9567 8–4A

"Like a trip to Bangkok without the airfare" – a "brilliant, authentic Thai" in a "tiny, no-frills" Bayswater basement, serving a "varied menu" ("heavy spice available for the brave") at "incredible, low prices". / W2 2DN; no website; 11 pm.

Hibiscus W1 £126 443
29 Maddox St 7629 2999 3–2C
Stronger showing this year for Claude Bosi's low-key foodie temple in Mayfair; a few critics still "expected more" at the "astronomical" prices, but overall there was much more consistent praise for his famously "adventurous" approach, "exciting" tastes, and "beautiful" presentation. Top Tip – "give the fantastic chef's table a try". / W1S 2PA; www.hibiscusrestaurant.co.uk; @HibiscusLondon; 11 pm; closed Mon & Sun; set weekday L £56 (FP).

High Road Brasserie W4 £50 113
162-166 Chiswick High Rd 8742 7474 7–2A
All the worst DNA of the Soho House group is expressed by its "pretentious" W4 offshoot; the Chiswick set still like posing on the terrace at brunch, but prices are "sky high", and even those who "love the genuine local buzz" say its standards are "very disappointing". / W4 1PR; www.brasserie.highroadhouse.co.uk; @sohohouse; 10.45 pm, Fri & Sat 11.45 pm, Sun 10 pm.

High Timber EC4 £62 223
8 High Timber 7248 1777 9–3B
"Excellent South African wines can be chosen after a wander through the wine cellars" at this Thames-side spot (owned by a Stellenbosch vineyard), near the Wobbly Bridge (fab views, but only from the outside tables); as for the "rustic" sustenance, it's pricey and "nothing exceptional". / EC4V 3PA; www.hightimber.com; @HTimber; 10 pm; closed Sat & Sun.

Hill & Szrok E8 £42 544
60 Broadway Mkt 7833 1933 1–2D
"Sitting around a big butcher's block doesn't sound very romantic, but it gives you lots to talk about!" – this "butcher-by-day, meat-feast-at-night" in Broadway Market provides "an unusual and well-lit setting" for "a fantastic meat experience". / E8 4QJ; www.hillandszrok.co.uk; @hillandszrok; 11 pm, Sun 9 pm.

Hilliard EC4 £28 443
26a Tudor St 7353 8150 9–3A
"Full of lawyers getting a health fix" – a "busy", all-day Temple haunt where "they care about the details, reflecting their demanding customers!"; "wonderful fresh ingredients" from a "menu that changes daily", plus superior coffee and "excellent cakes". / EC4Y 0AY; www.hilliardfood.co.uk; 6 pm; L only, closed Sat & Sun; no booking.

Hix W1 £65 222
66-70 Brewer St 7292 3518 3–2D
As the HQ of a 'name' chef, Mark Hix's potentially "stylish" and "buzzy" Soho venture (with basement bar) is a total yawn nowadays, and monumentally overpriced for what you get – i.e. so-so service, and food that's "nothing special". / W1F 9UP; www.hixsoho.co.uk; @HixRestaurants; 11.30 pm, Sun 10.30 pm.

Hix Oyster & Chop House EC1 £58 333
36-37 Greenhill Rents, Cowcross St 7017 1930 9–1A
"Great British dishes using the highest quality of raw materials" (eg "Barnsley chop to die for", and a wide selection of oysters) do win fans for Mark Hix's Smithfield operation; there are quibbles though – primarily that it's "not cheap". / EC1M 6BN; www.restaurantsetcltd.com; @HixRestaurants; 11 pm, Sun 10 pm; closed Sat L.

HKK EC2 £70 543

Broadgate Quarter, 88 Worship St 3535 1888 12–2B

"Challenging, interesting and fun" – the Chinese cuisine (much of it served from extensive multi-course tasting menus) at this Hakkasan-cousin, near Liverpool Street, is London's highest rated; the interior "looks lovely" but is "a little quiet". Top Menu Tip – "the best duck ever". / EC2A 2BE; www.hkklondon.com; @HKKlondon; 10 pm; closed Sun.

Hoi Polloi
Ace Hotel E1 £56 234

100 Shoreditch High St 8880 6100 12–1B

"Achingly trendy" Shoreditch hotel, where the grub's overseen by the team that created Bistrotheque; like its forebear, it's more the scene you go for – the "innovative" food's arguably too "expensive". / E1 6JQ; hoi-polloi.co.uk; @wearehoipolloi; Sun-Wed midnight, Thu-Sat 1 am; cancellation charge for larger bookings.

Holborn Dining Room
Rosewood London WC1 £62 234

252 High Holborn 3747 8633 2–1D

With its "old school glamour", this "impressive"-looking operation (on the site that was once Pearl, RIP) is quite "a wow", and its "spacious" and "buzzy" quarters are ideal for business; food-wise, however, it's "nothing out of this world". Top Tip – Check out the "wonderful" adjoining Scarfes Bar. / WC1V 7EN; www.holborndiningroom.com; @HolbornDining; 11.15 pm, Sun 10.30 pm.

Homeslice £24 544

52 Wells St, W1 3151 7488 2–1B NEW
13 Neal's Yd, WC2 7836 4604 4–2C

"Awesome pizza" – "huge", and with "obscure combinations that work" – are well "worth the wait" (you can't book) at these "fun", but "crammed" and "loud" pit stops, whose Fitzrovia outpost opened in August 2015.

Honest Burgers £28 443

Branches throughout London

"Not fancy, just bloody good!" – "of all the burger chains that have proliferated in recent years, this is the tops" (the original Brixton branch rating particular mention). Why? – they're "brilliantly sourced", "the specials are more special", and the "unique" rosemary flavoured fries are "seriously addictive". Queues, though, are "daunting". / www.honestburgers.co.uk; @honestburgers; 10 pm - 11 pm; SW9 closed Mon D.

Honey & Co W1 £48 542

25a, Warren St 7388 6175 2–1B

"Exhilarating" modern Middle Eastern dishes (not least the "extraordinary cakes") inspire adulatory reviews for this "Lilliputian-sized" café, near Warren Street tube; size constraints mean "it's hard to get a table" though, and once you have, conditions are "squashed". / W1T 5JZ; www.honeyandco.co.uk; @Honeyandco; Mon-Sat 10.30 pm; closed Sun.

Hood SW2 NEW £42 4 4 2

67 Streatham Hill 3601 3320 10–2D

"Already a regular haunt in Streatham Hill (book!)" – a welcoming "if slightly spartan" new, little neighbourhood café with a "small but well-cooked" menu, plus an "interesting" list of English wines and craft beers; brunch with kids "is a real winner" too. / SW2 4TX; www.hoodrestaurants.com; @hoodStreatham; 11 pm.

Hoppers W1 NEW

49 Frith St 3040 0887 4–2A

The sharp-eyed Sethi siblings – the team behind Gymkhana and Trishna (as well as backers of Bao, Lyle's and Bubbledogs) – aim to turn their Midas touch to street food, with this Soho café inspired by the road shacks of Tamil Nadu and Sri Lanka, due to open October 2015. / W1D 4SG; www.hopperslondon.com; 10.30 pm.

The Horseshoe NW3 £48 3 2 3

28 Heath St 7431 7206 8–2A

The "unbeatable combination" of Camden Brewery beers (which used to be brewed on this very site), and some of Hampstead's better pub grub win praise for this popular hostelry. / NW3 6TE; www.thehorseshoehampstead.com; @getluckyatthehorseshoe; 10 pm, Fri & Sat 11 pm.

Hot Stuff SW8 £22 4 4 2

23 Wilcox Rd 7720 1480 10–1D

"Top curries at super-cheap prices" continue to win enthusiastic recommendations for this BYO Indian, in deepest Vauxhall (on the stretch of road immortalised in 'My Beautiful Laundrette'). / SW8 2XA; www.eathotstuff.com; 9.30 pm; closed Mon; no Amex.

House of Ho £57 3 2 2

1 Percy St, W1 awaiting tel 2–1C NEW

57-59 Old Compton St, W1 7287 0770 4–3A

Fans praise "an interesting take on Vietnamese food" and "funky" styling at this well-publicised yearling; but critics say the nosh is "nothing special", that service is "not up to much", and think "the feel of the place is frankly depressing". A new HQ (on the site of Bam-Bou, RIP) is expected late-2015.

House Restaurant National Theatre SE1 NEW £52 2 3 2

Royal National Theatre, Belvedere Rd 7452 3600 2–3D

Views divide on this re-staging of the National's main restaurant space (fka 'Mezzanine'); undoubtedly it's "useful for a show", but while fans say it's "a lot better than its predecessor", those who found it "inconsistent" say "work is needed if we are to return for an encore". / SE1 9PX; @NT_House; 10 pm.

The Hoxton Grill EC2 £52 2 3 4

81 Great Eastern St 7739 9111 12–1B

"Everything is slick" at this large and "very cool" Shoreditch venue, serving "enjoyable" diner-style grub; not everyone 'gets it' though – "with its DJ and noise from drinkers, it doesn't know if it's a disco, bar or restaurant!" / EC2A 3HU; www.hoxtongrill.co.uk; @hoxtongrill; 11.45 pm.

Hubbard & Bell
Hoxton Hotel WC1 £56 334

199-206 High Holborn 7661 3030 2–1D

Soho House's "fun cross between a diner and a grill" is great for "people watching" and gets "very lively" ("noisy") in the evenings with a DJ and large groups; the food "can become incidental", so "better to go at lunchtime" (or for the excellent breakfasts). / WC1V 7BD; www.hubbardandbell.com; @hubbardandbell; 2 am, Sunday midnight.

Hunan SW1 £79 521

51 Pimlico Rd 7730 5712 5–2D

"Let the owner order for you", then sit back for "a roller coaster ride of endless one-mouthful plates" when you visit this "cramped" Pimlico veteran. The "truly original and exciting" cooking is arguably "London's best Chinese food" and the Peng family's "haphazard, grace-under-pressure" service helps create "an experience like no other". / SW1W 8NE; www.hunanlondon.com; 11 pm; closed Sun; set weekday L £56 (FP).

Hungry Donkey E1 NEW £42

56 Wentworth St 7392 9649 9–2D

Attractive-looking, airy, all-day operation in Aldgate inspired by Hellenic street food (eat in or take out), majoring in souvlaki cooked on the Josper grill and a wide range of Greek tipples; it opened too late for the survey, hence it's un-rated. / E1 7AL; www.hungrydonkey.co.uk; @thehungrydonkey; Mon-Wed 10 pm, Thu-Sat 10.30 pm, Sun 6 pm.

Hush £61 233

8 Lancashire Ct, W1 7659 1500 3–2B
95-97 High Holborn, WC1 7242 4580 2–1D

A "posh" location (tucked-away off Bond Street, with a large terrace), "buzzy" bar and "spacious" dining room have won a fashionable following for the Mayfair original of this small group, even if it's "not as good as it thinks it is"; its straightforward Holborn spin-off is akin to an upmarket Côte. / www.hush.co.uk; @Hush_Restaurant; W1 10.45 pm; WC1 10.30 pm, Sun 9.30 pm; WC1 closed Sun.

Hutong
The Shard SE1 £87 224

31 St Thomas St 3011 1257 9–4C

"Up high, overlooking London is breathtaking", at this "slick and graceful" 33rd-floor perch; but while fans find the Chinese cuisine "astonishingly good" for a room with a such an "exceptional" view, others find it "unspectacular" especially given the "crazy prices". / SE1 9RY; www.hutong.co.uk; @HutongShard; 11 pm.

Ibérica £46 334

Zig Zag Building, 70 Victoria St, SW1 7636 8650 2–4B NEW
195 Great Portland St, W1 7636 8650 2–1B
12 Cabot Sq, E14 7636 8650 11–1C
89 Turnmill St, EC1 7636 8650 9–1A

These "cool-ish" modern Spaniards offer an "inexpensive and delicious" selection of tapas; "for a fairly quick business lunch" the E14 branch is one of the Wharf's better options, and the "large" and "lively" Clerkenwell outlet is perhaps their best opening yet. A further outpost opened in Victoria as this guide went to press. / 11 pm; W1 closed Sun D.

Iddu SW7 NEW **£49** 2 1 2
44 Harrington Rd 7581 8088 5–2B
Not far from Gloucester Road tube, a new café and wine bar; its "interesting" Sicilian dishes and wines show some promise, but it can seem "pricey", and service can be "hopeless". / SW7 3ND; www.iddulondon.com; 10 pm.

Imli Street W1 **£40** 3 2 2
167-169 Wardour St 7287 4243 3–1D
With its "interesting", affordable Indian street food 'tapas', plus the odd cocktail if you so fancy, this sizeable Soho operation is "a handy drop-in", and one that can be "fun" too. / W1F 8WR; www.imlistreet.com; @imlistreet; 11 pm, Sun 10 pm.

Inaho W2 **£44** 5 1 5
4 Hereford Rd 7221 8495 6–1B
"Better than Nobu!" might seem a surprising claim for this "eccentric", "little" Japanese shed in Bayswater, but it's regularly praised for "the best sushi and sashimi ever"; the service though could not be described as 'rapid'. / W2 4AA; 10.30 pm; closed Sat L & Sun; no Amex or Maestro.

Inamo **£46** 2 2 2
4-12 Regent St, SW1 7484 0500 3–3D
134-136 Wardour St, W1 7851 7051 3–1D
The "quirky" touchscreen table ordering system is by far the best feature of this Asian chain – the food is secondary (but "tasty nonetheless"); the odd critic says it's "a rubbish concept", but for most reporters it's "fun for a night out with friends, or with kids, or maybe even a date". / www.inamo-restaurant.com; @InamoRestaurant; W1: Mon - Thu 11.30pm, Fri & Sat midnight, Sun 10.30 pm – SW1: Mon - Thu 11pm, Fri & Sat 12.30pm, Sun 10.30pm.

India Club
Strand Continental Hotel WC2 **£29** 3 2 1
143 Strand 7836 4880 2–2D
A scruffy old relic, near the Indian High Commission (where you BYO, or pick up a pint in the hotel bar); "it's the authenticity of the cooking, the eternal pre-war atmosphere, and very fair prices that keep us going back". / WC2R 1JA; www.strand-continental.co.uk; 10.50 pm; no credit cards; booking: max 6.

Indian Moment SW11 **£35** 3 4 3
44 Northcote Rd 7223 6575 10–2C
"A pre-drink curry, rather than a post-session, end-of-the-night filler!", say fans of this much-appreciated Battersea local, with its "interesting" cooking and "classy and modern" interior. / SW11 1NZ; www.indianmoment.co.uk; @indianmoment; 11.30 pm, Fri & Sat midnight; no Amex.

Indian Ocean SW17 **£33** 4 5 3
214 Trinity Rd 8672 7740 10–2C
"It never ever fails!" – a "stalwart" Wandsworth Indian, acclaimed for its "very tasty" cooking, and "some of the best service ever". / SW17 7HP; www.indianoceanrestaurant.com; 11.30 pm.

Indian Rasoi N2 £36 4 3 3
7 Denmark Ter 8883 9093 1–1B
"If you don't know it, you're missing out!"; this "tiny" Muswell Hill Indian draws fans from across north London for its "unusual" cooking with "lovely, individual flavours". / N2 9HG; www.indian-rasoi.co.uk; 10.30 pm; no Amex.

Indian Veg N1 £11 4 3 3
92-93 Chapel Mkt 7833 1167 8–3D
"Colourful, veggie propaganda posters all over the walls make for a diverting read" at this age-old, self-service, "buffet-style" vegan in Islington, where it's "hard not to overeat", given the "tasty curries at crazy prices". / N1 9EX; 11.30 pm.

Indian Zilla SW13 £46 3 3 2
2-3 Rocks Ln 8878 3989 10–1A
"Ace" and "original" cooking continues to win many fans for this Barnes sibling to Indian Zing; its ratings slipped this year though – a couple of reporters had "iffy" meals, and the ambience has suffered when it's empty. / SW13 0DB; www.indianzilla.co.uk; 11 pm; closed weekday L.

Indian Zing W6 £49 5 3 2
236 King St 8748 5959 7–2B
"Even my Punjabi mother-in-law swooned!" – Manoj Vasaikar's "very distinctive" modern Indian cuisine remains "worth the trip" to this very well-known, but somewhat "oddly located" little "gem", near Ravenscourt Park. / W6 0RS; www.indianzing.co.uk; @IndianZing; 11 pm, Sun 10 pm.

Indigo
One Aldwych WC2 £65 2 4 3
1 Aldwych 7300 0400 2–2D
A "dependable spot for a quick bite to eat pre-theatre" – this Theatreland mezzanine dining room benefits from the buzz of the foyer below and is "all-round a very good experience", enhanced by a successful revamp in spring 2015. / WC2B 4BZ; www.onealdwych.com; @OneAldwych; 10.15 pm.

Inside SE10 £45 4 4 1
19 Greenwich South St 8265 5060 1–3D
Guy Awford's "sparkling gem" is "still the best in Greenwich", serving "excellent-value" cuisine (both "classic and with a twist"); its premises aren't a huge plus however – they're "cramped, noisy and dowdy". / SE10 8NW; www.insiderestaurant.co.uk; @insideandgreenwich; Tue-Sat 10 pm, Sun 3 pm; closed Mon & Sun D; SRA-1.*

Ippudo London £38 2 3 2
Central St Giles Piazza, WC2 7240 4469 4–1B NEW
1 Crossrail Pl, E14 3326 9485 11–1C NEW
"It shouldn't be hard to take a reliable international formula and clone it", but these new outposts of the global Japanese tonkotsu chain get a mixed rep – even those who rate its first branch as "very good" say "it's inferior to Kanada-Ya across the road", and the worst reports are of food that's "watery and greasy". / www.ippudo.co.uk; @IppudoLondon.

Isarn N1 £46 4 3 2

119 Upper St 7424 5153 8–3D

"They put love into their authentic cooking" at this "tranquil" and affordable Thai – a very "dependable" feature of the Islington restaurant strip. / N1 1QP; www.isarn.co.uk; 11 pm, Sat & Sun 10 pm.

Ishtar W1 £46 3 3 2

10-12 Crawford St 7224 2446 2–1A

"Steady cooking, kind staff, fair prices… and that's over a dozen visits – what more can you ask?", say fans of this "accommodating" Turkish "gem", in Marylebone. / W1U 6AZ; www.ishtarrestaurant.com; 11.30 pm, Sun 10.30 pm; set weekday L £28 (FP).

The Italian Job W4 NEW £30 2 2 4

13 Devonshire Rd 8994 2852 7–2A

"The food's not really the point here (even if it's very serviceable none the less)" – it's the rotating list of Italian craft beer that makes this new Chiswick bar, just beside La Trompette, worth seeking out. / W4 2EU; www.theitalianjobpub.co.uk; @TheItalianJobW4.

Itsu £33 2 3 3

Branches throughout London

"A gym day feels more healthy" if you snack at these "refreshingly Lo-Cal" Pan-Asian pit-stops, whose sushi, "slurpy soups" and other "innovative bites" are "not the tastiest, but generally good quality". / www.itsu.co.uk; 11 pm, E14 10 pm; some are closed Sat & Sun; no booking.

The Ivy WC2 £69

1-5 West St 7836 4751 4–3B

Richard Caring's famous Theatreland idol – now the original of a fast expanding brand – emerged from a massive overhaul too late to be rated (just before the survey closed). Too often a let down in recent years, a handful of first-days reports say its "beautiful refurb" is "superb in every detail" – "wow, wow, wow!" / WC2H 9NQ; www.the-ivy.co.uk; @CapriceHoldings; 11 pm, Sun 10 pm; no shorts; booking: max 6; set weekday L & pre-theatre £45 (FP).

The Ivy Café W1 NEW

96 Marylebone Ln 3301 0400 2–1A

Richard Caring continues to expand his most bankable brand, The Ivy, with a casual café offering due to open November-2015 on the former site of Union Café (RIP) in Marylebone; let's hope it has better food than the other recent spin-offs. / W1U 2QA; www.theivycafemarylebone.com; 11 pm, Fri & Sat 11.30 pm, Sun 10.30 pm.

The Ivy Chelsea Garden SW3 NEW £57 2 2 5

197 King's Rd 3301 0300 5–3C

You need to be "Prince William or Lady Gaga to get a table before 2050", at the Ivy's new, all-day west London cousin (on the site that in the late '80s was famous as Henry J Beans). "Like the original Ivy, the food's not the point" – in fact, it's really "dreary" here – "it's the beautiful design and glorious, not-so-secret garden that make it a sublime addition to the King's Road". / SW3 5ED; www.theivychelseagarden.com; @ivychelsgarden; 11.30 pm.

The Ivy Kensington Brasserie W8 NEW
96 Kensington High St awaiting tel 5–1A
On the site of Jon (Foxtons) Hunt's short-lived Pavilion (RIP), yet another Ivy spin-off from the Caprice Group, due to open late-2015; whatever the outcome food-wise, it's good to know that more will be made of this barmily luxurious, but previously under-utilised, space. / W8 4SG.

The Ivy Market Grill WC2 NEW £57 223
1a Henrietta St 3301 0200 4–3D
If you're going to roll out a brand like 'The Ivy', for Pete's sake, do better than this new lukewarm knock-off, right by Covent Garden market; apologists say it's handy with a "nice al fresco" area, but given its "bland" food, "perfunctory" service and "lack of ambience" you "expect better of the Caprice stable". / WC2E 8PS; www.theivymarketgrill.com; @ivymarketgrill; midnight, Sun 11.30 pm; set weekday L £36 (FP).

Izgara N3 £34 322
11 Hendon Lane 8371 8282 1–1B
A recently refurbished Turkish grill in Finchley with a "wonderful array of meat skewers", and a "buzzy" (if rather "noisy") setting. / N3 1RT; www.izgararestaurant.net; midnight; no Amex.

Jackson & Rye £46 123
56 Wardour St, W1 7437 8338 3–2D
219-221 Chiswick High Rd, W4 8747 1156 7–2A NEW
Hotham House, 1 Heron Sq, TW9 8948 6951 1–4A
"A trick missed" – these "smart", US-style diners are a case of "style over substance"; they're "buzzing" (and Richmond has "a lovely riverside location"), but the food is "poor" (stick to breakfast) and service is "friendly" but "lackadaisical" – "employ some Americans!" / www.jacksonrye.com.

Jaffna House SW17 £16 542
90 Tooting High St 8672 7786 10–2C
"Despite its humble interior, well worth a visit" – a family-run Tooting Sri Lankan (the dining space is a converted living room) where the "tasty" grub is "ridiculously good value". / SW17 0RN; www.jaffnahouse.co.uk; midnight.

Jago
Second Home E1 NEW £49 323
60-80 Hanbury St 3818 3241 12–2C
If you're a lover of '70s SciFi movies, you'll love this "slightly weird" (and very orange) new conservatory annex to a so-now East End tech office space. Arguably "it's trying too hard to be hip", and the modern Middle Eastern-inspired food is "a bit mixed", but some dishes are "brilliantly executed". (The name? apparently slang for the slums that once inhabited this part of Shoreditch). / E1 5JL; www.jagorestaurant.com; @jagorestaurant; 10.30 pm.

Jamaica Patty Co. WC2 £10 332
26 New Row 7836 3334 4–3C
A handy Covent Garden pit stop, serving "above average patties" – "good grub, good prices, great tastes!" / WC2N 4LA; www.jamaicapatty.co.uk; @JamaicaPattyCo; 11 pm, Sun 7 pm.

Jamie's Diner W1 **£48** 222
23a, Shaftesbury Ave 3697 4117 3–3D
Jamie Oliver's year-old, family-friendly Soho diner disappoints half those who comment on it – it's "ordinary at best". / W1D 7EF; www.jamieoliversdiner.com; @jamiesdiner; Mon-Fri 11 pm, Sat & Sun 10.30 pm.

Jamie's Italian **£44** 112
Branches throughout London
"Avoid!"; Jamie Oliver risks becoming "synonymous with poor food" with his chain of Italian diners, which inspire far too many "embarrassingly bad" reports of "really weak" results, and "shrugging" service. / www.jamiesitalian.com; @JamiesItalianUK; 11.30 pm, Sun 10.30 pm; booking: min 6.

Jar Kitchen WC2 NEW **£48** 333
Drury Ln 7405 4255 4–1C
The owners are first-time restaurateurs, so there are still "some things to iron out" at this tiny rookie, on the fringes of Covent Garden; that said, it has "tasty home cooking" and "lovely staff" to recommend it. / WC2B 5QF; www.jarkitchen.com; @JarKitchen; 11.30 pm.

Jashan N8 **£32** 542
19 Turnpike Ln 8340 9880 1–1C
"Incredibly popular with anyone within easy reach of Turnpike Lane" – a "fantastic" (if slightly "tired"-looking) Indian, whose "extensive, wide-ranging menu is a departure from what you'd expect of a local", and "amazing for the price". / N8 0EP; www.jashanturnpikelane.co.uk; 11.30 pm; D only; no Amex; need 6+ to book, Sat & Sun.

Jin Kichi NW3 **£44** 543
73 Heath St 7794 6158 8–1A
"Just like Tokyo!"; this "real Japanese" in the heart of Hampstead may be "tiny" and "cramped", but "it never fails to deliver wonderful food" and "without ridiculous prices" too. / NW3 6UG; www.jinkichi.com; 11 pm, Sun 10 pm; closed Mon L.

Jinjuu W1 NEW **£47** 333
16 Kingly St 8181 8887 3–2C
Korean-inspired bar snacks and larger dishes "are not quite elevated to an art form, but to a good level" at the first solo venture from TV Iron Chef star Judy Joo, where you can eat in the ground floor bar (DJs on some nights), or basement dining room. / W1B 5PS; www.jinjuu.com; @JinjuuLDN; midnight.

Joanna's SE19 **£44** 334
56 Westow Hill 8670 4052 1–4D
An "institution" in Crystal Palace – this atmospheric neighbourhood stalwart of three decades' standing remains "a firm favourite" thanks to its "consistently good" all-round standards; just one gripe – "bring back the table cloths!" / SE19 1RX; www.joannas.uk.com; @JoannasRest; 10.45 pm, Sun 10.15 pm.

Joe Allen WC2 £53 124
13 Exeter St 7836 0651 4–3D
A "Theatreland favourite since it opened in the mid-'70s" – this "fun and buzzy", occasionally star-studded, old, Covent Garden basement hangs on to its fan club despite perennially "tired" cooking. Top Menu Tip – the "delicious under-the-counter burgers" which "strangely have never made the menu". / WC2E 7DT; www.joeallen.co.uk; @JoeAllenWC2; Sun-Thu 11.45 pm, Fri & Sat 12.45 am; set weekday L £34 (FP).

Joe's Brasserie SW6 £43 233
130 Wandsworth Bridge Rd 7731 7835 10–1B
The "comfort food" is "good standard stuff" and there's "very well-priced wine" at John Brinkley's stalwart brasserie in deepest Fulham; "enjoyable outside terrace" too. / SW6 2UL; www.brinkleys.com; @BrinkleysR; 11.30 pm, Sun 10.30 pm.

John Doe W10 NEW £49 433
46 Golborne Rd 8969 3280 6–1A
On-trend for slow-cooking and smoking, but doing it rather better than most – a "wonderful" north Kensington newcomer serving "fabulous game, fish, bone marrow and veg" straight from the charcoal grill; "sit at the bar and watch your meal being prepared". / W10 5PR; www.johndoerestaurants.com; @johndoegolborne; midnight, Sun 4 pm.

The Joint £26 532
19 New Cavendish St, W1 7486 3059 2–1A NEW
87 Brixton Village, Coldharbour Ln, SW9 07717 642812 10–1D
"The best pulled pork this side of anywhere", and "ribs and wings like you get in the deep South" are plain "brilliant" at this "lip-smackin'" BBQ duo; "you have to queue around the block at the hustling and bustling Brixton Market original, but boy is it worth it!" / www.the-joint.co; SW9 closed Mon.

Jolly Gardeners SW18 £49 433
214 Garratt Ln 8870 8417 10–2B
"MasterChef winner Dhruv Baker uses seasonal produce to create interesting alternatives to traditional pub fare" at this "stark" Earlsfield gastropub, which wins ringing endorsements from most (if not quite all) who report on it. / SW18 4EA; www.thejollygardeners.co.uk; @JollyGardeners; 11 pm, Sun 6 pm.

Jones & Sons E8 NEW £54 444
22-27 Arcola St 7241 1211 1–1C
"Many places in smarter postcodes would charge a heck of a lot more" than this open-kitchen operation, in a converted Dalston factory (nowadays trendy studios), which fans say "deserves proper recognition" for its cooking, in particular "outstanding" char-grilled steaks. / E8 2DJ; www.jonesandsonsdalston.com; 10 pm, Fri & Sat 11 pm.

The Jones Family Project EC2 £50 243
78 Great Eastern St 7739 1740 12–1B
"Staff couldn't be friendlier" at this sizeable Shoreditch bar (street level) / restaurant (basement); steak is the menu highlight, but top billing goes to the "fab cocktails". / EC2A 3JL; www.jonesfamilyproject.co.uk; @jonesshoreditch; 10.30 pm, Sun 6 pm.

José SE1 £47 555

104 Bermondsey St 7403 4902 9–4D

"It's worth fighting to get in" to José Pizarro's "tiny" and "cramped" little "piece of Spain" in Bermondsey – you enjoy "masterful" tapas, served by "staff who take tremendous pride in their work", in a marvellously "vibrant" setting. / SE1 3UB; www.josepizarro.com; @Jose_Pizarro; 10.15 pm, Sun 5.15 pm; closed Sun D.

José Pizarro EC2 NEW £58 443

Broadgate Circle 3437 0905 12–2B

From hip Bermondsey (José, Pizarro) to the heart of the Square Mile – cynics might say JP has sold out with this Broadgate Circle newcomer; early reports though say "it's a great addition to the City", with an "extensive" array of "superb" tapas, and "a super terrace for a sunny day". / EC2M 2QS; www.josepizarro.com; @JP_Broadgate; 10.45 pm, Sun 9.45 pm.

Joy King Lau WC2 £38 322

3 Leicester St 7437 1132 4–3A

"Four crowded floors of bustle" that are "very much better-than-average for Chinatown", if "looking a bit dated now"; the Cantonese chow's "not the most sophisticated", but "dim sum and char sui are all excellent". / WC2H 7BL; www.joykinglau.com; 11.30 pm, Sun 10.30 pm.

The Jugged Hare EC1 £66 323

49 Chiswell St 7614 0134 12–2A

"Really good game in season" is a highlight at this "countryman's oasis" near The Barbican – a "stylish" and "buzzy" ("packed") gastropub serving "lovely" British food. / EC1Y 4SA; www.thejuggedhare.com; @juggedhare; Mon-Wed 11 pm, Thu-Sat midnight, Sun 10.30 pm.

Julie's W11 £65

135 Portland Rd 7229 8331 6–2A

"Those cubbyhole niches have seen a lot of action" over the years, at this famously sexy, '70s basement warren in Holland Park; just as the food (never great) showed some signs of improving, they closed it till Spring 2016 for a huge refurb – let's hope it emerges as the knockout place it has the potential to be. / W11 4LW; www.juliesrestaurant.com; @JuliesW11; 11 pm.

Jun Ming Xuan NW9 £42 442

28 Heritage Ave 8205 6987 1–1A

In the new Beaufort Park area of Colindale, a modern Chinese at the foot of a recent development; even if The Times review hailing it as the UK's best is a tad wide of the mark, it wins enthusiastic praise for its "terrific dim sum and other classic dishes". / NW9 5GE; 11 pm.

The Junction Tavern NW5 £48 333

101 Fortess Rd 7485 9400 8–2B

A "high-quality gastropub" on the Tufnell Park/Kentish Town borders, that generates consistently upbeat feedback; cute courtyard. / NW5 1AG; www.junctiontavern.co.uk; @Junction Tavern; 11 pm, Mon 10.30 pm; Mon-Thu D only, Fri-Sun open L & D; no Amex.

K10 £38 332

20 Copthall Ave, EC2 7562 8510 9–2C
3 Appold St, EC2 7539 9209 12–2B
Minster Ct, Mincing Ln, EC3 3019 2510 9–3D NEW

"Better than the big-name conveyor chains" – these well-run, slightly "spartan" City operations have very "decent" standards, and serve "a great selection of sushi and other delicacies"; "arrive early to avoid the queues". / www.k10.com; Appold 9 pm, Wed-Fri 9.30 pm.

Kadiri's NW10 £24 432

26 High Rd 8459 0936 1–1A

"Every dish – mild or very hot – is delicious", say fans of this cramped, '70s subcontinental in Willesden; there's the odd gripe though that "they've pared back on what was a very varied menu to something more bog standard". / NW10 2QD; www.kadiris.com; @kadirislondon; 11 pm.

Kaffeine £12 455

15 Eastcastle St, W1 7580 6755 3–1D NEW
66 Great Titchfield St, W1 7580 6755 3–1C

"The coffee never disappoints" – "it's the best, no doubts" – at these "always packed" Fitzrovia haunts; "inventive" nibbles too, and "an amazing emphasis on top-quality service". / www.kaffeine.co.uk.

Kai Mayfair W1 £97 322

65 South Audley St 7493 8988 3–3A

This luxurious Chinese is "all a bit Mayfair", especially its claret-heavy wine list, non-oriental waiters, and prices off the Richter scale; perhaps surprisingly though, it's generally "worth it". / W1K 2QU; www.kaimayfair.co.uk; @kaimayfair; 10.45 pm, Sun 10.15 pm.

Kaifeng NW4 £62 323

51 Church Rd 8203 7888 1–1B

Hendon's stalwart kosher Chinese restaurant is, say fans, "as good as ever", and unusually flexible (they "cater for coeliacs" and "even a guest who didn't fancy Chinese was given a suitable dinner!"); not everyone's wowed though, especially by prices some consider a "rip off". / NW4 4DU; www.kaifeng.co.uk; 10 pm; closed Fri & Sat.

Kanada-Ya £19 532

3 Panton St, SW1 awaiting tel 4–4A NEW
64 St Giles High St, WC2 7240 0232 4–1B NEW

"The hoards queuing outside know they're in for a treat" at these cheap, "truly genuine", "cheek-by-jowl" ramen newcomers in the West End (outposts of a chain originating in Fukuoka, in southern Japan); "the broth is so rich, the meat so unctuous, you'll finish the bowl, even if you feel you're about to burst!" / www.kanada-ya.com/home/.

Kaosarn £26 343

110 St Johns Hill, SW11 7223 7888 10–2C
Brixton Village, Coldharbour Ln, SW9 7095 8922 10–2D

"Always hopping" – these "vibrant" ("if not exactly plush") cafés in Brixton Village and Battersea, are "spot on", with "fresh, home-cooked Thai flavours" ("no hint of generic gloop") and "a BYO policy that keeps prices down". / SW9 10 pm, Sun 9 pm; SW11 closed Mon L.

Kappacasein SE16 £6 532

1 Voyager Industrial Estate 07837 756852 11–2A

"The best toasted cheese sandwich in the history of the world" (and also "very good raclettes") inspire love (and long queues) for the Borough Market stall of this Bermondsey dairy (which itself opens on Saturdays). / SE16 4RP; www.kappacasein.com; Thu 5 pm, Fri 6 pm, Sat 5 pm.

Karma W14 £40 432

44 Blythe Rd 7602 9333 7–1D

"In a hidden corner of Olympia", this "quiet" Indian is well worth discovering – "decidedly not your average cuzza", it serves "superb, authentic curries". / W14 0HA; www.k-a-r-m-a.co.uk; @KarmaKensington; 11 pm; no Amex.

Kaspar's Seafood and Grill Savoy Hotel WC2 £79 333

100 The Strand 7836 4343 4–3D

Critics decry a "characterless" space and "unspectacular" cooking at the Savoy's former River Restaurant; on balance, though, most reporters approve of its "OTT" Deco decor and say the food is "excellent, if pricey". Top Tip – "good-value pre-theatre menu". / WC2R 0EU; www.kaspars.co.uk; @KasparsLondon; 11 pm.

Kateh £43 542

9 Knightsbridge Grn, SW1 7289 3393 5–1D NEW

5 Warwick Pl, W9 7289 3393 8–4A

A tiny outfit in Little Venice, which comes "absolutely recommended" thanks to the "beautiful blend of magical Persian dishes, served by its attentive and friendly staff"; it's "very (perhaps too) cosy" too – "it's hard to fit all the plates on the table!"; still no feedback on its year-old Knightsbridge branch. / www.katehrestaurant.co.uk; @KatehRestaurant.

Kazan £48 342

77 Wilton Rd, SW1 7233 8298 2–4B

93-94 Wilton Rd, SW1 7233 7100 2–4B

"Deservedly successful", "very busy" Pimlico duo, with restaurant and café spin-off on the same street; their looks are "quite ordinary", but service is "accommodating", and there's high praise for the "sparkling fresh" salads and mezze and other well-prepared Turkish fare. / www.kazan-restaurant.com; 10 pm.

The Keeper's House Royal Academy W1 £65 222

Royal Academy Of Arts, Piccadilly 7300 5881 3–3D

"It's handy when visiting an exhibition", but many reporters "expected more" of this "prestigious" basement two-year-old ("tucked away" below the RA) – the food "goes from excellent to meh", service can be "novice", and overall it can all seem "fairly ordinary". / W1J 0BD; www.keepershouse.org.uk; @KHRestaurant; 11.30 pm; closed Sun; set pre theatre £41 (FP).

Ken Lo's Memories SW1 **£60** 342

65-69 Ebury St 7730 7734 2–4B

"I love the place, and so do many regulars!" – this once-famous Belgravia Chinese remains a "calm and civilised" venue, and though oft-accused of "living on its past reputation", its ratings are remarkably steady; the food is "unadventurous by the standards of some newer Chinese places, but high quality". / SW1W 0NZ; www.memoriesofchina.co.uk; 10.45 pm, Sun 10 pm.

Kennington Tandoori SE11 **£45** 333

313 Kennington Rd 7735 9247 1–3C

"Preppy young locals rub shoulders with older politicos" at this "neighbourhood gossip shop" – a "consistently good local curry house", within easy striking distance of the Palace of Westminster. / SE11 4QE; www.kenningtontandoori.com; @TheKTL; 11 pm; no Amex.

Kensington Place W8 **£60** 333

201-209 Kensington Church St 7727 3184 6–2B

This seminal '90s venue, off Notting Hill Gate – with its "bright windows and open interior" – was "reinvented after the post-Rowley Leigh wilderness years" and is now biased to "delicious" fish and seafood (with shop attached); sceptics still find the food a tad "ordinary" however, and the setting's "noisy" as ever. / W8 7LX; www.kensingtonplace-restaurant.co.uk; @kprestaurantW8; 10.30 pm; closed Mon L & Sun D; set weekday L £45 (FP).

Kensington Square Kitchen W8 **£33** 343

9 Kensington Sq 7938 2598 5–1A

For "a top brunch in Kensington" (or an affordable "straightforward" bite at any time), winkle out this cute, cramped little indie café, tucked away off a picturesque old square. / W8 5EP; www.kensingtonsquarekitchen.co.uk; @KSKRestaurant; 4.30 pm, Sun 4 pm; L only; no Amex.

The Kensington Wine Rooms W8 **£55** 223

127-129 Kensington Church St 7727 8142 6–2B

"I'm at the age when reading wine lists is my form of porno, and a long lunch here is very enjoyable…!"; this Kensington bar-dining room provides an "extensive and varied list" (including plenty of wines by the glass), washed down with tapas-style food that's "pleasant". / W8 7LP; www.greatwinesbytheglass.com; @wine_rooms; 10.45 pm.

(Brew House)
Kenwood House NW3 **£32** 224

Hampstead Heath 8348 4073 8–1A

"Luxuriate in the sunshine at the outdoor tables" of Kenwood's beautifully located self-service café, at the top of Hampstead Heath; stick to breakfasts, coffee and cakes though – other options are "very variable and not great value, but the surroundings make every latte a joy!" / NW3 7JR; www.companyofcooks.com; @EHKenwood; 6 pm (summer), 4 pm (winter); L only.

Kerbisher & Malt £20 332

53 New Broadway, W5 8840 4418 1–2A
164 Shepherd's Bush Rd, W6 3556 0228 7–1C
170 Upper Richmond Road West, SW14 8876 3404 1–4A
50 Abbeville Rd, SW4 3417 4350 10–2D
59-61 Rosebery Ave, EC1 7833 4434 9–1A NEW

"Flaky, fresh fish, and proper fat chips" – plus funkier menu options (eg fennel salad!) – have fuelled growth at this chippy-chain, which fans say is "traditional where it counts, but stylish and modern too"; the design can seem "a bit dull" however, and sceptics say they're "only a bit better than an average chippy". / www.kerbisher.co.uk; 10 pm - 10.30pm, Sun 9 pm - 9.30 pm; W6 closed Mon; no booking.

Kettners W1 £58

29 Romilly St 7734 6112 4–2A

Will the Soho House group finally succeed where all else have failed in revivifying this magnificent Victorian landmark in Soho (founded in 1867), which – aside from its jolly champagne bar – has been perennially disappointing for as long as most folk can remember. When it re-opens in 2018, it will be as part of a new hotel complex. / W1D 5HP; www.kettners.com; @KettnersLondon; 11 pm, Fri & Sat 11.30 pm, Sun 9.30 pm.

Khan's W2 £23 332

13-15 Westbourne Grove 7727 5420 6–1C

For a "cheap 'n' cheerful" Indian meal, this large veteran canteen in Bayswater has its plus points; it's hectic though, and don't go if you want to booze (it's alcohol free). / W2 4UA; www.khansrestaurant.com; @khansrestaurant; 11.30 pm, Sat-Sun midnight.

Kiku W1 £55 432

17 Half Moon St 7499 4208 3–4B

"Marvellous sushi" is the draw to this "bustling" but "bland"-looking Mayfair fixture; a catch? – it's really "not cheap". / W1J 7BE; www.kikurestaurant.co.uk; 10.15 pm, Sun 9.45 pm; closed Sun L.

Kikuchi W1 £52 532

14 Hanway St 7637 7720 4–1A

"To-die-for sushi" – "better than much of what I tasted in Japan" – is the (only) reason to seek out this "simple" venture, tucked-away off Tottenham Court Road; it's "expensive" though, and with the service "there are some language barriers". / W1T 1UD; 10.30 pm; closed Sun.

Kimchee WC1 £42 322

71 High Holborn 7430 0956 2–1D

"The Korean Wagamama" in 'Midtown' is consistently well-rated, for both food that's "OK, rather than exceptional", and also its "well-designed space", but not for its sometimes "lousy" service. / WC1V 6EA; www.kimchee.uk.com; @kimcheerest; 10.30 pm.

Kintan WC1 £44 433

34-36 High Holborn 7242 8076 9–2A

London's first yakiniku-style outpost (a Japanese take on Korean BBQ) – this Holborn yearling wins praise for its "great-tasting" meaty fare; "kids love cooking their own dinner at the table too". / WC1V 6AE; www.kintan.uk/about; 10 pm.

Kipferl N1 **£45** 3 3 3

20 Camden Pas 77041 555 8–3D

"Without all the kitsch of lederhosen and dirndls" – an "obliging" Islington deli-restaurant offering "lovely Austrian food that's authentic but not too heavy" (eg schnitzels, Bergkäse omelette) plus "top coffee", and a "great selection of gateaux and Austrian wines"; just the job for brunch. / N1 8ED; www.kipferl.co.uk; @KipferlCafe; 9.30 pm; closed Mon.

Kiraku W5 **£35** 5 3 2

8 Station Pde 8992 2848 1–3A

"Exceptional Japanese food justifies the trek to this friendly, izakaya-style café", near Ealing Common tube, "hence why it's always packed", typically with the local Japanese community. / W5 3LD; www.kiraku.co.uk; @kirakulondon; 10 pm; closed Mon; no Amex.

Kishmish SW6 **£50** 4 4 3

448-450 Fulham Rd 7385 6953 5–4A

Not far from Stamford Bridge – a "non-standard" Indian whose interesting menu offers a "different take" on the average curry ("delicious buffalo vindaloo" for example). / SW6 1DL; www.kishmish.biz; @KishmishFulham; 11 pm.

Kitchen National Theatre SE1 NEW **£26** 2 2 2

South Bank 7452 3600 2–3D

"Not fine dining", and "not with a lot of choice", but "for a quick bite before a play" or when on the South Bank, the NT's "very reasonably priced" new "cheap 'n cheerful self-service option" is "worth considering". / SE1 9PX; www.nationaltheatre.org; 8 pm, Sun 6 pm.

Kitchen W8 W8 **£69** 5 4 3

11-13 Abingdon Road 7937 0120 5–1A

"Phil Howard has worked his magic" in overseeing this "smart but unpretentious" neighbourhood spot, just off Ken' High Street; "nuanced" and "very fine" cuisine is "excellently served" in a setting that's "not hugely distinctive" but "calm and serene". / W8 6AH; www.kitchenw8.com; @KitchenW8; 10.30 pm, Sun 9.30 pm; set weekday L £42 (FP), set pre-theatre £44 (FP), set Sun L £52 (FP).

Kitty Fisher's W1 NEW **£67** 4 4 4

10 Shepherd's Mkt 3302 1661 3–4B

If you can nab a table (ay, there's the rub), you should find your efforts amply-rewarded by this "cramped" newcomer in Mayfair's Shepherd's Market – one of 2015's hottest tickets thanks to its "genial" service, "romantic" style, and Tomos Parry's "very different and impressive, yet un-fussy cooking". Top Menu Tip – "the burnt onion butter alone is worth a trip". / W1J 7QF; www.kittyfishers.com; @kittyfishers; 9.30 pm.

Koba W1 **£42** 3 3 3

11 Rathbone St 7580 8825 2–1C

"Fun for a change" – a Korean table-BBQ celebrating its 10th year, that makes a good introduction to the cuisine, and is consistently well-rated. / W1T 1NA; 11 pm; closed Sun L.

Koffmann's
The Berkeley SW1 £86 553

The Berkeley, Wilton Pl 7107 8844 5–1D

"Masterful" veteran chef, Pierre Koffmann, uses his "magic touch" to render "fabulous flavours from relatively humble ingredients" via an "old-school", "gutsy" French menu at this Knightsbridge basement, where "wonderful" service helps enliven the potentially "sterile" interior. Top Menu Tip – "pistachio soufflé is an attraction in itself". / SW1X 7RL; www.the-berkeley.co.uk; @TheBerkeley; 10.30 pm; set weekday L £50 (FP), set pre-theatre £52 (FP).

Kolossi Grill EC1 £33 343

56-60 Rosebery Ave 7278 5758 9–1A

"Almost as good as a Greek holiday", say fans of this "cheap 'n' cheerful" taverna near Sadler's Wells – "ancient waiters" provide "a warm welcome" and the nosh has been "consistent over decades". / EC1R 4RR; www.kolossigrill.com; 11 pm; closed Sat L & Sun; set weekday L £17 (FP).

Konditor & Cook £22 332

Curzon Soho, 99 Shaftesbury Ave, W1 0844 854 9367 4–3A
46 Gray's Inn Rd, WC1 0844 854 9365 9–1A
10 Stoney St, SE1 0844 854 9363 9–4C
22 Cornwall Road, SE1 0844 854 9361 9–4A
30 St Mary Axe, EC3 0844 854 9369 9–2D

"Exquisite cakes", "top sarnies" and "fabulous" coffee are a particular danger at these "cramped" cafés – "I'd be fat as a barrel if I lived nearby!". / www.konditorandcook.com; 6 pm, W1 11 pm; WC1 & EC3 closed Sat & Sun; SE1 closed Sun; no booking.

Kopapa WC2 £65 222

32-34 Monmouth St 7240 6076 4–2B

For brunch especially, Peter Gordon's "busy" Pacific-fusion café in Theatreland is often recommended; one or two reporters really don't dig it though, describing "supposedly Maori-influenced" food that "sounds much better than it tastes". / WC2H 9HA; www.kopapa.co.uk; @Kopapacafe; 11 pm, Sun 9.45 pm; set pre theatre £42 (FP).

Koya-Bar W1 £34 444

50 Frith St 7434 4463 4–2A

Koya's gone, but its neighbouring atmospheric, if utilitarian bar sails on, serving "always interesting" udon noodle and donburi (rice-based) dishes; expansion beyond Soho is on the cards, with a spin-off planned for 2016. / W1D 4SQ; www.koyabar.co.uk; @KoyaBar; Mon-Wed 10.30 pm, Thu-Sat 11 pm, Sun 10 pm; no Amex.

Kricket
Pop Brixton SW9 NEW £44

53 Brixton Station Rd no tel 10–1D

Part of a Brixton community project built around old freight containers and championing budding food and drink entrepreneurs – a new Indian-inspired concept mixing small plates and cocktails, that wins positive early reports. / SW9 8PQ; www.kricket.co.uk; @KricketBrixton; 10 pm.

Kulu Kulu £32 3 1 2
76 Brewer St, W1 7734 7316 3–2D
51-53 Shelton St, WC2 7240 5687 4–2C
39 Thurloe Pl, SW7 7589 2225 5–2C
"Don't go if you're a sushi aficionado", but "for a quick fix" these "old-timer" conveyor-cafés "tick every box for easy grub". / 10 pm, SW7 10.30 pm; closed Sun; no Amex; no booking.

Kurobuta £55 4 2 3
Harvey Nichols, Knightsbridge, SW1 7920 6440 5–1D NEW
312 King's Rd, SW3 3475 4158 5–3C
17-20 Kendal St, W2 3475 4158 6–1D
"Super oishi!" (as they say in Japan) – ex-Nobu supremo Scott Hallsworth's "funky, young and vibey" izakayas have won fame with "amazing dishes, bursting with big bold flavours". Staff can be "overwhelmed" though, and his W2 branch dished up some "disastrous" meals this year, in contrast to his well-rated newcomer in SW3 (near his original pop-up). / www.kurobuta-london.com.

The Ladbroke Arms W11 £53 4 3 4
54 Ladbroke Rd 7727 6648 6–2B
"One of the prettiest pubs in London" – this fine Notting Hill tavern "never fails to come up trumps" with its "always delicious" food and "friendly" (if occasionally "disorganised") service; "try to get a table outside". / W11 3NW; www.capitalpubcompany.com; @ladbrokearms; 11 pm, Sun 10.30 pm; no booking at D.

The Lady Ottoline WC1 £50 3 3 3
11a Northington St 7831 0008 2–1D
Centrally located (Bloomsbury) yet somehow still feeling "tucked away", this handsomely restored Victorian pub is "more restaurant than boozer" with a "comforting", "seasonal" menu that's "not overly elaborate". / WC1N 2JF; www.theladyottoline.com; @theladyottoline; 10 pm, Sun 8 pm.

Lahore Karahi SW17 £23 4 1 2
1 Tooting High Street, London 8767 2477 10–2C
"Cheap thrills in Tooting" – even if service is "patchy", the food at this "buzzing", "no-frills" Pakistani canteen-landmark is worth queueing for; BYO. / SW17 0SN; www.lahorekarahi.co.uk; midnight; no Amex.

Lahore Kebab House £24 4 1 2
668 Streatham High Rd, SW16 8765 0771 10–2D
2-10 Umberston St, E1 7481 9737 11–1A
"A place of pilgrimage" for decades, this "noisy and frantic" Pakistani "bedlam" in Whitechapel is renowned for its "incredible food at incredible prices" (in particular its "stupendous lamb chops"); it provoked a couple of 'off' reports this year though – hopefully just a blip. It also has a well-rated, but much less well-known Streatham sibling. BYO. / midnight.

Lamberts SW12 £50 5 5 4
2 Station Pde 8675 2233 10–2C
"Approaching Chez Bruce standards but less expensive!" – this Balham neighbourhood favourite "hits all the right notes", with its "subtle" decor, "helpful" service and "unfailingly impressive" cooking that's "really exceptional value". / SW12 9AZ; www.lambertsrestaurant.com; @lamberts_balham; 10 pm, Sun 5 pm; closed Mon & Sun D; no Amex; set always available £36 (FP); SRA-3.*

(Winter Garden)
The Landmark NW1 **£78** 2 3 4

222 Marylebone Rd 7631 8000 8–4A

The "formidable" Sunday brunch – with "unlimited champagne, live music and excellent food" – satisfies visitors to this "beautiful" Marylebone destination time and again, as does the ambience of the "wonderful, light atrium" with "lights twinkling in the trees". / NW1 6JQ; www.landmarklondon.co.uk; @landmarklondon; 10.15 pm; no trainers; booking: max 12; set always available £55 (FP).

Langan's Brasserie W1 **£68** 2 2 4

Stratton St 7491 8822 3–3C

With its "chatterbox-y" buzz, this famous and "delightfully furnished" old-timer, near The Ritz, is "a long time favourite" for its older fan club, in particular as an "impressive but laid back venue for business"; its culinary standards, however, have long been well "past it". / W1J 8LB; www.langansrestaurants.co.uk; @langanslondon; 11 pm, Fri & Sat 11.30 pm; closed Sun.

Lantana Cafe **£35** 3 3 3

13-14 Charlotte Pl, W1 7323 6601 2–1C
45 Middle Yd, Camden Lock Pl, NW1 7428 0421 8–2B NEW
Unit 2, 1 Oliver's Yd, 55 City Rd, EC1 7253 5273 12–1A

"Sweet mate!"; one of the first Aussie-style coffee bars to bring Antipodean-style brunching to the capital – the Fitzrovia side street original is still "the best" ("be prepared to queue at weekends"), but the "EC1 canteen for Shoreditch hipsters" is gaining fans too. / www.lantanacafe.co.uk.

Lardo **£40** 3 3 4

158 Sandringham Rd, E8 3021 0747 1–1D NEW
197-201 Richmond Rd, E8 8965 2683 1–2D

"Tattooed diners and china crockery" abound at this "classic Hackney hipster venue" near London Fields (now with nearby offshoot, Lardo Bebé) – but if you can withstand the beards and beanies then you'll enjoy "pizza with gravitas". / www.lardo.co.uk; @lardolondon.

Latium W1 **£53** 4 5 3

21 Berners St 7323 9123 3–1D

"There's nothing in your face" about Maurizio Morelli's "grown up" and "unpretentious" Fitzrovia favourite; "subtle" cooking ("awesome ravioli") is very professionally served in a "spacious" room that's "smart, if slightly austere". / W1T 3LP; www.latiumrestaurant.com; @LatiumLondon; 10.30 pm, Sat 11 pm; closed Sat L & Sun L.

Launceston Place W8 **£79** 4 5 4

1a Launceston Pl 7937 6912 5–1B

In a Kensington backstreet, this "very quiet and romantic" townhouse is a classic choice for an "intimate" date; it's currently on a high – "nothing seems too much trouble" for the "attentive" staff, and the cuisine has been consistently "excellent" in recent times – let's hope it survives the August 2015 departure of chef Tim Allen. / W8 5RL; www.launcestonplace-restaurant.co.uk; @LauncestonPlace; 10 pm, Sun 9.30 pm; closed Mon & Tue L; set weekday L £55 (FP), set Sun L £62 (FP).

THE LEDBURY W11 £133 555
127 Ledbury Rd 7792 9090 6–1B
"Brett Graham simply doesn't falter" at this "utterly brilliant" Notting Hill champion – yet again London's No. 1 foodie address thanks to his "adventurous" culinary creations "perfectly executed with panache". The "muted luxury" of the room is all part of an experience combining "subtle understated elegance, and care given to every detail". / W11 2AQ; www.theledbury.com; @theledbury; 9.45 pm; closed Mon L & Tue L; set weekday L £82 (FP).

Lemonia NW1 £45 245
89 Regent's Park Rd 7586 7454 8–3B
"What do they put in the water?" to drive the "terrific" buzz at this "always packed" Primrose Hill mega-taverna; "obliging" long-serving staff ("you feel like they know you") are key to its magic, but less so the Greek fodder – "I've complained about the boring, unchanging food since about 1975, but keep on going back!" / NW1 8UY; www.lemonia.co.uk; @Lemonia_Greek; 11 pm; closed Sun D; no Amex; set weekday L £29 (FP).

Leon £26 232
Branches throughout London
"Fast food as in quick, not cheap and nasty" – so say devotees of the "wholesome", "healthy" snacks at this much-lauded chain; no escaping, however, that a fair few old fans feel it's "losing its edge", offering "nothing overly exciting" these days. / www.leonrestaurants.co.uk; 10 pm, W1 8.45 pm, E14 8 pm; EC4 closed Sun, W1 closed Sat & Sun; no booking L.

Leong's Legends W1 £37 422
3 Macclesfield St 7287 0288 4–3A
"Wow those soup dumplings are good!" – Chinatown Taiwanese with "consistently interesting food, especially the signature Xiao Long Bao"; "you knock on the door to get in" – it's "not very comfortable, but who cares with tastes and flavours like this". / W1D 6AX; www.leongslegend.com; 11 pm, Sat 11.30 pm; no booking.

The Lido Café
Brockwell Lido SE24 £43 334
Dulwich Rd 7737 8183 10–2D
"It's fun watching the early swimmers" if you try the "wonderful breakfast" at this "relaxing" café, which enjoys "a lovely setting next to the Lido"; at other times the Mediterranean fare is "of a good standard and fairly priced" too. / SE24 0PA; www.thelidocafe.co.uk; @thelidocafe; 9.30 pm; closed Sun D; no Amex.

The Light House SW19 £56 222
75-77 Ridgway 8944 6338 10–2B
"Innovative dishes, from an ever-changing menu" still lead some fans to tip this airy ("noisy") fixture as "Wimbledon's premier dining experience"; "it's time for a shake-up" though – too many other reports suggest "it's lazy, and resting on its laurels". / SW19 4ST; www.lighthousewimbledon.com; 10.30 pm; closed Sun D.

Lima W1 £65 332

31 Rathbone Pl W1 3002 2640 2–1C
'Lima Floral': 14 Garrick St WC2 7240 5778 4–3C
"Sensational" ceviches and other "mind-blowing" Peruvian fare – with "unfamiliar ingredients" and "a bit of a kick" – quickly won renown for the Fitzrovia original, but both it, and its new Covent Garden ('Lima Floral') spin-off can suffer from seeming "over-hyped", not helped by slightly "soulless" decor. / W1T 1JH; www.limalondon.com; @lima_london; 10.45 pm, Sun 3.30 pm; closed Sun D; set weekday L £40 (FP).

Linnea TW9 £50 443

Kew Green 8940 5696 1–3A
"Wonderful simple food, well presented" again wins lofty ratings for Jonas Karlsson's Kew Green yearling; but while fans "are amazed it's not more popular" there are quibbles – "the room is a little bleak", and the odd reporter finds prices "toppy". / TW9 3BH; www.linneakew.co.uk; 10 pm; closed Mon & Sun; set weekday L £30 (FP).

Lisboa Pâtisserie W10 £10 335

57 Golborne Rd 8968 5242 6–1A
"A trip to Portobello market is incomplete without a visit to this mythical café"; "it's like walking into somewhere in Lisbon itself", with "strong coffee, lots of chatter, and piles of heavenly, sticky sweet cakes". / W10 5NR; 7 pm; L & early evening only; no booking.

Little Bay £28 235

228 Belsize Rd, NW6 7372 4699 1–2B
171 Farringdon Rd, EC1 7278 1234 9–1A
"Its all about the ambience in these eccentric and outlandish theatre-themed bistros (just the right side of tacky)"; the food's not award-winning, but "it's so cheap and excellent for the price, there are never any complaints!" / www.little-bay.co.uk; @TheLittleBay; 11.30 pm, Sun 11 pm; no Amex, NW6 no credit cards.

Little Georgia Café £35 334

14 Barnsbury Rd, N1 7278 6100 8–3D
87 Goldsmiths Row, E2 7739 8154 1–2D
"The unusual combinations of flavours all seem to work", when it comes to the "solid Georgian cooking" at these "very cute" cafés, in Hackney and Islington. / www.littlegeorgia.co.uk; 10 pm.

Little Social W1 £76 333

5 Pollen St 7870 3730 3–2C
The "petite and cosy" style of this Mayfair mews haunt can make it seem a more "easygoing" choice than its showier sibling, Pollen Street Social, opposite; it too serves some "classy" and "clever" cooking, but like other Atherton places is drawing increasing flak for being "overpriced" and "underwhelming". / W1S 1NE; www.littlesocial.co.uk; @_littlesocial; 10.30 pm; closed Sun; set weekday L £48 (FP).

Lobster Pot SE11 £62 433

3 Kennington Ln 7582 5556 1–3C
An "idiosyncratic but charming", family-run stalwart in a "terrible" Kennington location, where you eat surrounded by engagingly "weird" nautical decor ("complete with seagull noises"); the overall effect is "very French", helped by the "splendid", "real" Breton fish and seafood. / SE11 4RG; www.lobsterpotrestaurant.co.uk; 10.30 pm; closed Mon & Sun; booking: max 8.

We've turned our ratings system upside down!

As always Harden's will assess:

F – Food

S – Service

A – Ambience

But now high numbers are better…

5 – Exceptional

4 – Very good

3 – Good

2 – Average

1 – Poor

Locanda Locatelli
Hyatt Regency W1 £78 333
8 Seymour St 7935 9088 2–2A
"Creative and expertly presented cuisine" has long made Giorgio Locatelli's "civilised" Marylebone dining room one of London's better-known Italian destinations; it is "hugely expensive" though, and while it feels "romantic" to some, it's "too corporate" for other tastes. / W1H 7JZ; www.locandalocatelli.com; @LocLocatelli; 11 pm, Thu-Sat 11.30 pm, Sun 10.15 pm; booking: max 8.

Locanda Ottomezzo W8 £67 343
2-4 Thackeray St 7937 2200 5–1B
"An excellent range of food and enthusiastic staff" help win praise for this Kensington Italian, whose "niche-y" interior is "somewhat cramped" but pleasantly "rustic". / W8 5ET; www.locandaottoemezzo.co.uk; 10.30 pm; closed Mon L, Sat L & Sun.

Loch Fyne £45 223
Branches throughout London
"You go knowing what to expect" to this fish and seafood franchise – even if the performance is rather "formulaic", there's "a very good range of options" and for "a decent meal in nice surroundings" it is "unexceptional but reliable". / www.lochfyne-restaurants.com; 10 pm, WC2 10.30 pm.

The Lockhart W1 £56 222
22-24 Seymour Pl 3011 5400 2–2A
"A different style of food for London" – "real American cooking" from the Deep South, served in an increasingly hip corner of Marylebone; fans love the "refined big flavours", but sceptics say dishes can "lack delicious-ness". Top Menu Tip – all agree on one thing: "the corn bread is phenomenal". / W1H 7NL; www.lockhartlondon.com; @LockhartLondon; 10 pm, Sun 3.30 pm; closed Mon & Sun D.

Lola Rojo SW11 £43 434
78 Northcote Rd 7350 2262 10–2C
"A fantastic Spanish spot" in Battersea, with a crisp modern interior, where "excellent tapas are creative yet authentic" and "superb value". / SW11 6QL; www.lolarojo.net; @LolaRojoSW11; 10.30 pm, Sat & Sun 11 pm; no Amex.

London House SW11 £62 332
7-9 Battersea Sq 7592 8545 10–1C
Gordon Ramsay's Battersea yearling splits opinion; fans say it's "an unexpected pleasure" with "stylish" looks and "complex and rich" cuisine – to sceptics though, it's "missing that certain je ne sais quoi". / SW11 3RA; www.gordonramsay.com/london-house; @londonhouse; Tue-Fri 10 pm; closed Mon, Tue L & Wed L.

The Lord Northbrook SE12 £39 444
116 Burnt Ash Rd 8318 1127 1–4D
There's "a great community feel" to this large Lea Green hostelry which "underwent a 1000% makeover a few years ago"; "in an area lacking good eating options", it "always comes up trumps". / SE12 8PU; www.thelordnorthbrook.co.uk; @LordNorthbrook; 9 pm, Fri & Sat 10 pm.

Lorenzo SE19 **£46** 2 2 3
73 Westow Hill 7637 0871 1–4D
This "bustling", Italian local is an Upper Norwood "staple", liked for its "lively" style and "reasonable prices"; food-wise, it "can be disappointing nowadays", but most reports say it's still "reliable". Top Tip – avoid the "crowded and slightly claustrophobic basement". / SE19 1TX; www.lorenzo.uk.com; 10.30 pm.

Luce e Limoni WC1 **£52** 4 4 4
91-93 Gray's Inn Rd 7242 3382 9–1A
"Sister restaurant of nearby Fabrizio" in Bloomsbury, but "quieter" and more "high end"; it's a very solid all-rounder combining "a hugely congenial" interior with "welcoming" service and accomplished Sicilian food at "honest prices". / WC1X 8TX; www.luceelimoni.com; 10 pm, Fri-Sat 11 pm.

Lucio SW3 **£68** 3 3 3
257 Fulham Rd 7823 3007 5–3B
"Lucio is there to greet and meet" at his "friendly" Chelsea Italian, where the food and "excellent" wines are rather toppishly priced but "never fail to deliver". Top Tips – "amazing" pasta, and "incredible value" set lunch. / SW3 6HY; www.luciorestaurant.com; 10.45 pm; set weekday L £38 (FP).

The Lucky Pig Fulham SW6 NEW **£50**
374 North End Rd 7385 1300 5–4A
Regular music is a feature at this slightly glam new bar-cum-restaurant (a spin-off from a Fitzrovia cocktail den), occupying the large site that was once Sugar Hut (long RIP); no feedback yet for a rating. / SW6 1LY; www.theluckypig.co.uk; @LuckyPigFulham; midnight; set weekday L £29 (FP).

Lucky Seven W2 **£35** 3 3 3
127 Westbourne Park Rd 7727 6771 6–1B
Teleport yourself to '50s America at Tom Conran's vintage US diner, on the fringe of Notting Hill; expect to queue and share a booth, but its yummy burgers and shakes "justify the wait". / W2 5QL; www.lucky7london.co.uk; @Lucky7London; 10.15 pm, Sun 10 pm; no Amex; no booking.

Lupita WC2 **£44** 3 3 2
13-15 Villiers St 7930 5355 4–4D
For a "snappy" bite right in the heart of town – an "unpretentious and good value" Mexican, with "unusual" and "authentic" dishes – a "surprise find" in the grungy, touristy environs of Charing Cross station. / WC2N 6ND; www.lupita.co.uk; @LupitaUK; 11 pm, Fri & Sat 11.30 pm, Sun 10 pm.

Luppolo E11 NEW **£32**
34-38 High St 8530 8528 1–2D
Deriving its name from the Italian word for hops – a new Wanstead pizzeria specialising in craft beers, including their own-brand pale ale. / E11 2RJ; www.luppolopizza.com; @LuppoloWanstead; 11 pm, Sun 10.30 pm.

Lure NW5 **£40** 4 3 3
56 Chetwynd Rd 7267 0163 8–1B
"A beautiful range of fish, and some interesting sides" have won instant raves for this Aussie-run, "upmarket chippy with a twist" – "a welcome arrival" to Dartmouth Park. / NW5 1DJ; www.lurefishkitchen.co.uk; 10 pm.

Lurra W1 NEW **£52**

9 Seymour Pl 7724 4545 2–2A

Just as this guide went to the printers, a sister to the highly-esteemed Donostia in Marble Arch opened up nearby, offering food from the 'erretegia' (charcoal and wood grills, traditional to the Basque Country). / W1H 5BA; www.lurra.co.uk; @LurraW1.

Lutyens EC4 **£74** 2 2 2

85 Fleet St 7583 8385 9–2A

As "a very solid business lunch venue", Sir Terence Conran's "smart" City-fringe brasserie is a reasonably "classy" choice; given its "antiseptic" ambience and cuisine that's "OK, but no more", there's no other reason to seek it out. / EC4Y 1AE; www.lutyens-restaurant.com; @LutyensEC4; 9.45 pm; closed Sat & Sun.

Lyle's E1 **£66** 5 5 3

The Tea Building, 56 Shoreditch High St 3011 5911 12–1B

"The food speaks for itself" – "memorable" combinations, sourced "with real care", prepared with "passion" and presented "with a lack of hype" – when you visit this agreeably "austere" and "honest" Shoreditch yearling (founded by alumni of St John). / E1 6JJ; www.lyleslondon.com; @lyleslondon; 10 pm; closed Sat L & Sun.

M Restaurants **£74** 4 3 3

Zig Zag Building, Victoria St, SW1 3327 7770 2–4B NEW

2-3 Threadneedle Walk, EC2 3327 7770 9–2C

Ex-Gaucho supremo, Martin Williams, is the man behind this large, extremely ambitious City entertaining complex, incorporating a sushi-to-ceviche 'Raw' restaurant, alongside a more familiar 'Grill', the latter acclaimed for its formidable selection of steaks; to critics it can all seem "too like Las Vegas", but fans – particularly for a "discreet" business occasion – say it's "wonderful". A Victoria outpost is due to open in November 2015. / www.mrestaurants.co.uk.

Ma Cuisine TW9 **£43** 2 2 2

9 Station Approach 8332 1923 1–3A

"No effort to be modern or fashionable" is a plus-point for fans of this "'70s-style bistro throwback", near Kew Gardens station; sceptics say "it owes its popularity to a lack of local oppo'", but most reporters applaud its "timeless" appeal and "reasonable prices". / TW9 3QB; www.macuisinekew.co.uk; @MaCuisineKew; 10 pm, Fri & Sat 10.30 pm; no Amex.

Ma Goa SW15 **£40** 4 4 2

242-244 Upper Richmond Rd 8780 1767 10–2B

"There's a good reason it's been around for years!" – this family-run, "hidden gem" in Putney has "charming" service and "offbeat Indian home cooking" featuring "distinctly Goan flavours" at "great prices"; it's not quite as highly rated as it once was though. / SW15 6TG; www.ma-goa.com; @magoarestaurant; 10.30 pm, Fri-Sat 11 pm, Sun 10pm.

MacellaioRC SW7 **£52** 5 3 4

84 Old Brompton Rd 7589 5834 5–2B

"Knocking more macho steak houses into a cocked hat" – this offbeat grill occupies an Italian butcher's shop in South Kensington, where "an enthusiastic owner" serves "the best steaks ever", and where the ingenious wine list is arranged according to how rare or well done you like your meat. Staff can be a tad "patronising" though – "Italians who assume we all live on Spam and Sunblest!" / SW7 3LQ; www.macellaiorc.com; @MaxelaUk; 11 pm.

Made In Camden
Roundhouse NW1 **£44** 2 2 2

Chalk Farm Rd 7424 8495 8–2B

"For a casual meal after the Roundhouse (in whose entrance it's located)", this well-designed bar/dining room is ideal; but while its cooking can come as "a pleasant surprise", it's not as highly-rated as once it was. / NW1 8EH; www.madeincamden.com; 10.15 pm.

Made in Italy **£40** 3 3 3

50 James St, W1 7224 0182 3–1A

249 King's Rd, SW3 7352 1880 5–3C

"Excellent pizzas" (served by the metre), "switched on" service and "good VFM" continue to impress at this small Italian chain; as always the "buzzy King's Road classic" is tops (but SW19 also got a thumbs-up this year). / www.madeinitalygroup.co.uk; 11 pm, Sun 10 pm; SW3 closed Mon L.

Madhu's UB1 **£36** 4 3 3

39 South Rd 8574 1897 1–3A

A legendary Southall curry house, whose "minimalist interior makes a refreshing change from typical chintz", and which provides "friendly" service and high-quality cooking; (it's part of an eponymous empire incorporating outside catering, and a branch at the Sheraton Skyline Heathrow). / UB1 1SW; www.madhus.co.uk; 11.30 pm; closed Tue, Sat L & Sun L.

The Magazine Restaurant
Serpentine Gallery W2 **£57** 3 4 5

Kensington Gdns 7298 7552 6–2D

"If you want something a bit different for a romantic meal", Zaha Hadid's "sleek" structure, leafily located in Hyde Park, is "a very pleasant place to eat, drink and while away time", and the food's not bad either. / W2 2AR; www.magazine-restaurant.co.uk; @TheMagazineLDN; Tue & Sun 6 pm, Wed-Sat 10.45 pm; closed Mon, Tue D & Sun D.

Magdalen SE1 **£55** 4 4 3

152 Tooley St 7403 1342 9–4D

"An oasis in a desert of mediocrity around London Bridge" – this "grown up" gem has won a strong following over the years with its "unobtrusive" service, "understated" style, and – last but not least – its "rich and complex" cuisine (emphasising meat and offal), matched with "lovely" wine. / SE1 2TU; www.magdalenrestaurant.co.uk; @Magdalense1; 10 pm; closed Sat L & Sun; set weekday L £37 (FP).

Maggie Jones's W8 £55 2 3 5
6 Old Court Pl 7937 6462 5–1A
With its "intimate wooden booths and rustic fare" (in "hearty portions"), this "quirky" hideaway, near Kensington Palace (named for the pseudonym Princess Margaret used to book under) is "one of the cosiest restaurants in London". It's fair to say, however, that the cooking is a little "'70s-bistro… and that's not a compliment".
/ W8 4PL; www.maggie-jones.co.uk; 11 pm, Sun 10.30 pm.

Maguro W9 £38 3 4 3
5 Lanark Pl 7289 4353 8–4A
A "tiny" Maida Vale Japanese, serving "delicious" sushi and other fare; "it's clearly doing something right as it's always busy and buzzy".
/ W9 1BT; www.maguro-restaurant.com; 11 pm, Sun 10.30 pm; no Amex.

Maison Bertaux W1 £16 4 2 3
28 Greek St 7437 6007 4–2A
"So oblivious of trends and fashions"; "there's nowhere else like" this "eccentric" Soho treasure (est 1871) – "just a great place to sit for a really good, big cup of black coffee and a croissant or cake".
/ W1D 5DQ; www.maisonbertaux.com; @Maison_Bertaux; 10.15 pm, Sun 8 pm.

Malabar W8 £42 4 4 2
27 Uxbridge St 7727 8800 6–2B
"Going great guns after over 25 years" – this curry house just off Notting Hill Gate is "a neighbourhood classic", and, though its "graceful", "modern" decor is a tad "soulless", service is "charming" and the cooking is "very strong". / W8 7TQ; www.malabar-restaurant.co.uk; 11.30 pm.

Malabar Junction WC1 £41 3 4 3
107 Gt Russell St 7580 5230 2–1C
"Don't be fooled by the modest entrance" if you seek out this calming Keralan, near the British Museum – even those who find the interior "hotel-y" approve of its "very attentive" service and high-quality South Indian fare. / WC1B 3NA; www.malabarjunction.com; 11 pm.

Mamma Dough £28 3 3 3
76-78 Honor Oak Pk, SE23 8699 5196 1–4D NEW
354 Coldharbour Ln, SW9 7095 1491 10–1D NEW
The Honor Oak Park original may be "overrun by children with beardy fathers – but the pizzas make it worth it!", as do the "brilliant staff"; a Brixton branch opened in September 2015.

Mandalay W2 £30 2 2 1
444 Edgware Rd 7258 3696 8–4A
"Scuzzy in looks, but packed for a reason!" – the Ally family's "small and friendly" shop-conversion, near Edgware Road tube still draws a crowd thanks to its "fresh and inexpensive" Burmese chow (think Indian meets Chinese). / W2 1EG; www.mandalayway.com; 10.30 pm; closed Sun.

Mandarin Kitchen W2 £41 4 2 2
14-16 Queensway 7727 9012 6–2C
"Very busy" and "very crowded" Bayswater Chinese, famous for its seafood, and in particular its "succulent" lobster noodles; what a loss though – the hilariously bad decor "had a bit of a spruce up" this year. / W2 3RX; 11.15 pm.

Mangal 1 E8 £31 544

10 Arcola St 7275 8981 1–1C

"The smell alone gets my vote!" – "the huge, roaring furnace of a charcoal grill" produces some of London's best kebabs at this "consistently brilliant" Turk, which was a cheap 'n' cheerful, cross-town destination long before Dalston was trendy; "BYO is a bonus". / E8 2DJ; www.mangal1.com; @Mangalone; midnight, Sat & Sun 1 am; no credit cards.

Mangal II N16 £35 432

4 Stoke Newington Rd 7254 7888 1–1C

Although less acclaimed than the nearby original, this Dalston spin-off "continues to excel in Turkish grills and salads in an area with many competitors" – "it is what it is, but it's always fun, always consistent". / N16 8BH; www.mangal2.com; 1 am, Sun midnight.

Manicomio £60 223

85 Duke of York Sq, SW3 7730 3366 5–2D

6 Gutter Ln, EC2 7726 5010 9–2B

"The best al-fresco dining" – particularly at SW3 – is a major boost to the popularity of these "safe, if pretty unremarkable" Italians, ideal for a light lunch over business (in the City) or "as a hideaway for a break from shopping" (in Chelsea). / www.manicomio.co.uk; SW3 10.30 pm, Sun 10 pm; EC2 10 pm; EC2 closed Sat & Sun.

Manna NW3 £57 332

4 Erskine Rd 7722 8028 8–3B

The UK's oldest veggie is an obscure little café in Primrose Hill; reports from its tiny fan club are all upbeat though – they say it's "enjoying a new lease of life", with "great vegan dishes". / NW3 3AJ; www.mannav.com; @mannacuisine; 10 pm; closed Mon.

The Manor SW4 £57 543

148 Clapham Manor St 7720 4662 10–2D

With the opening of this "stellar" new sibling to the nearby Dairy, this "underwhelming corner of Clapham" now has two stand-out venues; "genuinely passionate" staff provide "terrific" small plates that are "ingenious without being daft" in a "designer-grungy" setting. Top Menu Tip – "incredible tasting menu here" too. / SW4 6BS; www.themanorclapham.co.uk; @TheManorClapham; 10 pm, Sun 4pm.

Manuka Kitchen SW6 £45 444

510 Fulham Rd 7736 7588 5–4A

With its "concise but perfect" wine list, "exceptional quality" menu and overall "incredible value", this "tiny" New Zealand-inspired two-year-old in Fulham is already a firm favourite, with brunch a particular highlight; don't forget to check out the downstairs gin bar. / SW6 5NJ; www.manukakitchen.co.uk; @ManukaKitchen; 11 pm, Sun 5 pm.

Mar I Terra SE1 £31 232

14 Gambia St 7928 7628 9–4A

"A very unpretentious, friendly and reliable, hidden-away Spanish place", near Southwark tube, praised for its "authentic", if "basic", tapas and other fare. / SE1 0XH; www.mariterra.co.uk; 11 pm; closed Sat L & Sun.

Marcus
The Berkeley SW1 £118 2 3 2
Wilton Pl 7235 1200 5–1D
Since its March 2014 refit, Marcus Wareing's celebrated Knightsbridge chamber has lost its momentum. Fans do still extol a "completely fabulous" experience with "cracking" cuisine, but even they often note how "expensive" it is. And there are now far too many critics – citing a "pompous" approach and cooking "lacking wow factor" – who say its prices are plain "outrageous". / SW1X 7RL; www.marcus-wareing.com; @Marcussw1; 10.45 pm; closed Sun; no jeans or trainers; booking: max 8; set weekday L £82 (FP).

Margaux SW5 £64 3 2 3
152 Old Brompton Rd 7373 5753 5–2B
"A good addition to Earl's Court" – a "bare-brick" local yearling, with "delicious" cooking and an enjoyable wine selection. See also Bandol. / SW5 0BE; www.barmargaux.co.uk; @BarMargaux; 11 pm, Sun 10 pm.

Mari Vanna SW1 £70 2 3 4
116 Knightsbridge 7225 3122 5–1D
"The splendid recreation of a Russian interior" ("like your rich grandma's beautiful dacha") is a highpoint of this luxurious Knightsbridge haunt; the "very expensive" Russian scoff is middling, but "add vodka in all its varieties" and the experience can be "fun". / SW1X 7PJ; www.marivanna.co.uk; @marivannalondon; 11.30 pm.

Marianne W2 £122 4 5 4
104 Chepstow Rd 3675 7750 6–1B
Marianne Lumb's "tiny treasure" (just 14 covers) in Bayswater is "an absolute joy that's worth every penny!", with "passionate" personal service, and "confident", "exquisite" cooking, which create a "wonderfully intimate" experience; "it's easier to get into Downing Street than to reserve" though. / W2 5QS; www.mariannerestaurant.com; @Marianne_W2; 11 pm; closed Mon.

Market NW1 £50 3 3 2
43 Parkway 7267 9700 8–3B
"We envy the locals!", say further-afield fans of this well-established brasserie in the centre of Camden Town; "the tables are almost on top of one another", but it's "buzzy and fun", and the cooking's "really good, honest fare". / NW1 7PN; www.marketrestaurant.co.uk; @MarketCamden; 10.30 pm, Sun 3 pm; closed Sun D; set weekday L £30 (FP).

The Marksman E2 NEW £50
254 Hackney Rd 7739 7393 1–2D
There's some pedigree behind this freshly refitted and relaunched Hackney pub with Tom Harris and Jon Rotheram – alumni of the St John Hotel, Nobu and Fifteen – at the helm; we await the survey, for a full report next year. / E2 7SJ; www.marksmanpub.com; @marksman_pub; midnight, Sun 11 pm.

F S A

Maroush £53 322

I) 21 Edgware Rd, W2 7723 0773 6–1D
II) 38 Beauchamp Pl, SW3 7581 5434 5–1C
V) 3-4 Vere St, W1 7493 5050 3–1B
VI) 68 Edgware Rd, W2 7224 9339 6–1D
'Garden') 1 Connaught St, W2 7262 0222 6–1D

"Consistent quality over numerous years" has won a big following for this well-known Lebanese chain, some of whose branches (I & II) have bustling café/take-aways alongside more serious restaurants; especially at the latter however, "the decor could be fresher". Top Menu Tip – in the cafés, if you're on a budget, ask for the menu of wraps. / www.maroush.com; most branches close between 12.30 am-5 am.

Masala Grill SW10 NEW £54 444

535 King's Rd 7351 7788 5–4B

Though in a simpler vein, "standards are being maintained at the former Chutney Mary"; this new Indian (same owners) offers "a different slant to the original on the site" but is "very professional" with some "excellent and unusual" dishes. / SW10 0SZ; www.masalagrill.co.

Masala Zone £32 233

Branches throughout London

"For a quick, cheap 'n' cheerful meal", this "bustling", "interestingly decorated", Indian-street-food chain is just the job, with its "good-value thalis" and other "simple" fare; WC2 in particular is "ideal pre-theatre". / www.realindianfood.com; 11 pm, Sun 10.30 pm; no Amex; booking: min 10.

MASH Steakhouse W1 £83 221

77 Brewer St 7734 2608 3–2D

No-one doubts the quality of the meat at this "swanky" steakhouse, "deep underground" near Piccadilly Circus; it's so "overpriced" it can seem "average" however, and the "cavernous" interior is "too large" and "brash". / W1F 9ZN; www.mashsteak.co.uk; @mashsteaklondon; 11.30 pm, Sun 11 pm; closed Sun L.

Massimo
Corinthia Hotel WC2 £76 243

10 Northumberland Ave 7998 0555 2–3D

Few chambers boast such dazzlingly OTT decor as this luxurious five-star dining room, near Embankment tube; its "high-end Italian fare" has always struggled to find a constituency, but fans say "the pre-theatre meal is a great experience". / WC2N 5AE; www.corinthia.com; @massimorest; 10.45 pm; closed Sun; set weekday L £55 (FP).

Masters Super Fish SE1 £25 422

191 Waterloo Rd 7928 6924 9–4A

"Queues of parked cabs while drivers grab a refuel say all you need to know" about the "terrific" fish 'n' chips at this "basic" SE1 pit-stop – "the wonderfully light batter and perfectly crispy chips are a thing of joy, while the mustard-crust option is ideal for carb-avoiders". / SE1 8UX; @MSuperfish; 10.30 pm; closed Sun; no Amex; no booking, Fri D.

Matsuba TW9 £46 443
10 Red Lion St 8605 3513 1–4A
"A small room" hosts this "independent Japanese" on the fringes of Richmond town centre; its sushi and other Japanese/Korean fare is "decent rather than great", but there's no doubting that it's "a real treat for the 'burbs". / TW9 1RW; www.matsuba-restaurant.com; @matsuba; 10.30 pm; closed Sun.

Matsuri SW1 £85 331
15 Bury St 7839 1101 3–3D
"Great teppanyaki in the traditional style" is an "entertaining experience" (especially for a business occasion) at this pricey St James's Japanese; not so the "drab" interior however. / SW1Y 6AL; www.matsuri-restaurant.com; @MatsuriJ; 10.30 pm, Sun 10 pm.

Max's Sandwich Shop N4 NEW £20 422
19 Crouch Hill awaiting tel 1–1C
Not your traditional sandwich shop; this Crouch Hill creation serves hot sarnies and boozy cocktails till midnight – "not flashy, but highly underrated!". / N4 4AP; @lunchluncheon; 11 pm, Sun 6 pm.

Mayfair Pizza Company W1 NEW £47 334
4 Lancashire Ct 7629 2889 3–2B
"Tucked away" in a cute enclave off Bond Street, a "lovely pizza spot" (formerly a branch of Rocket) that's "consistently good value for Mayfair". / W1S 1EY; www.mayfairpizzaco.com; 11 pm.

maze W1 £84 222
10-13 Grosvenor Sq 7107 0000 3–2A
It seems a long time since this Gordon Ramsay operation in Mayfair was the talk of the town; fans do still proclaim its "well-executed fusion combinations", but oftentimes reporters think it's borderline "awful", and "hugely overpriced". / W1K 6JP; www.gordonramsay.com/maze; @mazerestaurant; 11 pm; set always available £56 (FP).

maze Grill W1 £76 222
10-13 Grosvenor Sq 7495 2211 3–2A
Gordon Ramsay's Mayfair grill room is a shadow of its former self nowadays, attracting few and mixed reports; but while too many critics still gripe about the cooking ("rubbish") or the prices ("really??!!"), more positive types say its steaks and sides are "reliably good" and that it makes "a discreet venue for business". / W1K 6JP; www.gordonramsay.com; @mazegrill; 11 pm; no shorts; set always available £50 (FP).

maze Grill SW10 £74 222
11 Park Wk 7255 9299 5–3B
Gordon Ramsay's return to the Chelsea site where he earnt his stripes (when it was Aubergine) – a new offshoot of his maze brand – is a bit of a damp squib; fans do say it's "lovely", with "excellent steak", but feedback is muted, and even supporters say "it's highly priced for what's only good execution". / SW10 0AJ; www.gordonramsay.com/mazegrill/park-walk; @mazegrill; 11 pm; set always available £47 (FP).

Mazi W8 **£62** 3 3 4

12-14 Hillgate St 7229 3794 6–2B

"Sophisticated Greek-inspired cooking with a twist" has won quite a fan club for this "cheap 'n' cheerful" (quite cramped) two-year-old, off Notting Hill Gate. / W8 7SR; www.mazi.co.uk; @mazinottinghill; 10.30 pm; closed Mon L & Tue L; set weekday L £34 (FP).

Meat Mission N1 **£33** 3 3 4

14-15 Hoxton Mkt 7739 8212 12–1B

"When a dirty burger is required", you're "up to your elbows in deliciousness" at this "cracking" Hoxton Square operation (part of the 'Meat' franchise); it's "fun" (if "noisy") too. / N1 6HG; www.meatmission.com; @MEATmission; midnight, Sun 10 pm.

MEATLiquor **£38** 3 2 4

74 Welbeck St, W1 7224 4239 3–1B

133b Upper St, N1 awaiting tel 8–3D NEW

The self-consciously "dingy", "so-loud" vibe – "like a cross between a biker bar and a branch of Hollisters" – underpins the "hip" appeal of these notorious dives; "the long queues are justified" though for a fix of the "brill cocktails", "lovely dirty burgers" and other cholesterol-laden treats.

MEATmarket WC2 **£30** 4 2 2

Jubilee Market Hall, 1 Tavistock Ct 7836 2139 4–3D

"Forget the fakery of crinkly sided food trucks with old Etonian owners" – for "a rough and ready, but brilliant burger", this "honest" Covent Garden joint makes a superb "guilty treat"; "great rum cocktails too". / WC2E 8BD; www.themeatmarket.co.uk; @MEATLiquor; midnight, Sun 10 pm; no Amex.

Mediterraneo W11 **£60** 3 3 4

37 Kensington Park Rd 7792 3131 6–1A

Even devotees concede this "long-time favourite" in Notting Hill is "a bit dear for a local", but they say it's "worth it" thanks to its "warm, lively and intimate" atmosphere, and "traditional Italian fare that's very well done". / W11 2EU; www.mediterraneo-restaurant.co.uk; 11.30 pm, Sun 10.30 pm; booking: max 10.

Medlar SW10 **£71** 4 4 3

438 King's Rd 7349 1900 5–3B

"Well-hidden in the red-trouser-wearing Chelsea hinterlands", this unexpectedly accomplished neighbourhood spot (run by some alumni of Chez Bruce) has won an impressive fan club. Perhaps the interior is a tad "subdued", but staff are "incredibly friendly and efficient", the "sensitive" cooking is "stunning", and there's a "remarkably varied" wine list. Top Tip – "amazing value lunch". / SW10 0LJ; www.medlarrestaurant.co.uk; @medlarchelsea; 10.30 pm; set weekday L £51 (FP).

Megan's **£45** 2 2 4

571 Kings Rd, SW6 7371 7837 5–4A

120 St John's Wood High St, NW8 7183 3138 8–3A

"The enchanting, tucked-away covered garden keeps us going back for more", but the provisions at this Chelsea neighbourhood haunt – which now also has a very cute St John's Wood spin off – has "lost a little sparkle since its change of management". / www.megans.co.uk.

Mele e Pere W1 **£50** 3 3 3

46 Brewer St 7096 2096 3–2D

"Why is it not more popular?"; this (slightly "dull-looking") Soho basement is "worth knowing about in this bit of town" – the food's "reliable" and "reasonably priced" and it's "noisy" but "great fun". Top Menu Tips – "to-die-for gelatos", "Prosecco on tap", and an interesting list of vermouths. / W1F 9TF; www.meleepere.co.uk; @meleEpere; 11 pm; set weekday L £31 (FP).

The Melt Room W1 NEW **£18**

26 Noel St 7096 2002 3–1D

Single concept restaurants are all the rage, but perhaps we have reached the fashion's ne plus ultra with this May 2015 Soho arrival? – a restaurant dedicated to the art of the cheese toastie! / W1F 8GY; www.meltroom.com; @melt_room; 9 pm, Sun 6.30 pm.

Menier Chocolate Factory SE1 **£52** 1 2 3

51-53 Southwark St 7234 9610 9–4B

"Excellent-value, meal-and-show ticket deals" are the way to go at this intriguing South Bank venue, which combines a restaurant and small theatre; otherwise "you wouldn't make the trip" for its "no-frills" fodder from a "limited" menu. / SE1 1RU; www.menierchocolatefactory.com; @MenChocFactory; 11 pm; closed Mon & Sun D.

The Mercer EC2 **£62** 2 2 2

34 Threadneedle St 7628 0001 9–2C

"There's elbow room to talk shop" at this "airy", City "staple" – a converted banking hall, in the heart of the Square Mile, with a "very strong business clientele"; its ratings have drifted though – the "broadly British" food is "OK, but nothing special", and service "patchy at times". / EC2R 8AY; www.themercer.co.uk; 9.30 pm; closed Sat & Sun.

Merchants Tavern EC2 **£58** 3 3 4

36 Charlotte Rd 7060 5335 12–1B

Angela Hartnett's "superbly buzzy and attractive" Shoreditch two-year-old – complete with large open kitchen – continues to draw enthusiastic praise for its "relaxed" vibe and "unpretentious and delicious" (if sometimes "variable") cooking. Top Tip – superior quick bites in the front bar. / EC2A 3PG; www.merchantstavern.co.uk; @merchantstavern; 11 pm, Sun 9 pm; set weekday L £38 (FP), set Sun L £43 (FP).

Le Mercury N1 **£32** 2 3 4

154-155 Upper St 7704 8516 8–2D

"No frills", but "cosy" bistro that's been a "cheap 'n' cheerful" Islington institution for as long as most people can remember; the scoff is only "standard French fare", but "for the price you can't beat it". / N1 1QY; www.lemercury.co.uk; @Le_Mercury; 12 pm, Sun 11 pm; Mon-Thu D only, Fri-Sun open L & D.

Meson don Felipe SE1 **£40** 2 2 3

53 The Cut 7928 3237 9–4A

A "very old-school, and over-crowded tapas bar, with haphazard service"; "excellent, keenly-priced wines" add to an overall effect that's surprisingly pleasing (especially when the Flamenco guitarist is playing) and it's "a really fun place to eat around a show at the Old Vic". / SE1 8LF; www.mesondonfelipe.com; @MesonDonFelipe1; 11 pm; closed Sun; no Amex; no booking at D.

Mews of Mayfair W1 £68 2 3 4

10 Lancashire Ct, New Bond St 7518 9388 3–2B

Luscious cocktails fuel the "great buzz" at this well-located Mayfair haunt, tucked-away just off Bond Street, and with "lovely outside tables in summer"; the food though is "pretty average" and (unless you go on an offer) "pricey" too. / W1S 1EY; www.mewsofmayfair.com; @mewsofmayfair; 10.45 pm; closed Sun D; SRA-3.*

Meza £30 5 3 2

34 Trinity Rd, SW17 0772 211 1299 10–2C

70 Mitcham Rd, SW17 8672 2131 10–2C

"The cat is well and truly out of the bag on this one!" – this "teeny-tiny" Tooting Lebanese is permanently "full to bursting" thanks to its "hospitable" style, and "simple", but "unfailingly good", mezze and other "delicious" fare at "startlingly cheap" prices. There's now a second site nearby.

Michael Nadra £57 4 3 2

6-8 Elliott Rd, W4 8742 0766 7–2A

42 Gloucester Ave, NW1 7722 2800 8–2B

Michael Nadra's "first class" modern French cuisine wins high acclaim for both his very "cramped" Chiswick original, and also for his cavernous two-year-old spin-off in Camden Town; NW1 isn't quite as well-rated or well-known as W4, but more worth knowing about in the locale. / www.restaurant-michaelnadra.co.uk; @michaelnadra; W4 10 pm, Fri-Sat 10.30 pm, NW1 10.30 pm, Sun 9 pm; NW1 closed Mon, W4 closed Sun.

Mien Tay £31 3 1 1

180 Lavender Hill, SW11 7350 0721 10–1C

122 Kingsland Rd, E2 7729 3074 12–1B

"Massive bowls of pho and two can eat until stuffed for about £20" – that's the attraction of these "busy and buzzy" pitstops in Battersea and Shoreditch; the trade-offs are "shabby" decor and "perfunctory" service. / 11 pm, Fri & Sat 11.30 pm, Sun 10.30 pm; cash only.

Mildreds W1 £42 3 3 2

45 Lexington St 7494 1634 3–2D

"Reliable", "buzzy" veggie canteen that's something of a Soho institution; it serves "hearty food that really fills you up", "if you don't mind a queue..." / W1F 9AN; www.mildreds.co.uk; @mildredssoho; 10.45 pm; closed Sun; no Amex; no booking.

Milk SW12 £14 4 4 4

20 Bedford Hill 8772 9085 10–2C

"So lucky to have this great independent in Balham" – a "little (and I do mean little)" caff serving "amazing coffee and inspirational all-day brunch"; "you inevitably queue, but it's worth the wait". / SW12 9RG; www.milk.london.

Mill Lane Bistro NW6 £53 2 3 2

77 Mill Ln 7794 5577 1–1B

Mixed reports of late on this "little bit of France in West Hampstead", whose repertoire includes "Full French Breakfast"; to many it's still "an all-round great local", but a worrying number this year were "totally underwhelmed". / NW6 1NB; www.milllanebistro.com; @millanebistro; 10 pm; closed Mon & Sun D; no Amex.

Min Jiang
The Royal Garden Hotel W8 **£77** 4 3 5
2-24 Kensington High St 7361 1988 5–1A
"Peking duck to die for", "fantastic dim sum", and "a superb panorama as a bonus" – that's the "rare combination" at this 8th-floor dining room overlooking Kensington Gardens, which – as one of London's top Chinese destinations – breaks all the rules for rooms with a view. / W8 4PT; www.minjiang.co.uk; @royalgdnhotel; 10 pm.

Mint Leaf **£51** 3 3 2
Suffolk Pl, Haymarket, SW1 7930 9020 2–2C
Angel Ct, Lothbury, EC2 7600 0992 9–2C
The low profile of these designer Indians – in a "dim-lit" basement near Trafalgar Square, and near Bank – is at odds with the big sums lavished on their slick decor; feedback is thin but upbeat – the food's "not cheap" but "very well prepared", and they serve "great bar snacks along with full meals". / www.mintleafrestaurant.com; SW1 11 pm, Sun 10.30 pm – EC2 10.30 pm; SW1 closed Sat & Sun L, EC2 closed Sat & Sun.

Mirch Masala SW17 **£25** 5 2 1
213 Upper Tooting Rd 8767 8638 10–2D
"You get no pretentions, just great flavours" at this "high turnover", "café-style Pakistani" in Tooting, serving "really tasty food at incredible prices". / SW17 7TG; www.mirchmasalarestaurant.co.uk; midnight; no credit cards.

Mishkin's WC2 **£43** 1 2 3
25 Catherine St 7240 2078 4–3D
"They wouldn't know their challah from their cholent" at Russell Norman's "trendy" Covent Garden diner; admittedly "it's no small trick making Jewish food cool", but its "deli treats" are "lacklustre" and "couldn't be much less authentic". / WC2B 5JS; www.mishkins.co.uk; @MishkinsWC2; 11.15 pm, Sun 10.15 pm.

Mission E2 NEW **£55** 2 3 4
250 Paradise Row 7613 0478 12–1D
"What a list! What a venue!" – the team behind Sager + Wilde have created a "fantastic" new space, in this Bethnal Green railway arch, where the focus is on a "brilliant and interesting wine selection" dominated by Californian vintages; the sharing plates? – a mite "unremarkable". / E2 9LE; missione2.com; @mission-e2; midnight.

The Modern Pantry **£58** 3 3 4
47-48 St Johns Sq, EC1 7553 9210 9–1A
14 Finsbury Sq, EC2 7553 9210 12–2A NEW
"You could be in Sydney", say fans of the "exciting combinations" at Anna Hansen's foodie hotspot in Clerkenwell, known particularly as a top brunch destination; critics complain of "bland" results though, and say the interior's "not the most luxurious". New City-fringe branch opened in September 2015. / www.themodernpantry.co.uk; @TheModernPantry; SRA-3.*

MOMMI SW4 NEW **£39**
44 Clapham High St 3814 1818 10–2D
Another Japanese–South American fusion hang-out, this time in Clapham; it opened too late for our survey, but apparently marries the 'vibrancy of Miami and the eclecticism of Venice Beach'. / SW4 7UR; www.wearemommi.com; @wearemommi; 11 pm, Thu-Sun midnight.

Momo W1 £69 2 2 3

25 Heddon St 7434 4040 3–2C

"Lovely" (if "loud and squashed") souk-style, glam-crowd, party-Moroccan, off Regent Street, with a vibey basement bar, and "great summer terrace"; service is very "variable" however, and the food is "totally overpriced" and "just not worth it..." / W1B 4BH; www.momoresto.com; @momoresto; 11.30 pm, Sun 11 pm.

Mon Plaisir WC2 £59 2 2 4

19-21 Monmouth St 7836 7243 4–2B

This "delightful" 70-year-old, Gallic veteran in Covent Garden, is "a staunch friend" to its big, devoted following; especially compared with yesteryear however, the "classic" brasserie fare is "never going to set the world alight", but it's certainly still "good value pre-theatre". / WC2H 9DD; www.monplaisir.co.uk; @MonPlaisir4; 11 pm; closed Sun; set pre-theatre £32 (FP), set weekday L £33 (FP).

Mona Lisa SW10 £28 3 3 2

417 King's Rd 7376 5447 5–3B

"It's cheap as chips, so long as you don't stray from the set offer", at this veteran World's End greasy spoon, whose ace three-courses-for-a-tenner evening deal draws in a 'dukes-to-dustmen' clientele. / SW10 0LR; 11 pm, Sun 5.30 pm; closed Sun D; no Amex.

Monmouth Coffee Company £12 5 5 4

27 Monmouth St, WC2 7232 3010 4–2B

Arches Northside, Dockley Rd, SE16 7232 3010 9–4D

2 Park St, SE1 7232 3010 9–4C

The coffee is "a miracle" – and "there's a wonderful range" too (plus "super" pastries, and at SE1 "fabulous bread 'n' jam") – at these "totally friendly", if "crowded" communal café-classics. / www.monmouthcoffee.co.uk; 6 pm-6.30 pm, SE16 12 pm; closed Sun; SE16 open Sat only; no Amex; no booking.

Morada Brindisa Asador W1 NEW £43 2 2 4

18-20 Rupert St 7478 8758 4–3A

Opinions split on this "ambitious" (and pricey) new Hispanic venture, just off Shaftesbury Avenue, with its "huge central bar". To fans it's "a triumphant opening" with "wonderful BBQ meats and fish" ("the roasted whole leg of suckling pig is quite a centrepiece"), plus "super sherries and wines". "Ragged" service is a repeat complaint however, as is "unexciting" results. / W1D 6DE; www.brindisatapaskitchens.com/morada; @Brindisa.

Morden & Lea W1 NEW £43

17 Wardour St 3764 2277 4–3A

Ex-Ramsay henchman, Mark Sargeant, is the driving force behind this two-floor Soho newcomer (ground floor, sharing plates – upstairs, proper dining room), whose staid, trad' looks (lots of leather and Farrow & Ball) might seem more at home in Bath than just by Chinatown; no feedback yet for a rating. / W1D 6PJ; www.mordenandlea.com; @MordenAndLea; 11 pm, Sun 10 pm.

Morelli's Gelato WC2 NEW £22

20a The Piazza, The Mkt 07479 856889 4–3D

Surprisingly few mentions for this recent addition to Covent Garden Market – an outpost of a much-loved Broadstairs ice cream institution (est 1932); as well as gelato you'll find prosecco and coffee. / WC2 8RB; @morellisgelato; 8 pm.

The Morgan Arms E3 £50 433

43 Morgan St 8980 6389 1–2D

After a recent update, locals feel this "brilliant" Mile End gastropub is "coming back" into its own – the grub is "about as good as it gets", and at "reasonable" prices too. / E3 5AA; www.morganarmsbo.com; @TheMorganArms; 10 pm.

Morito EC1 £36 432

32 Exmouth Mkt 7278 7007 9–1A

"If you're looking for a not-too-pricey quality bite", try to grab one of the "small stools" at Moro's "buzzy" little sister – it's a bit "cramped and uncomfortable", but the tapas are "truly scrumptious". / EC1R 4QE; www.morito.co.uk; @moritotapas; 11 pm, Sun 4 pm; closed Sun D; no Amex; no booking at D.

MORO EC1 £60 543

34-36 Exmouth Mkt 7833 8336 9–1A

"Amazingly consistent over the years, and still in a league of its own" – this "mad busy", but "laid back and friendly" Exmouth Market favourite "still retains its zing", serving "inventive riffs on Spanish/North African dishes" showcasing "clear, clean flavours", and "an exciting wine list" that's "particularly strong on sherries"; "it's still too noisy", though. / EC1R 4QE; www.moro.co.uk; @RestaurantMoro ; 10.30 pm; closed Sun D.

Motcombs SW1 £62 233

26 Motcomb St 7235 6382 5–1D

"You will meet interesting rogues and nobs mixing happily together in the upstairs wine bar, before winding your way downstairs to the 'serious' restaurant below", at this long-established Belgravia den; food-wise it's "very reliable, but never exceptional". / SW1X 8JU; www.motcombs.co.uk; @Motcombs; 11 pm; closed Sun D.

Moti Mahal WC2 £65 332

45 Gt Queen St 7240 9329 4–2D

A "classic West End Indian" on the fringe of Covent Garden that's part of a Delhi-based chain; its cooking "doesn't quite blow the lights out, but is reliably interesting". / WC2B 5AA; www.motimahal-uk.com; @motimahal59; 10.45 pm; closed Sat L & Sun.

Mr Chow SW1 £86 333

151 Knightsbridge 7589 7347 5–1D

Still inspiring loyalty after nearly 50 years, this once-glamorous Knightsbridge haunt pleases its dedicated fan club; whether it's still truly, as some suggest, "a place to be seen" is very debatable, but its "very expensive" Chinese fare remains solidly rated. / SW1X 7PA; www.mrchow.com; @MRCHOW; midnight; closed Mon L.

Murakami WC2 NEW £45

63-66 St Martin's Ln 3417 6966 4–3B

A big, Japanese newcomer in Covent Garden, offering a wide menu incorporating sushi, sashimi and robata-grilled meats; limited feedback so far (but all upbeat). / WC2N 4JS; www.murakami-london.co.uk; @hello_murakami; 10.30 pm.

Murano W1 £95 333

20-22 Queen St 7495 1127 3–3B

Angela Hartnett's "quietly sophisticated" Mayfair flagship is a "classy" mix of "sleek" (slightly anonymous) decor and "superb" cuisine (that's "not really that Italian"); its ratings were hit this year however, by incidents of "inattentive" cooking and "disinterested" service. / W1J 5PP; www.muranolondon.com; @muranolondon; 11 pm; closed Sun; set weekday L £57 (FP).

Namaaste Kitchen NW1 £44 442

64 Parkway 7485 5977 8–3B

A comfortable, Camden Town curry house that's consistently well-rated for its "excellent and different modern Indian cooking". / NW1 7AH; www.namaastekitchen.co.uk; @NamaasteKitchen; 11 pm.

The Narrow E14 £50 113

44 Narrow St 7592 7950 11–1B

Gordon Ramsay, please either ditch or sort out this under-performing Limehouse pub – with its "laid-back" style and smashing views from the conservatory, it could be a Docklands destination, but too often its standards are "truly dreadful". / E14 8DP; www.gordonramsay.com/thenarrow/; @thenarrow; 10.30 pm, Sun 8 pm.

The National Dining Rooms National Gallery WC2 £51 113

Sainsbury Wing, Trafalgar Sq 7747 2525 2–2C

"Lovely space, shame about the food!"; as "a convenient option for a light bite", this attractive dining room "overlooking bustling Trafalgar Square" would be ideal... were it not for Peyton & Byrne's "atrocious" service and inept catering. / WC2N 5DN; www.thenationaldiningrooms.co.uk; @PeytonandByrne; 5 pm, Fri 8.30 pm; Sat-Thu closed D, Fri open L & D; no Amex.

Naughty Piglets SW2 NEW £46 452

28 Brixton Water Ln 7274 7796 10–2D

A "lovely new local" in the "unpromising area between Brixton and Herne Hill" featuring "amazing wine options" (many of them "natural and unusual"); "it's the sort of place you want to do well", with "ultra-charming" service and "simple" tapas. / SW2 1PE; www.naughtypiglets.co.uk; 11 pm, Sun 4 pm.

Nautilus NW6 £41 441

27-29 Fortune Green Rd 7435 2532 1–1B

"The matzo meal batter is so light and the fish always so über fresh" that it's inevitably a delight to visit this "truly excellent" – if "basic and functional" – West Hampstead chippy. / NW6 1DU; 10 pm; closed Sun; no Amex.

Nayaab SW6 £36 432

309 New King's Rd 7731 6993 10–1B

"Proper Indian cooking from a wide-ranging menu" wins high praise for this well-established Punjabi, near Parsons Green. / SW6 4RF; 11 pm.

Needoo E1 £28 422

87 New Rd 7247 0648 12–2D

"You could walk past it and not look twice", but this East End Pakistani (somewhat eclipsed by its near neighbour Tayyabs) offers "cheap 'n' cheerful meals in abundance" – "great, simple curries" and magnificent lamb chops. / E1 1HH; www.needoogrill.co.uk; @NeedooGrill; 11.30 pm.

New Mayflower W1 £42 322
68-70 Shaftesbury Ave 7734 9207 4–3A
"You don't go for the average service or ambience", but for the "reliably good Cantonese/Peking cuisine" offered by this "reliable" Chinatown stalwart, which serves well into the wee hours of early morning. / W1D 6LY; www.newmayflowerlondon.com; 4 am; D only; no Amex.

New Street Grill EC2 £59 233
16a New St 3503 0785 9–2D
D&D London's spacious, characterful and well-appointed warehouse conversion near Liverpool Street is primarily tipped for business occasions; but while fans applaud its "excellent" steaks, its ratings are held back by a minority who find the whole package "expensive" and "unimpressive". / EC2M 4TR; www.newstreetgrill.co.uk; @newstreetgrill; 10.30 pm; closed Sun D.

New World W1 £38 323
1 Gerrard Pl 7434 2508 4–3A
"Old-school Hong Kong dim sum on a trolley – the only way to have it!"; "be prepared to queue" for this massive Chinatown landmark – "there are classier restaurants by far", but "the fun factor of the circulating food makes the experience". / W1D 5PA; www.newworldlondon.com; 11.30 pm, Sun 11 pm.

The Newman Arms W1 £46
Rathbone St 3643 6285 3–1A
Apparently Orwell's 'proles pub' in 1984, this old Fitzrovian boozer was taken over by the owner of The Cornwall Project, Matt Chatfield, too late for significant survey feedback; enthusiastic early press reports on its farm-to-fork approach (with the aim of 'providing the freshest Cornish fish and veg'). / W1T 1NG; www.newmanarms.co.uk; @NewmanArmsPub; 11 pm.

Newman Street Tavern W1 £45 334
48 Newman St 3667 1445 3–1D
It's "under-appreciated", say fans of this "classic gastropub" in Marylebone, applauded for its "grown-up" cooking – with a strong emphasis on "always being fresh and seasonal" – and "genial" style. / W1T 1QQ; www.newmanstreettavern.co.uk; @NewmanStTavern; 10.30 pm; closed Sun D; SRA-2.*

Nobu
Metropolitan Hotel W1 £90 332
19 Old Park Ln 7447 4747 3–4A
"Still doing amazing sushi… still incredibly expensive" – London's original Japanese-fusion haunt is increasingly overlooked nowadays, but it remains a "classic" for some reporters; the odd celeb still pops up now and again, but even so the dining room "lacks atmosphere". / W1K 1LB; www.noburestaurants.com; @NobuOldParkLane; 10.15 pm, Fri & Sat 11 pm, Sun 10 pm; set weekday L £58 (FP).

Nobu Berkeley W1 £90 322
15 Berkeley St 7290 9222 3–3C
"Expensive but amazing" sushi and other "fabulous" fusion fare underpins support for this large, showy Mayfair Japanese; it can seem "impersonal" and "charmless" however, and sceptics say it's overrun by a "selfie-stick clientele" nowadays. / W1J 8DY; www.noburestaurants.com; @NobuBerkeleyST; 11 pm, Sun 9.45 pm; closed Sun L; set weekday L £58 (FP).

F S A

Noor Jahan £40 433

2a Bina Gdns, SW5 7373 6522 5–2B
26 Sussex Pl, W2 7402 2332 6–1D

These gloomily "upmarket", "always busy" neighbourhood curry houses are the "perfect" local for the well-heeled denizens of Earl's Court and Bayswater looking for a "reliable" fix of "classic Indian tandoori fare". / 11.30 pm, Sun 10 pm.

Nopi W1 £70 322

21-22 Warwick St 7494 9584 3–2D

"Sublime flavour combos that both excite and comfort" have carved a huge name for Yotam Ottolenghi's modern Middle Eastern spot, just off Regent Street; ratings slid across the board this year though, and it took flak for some "ordinary" meals, its "eye-watering" expense, "offhand" service and "sterile" ambience. / W1B 5NE; www.nopi-restaurant.com; @ottolenghi; 10.15 pm, Sun 4 pm; closed Sun D.

Nordic Bakery £15 333

14a Golden Sq, W1 3230 1077 3–2D
37b New Cavendish St, W1 7935 3590 2–1A
48 Dorset St, W1 7487 5877 2–1A

You suffer "Soho media types networking over a coffee and a delicious cinnamon bun" but it's worth "squeezing yourself into" one of these "authentic" Scandi coffee shops. / Golden Square 8 pm, Sat 7 pm, Sun 7 pm, Cavendish Street & Dorset Street 6 pm.

The Norfolk Arms WC1 £44 433

28 Leigh St 7388 3937 8–4C

"A real find near King's Cross" – a "pleasantly chaotic" hybrid of gastropub and tapas bar, serving "unpretentious but delicious" Spanish-inspired food. / WC1H 9EP; www.norfolkarms.co.uk; 10.15 pm.

North China W3 £42 432

305 Uxbridge Rd 8992 9183 7–1A

One of Acton's few claims to gastronomic heights, this long-established, family-run Chinese is "so busy" because it's unusually good for somewhere out in the boonies, and "prices are more than reasonable". / W3 9QU; www.northchina.co.uk; 11 pm, Fri & Sat 11.30 pm.

The North London Tavern NW6 £46 333

375 Kilburn High Rd 7625 6634 1–2B

Handy for Kilburn's Tricycle Theatre – a "surprisingly good gastropub", with "genuine service" and "very decent food"; it's part of the Metropolitan Pub Company. / NW6 7QB; www.northlondontavern.co.uk; @NorthLondonTav; 10.30 pm, Sun 9.30 pm.

North Sea Fish WC1 £38 332

7-8 Leigh St 7387 5892 8–4C

"Some of the customers may look on their last legs, but for fine fish 'n' chips at fair prices" seek out this old-fashioned Bloomsbury chippy, whose "faded '70s decor has its own character". / WC1H 9EW; www.northseafishrestaurant.co.uk; 10 pm, Sun 5.30 pm; closed Sun D; no Amex.

The Northall
Corinthia Hotel SW1 **£85** 3 4 4

10a Northumberland Ave 7321 3100 2–3C

"No need to worry about the office bean counters getting stressed over pricey client lunches" if you entertain at this "very classy"-looking brasserie, near Embankment; "for part of such an extravagant 5-star hotel" it's "not too expensive" (set lunch in particular) and the grub's very "decent". / SW1A 2BD; www.thenorthall.co.uk; @CorinthiaLondon; 10.45 pm; set L & pre-theatre £56 (FP).

Northbank EC4 **£56** 3 4 4

1 Paul's Walk 7329 9299 9–3B

"Great views of the Shard and Tate Modern" are the star turn at this business-friendly bar-restaurant, by the Wobbly Bridge; the food can still be "lovely", but it's looking "a little tired" these days with "haphazard" service – time for a revamp? / EC4V 3QH; www.northbankrestaurant.co.uk; @NorthbankLondon; 10 pm; closed Sun.

Novikov (Asian restaurant) W1 **£102** 1 1 2

50a Berkeley St 7399 4330 3–3C

"Glamorous… if you're into big tables of overdressed Euros, yelling at the top of their voices!" – this Russian-owned Pan-Asian is praised by fans for its "stunning" food and "electric" ambience, but dismissed by critics for its "inferior" fare, and prices on a par with an EU bailout. / W1J 8HA; www.novikovrestaurant.co.uk; @NovikovLondon; 11.15 pm; set weekday L £57 (FP).

Novikov (Italian restaurant) W1 **£110** 2 2 2

50a Berkeley St 7399 4330 3–3C

That it's "ludicrously expensive", is the main drawback of the "OTT" Italian section of this ostentatious, Russian-run Mayfair bling-fest – the food's actually "better than you'd imagine"; and if you like this sort of thing, it's "great for people watching". / W1J 8HA; www.novikovrestaurant.co.uk; @NovikovLondon; 11.15 pm.

Numero Uno SW11 **£53** 4 4 4

139 Northcote Rd 7978 5837 10–2C

A quintessential "neighbourhood Italian" bordering the Nappy Valley – "friendly and authentic", with "slick service, matched by a range of traditional dishes". / SW11 6PX; 11.30 pm; no Amex.

Nuovi Sapori SW6 **£45** 3 4 3

295 New King's Rd 7736 3363 10–1B

"Friendly and welcoming" owners contribute much to the appeal of this well-established local near Parsons Green, serving a "reliable" menu of "traditional Italian cuisine". / SW6 4RE; 11 pm; closed Sun.

Nusa Kitchen **£12** 4 4 3

9 Old St, EC1 7253 3135 9–1B
2 Adam's Ct, EC2 7628 1149 9–2C
88 Cannon St, EC4 7621 9496 9–3C

"Transforming the lunch time soup experience" – City and Farringdon pit stops which serve "utterly amazing" Asian broths. / www.nusakitchen.co.uk; 4 pm; closed Sat & Sun; no booking.

Oak £50 4 2 4

243 Goldhawk Rd, W12 8741 7700 7–1B
137 Westbourne Park Rd, W2 7221 3355 6–1B
There's something so "cool" about the "really buzzing" style of these "transformed old boozers" in Bayswater and Shepherd's Bush, which serve "scrumptious", "thin and crispy" pizza – "some of the finest in town!" Top Tip – the upstairs bar in W2 is "a real gem". / W12 Mon - Sat 10:30pm / SUn 9:30pmW2 Mon-Thurs 10:30pm / Fri - Sat 11pm / Sun 10pm.

Obicà £46 3 3 2

11 Charlotte St, W1 7637 7153 2–1C
19-20 Poland St, W1 3327 7070 3–1D
96 Draycott Ave, SW3 7581 5208 5–2C
35 Bank St, E14 7719 1532 11–1C
"For some reason they've changed their name (from Obika)", but these 'Mozzarella bars' "make a solid choice for some excellent produce and a drink or two", and win tips for their superior pizza too. / www.obika.co.uk; 10 pm - 11 pm; E14 Closed Sun.

Oblix
The Shard SE1 £88 2 2 4

31 St Thomas St 7268 6700 9–4C
"To woo a date" the view is "stunning" at this 32nd-floor South Bank roost (run by the owners of Zuma, et al); so are the "extortionate" prices though, and sceptics suggest you "go to the bar, and eat elsewhere". (Stop Press – will new Pied à Terre chef, Marcus Eaves – who joined in September 2015 – finally make it a foodie hotspot?) / SE1 9RY; www.oblixrestaurant.com; @OblixRestaurant; 11 pm.

Odette's NW1 £62 3 3 3

130 Regent's Park Rd 7586 8569 8–3B
"For an unhurried journey of sensory delight", Bryn William's "cosy", "slightly old-fashioned" romantic classic in Primrose Hill remains well-rated as "a lovely all-round experience" with "first-rate" cuisine; for a few doubters though, it "just doesn't quite hit the spot". / NW1 8XL; www.odettesprimrosehill.com; @Odettes_rest; 10 pm, Fri & Sat 10.30 pm; closed Mon; no Amex.

Ognisko Restaurant SW7 £51 3 3 4

55 Prince's Gate, Exhibition Rd 7589 0101 5–1C
"The old-fashioned dining room is a delight", at this émigrés club near the Science Museum, which also boasts "a wonderful rear terrace, on a garden square"; Jan Woroniecki's year-old regime doesn't please all its old regulars, but the "hearty" Polish fare and "exotic house cocktails" were well-rated this year. / SW7 2PN; www.ogniskorestaurant.co.uk; 11.15 pm ; closed Mon L; no trainers.

Oka £47 4 3 3

Kingly Court, Kingly St, W1 7734 3556 3–2D NEW
71 Regent's Park Road, NW1 7483 2072 8–3B
In Soho and Primrose Hill, a duo of Pan-Asian restaurants offering "excellent quality" sushi and a smattering of "unusual" but "clever" dishes – Marmite chicken anyone? / www.okarestaurant.co.uk; @RestaurantOka; 10.30 pm.

Old Tom & English W1 NEW **£49**
187b Wardour St 7287 7347 3–1D
A Soho hang-out that only takes reservations? – a nowadays radical premise for this low-lit basement hideaway, entered speakeasy-style via a "discreet" entrance, and with "quirky" '60s styling; cocktails are a big deal here, but early reports say the food is better than incidental. / W1F 8ZB; oldtomandenglish.com/; @oldtomsoho; 11.30 pm, Sat midnight.

Oldroyd N1 NEW **£42**
344 Upper St 8617 9010 8–3D
Tom Oldroyd (formerly chef-director of Polpo group) goes it alone at this pocket-sized, new modern bistro in Islington, serving a variety of funky sharing plates; it opened too late for our survey, but early press feedback hails it as a bargain. / N1 0PD; www.oldroydlondon.com; @oldroydlondon.

Oliveto SW1 **£63** 4 2 2
49 Elizabeth St 7730 0074 2–4A
"Wonderful pizza and pasta, at prices that don't frighten Belgravians one little bit" make this "family-friendly" Sardinian a choice that's relatively "cheap 'n' cheerful", if only by the standards of this swanky 'hood. / SW1W 9PP; www.olivorestaurants.com/oliveto; @OlivoGroup; 10.30 pm; booking: max 7 at D.

Olivo SW1 **£58** 3 4 2
21 Eccleston St 7730 2505 2–4B
"Dated" '90s Belgravian, with "tables too close together and dreadful acoustics"; "it's very popular for good reason" though – its Sardinian cuisine is "consistently excellent" and matched with "interesting Sardinian wines". / SW1 9LX; www.olivorestaurants.com/olivo; @OlivoGroup; 10.30 pm; closed Sat L & Sun L.

Olivocarne SW1 **£61** 4 4 2
61 Elizabeth St 7730 7997 2–4A
"Upscale sister to Olivo, Oliveto etc. with more of a focus on meat" – this Belgravia's Sardinian has "excellent" cooking to offset its rather "reserved" ambience. / SW1W 9PP; www.olivorestaurants.com/olivocarne; @OlivoGroup; 11 pm, Sun 10.30 pm.

Olivomare SW1 **£61** 4 3 2
10 Lower Belgrave St 7730 9022 2–4B
Stark, "Barbarella-esque" decor creates a "bare-bones" ambience at this very "contemporary" Belgravian; this "does nothing to detract", however, from the "brilliant and resolutely Sardinian menu", majoring in "super-fresh" fish and seafood; the wine list's "a joy" too. / SW1W 0LJ; www.olivorestaurants.com/olivomare; @OlivoGroup; 11 pm, Sun 10.30 pm; booking: max 10.

Olympic
Olympic Studios SW13 **£50** 2 2 4
117-123 Church Rd 8912 5170 10–1A
"A roaring success among trendier Barnes types" – this converted Edwardian cinema (for much of its life, famous recording studios, but nowadays again also showing movies) makes "a great local meeting place", especially for brunch; "both food and service are hit-and-miss though… when they get it right it's really good, but it's very inconsistent". / SW13 9HL; www.olympiccinema.co.uk; @Olympic_Cinema; 11 pm, Sat & Sun midnight.

Olympus Fish N3 £34 452

140-144 Ballards Ln 8371 8666 1–1B

"Wonderful, fresh, char-grilled fish" is an alternative to the "succulent non-greasy fish 'n' chips" at this "unpretentious" Finchley chippy, whose longstanding owners give a notably "warm welcome". Top Menu Tip – "divine sea bass cooked in sea salt". / N3 2PA; www.olympusrestaurant.co.uk; @Olympus_London; 11 pm; set weekday L £17 (FP).

On The Bab £36 432

39 Marylebone Ln, W1 7935 2000 2–1A NEW

36 Wellington St, WC2 7240 8825 4–3D NEW

305 Old St, EC1 7683 0361 12–1B

"Korean food is so hot right now", and these energetic, "cheap 'n' cheerful" pit-stops and their "delicious" anju (street-food dishes) are a "must try"; very handy new Covent Garden branch that "makes a good fist of fast turnarounds". / www.onthebab.co.uk; @onthebab.

One Canada Square E14 £58 222

1 Canada Sq 7559 5199 11–1C

For a business lunch this two-year-old bar/brasserie, in the lobby of Canary Wharf's main skyscraper, couldn't have a better location; it's "a bit of a goldfish bowl" however (which at night is "rammed with loud City types"), and the "pricey" food is "not as good as they think it is". / E14 5AB; www.onecanadasquarerestaurant.com; @OneCanadaSquare; 10.45 pm; closed Sun; set pre theatre £36 (FP).

101 Thai Kitchen W6 £33 421

352 King St 8746 6888 7–2B

"Mind-blowing spicing" ("not for the faint hearted!") vouches for the authenticity of this Thai caff near Stamford Brook; it's a "no-nonsense, straightforward place" but "look past the decor – you'll be in south east Asia!". / W6 0RX; www.101thaikitchen.com; 10.30 pm, Fri & Sat 11 pm; no Amex.

1 Lombard Street EC3 £69 233

1 Lombard St 7929 6611 9–3C

"The buzz is returning to pre-crash heights" at this Square Mile linchpin; OK, the food is only "satisfactory" and the ex-banking-hall interior is a "bit cavernous and plain", but tables are "well-spaced", and its "capable" style and central location make it "a perfect setting for the City". / EC3V 9AA; www.1lombardstreet.com; @1lombardstreet; 10 pm; closed Sat & Sun; booking: max 6.

One Sixty Smokehouse £52 443

291 West End Ln, NW6 7794 9786 1–1B

9 Stoney Ln, E1 7283 8367 9–2D NEW

"Comfort food at its American best" – "sensational" ribs, wings, soft-shell crab burgers, etc – wins raves for David Moore and Sean Martin's year-old "edgy West Hampstead smokehouse", now also with a branch in the City. / www.one-sixty.co.uk; @onesixtylondon.

One-O-One
Sheraton Park Tower SW1 £100 5 2 1
101 Knightsbridge 7290 7101 5–1D
"Off-the-charts-good" Breton fish cuisine makes Pascal Proyart's Knightsbridge HQ "London's best-kept secret for seafood"; there is, however, a catch – the hotel dining room it occupies is "absolutely ghastly", with a "dead", "business-lounge" ambience. / SW1X 7RN; www.oneoonerestaurant.com; @oneoone; 10 pm; closed Mon & Sun; booking: max 6; set weekday L £55 (FP).

The Only Running Footman W1 £61 3 3 3
5 Charles St 7499 2988 3–3B
"There's plenty of elbow room in the spacious dining room" of this boozer, near Berkeley Square – "very handy for a Mayfair working lunch", or indeed any other kind of occasion. / W1J 5DF; www.therunningfootmanmayfair.com; @theorfootman; 10 pm.

Opera Tavern WC2 £46 4 4 4
23 Catherine St 7836 3680 4–3D
"The best ever small tasty treats" are provided by "willing" staff at this "very cute" (but at times very "noisy") pub-conversion sibling to Salt Yard, well-located near Covent Garden. Top Menu Tips – "Morcilla Scotch eggs to die for"; and "outstanding mini Ibérico pork and foie gras burgers". / WC2B 5JS; www.operatavern.co.uk; @saltyardgroup; 11.15 pm, Sun 9.45 pm; SRA-2.*

Opso W1 £44 2 2 4
10 Paddington St 7487 5088 2–1A
All acknowledge the "beautiful" interior of this Marylebone yearling, but its modern Greek cooking splits opinion – to fans it's a solid "cheap 'n' cheerful" choice, but to critics it's "disappointing" and "highly priced". / W1U 5QL; opso.co.uk; @OPSO_london; 10 pm, Fri & Sat 10.30 pm; closed Sun D.

The Orange SW1 £59 3 3 4
37 Pimlico Rd 7881 9844 5–2D
"Fun and atmospheric" Pimlico gastropub which "draws an attractive younger crowd" with its "fab" pizza, and other fare. / SW1W 8NE; www.theorange.co.uk; @TheOrangeSW1; 10 pm, Sun 9.30 pm.

Orange Pekoe SW13 £26 3 4 4
3 White Hart Ln 8876 6070 10–1A
"A unique and lovely tea room and café" in Barnes – a "superb selection of teas" is served "with flair", plus "well-chosen" bites including "salads to die for", "filling sarnies" and "very good cakes". / SW13 0PX; www.orangepekoeteas.com; @OrangePekoeTeas; 5 pm; L only.

The Orange Tree N20 £46 2 2 3
7 Totteridge Ln 8343 7031 1–1B
A popular Totteridge linchpin that again divides the locals – to critics it's "a waste of a prime location", but fans say it's "always good". / N20 8NX; www.theorangetreetotteridge.co.uk; @orangetreepub; 9.45 pm, Fri & Sat 10.30 pm, Sun 9 pm; set weekday L £28 (FP).

Orpheus EC3 £48 4 3 1
26 Savage Gdns 7481 1931 9–3D
"It looks awful, but that's a good thing – I don't want anyone else to know about it!"; this "throwback" in a railway arch near Tower Hill is little known, but its fish dishes are "unusually good", featuring "simple yet elegant saucing". / EC3N 2AR; www.orpheusrestaurant.co.uk; 3 pm; L only, closed Sat & Sun.

Orrery W1 £80 3 4 3

55 Marylebone High St 7616 8000 2–1A

A "bright and airy" first-floor room – above Marylebone's Conran Shop, and overlooking a churchyard – provides the "spacious" and "calm" setting for this well-known D&D London venture, whose "efficient" service further boosts its appeal for business; the food is "expensive" but usually "lovely" too. / W1U 5RB; www.orreryrestaurant.co.uk; @orrery; 10.30 pm, Fri & Sat 11 pm; set weekday L £52 (FP), set Sun L £55 (FP).

Orso WC2 £55 2 2 2

27 Wellington St 7240 5269 4–3D

"Very convenient for the ROH" – this once-exciting, Covent Garden basement remains a treasured "stalwart" for a devoted fan club, who say it's "charming" and "solid"; ratings-wise, it "continues to go downhill", however – its performance can just seem too "stale". / WC2E 7DB; www.orsorestaurant.co.uk; @Orso_Restaurant; 11.30 pm; set always available £36 (FP).

Oslo Court NW8 £62 3 5 4

Charlbert St, off Prince Albert Rd 7722 8795 8–3A

"It is as though the last 30 years never happened", at this "unique" time-warp at the foot of a Regent's Park apartment block – a fave rave for silver-haired north Londoners with birthdays to celebrate. For most reporters, it remains an utter "treasure" thanks to its "wonderful", "retro" '70s menu, "fun" style and "long serving staff" who help "put a smile on your face", but for a few (including former fans) it's starting to feel like it's "gone over". Top Menu Tip – "the famed dessert trolley". / NW8 7EN; www.oslocourtrestaurant.co.uk; 11 pm; closed Sun; no jeans or trainers.

Osteria Antica Bologna SW11 £43 4 3 3

23 Northcote Rd 7978 4771 10–2C

"A light and accessible makeover" has revivified this "busy and cheerful" age-old osteria, near Clapham Junction – the food's "nothing fancy, but genuine northern Italian cuisine, mixing staples and specials of the day". / SW11 1NG; www.osteria.co.uk; @OsteriaAntica; 10.30 pm, Sun 10 pm.

Osteria Basilico W11 £58 3 2 4

29 Kensington Park Rd 7727 9957 6–1A

An enduring pillar of Notting Hill dining that's still "consistently good", particularly its "fun atmosphere"; "don't forget to book if you want a table on the ground floor". / W11 2EU; www.osteriabasilico.co.uk; 11.30 pm, Sun 10.15 pm; no booking, S.

Osteria Tufo N4 £47 4 5 3

67 Fonthill Rd 7272 2911 8–1D

"There's no need to go to the West End any more", when you can visit this "fabulous" two-year-old in Finsbury Park – "the best kind of neighbourhood place", "run with love" and with "top-notch", "reasonably priced" Italian cooking. / N4 3HZ; www.osteriatufo.co.uk; @osteriatufo; 10.30 pm; closed Mon & Sun L; no Amex.

FSA

Ostuni NW6 £49 334

43-45 Lonsdale Rd 7624 8035 1–2B

A converted Victorian workshop, in Queen's Park, provides a "very attractive and very spacious" venue for this "lively" two-year-old Puglian, whose "authentically Italian" decor is carried off with "pizzazz", and which serves "great food at reasonable prices". / NW6 6RA; www.ostunirestaurant.co.ukwww.ostunirestaurant.co.uk; @OstuniLondon; 10 pm, Sun 9 pm.

Otto's WC1 £65 454

182 Grays Inn Rd 7713 0107 2–1D

"The old-school French cuisine you thought had died a death" makes an unlikely find behind an unassuming façade in an "out-of-the-way" corner of Bloomsbury; the "eccentric" interior is "charming in a quiet, old-fashioned way", but the stand-out attractions are "Otto himself, who's a star", "superb" food and "excellent" wine. Top Menu Tips – "sublime" steak tartare, and the "to die for" Canard à la Presse (for which you must pre-order). / WC1X 8EW; www.ottos-restaurant.com; @OttosRestaurant; 9.45 pm; closed Sat L & Sun; set weekday L £47 (FP).

Ottolenghi £52 422

13 Motcomb St, SW1 7823 2707 5–1D
63 Ledbury Rd, W11 7727 1121 6–1B
1 Holland St, W8 7937 0003 5–1A
287 Upper St, N1 7288 1454 8–2D
50 Artillery Pas, E1 7247 1999 9–2D

"You discover tastebuds you never knew existed!", say fans of the "revelatory" salads and "insanely good" cakes at Yotam Ottolenghi's "chic" (but slightly "sterile") communal deli/cafés; "ridiculous queues" are a perennial hazard however, and a dip in ratings supports those who say "it's suffering from its own success". / www.ottolenghi.co.uk; N1 10.15 pm, W8 & W11 8 pm, Sat 7 pm, Sun 6 pm; N1 closed Sun D; Holland St take-away only; W11 & SW1 no booking, N1 booking for D only.

Outlaw's Seafood and Grill
The Capital Hotel SW3 £84 442

22-24 Basil St 7589 5171 5–1D

Nathan Outlaw's "rare and outstanding" treatment of fish and seafood underpins the "first class" experience at this "calm" chamber, just a stone's throw from Harrods, although the room is too small and "too formal" for some tastes. Top Tip – on Thursday you can BYO with no corkage. / SW3 1AT; www.capitalhotel.co.uk; @hotelcapital; 10 pm; closed Sun; set weekday L £52 (FP).

(Brasserie)
Oxo Tower SE1 £73 112

Barge House St 7803 3888 9–3A

"Urgh!" – the brasserie section of this South Bank landmark "consistently trades on its name and great Thames view" with "terrible service and very ordinary food"; what's more it's "very, very expensive". / SE1 9PH; www.harveynichols.com/restaurants/oxo-tower-london; @OXO_Tower; 11 pm, Sun 10 pm; set weekday L & pre-theatre £51 (FP).

(Restaurant)
Oxo Tower SE1 **£89** 1 1 1
Barge House St 7803 3888 9–3A
"Stunning view, shame about the food" – year-in-year-out it's plus ça change at this famous South Bank fixture, whose "rubbish" cooking, "purposeless" service and hefty bills make it nigh on "the worst bang for your buck in town". / SE1 9PH; www.harveynichols.com/restaurants; @OXO_Tower; 11 pm, Sun 10 pm; set weekday L £59 (FP); SRA-3.*

Pachamama W1 **£56** 3 3 2
18 Thayer St 7935 9393 2–1A
"Intriguing sharing plates inspired by Peru", all "washed down with good Pisco cocktails" win a big thumbs-up for this Marylebone yearling; on the downside, its basement setting is "soulless", and "the acoustics are terrible". / W1U 3JY; www.pachamamalondon.com; @pachamama_ldn; 10.45 pm; closed Mon L.

Le Pain Quotidien **£31** 2 2 4
Branches throughout London
"Nothing to get too excited about", but this "rustic" chain makes a great standby for a bowlful of coffee, or "handy refuel" (especially breakfast) – "there's just something about the ambience… it feels very relaxed". / www.painquotidien.com; most branches close between 7 pm-10 pm; no booking at some branches, especially at weekends.

The Painted Heron SW10 **£56** 4 4 3
112 Cheyne Walk 7351 5232 5–3B
"Hidden away but worth finding" – this "understated but excellent" Indian fixture off the Chelsea Embankment provides "friendly and eager" service and "is an oasis of adventurous, impeccably spiced cuisine". / SW10 0DJ; www.thepaintedheron.com; @thepaintedheron; 10.30 pm, Sun 10 pm; no Amex.

The Palmerston SE22 **£55** 4 3 3
91 Lordship Ln 8693 1629 1–4D
Superior East Dulwich gastropub that's a haven of "good value", "great seasonal pub food" and "a big range of wines by the glass" – the kind of place "you'd happily eat almost everything on the menu". / SE22 8EP; www.thepalmerston.co.uk; @thepalmerston; 10 pm, Sun 9.30 pm; no Amex; set always available £31 (FP).

The Palomar W1 **£48** 4 4 4
34 Rupert St 7439 8777 4–3A
"Israeli cooking as in Jerusalem" ("brilliant, punchy, sparky" small dishes), plus "super-keen and knowledgeable" service have made a smash-hit of this "bare-walled" yearling, in the heart of the West End – "the joint is jumping!" and it's superb "fun" (if "squashed" and "extremely noisy"). There's a little, tough-to-book, dining room, or sit at the bar and watch the chefs in action. / W1D 6DN; www.thepalomar.co.uk; @palomarsoho; 11 pm, Fri-Sat 11.30 pm; closed Sun L; SRA-1.*

The Pantechnicon SW1 **£58** 3 3 4
10 Motcomb St 7730 6074 5–1D
This "professionally run" Belgravian combines a "buzzy ground floor bar", with a "quieter", grand and comfortable upstairs dining room, which "still feels like a pub… just". / SW1X 8LA; www.thepantechnicon.com; @ThePantechnicon; 10 pm, Sun 9.30 pm.

Pappa Ciccia £34 444

105 Munster Rd, SW6 7384 1884 10–1B
41 Fulham High St, SW6 7736 0900 10–1B
"Outstanding pizza (crispy and doughy without being burnt)" is a highlight of the "tasty, traditional Italian fare, in generous portions" at these BYO spots in Fulham – "for the price you pay, the food's extremely good". / www.pappaciccia.com; 11 pm, Sat & Sun 11.30 pm; Munster Rd no credit cards.

Paradise by Way of Kensal Green W10 £50 225

19 Kilburn Ln 8969 0098 1–2B
Rambling, "shabby-chic" Kensal Green landmark, still ticking all the right boxes for its glam' 20/30-something following; in its large, "laid-back" dining room, the food's "nothing too exciting" but "enjoyable". / W10 4AE; www.theparadise.co.uk; @weloveparadise; 10.30 pm, Fri & Sat 11 pm, Sun 9 pm; closed weekday L; no Amex.

Paradise Garage E2 NEW £45

254 Paradise Row 7613 1502 12–1D
New debut from foodie darling Robin Gill (he of Clapham's The Manor, and The Dairy) in an oh-so-hip railway arch, in the beating heart of trendy Bethnal Green; it opened too late for survey feedback on its funky small plates, but the word on the street is encouraging. / E2 9LE; paradise254.com; @ParadiseRow254; 9.30 pm; closed Mon, Tue L & Sun D.

Paradise Hampstead NW3 £33 454

49 South End Rd 7794 6314 8–2A
"The friendly owner goes the extra mile" at this "classic, traditional, British Indian of decades' standing" – an "insufferably popular" neighbourhood "hotspot" by Hampstead Heath overground; everything about the place is "a cut above". / NW3 2QB; www.paradisehampstead.co.uk; 10.45 pm.

El Parador NW1 £38 454

245 Eversholt St 7387 2789 8–3C
"It looks nothing from the outside", but this "terrific" spot, near Mornington Crescent, is a great all-rounder, not least its "dreamy" tapas ("there's always something new and different") that's "well-priced" to boot; "cosy little courtyard in summer". / NW1 1BA; www.elparadorlondon.com; 11 pm, Fri & Sat 11.30 pm, Sun 9.30 pm; closed Sat L & Sun L; no Amex.

Parlour NW10 £49 444

5 Regent St 8969 2184 1–2B
Jesse Dunford Wood's "unique and quirky venue" occupies "a converted Kensal Rise boozer", but "it's no normal gastropub" – the food's "really interesting and delicious". Top Tips – the "amazing cow pie in huge portions" (and a meal at the chef's personal table). / NW10 5LG; www.parlourkensal.com; @ParlourUK; 10 pm; closed Mon.

Patara £56 333

15 Greek St, W1 7437 1071 4–2A
5 Berners St, W1 8874 6503 3–1D NEW
7 Maddox St, W1 7499 6008 3–2C
181 Fulham Rd, SW3 7351 5692 5–2C
9 Beauchamp Pl, SW3 7581 8820 5–1C
"Delicate" cooking, "unobtrusive" service and "subtle" decor combine to make this popular and rather superior Thai chain "an all-round good effort". / www.pataralondon.com; 10.30 pm; Greek St closed Sun L.

Paternoster Chop House EC4 £55 332

Warwick Ct, Paternoster Sq 7029 9400 9–2B

Mixed feedback this year, on this "expensive" D&D London steakhouse, which critics feel seems to "trade on its location" (it's right by St Paul's, with many al fresco tables); "at lunch, it's 95% business", and hard to give it any wider recommendation. / *EC4M 7DX; www.paternosterchophouse.co.uk; @paternoster1; 10.30 pm; closed Sat & Sun D.*

Patio W12 £36 355

5 Goldhawk Rd 8743 5194 7–1C

"Old-fashioned, in the nicest possible way" – a "warm and cosy" spot, right by Shepherd's Bush Green, that's a top budget choice thanks to its super-friendly service, affordable Polish fodder, and wide range of flavoured vodkas. / *W12 8QQ; www.patiolondon.com; 11 pm, Sat & Sun 11.30 pm; closed Sat L & Sun L.*

Pâtisserie Valerie £28 222

Branches throughout London

Luke Johnson is laughing all the way to the bank with his partial June 2015 sale of this once-tiny pâtisserie chain; some reporters think it can be "dire" nowadays (the new branches in particular), but others do praise the "wonderful" cakes and "yummy brunches", especially at the "tatty but charming Old Compton Street original". / *www.patisserie-valerie.co.uk; most branches close between 5 pm-8 pm; no booking except Old Compton St Sun-Thu.*

Patogh W1 £22 444

8 Crawford Pl 7262 4015 6–1D

A "lovely, little Middle Eastern spot", just off the Edgware Road – "simple but very atmospheric", serving "authentic, basic dishes" featuring "large portions of freshly grilled meat"; BYO. / *W1H 5NE; 11 pm; no credit cards.*

Patron NW5 NEW £47 334

26 Fortress Rd 7813 2540 8–2C

A cute, little, new 'Cave à Manger' in Kentish Town, "already very busy" thanks to its "simple but good, traditional French fare". / *NW5 2HB; www.patronlondon.com.*

Patty and Bun £23 433

54 James St, W1 7487 3188 3–1A

22-23 Liverpool St, EC2 7621 1331 9–2D

"Just wow!"; the "revelatory" burgers are "a sloppy sensation" – "so juicy, moist and cooked to perfection" – at these "loud", "indie-vibe" pitstops, whose branch near Selfridges is the highest-rated burger-joint in town. / *www.pattyandbun.co.uk; Mon - Wed 10pm, Thu - Fri 11pm, Sat 9pm, Sun 6pm.*

The Pear Tree W6 £43 334

14 Margravine Rd 7381 1787 7–2C

A "lovely and intimate" little Victorian gastropub (with cute garden), tucked way behind the Charing Cross Hospital, serving a "limited" menu of "surprisingly good" food. / *W6 8HJ; www.thepeartreefulham.com; Mon-Thu D only, Fri-Sun open L & D.*

Pearl Liang W2 £47 432

8 Sheldon Sq 7289 7000 6–1C

A hotspot for dim sum – this big, dim-lit basement Chinese has an out-on-a-limb, Paddington Basin location, but is worth truffling out for its "top notch" cooking. / W2 6EZ; www.pearlliang.co.uk; @PearlLiangUK; 11 pm.

Peckham Bazaar SE15 £46 444

119 Consort Rd 7732 2525 1–4D

"Different… in a good way" – a "really interesting menu of mainly Greek Albanian food" (much of it barbecued) earns many recommendations for this "buzzy little Balkan place in an unlikely part of Peckham"; its "mysterious wines" add to the appeal – "I just do a lucky dip and it's always fine". / SE15 3RU; www.peckhambazaar.com; @PeckhamBazaar; 10 pm, Sun 8 pm; closed Mon, Tue-Fri D only, Sat & Sun open L & D; no Amex.

Peckham Refreshment Rooms SE15 £40 323

12-16 Blenheim Grove 7639 1106 1–4D

On a Friday and Saturday night this Peckham two-year-old can be "a bit too manic with young drinkers", but most locals cherish it as a "chilled" spot (notwithstanding the "uncomfortable bar stools") for a "quality", "casual" bite. / SE15 4QL; www.peckhamrefreshment.com; @PeckhamRefresh; midnight; closed Sun D.

Pedler SE15 NEW £37 324

58 Peckham Rye 3030 5015 1–4D

"A welcome addition to the trendy Peckham scene" – a "busy" if "crammed-in" bistro dishing up "simple, tasty" meals at "reasonable prices"; "fantastic brunch" too, with an "extremely impressive variety" of "thoughtful" options. / SE15 4JR; www.pedlerpeckhamrye.com; @pedlerpeckham; 10.45 pm; closed Mon, Tue L, Wed L, Thu L & Sun D.

Pellicano £59 343

19-21 Elystan St, SW3 7584 1789 5–2C

MyHotel, 35 Ixworth Pl, SW3 7589 3718 5–2C

"The move to myHotel hasn't made me love it any less!" – a Chelsea old favourite that was rehoused on the same street a couple of years ago, but is "as good as ever", with "well-prepared, reasonably priced Sardinian cooking". It leaves behind Pellicanino – a more informal spot for pizza and pasta on the original site.

E Pellicci E2 £19 345

332 Bethnal Green Rd 7739 4873 12–1D

"Lashings of Cockney charm" are on the menu of this "consistently marvellous" East End caff, known for its listed Art Deco interior, and "delicious, old-fashioned breakfast fry-ups". / E2 0AG; 4.15 pm; L only, closed Sun; no credit cards.

Pennethorne's Cafe Bar Somerset House WC2 NEW £38

The New Wing, Somerset Hs, Strand 3751 0570 2–2D

A recent addition to the increasingly well-served New Wing of Somerset House; not enough reviews for a rating this year, but initial reports tip it as a "smart, grown-up place to meet friends" for a glass of vino and a snack. / WC2R 1LA; www.pennethornescafe.co.uk; @pennethornes; 9.45 pm; closed Sun; no Amex.

Pentolina W14 £47 4 5 4

71 Blythe Rd 3010 0091 7–1C

"What a jewel!" – this "massively popular" Olympia spot is "heaven-around-the-corner" for locals; it's "cramped and noisy", but very "attractive" looking, with "extremely welcoming" service from the chef's wife and "fresh and imaginative" Italian cooking. / W14 0HP; www.pentolinarestaurant.co.uk; 10 pm; closed Mon & Sun; no Amex.

The Pepper Tree SW4 £30 3 3 3

19 Clapham Common S'side 7622 1758 10–2D

"There's no time to hang around", at this "always crowded" Clapham canteen; "you do have to queue, but give it a go for its modestly priced nosh that's simple, unfussy, and filling". / SW4 7AB; www.thepeppertree.co.uk; @PepperTreeSW4; 10.45 pm, Sun & Mon 10.15 pm; no booking.

Percy & Founders W1 NEW £54 3 3 3

1 Pearson Sq, Fitzroy Pl 3761 0200 2–1B

There's "a real wow factor" to the "smart and American-feeling" decor of this big new watering hole – the "open and spacious ground floor of a Fitzrovia office building"; fans say the food is "surprisingly good" too, but others – judging it "over-designed and inauthentic" – find its appeal "hollow". / W1T 3BF; percyandfounders.co.uk; @PercyFounders; 10.30 pm; closed Sun D.

Pescatori £56 3 2 2

11 Dover St, W1 7493 2652 3–3C

57 Charlotte St, W1 7580 3289 2–1C

These West End Italians may "lack that friendly local feel" but even their worst critic says the fish and seafood here is consistently "well done". / www.pescatori.co.uk; 11 pm; closed Sat L & Sun.

Petersham Hotel TW10 £65 3 4 5

Nightingale Ln 8940 7471 1–4A

"Unbeatable views of the Thames" are the stand-out feature of this "elegant" (if "rather dated") traditional dining room in a "lovely, old, grand hotel", near Richmond Park – a particular hit with its silver-haired clientele; service is "gracious" and "un-rushed", and it's just the job for a special family meal. / TW10 6UZ; www.petershamhotel.co.uk; @ThePetersham; 9.45 pm, Sun 8.45 pm; set Sun L £57 (FP).

Petersham Nurseries TW10 £72 2 2 4

Church Ln, Off Petersham Rd 8940 5230 1–4A

"Down a narrow lane, near Richmond Park, an idyllic and unique greenhouse setting, with earthen floor, greenery and pleasantly distressed antiques creates a magical atmosphere"; food-wise, though, this now-famous garden centre café "is not what it used to be" – "uninspiring", yet "priced like the West End". / TW10 7AG; www.petershamnurseries.com; @PetershamN; L only, closed Mon.

The Petite Coree NW6 NEW £39 5 4 2

98 West End Ln 7624 9209 1–1B

"A former Nobu chef brings his magic touch to NW6", with the opening of this "really sweet little neighbourhood find"; while the "cramped" interior "leaves something to be desired", the "unlikely sounding Korean/Euro fusion fare" is "somehow made to work" – "it's truly wonderful and inexpensive". / NW6 2LU; www.thepetitecoree.com.

La Petite Maison W1 £83 434
54 Brook's Mews 7495 4774 3–2B
"You're whisked to the South of France", when you visit this "sophisticated", "noisy" and "crowded" Mayfair haunt; few seem to begrudge the dizzying prices, as the "gimmick-free" Mediterranean-style sharing plates are "simply stunning" – "appealingly light" and so, so fresh. / W1K 4EG; www.lpmlondon.co.uk; @lpmlondon; 10.45 pm, Sun 9.45 pm.

Pétrus SW1 £108 343
1 Kinnerton St 7592 1609 5–1D
The "stunning" wine selection is the centrepiece of Gordon Ramsay's swish and discreet Belgravian; on most accounts it's "stunningly good in every way", but it's also "extremely expensive" and a tad "too corporate" for some tastes. / SW1X 8EA; www.gordonramsay.com/petrus; @petrus; 10.15 pm; closed Sun; no trainers; set weekday L £66 (FP).

Peyote W1 £70 223
13 Cork St 7409 1300 3–3C
Mayfair Latino overseen by Mexico City legend, chef Eduardo Garcia, that's not made huge waves, but undoubtedly has a "trendy, buzzing atmosphere"; fans do hail its "delicious" Mexican tucker, but even they say it's "dear" – to foes it's "disappointing with the owner's pedigree" and, at the price, "exorbitant". / W1S 3NS; www.peyoteresaurant.com; @Peyotelondon; Mon-Thu 1 am, Fri & Sat 2 am; closed Sat L & Sun.

Pham Sushi EC1 £36 531
159 Whitecross St 7251 6336 12–2A
"You don't go for the ambience!"; you go to this "basic" Barbican fixture for "fabulous" sushi and sashimi that's "incredible value". / EC1Y 8JL; www.phamsushi.co.uk; @phamsushi; 9.45 pm; closed Sat L & Sun.

Pho £35 223
Branches throughout London
"For a wholesome steaming hot bowl of noodles", these popular Vietnamese pitstops remain a "reliable option", but "quality has dropped since its early days" and its overall performance is now "OK but unspectacular". / www.phocafe.co.uk; EC1 10 pm, Fri & Sat 10.30 pm, W1 10.30 pm, W12 9 pm, Sat 7 pm, Sun 6 pm; EC1 closed Sat L & Sun, W1 closed Sun; no Amex; no booking.

The Phoenix SW3 £49 233
23 Smith St 7730 9182 5–2D
"Wonderfully atmospheric" backstreet boozer (part of Geronimo Inns) that's "always good fun", and with food that's "decently priced for Chelsea". / SW3 4EE; www.geronimo-inns.co.uk; @ThePhoenixSW3; 10 pm; SRA-3.*

Phoenix Palace NW1 £56 322
5-9 Glentworth St 7486 3515 2–1A
"Giant green and gold fixture", near Baker Street, that's "well-favoured by the Chinese community", particularly for dim sum; it's not as highly rated as it once was however – dishes can be "matchless" but they can also be "so-so" nowadays. / NW1 5PG; www.phoenixpalace.co.uk; 11.15 pm, Sun 10.15 pm.

Picture W1 £49 343
110 Great Portland St 7637 7892 2–1B
An "epic tasting menu" is a highlight of the "interesting" and "good value" small-plate formula, at this "sparse"-looking two-year-old near Broadcasting House, "decorated with the usual exposed brick, concrete and naked bulbs". / W1W 6PQ; www.picturerestaurant.co.uk; @picturerest; 10 pm; closed Sun.

Piebury Corner N7 £19 433
209-211 Holloway Rd 7700 5441 8–2D
It helps to be a fan of the Gunners if you visit this "small" 'pie deli' near the Emirates, whose "great range of pies, roasties and gravies" is named for members of the Arsenal team – "good grub at good prices", plus an "ever-changing" list of beers and wines. / N7 8DL; www.pieburycorner.com.

PIED À TERRE W1 £110 553
34 Charlotte St 7636 1178 2–1C
David Moore's "perennially excellent!" foodie temple in Fitzrovia remains one of London's prime gastronomic 'heavy hitters' – service is "outstanding", the "very clever" cuisine is "a joy", and a friendly sommelier oversees a "treasure trove" of wine. Stop Press – chef Marcus Eaves left in early September 2015, but David Moore has a good track record of attracting the best talent here. / W1T 2NH; www.pied-a-terre.co.uk; @PiedaTerreUK; 10.45 pm; closed Sat L & Sun; booking: max 7; set weekday L £60 (FP), set pre-theatre £64 (FP).

Pig & Butcher N1 £52 444
80 Liverpool Rd 7226 8304 8–3D
"Beautiful meats cooked to perfection" are the highlight of the daily changing menu of this "very decent" Islington gastropub – "it's very busy, and rightly so". / N1 0QD; www.thepigandbutcher.co.uk; @pigandbutcher; 10 pm, Sun 9 pm; Mon-Thu D only, Fri-Sun open L & D.

Pilpel £9 442
38 Brushfield Street, London, E1 7247 0146 12–2B
Old Spitalfields Mkt, E1 7375 2282 12–2B
146 Fleet St, EC4 7583 2030 9–2A
Paternoster Sq, EC4 7248 9281 9–2B
"Just really really good falafel" from this small chain – "crisp but never dry", "deeply flavoured", "always fresh", and pleasantly "fluffy". / www.pilpel.co.uk; (1) MON - FRI 4pm (2) Mon-Fri 4pm / Sun 5pm(3) Mon - Thirs 8pm / Fri 4pm(4) Mon - Thurs 9pm / Fri 4pm / Sun 6pm; some branches closed Sat & Sun.

Piquet W1 NEW £55
92-94 Newman St 3826 4500 3–1D
The first solo effort from chef Allan Pickett (last seen at D&D London's Plateau) is set to open in autumn 2015, backed by Bodean's founder André Blais – expect classic French-style cuisine using British ingredients. / W1T 3EZ; www.piquet-restaurant.co.uk.

El Pirata W1 £39 344
5-6 Down St 7491 3810 3–4B
"Mad, slightly Bohemian bar" (well, by Mayfair's stodgy standards anyway) whose "lively" style and "good-value tapas" makes for "a lot of fun at very reasonable prices" for such an expensive area. / W1J 7AQ; www.elpirata.co.uk; @ElPirataMayfair; 11.30 pm; closed Sat L & Sun.

Pitt Cue Co W1 £25 533

1 Newburgh St 7287 5578 3–2D

"Pulled pork the best this side of Austin, TX" and other meaty-licious treats induce severe "cravings" in fans of this "brilliant BBQ", just off Carnaby Street; "you find queues and end up sharing tables, but this is part of the experience!" / W1F 7RB; www.pittcue.co.uk; @PittCueCo.

Pizarro SE1 £50 344

194 Bermondsey St 7407 7339 9–4D

José P is "a genuine star" and his "ebullient" Bermondsey favourite inspires rave reviews for its "helpful" service and "absolutely delicious" cooking; it's somewhat overshadowed by its nearby tapas bar sibling however. See also José Pizarro, EC2. / SE1 3TQ; www.josepizarro.com/restaurants/pizarro; @Jose_Pizarro; 11 pm, Sun 10 pm.

Pizza East £48 434

310 Portobello Rd, W10 8969 4500 6–1A
79 Highgate Rd, NW5 3310 2000 8–1B
56 Shoreditch High St, E1 7729 1888 12–1B

"Get your skinnys on, brush up the face fur and maybe have a tattoo also" if you visit these "too-cool-for-school, hipster heavens". But it seems "you can have both style and substance" – staff are "friendly" and the pizza is "totally inauthentic yet utterly delicious". / www.pizzaeast.com; @PizzaEast; E1 Sun-Wed 11 pm, Thu 12 am, Fri-Sat 1am; W10 Mon-Thu 11.30 pm, Fri-Sat 12 am, Sun 10.30 pm.

Pizza Metro £43 432

64 Battersea Rise, SW11 7228 3812 10–2C
147-149 Notting Hill Gt, W11 7727 8877 6–2B

"Proper, Neapolitan wood-fired pizza" (served al metro) drags fans from all over town to this "busy" old-favourite in Battersea, which always delivers a "fun" (if "noisy") night out; it has a similar, but less well-known, sibling in Notting Hill. / SW11 1EQ; www.pizzametropizza.com; @pizzametropizza; 11 pm, Fri & Sat midnight; no Amex.

Pizza Pilgrims £33 334

102 Berwick St, W1 0778 066 7258 3–2D
11-12 Dean St, W1 7287 8964 3–1D
Kingly Ct, Carnaby St, W1 7287 2200 3–2C

"I don't like pizza, but I LOVE this pizza!" – the Elliot brothers' "funky and fun" Soho pitstops are "worth the pilgrimage" thanks to "authentic" fare that's "a slice above the chains". / Mon - Sat 10.30pm, Sun 9.30 pm.

PizzaExpress £41 222

Branches throughout London

"Still the Daddy!" – this "amazingly consistent", 50-year-old chain remains formidably successful, not least as an "ultra-reliable, go-to-destination with the kids"; its ambience rating took a swallow dive this year however – something about the management style of new owners Hony Capital? / www.pizzaexpress.co.uk; 11.30 pm - midnight; most City branches closed all or part of weekend; no booking at most branches; SRA-1.*

Pizzeria Oregano N1 £41 443

18-19 St Albans Pl 7288 1123 *8–3D*

"Shhh don't tell anyone!" – fans of this "tucked-away Italian, hidden off Upper Street", say "its pizzas can't be beat"; "one of the best places hereabouts for a family meal". / N1 0NX; www.pizzaoregano.co.uk; @PizzeriaOregano; 11 pm, Fri 11.30 pm, Sun 10.30 pm; closed weekday L.

Pizzeria Pappagone N4 £36 344

131 Stroud Green Rd 7263 2114 *8–1D*

"Make sure you book at the weekends", for this "bustling" Stroud Green Italian ("the perfect spot for any family that doesn't want to be the noisiest one there"); "speedy" service is "the friendliest ever", and "outstanding" pizza is the highlight of a wide menu. / N4 3PX; www.pizzeriapappagone.co.uk; @Pizza_Pappagone; midnight.

Pizzeria Rustica TW9 £41 443

32 The Quadrant 8332 6262 *1–4A*

"Genuinely 'home-made' pizza" wins fans for this "hectic, not exactly spacious, but efficient and jolly" outfit, handy for Richmond station. / TW9 1DN; www.pizzeriarustica.co.uk; @RusticaPizzeria; Mon-Sat 11 pm, Sun 10 pm; no Amex.

PJ's Bar and Grill SW3 £58 344

52 Fulham Rd 7581 0025 *5–2C*

"Great brunch on weekends" is a well-established Chelsea ritual at this large, polo-themed venue, where "fun at the bar" is a greater draw than the "wide choice of sometimes unimaginative fare". / SW3 6HH; www.pjsbarandgrill.co.uk; @PJsBARANDGRILL; 10.30 pm, Sun 10 pm.

Plateau E14 £70 233

Canada Pl 7715 7100 *11–1C*

"My go-to place for a business meal in Canary Wharf" is how many E14 worker bees think of D&D London's elevated vantage-point ("lovely views" of Docklands), despite its "hard furnishings" and food that's "good not great". Top Menu Tip – "super dinner-time special offers". / E14 5ER; www.plateau-restaurant.co.uk; @plateaulondon; 10.15 pm; closed Sat L & Sun; set menu £47 (FP).

The Plough SW14 £45 344

42 Christ Church Rd 8876 7833 *10–2A*

"After a walk in Richmond Park, this traditional East Sheen pub is a wonderful destination"; the food – "a combination of pub grub and 'smarter' dishes" – is "reliably good", service makes an effort, and as well as an atmospheric interior, there's a big outside area with heaters. / SW14 7AF; theplough.com; Mon-Thu 9.30 pm, Fri & Sat 10 pm, Sun 9 pm; no Amex.

Plum + Spilt Milk
Great Northern Hotel N1 £64 233

King's Cross 3388 0800 *8–3C*

"Very convenient for the Eurostar", this "comfortable" and "beautifully-lit" operation is "ideal for business meetings", or "to make the start of a journey special"; its cooking – if sometimes "uninspiring" – is "pretty solid" too. / N1C 4TB; www.plumandspiltmilk.com; @PlumSpiltMilk; 11 pm, Sun 10 pm; set weekday L £44 (FP).

Plum Valley W1 £51 323

20 Gerrard St 7494 4366 4–3A

"Rising above the mundane standards of Chinatown" – this somewhat superior venture particularly wins praise for its "great dim sum with a twist". / W1D 6JQ; www.plumvalleylondon.com; 11.30 pm.

Poissonnerie de l'Avenue SW3 £70 333

82 Sloane Ave 7589 2457 5–2C

"Just where to take an aged relative" – this "elegant" Brompton Cross stalwart is "reminiscent of a bygone age"; "the bill mounts up", but its loyal, silver-haired following just say "thank goodness for a place like this", with "courteous" service and "unfailingly good fish". / SW3 3DZ; www.poissonnerie.co.uk; 11.30 pm, Sun 10,30 pm.

POLLEN STREET SOCIAL W1 £95 222

8-10 Pollen St 7290 7600 3–2C

Eeeessh! – turns out Jason Atherton isn't superhuman after all, as falling ratings at his original solo venture give the first hints of growing pains amidst his burgeoning (but hitherto seemingly bulletproof) empire. This, the original Social, still has legions of fans who laud its "utterly inventive" cuisine and "buzzy" (if "downright noisy") vibe, but its performance has seemed more "generic" and "passionless" of late, with gripes over "unmemorable" meals at high prices, and "conveyor-belt" service. / W1S 1NQ; www.pollenstreetsocial.com; @PollenStSocial; 10.45 pm; closed Sun; set weekday L £63 (FP).

Polpetto W1 £48 333

11 Berwick St 7439 8627 3–2D

Fans of this Soho branch of Russell Norman's Venetian tapas empire say it's "easily his best" – "a great little 'bacaro', oozing atmosphere, matched by delicious small plates"; even so, there are one or two reporters for whom "it's not as good as expected". / W1F 0PL; www.polpo.co.uk; @PolpettoW1; 11 pm.

Polpo £40 223

41 Beak St, W1 7734 4479 3–2D
142 Shaftesbury Ave, WC2 7836 3119 4–2B
6 Maiden Ln, WC2 7836 8448 4–3D
Duke Of York Sq, SW3 7730 8900 5–2D NEW
126-128 Notting Hill Gate, W11 7229 3283 6–2B
2-3 Cowcross St, EC1 7250 0034 9–1A

"Are they starting to believe their own PR" at Russell Norman's NYC-style hang-outs? Legions of fans still say they're "such fun" with "tasty", "simple" Venetian tapas, but a growing number – citing "erratic" service and "mediocre" food – believe "it's all beginning to feel a little dispiriting and chain-y". / www.polpo.co.uk; W1 & EC1 11 pm; WC2 11 pm, Sun 10.30 pm; W1 & EC1 closed D Sun.

Le Pont de la Tour SE1 £80 224

36d Shad Thames 7403 8403 9–4D

It has "stunning views" of Tower Bridge, but D&D London's "elegant" landmark has seemed "stuck in the '90s" in recent years, and – aided by its "serious" wine list – appeals most as a business venue nowadays. In October 2015 it re-opens after a major two-month face-lift – let's hope they will pep up the "decent" but pricey cooking too. / SE1 2YE; www.lepontdelatour.co.uk; @lepontdelatour; 10.30 pm, Sun 9.30 pm; no trainers; set Sun L £54 (FP).

Popeseye £47 342

108 Blythe Rd, W14 7610 4578 7–1C
36 Highgate Hill, N19 3601 3830 8–1B
277 Upper Richmond Rd, SW15 8788 7733 10–2A

"Unerringly succulent steaks" plus "quality, affordable red wines" is a "straightforward" formula that's sustained these "cosy", if basic local bistros since way before the current steakhouse craze; the Olympia original has always eclipsed its Putney spin-off, but feedback is good on the new Highgate branch. / www.popeseye.com; 10.30 pm; D only, closed Sun; no credit cards.

Poppies £29 434

30 Hawley Cr, NW1 7267 0440 8–2B
6-8 Hanbury St, E1 7247 0892 12–2C

"No-frills", fish 'n' chip restaurants in Spitalfields and Camden Town where "you eat surrounded by Post-War memorabilia, and served by staff in period dress"; it's all done "with style and zing", and "serves better food than you might expect"; live music in NW1 too.

La Porchetta Pizzeria £34 233

33 Boswell St, WC1 7242 2434 2–1D
141-142 Upper St, N1 7288 2488 8–2D
147 Stroud Green Rd, N4 7281 2892 8–1D
74-77 Chalk Farm Rd, NW1 7267 6822 8–2B
84-86 Rosebery Ave, EC1 7837 6060 9–1A

Of all the wide variety of dishes, it's particularly the "genuine pizzas" in "good portions" (and at "fair value" prices) that keep packing in punters at these upbeat north London stand-bys; "lovely", "no fuss" service too. / www.laporchetta.net; Mon - Sat 11pm, Sun 10 pm; WC1 closed Sat L & Sun; N1,EC1 & NW1 closed Mon-Fri L; N4 closed weekday L; no Amex.

La Porte des Indes W1 £65 334

32 Bryanston St 7224 0055 2–2A

"From the outside it appears ordinary", but inside this "Tardis-like" space near Marble Arch is "vast, exotic and beautiful", complete with "a waterfall and costumed waiters"; it's all good "fun", and "complemented by great food" from an "upmarket" French-colonial Indian menu. / W1H 7EG; www.laportedesindes.com; @LaPorteDesIndes; 11.30 pm, Sun 10.30 pm.

Il Portico W8 £54 354

277 Kensington High St 7602 6262 7–1D

"You get treated like the prodigal son returning home", if you're one of the many regulars at this easily-missed, "convivial" stalwart, near Kensington Odeon, "run by the same family since its inception back in the 1970's"; "all the old favourites are on the menu" and realised to a very dependable standard. / W8 6NA; www.ilportico.co.uk; 10.45 pm; closed Sun.

Portland W1 NEW £58 553

113 Great Portland St 7436 3261 2–1B

Outstanding "new kid-on-the-foodie-block", which crept into Fitzrovia without fanfare, but is proving one of the year's gastronomic highlights; its "functional" and "echo-y" design covers the "bare essentials", the notably "genuine" service (led by co-owner Will Lander) is "spot on", and the "eclectic" cuisine is "novel" and "exciting". / W1W 6QQ; www.portlandrestaurant.co.uk; @portland113; 9.45 pm; closed Sun.

Portobello Ristorante W11 £50 333

7 Ladbroke Rd 7221 1373 6–2B

It's well worth knowing about this "very friendly and VERY Italian" spot, just off Notting Hill Gate; the welcome is "warm", they serve "wonderful" pizza, there's a superb outside terrace in summer, and it's a winner if you have kids too. / W11 3PA; www.portobellolondon.co.uk; 10 pm, Fri-Sat 11 pm.

**The Portrait
National Portrait Gallery WC2** £58 234

St Martin's Pl 7312 2490 4–4B

"Stunning views towards Nelson and Parliament" are the exceptional talking points of this top-floor dining room, by Trafalgar Square; fans say the cooking is "amazingly good for a gallery" too, but to harsher critics that translates as "reliable but unexciting" (maybe go for an "impressive brunch"). / WC2H 0HE; www.npg.org.uk/visit/shop-eat-drink.php; @NPGLondon; Thu-Fri 8.30 pm; Sun-Wed closed D.

Potli W6 £42 433

319-321 King St 8741 4328 7–2B

"No idea why it's still second to Indian Zing!" – this nearby, sparky-looking Hammersmith hang-out serves "inventive and big-flavoured" cuisine that's only a smidgeon less highly rated than at its better known local rival. Top Menu Tip – "fantastic fish curries". / W6 9NH; www.potli.co.uk; @Potlirestaurant; 10.30 pm, Fri & Sat 11.30 pm.

La Poule au Pot SW1 £63 335

231 Ebury St 7730 7763 5–2D

"For romantic gazing across a candle into the eyes of your beloved", there is no better choice than this famously "seductive" haven of "dark corners and intimacy" in Pimlico. The hearty, "classic" Gallic sustenance carries "no surprises", but it and the "colourful", "resolutely French" service all "add to the rustic charm". / SW1W 8UT; www.pouleaupot.co.uk; 11 pm, Sun 10 pm; set weekday L £45 (FP).

Prawn On The Lawn N1 £47 443

220 St Paul's Rd 3302 8668 8–2D

A short hop from Highbury & Islington tube, this fishmonger-cum-restaurant is well worth tracking down for its "amazingly fresh fish, simply prepared", and "knowledgeable owner and staff" – but you may have to squeeze in like the proverbial sardine! / N1 2LY; prawnonthelawn.com; @PrawnOnTheLawn; 11 pm; closed Mon & Sun; no Amex.

Primeur N5 £48 433

116 Petherton Rd 7226 5271 1–1C

"Just what N5 needed!" – an "amazing neighbourhood winner" that's "hard to find and hard to book" but serves "beautiful, simple dishes" and "very good", somewhat "esoteric" wine; negatives? – get on their wrong side, and staff can display a "bad attitude". / N5 2RT; www.primeurn5.co.uk; @Primeurs1; 10 pm; closed Mon, Tue L, Wed L, Thu L & Sun D; no booking.

The Prince Of Wales SW15 £48 434

138 Upper Richmond Rd 8788 1552 10–2B

Ratings are consistently positive for this local, near East Putney station – part of the dependable Food & Fuel chain – praised for its "excellent gastropub fare". / SW15 2SP; www.princeofwalesputney.co.uk; @princeofwalessw; 10 pm, Sun 9.30 pm.

Princess Garden W1 £50 333
8-10 North Audley St 7493 3223 3–2A
You're not in Chinatown now! – this "plush" Mayfair Chinese is an "elegant" ("slightly clinical") spot with "smartly dressed" staff and a "comfortable" interior; the Cantonese cooking is "consistent" and "surprisingly good value" too. / W1K 6ZD; www.princessgardenofmayfair.com; 11 pm.

Princess of Shoreditch EC2 £50 344
76 Paul St 7729 9270 12–1B
"Downstairs, they still know how to do proper pub food" – up the spiral stairs there's a "relaxed" restaurant serving "surprisingly good" grub – at this "unpretentious" but happening Shoreditch boozer. / EC2A 4NE; www.theprincessofshoreditch.com; @princessofs; 10 pm, Sun 8 pm; no Amex.

Princess Victoria W12 £46 333
217 Uxbridge Rd 8749 5886 7–1B
This "beautifully restored, Victorian gin palace" makes a "lovely" and "bustling" retreat from a busy highway, deep in Shepherd's Bush; it's become a major local destination thanks to its "enticing" food and "very strong wine list for a pub". / W12 9DH; www.princessvictoria.co.uk; @pvwestlondon; 10.30 pm, Sun 9.30 pm; no Amex.

Princi W1 £35 324
135 Wardour St 7478 8888 3–2D
"Late-night munchies?"... "pre-theatre snack?"... "need a quick light lunch?" – this "vibrant and fun" (if "jammed") Milanese-inspired deli-patisserie in Soho is just the job, with a "tempting" array of dishes ranging from "top" pizza to "sinful" cakes. / W1F 0UT; www.princi.com; midnight, Sun 10 pm; no booking.

Prix Fixe W1 £39 323
39 Dean St 7734 5976 4–2A
"For an enjoyable evening of classic French food that doesn't break the bank, this little bit of France in Soho delivers with remarkable reliability", and offers "good value for money". / W1D 4PU; www.prixfixe.net; @prixfixelondon; 11.30 pm.

Provender E11 £39 443
17 High St 8530 3050 1–1D
"Proof the east is on the up!" – well-known restaurateur, Max Renzland's "bourgeois" café/bistro in Wanstead is a "classic" Gallic venture, "with a proper French attitude" and very "well-executed" cooking. Top Menu Tip – the £16.50 set lunch menu is "amazing value for money". / E11 2AA; www.provenderlondon.co.uk; @ProvenderBistro; Sun 9 pm, Mon-Fri 10 pm; set weekday L £29 (FP).

The Providores W1 £70 332
109 Marylebone High St 7935 6175 2–1A
Increasingly it is the "consistently interesting" list of NZ wines, visiting makers and "phenomenal" wine dinners that reporters note at this first-floor Marylebone dining room; leaving aside its "terrific" and "innovative" brunch, the Pan-Pacific cuisine is less in the spotlight. / W1U 4RX; www.theprovidores.co.uk; 10.30 pm; SRA-2.*

(Tapa Room)
The Providores W1 **£58** 3 3 3
109 Marylebone High St 7935 6175 2–1A
"Still exciting!" – even after 15 years, support for Peter Gordon's "imaginative" Pan-Pacific Marylebone tapas bar is very solid – if you're prepared to be "squashed" into the "crowded" dining room, results can still "surprise". / W1U 4RX; www.theprovidores.co.uk; @theprovidores; 10.30 pm, Sun 10 pm.

Prufrock Coffee EC1 **£13** 3 4 4
23-25 Leather Ln 0785 224 3470 9–2A
"Much beard stroking" is a hazard at this "coffee geek heaven" near Chancery Lane, where "brews are pulled with excruciating care on a Marzocco machine" – a "buzzy" spot with "very decent" snacks too. / EC1N 7TE; www.prufrockcoffee.com; @PrufrockCoffee; L only; no Amex.

Pulia SE1 NEW **£38**
36 Stoney St 7407 8766 9–4C
Already an established chain of café/delis in its homeland, this Italian newcomer – right in the scrum of London's criminally busy Borough Market – has yet to inspire sufficient reports for a rating. / SE1 9AD; www.pulia.it/en; @Pulia; 8.30 pm.

The Punchbowl W1 **£48** 3 3 4
41 Farm St 7493 6841 3–3A
Serving the well-heeled residents of Mayfair since 1750, this characterful, tastefully revamped Georgian boozer (owned till recently by Madonna-ex, Guy Ritchie) wins decent ratings across the board, albeit from a smattering of reporters. / W1J 5RP; www.punchbowllondon.com; @ThePunchBowlLDN; closed Sun D.

Punjab WC2 **£32** 3 3 3
80 Neal St 7836 9787 4–2C
This "faded" Covent Garden veteran is "one of London's oldest" and "much better than you might expect from its touristy location"; service is good too, although "you do sometimes get the feeling that the quicker they can get it to you, the quicker you'll go". / WC2H 9PA; www.punjab.co.uk; 11 pm, Sun 10.30 pm.

Quaglino's SW1 **£65** 2 2 3
16 Bury St 7930 6767 3–3D
Fans hail the "third coming" of this "glitzy" D&D London veteran – relaunched in 2014 with more regular entertainment – applauding its "much busier and buzzier" vibe in particular; its ratings are still dragged down though by too many "very, very average" reports. / SW1Y 6AJ; www.quaglinos-restaurant.co.uk; @quaglinos; 10.30 pm, Fri & Sat 11 pm; closed Sun; no trainers; set dinner £43 (FP), set weekday L £47 (FP).

The Quality Chop House EC1 **£47** 3 5 3
94 Farringdon Rd 7278 1452 9–1A
"Retaining the era of a bygone age" – this restored 'Working Class Caterer' is a foodie linchpin of Farringdon, despite its "bum-numbingly, cripplingly-uncomfy, bench-seating booths"; "honest" British grub is "prepared with care", but it's somewhat secondary to the "brief but intriguing and fairly priced" wine list. / EC1R 3EA; www.thequalitychophouse.com; @QualityChop; 10.30 pm; closed Sun.

Quantus W4 £41 454

38 Devonshire Rd 8994 0488 7–2A

"Leo, the owner, is very entertaining" and the "amiable" staff set up a "welcoming" vibe at this "snug" Chiswick favourite; food-wise it's rather "in the shadow of La Trompette opposite", but the Latin-influenced cuisine is "always interesting". / W4 2HD; www.quantus-london.com; 10 pm; closed Mon L, Tue L & Sun.

Quattro Passi W1 £95 232

34 Dover St 3096 1444 3–3C

"The sister restaurant of one with the same name on the Amalfi coast" – this Mayfair yearling does win praise (especially from expense accounters) for its "proper Italian cooking" and "spacious" interior, but the "3-digit wine list" is a total shocker ("I actually gasped out loud"), and "at these prices, they must be having a laugh". / W1S 4NG; www.quattropassi.co.uk; @quattropassiuk; 10.30 pm; closed Sun D; set weekday L £38 (FP).

The Queens Arms SW1 £43 344

11 Warwick Way 7834 3313 2–4B

"Cheerful and helpful" staff contribute to the appeal of this popular Pimlico gastropub, where menu staples ("excellent burgers and fish 'n' chips") come particularly recommended; eat in the "crowded" bar or "quieter upstairs". / SW1V 1QT; www.thequeensarmspimlico.co.uk; @thequeensarms; 10 pm.

Queenswood SW11 NEW £46 223

15 Battersea Sq 7228 8877 5–4C

In deepest Battersea, a new bistro featuring extensive drinks options, and with a wider-than-usual array of veggie dishes; fans say it's a "lively addition to the area", but others give it a more lukewarm reception. / SW11 3RA; queenswoodldn.com; @QueenswoodLDN; 10.30 pm; no Amex.

Le Querce SE23 £38 443

66-68 Brockley Rise 8690 3761 1–4D

"The specials board is particularly interesting" at this "fantastic", "family-run" Sardinian – Brockley Park's greatest contribution to London gastronomy, with "very industrious" service. Top Menu Tips – "wonderful homemade pasta" and funky ice creams (e.g. beetroot and basil). / SE23 1LN; www.lequerce.co.uk; 10 pm, Sun 8.30 pm; closed Mon & Tue L.

Quilon SW1 £71 442

41 Buckingham Gate 7821 1899 2–4B

"It looks a little bit like an airport departure lounge", but the Taj Group's "understated", "well-spaced" and luxurious dining room, near Buck House, is a seriously good gastronomic destination with "fragrant", "delightfully subtle" Keralan cuisine that, at its best, is "unbeatable". / SW1E 6AF; www.quilon.co.uk; @TheQuilon; 11 pm, Sun 10.30 pm; set weekday L £50 (FP); SRA-1.*

Quirinale SW1 £60 332

North Ct, 1 Gt Peter St 7222 7080 2–4C

"You may spot the odd politico or two" at this Westminster basement, whose "bright, spacious, high-ceilinged interior" lifts its slightly "sterile" ambience; "in a neighbourhood without too many choices", its "fine" Italian cuisine is all the more notable. / SW1P 3LL; www.quirinale.co.uk; @quirinaleresto; 10.30 pm; closed Sat & Sun; set weekday L £42 (FP).

Quo Vadis W1 **£56** 3 5 4

26-29 Dean St 7437 9585 4–2A

Under the Hart Bros, this well-known Soho veteran is really on song, and the "particularly charming" staff contribute to the "bag-loads of character" in its "bright, spacious and gloriously flower-filled" dining room; Jeremy Lee's food is "not centre stage" but "unfussy, un-showy and very capable". / W1D 3LL; www.quovadissoho.co.uk; 10.45 pm; closed Sun; set pre-theatre £38 (FP), set weekday L £42 (FP).

Rabbit SW3 **£47** 4 4 4

172 King's Rd 3750 0172 5–3C

What is this "fun and original" sibling to Notting Hill's Shed doing in the heart of the King's Road? Its "innovative" British sharing plates can be a bit "microscopic", but are "superbly executed" with "farm-fresh" flavours, and the "creative", "barn-like" decor "works well in the crazy L-shaped space". / SW3 4UP; www.rabbit-restaurant.com; @RabbitResto; closed Mon L & Sun D.

Rabot 1745 SE1 **£58** 2 2 3

2-4 Bedale St 7378 8226 9–4C

"Not as gimmicky as it sounds, but not amazing either" – a fair summary of views on this Hotel Chocolat-backed yearling (with an atmospheric covered terrace overlooking Borough Market), that features "a very original menu with cocoa in every dish". / SE1 9AL; www.hotelcholcolat.com/uk/restaurant/rabot-1745; @rabot1745; 9.30 pm; closed Mon & Sun.

Radha Krishna Bhaven SW17 **£29** 3 3 2

86 Tooting High St 8682 0969 10–2C

Limited feedback on this well-established Tooting curry house – its South Indian cuisine is highly rated by those who do comment however. / SW17 0RN.

Ragam W1 **£28** 5 4 2

57 Cleveland St 7636 9098 2–1B

"Standing the test of time over many years" – this "bright-lit" gem "in the shadow of the Telecom Tower" is arguably "the best cheap curry in central London", serving "terrific South Indian food at great prices"; looks-wise it's always been totally "nondescript", but they refurbished in summer 2015. Top Menu Tip – "dosas are a revelation". / W1T 4JN; www.ragam.co.uk; 11 pm.

Rainforest Café W1 **£58** 1 2 3

20-24 Shaftesbury Ave 7434 3111 3–3D

"I hate it… but kids love it!"; animatronic jungle creatures and real rain are a hazard at this theme diner near Piccadilly Circus, but even those who say it's "severely overpriced" sometimes admit (if through gritted teeth) that it can be great fun! / W1V 7EU; www.therainforestcafe.co.uk; @RainforestCafe; 10 pm, Fri & Sat 8 pm.

Randall & Aubin W1 **£58** 4 4 4

16 Brewer St 7287 4447 3–2D

"It just rocks!"; this "cool little Soho haven" is "a bit cramped and insanely busy" thanks to its "fabulous" seafood ("proper fruits de mer") and "top rotisserie chicken"; in September 2015, its once notoriously uncomfortable tall stools received a plush makeover, making them an even better perch for people-watching! / W1F 0SG; www.randallandaubin.com; @randallandaubin; 11 pm, Sat midnight, Sun 10 pm; no booking at D.

Rani N3 £29 3 2 2
7 Long Ln 8349 4386 1–1B
Finchley's Gujarati veggie-veteran is (on most accounts), "an old favourite back on form", serving a "delicious and varied selection" of "great-value dishes", with "fab homemade condiments". / N3 2PR; www.raniuk.com; @RaniVegetarian; 10.30 pm.

Raoul's Café £46 2 2 3
105-107 Talbot Rd, W11 7229 2400 6–1B
13 Clifton Rd, W9 7289 7313 8–4A
"Perfect eggs" – and "when it's warm, being able to sit out" – are the key selling points of this laid-back brunch favourite in Maida Vale, where "you often queue even though it's not cheap"; the Hammersmith branch has closed, but there's also a (little-commented-on) Notting Hill spin-off. / www.raoulsgourmet.com; 10.15 pm, W11 6.15 pm; booking after 5 pm only.

Rasa £38 4 3 3
6 Dering St, W1 7629 1346 3–2B
Holiday Inn Hotel, 1 Kings Cross, WC1 7833 9787 8–3D
55 Stoke Newington Church St, N16 7249 0344 1–1C
56 Stoke Newington Church St, N16 7249 1340 1–1C
"Ridiculously affordable", "delicately flavoured" (and "relatively healthy") Keralan cooking still wins rave reviews for this small South Indian chain, whose Stokey original remains "a go-to local gem". / www.rasarestaurants.com; 10.45 pm; WC1 & W1 closed Sun.

Rasoi SW3 £99 4 2 3
10 Lincoln St 7225 1881 5–2D
"Set in a beautiful townhouse in a side street near Sloane Square" – Vineet Bhatia's "calm" and "elegant" Chelsea HQ is, for fans, "the definition of innovative Indian cuisine", with each dish "a symphonic composition"; not everyone's impressed though, and even supporters can find it "horrifically expensive". / SW3 2TS; www.rasoirestaurant.co.uk; @GujaratiRasoi; 10.30 pm, Sun 9.45 pm; closed Sat L; set weekday L £58 (FP).

Ravi Shankar NW1 £32 3 2 2
132-135 Drummond St 7388 6458 8–4C
"Mercifully, little changes at this Little India veggie stalwart" – "a complete bargain" that's "the best of the buffet choices hereabouts"; "amazingly cheap at lunch". / NW1 2HL; 10.30 pm.

Red Dog £41 3 2 3
37 Hoxton Sq, N1 3551 8014 12–1B
27-31 Bedford Rd, SW4 3714 2747 10–2D
The "Devastator Burger" is a hallmark of this "crowded and noisy" Kansas City BBQ concept, in Hoxton and now also in Clapham too, but like most of the fare here, while "substantial", it's "fairly expensive". / www.reddogsaloon.co.uk; @reddogsaloonn1.

Red Fort W1 £65 2 2 2
77 Dean St 7437 2525 4–2A
This landmark curry-stalwart in Soho has revamped over the years, but its ratings waned sharply this year; for fans it's still a big favourite, but for others it's now a big let-down – "it made me think of an averagely 'premium' restaurant, in an averagely 'premium' hotel". / W1D 3SH; www.redfort.co.uk; @redfortlondon; 11.15 pm, Sun 10.15 pm; closed Sat L & Sun L; set weekday L & pre-theatre £38 (FP).

The Red Pepper W9 £48 322

8 Formosa St 7266 2708 8–4A

"Shame it's so cramped and uncomfortable", and "very noisy" too – the wood-fired pizza at this long-running Maida Vale fixture can be "excellent". / W9 1EE; www.theredpepperrestaurant.co.uk; Sat 11 pm, Sun 10 pm; closed weekday L; no Amex.

The Refinery NW1 NEW £49 233

5 Brock St, Regent's Pl 3002 5524 8–4C

Part of the Drake & Morgan empire (and sharing its name with the group's Bankside branch), this "light and spacious" arrival is a handy option near Euston station, serving "British staples at reasonable prices". / NW1 3FG; www.therefinerybar.co.uk; @therefinerybar; 10 pm; closed Sun; SRA-3.*

Le Relais de Venise L'Entrecôte £46 322

120 Marylebone Ln, W1 7486 0878 2–1A

18-20 Mackenzie Walk, E14 3475 3331 11–1C

5 Throgmorton St, EC2 7638 6325 9–2C

"A very simple concept that works every time" – this Gallic steakhouse chain offers little choice – you get "a rather tasty green salad", steak with secret sauce, "addictive fries", and second helpings if needed; the setting is "bustling", but "brusque-verging-on-rude" service can leave branches feeling "soulless". / www.relaisdevenise.com; W1 11 pm, Sun 10.30 pm; EC2 10 pm; EC2 closed Sat & Sun; no booking.

Resident Of Paradise Row E2 NEW £46

Arch 252 Paradise Row 7729 9609 12–1D

Locals tip it as a "great Sunday roast and brunch" spot, but otherwise there's limited feedback for this year-old bar/restaurant in Bethnal Green, sheltered by increasingly fashionable railway arches (and with a sizeable outside terrace). / E2 9LE; www.residentlondon.com; @ResidentPR; Tue-Sat 10.15 pm, Sun 8 pm; Kitchen is closed on Mondays but they still serve snacks.

Le Restaurant de Paul £38 443

29-30 Bedford St, WC2 7836 3304 4–3C

Tower 42, Old Broad St, EC2 7562 5599 9–2C NEW

Covent Garden HQ of the famous pâtisserie chain, where fans "are delighted they have a full-blown restaurant" – a civilised chamber, off the main shop. "Ideal for an afternoon-tea break" or light bite anytime (salads, charcuterie, omelettes, etc), a second full-service outpost opened in the City's Tower 42 as we went to press. / WC2E 9ED; www.paul-uk.com; @Paul_Bakery; Sun-Thu 9 pm, Fri & Sat 9.30 pm.

Reubens W1 £55 332

79 Baker St 7486 0035 2–1A

The "best salt beef in London" is hailed by fans of this long-established Marylebone deli-restaurant (the latter in the basement), serving "delicious kosher food in massive portions". / W1U 6RG; www.reubensrestaurant.co.uk; 9.45 pm; closed Fri D & Sat; no Amex.

Rex & Mariano W1 NEW £47 543

St Anne's Ct 7437 0566 4–2A

"A great attempt to redefine seafood dining!"; the Goodman Group have hit another home run with this "bright and airy" newcomer, tucked away down a Soho alleyway, where "sensational" dishes are "extraordinary value". The "waiter-free", iPad ordering can be "confusing", but fans say "it puts the diner at the heart of the meal". Top Menu Tip – raw items, grills, plus "outstanding" salads, ceviches, and courgette fries. Stop Pess – In September 2015, it was announced that Rex & Mariano would move elsewhere – these premises will become another new concept: Zelman Meats.
/ W1F 0BD; rexandmariano.com; @RexandMariano; Sun-Thu 10.30 pm, Fri & Sat 11 pm.

Rextail W1 £83 333

13 Albermarle St 3301 1122 3–3C

Arkady Novikov's year-old basement (a stylish, but "cramped" space of railway-carriage proportions) put in a better performance this year – "the price reflects its Mayfair setting", but it's overall "very enjoyable". / W1S 4HJ; www.rextail.co.uk; @Rextail_London; midnight; closed Sun.

The Rib Man E1 £12 53–

Brick Lane, Brick Lane Market no tel 12–2C

Mark Gevaux's "meltingly tender ribs and rolls of porky greatness" can no longer be found at KERB – now you need to go to Brick Lane on Sundays instead; his "fiery" sauces are the stuff of urban legend – "Look out! They'll blow your head off!" / E1 6HR; www.theribman.co.uk; @theribman.

Rib Room
Jumeirah Carlton Tower Hotel SW1 £103 342

Cadogan Pl 7858 7250 5–1D

"A real treat in every respect" – this luxurious, well-spaced Belgravia dining room is firing on all cylinders after its revamp last year; as well as the top-quality roast beef and grills for which it's long been famous, the "seasonal menus show true skill and inventiveness".
/ SW1X 9PY; www.theribroom.co.uk; @RibRoomSW1; 11 pm, weekends 10.30 pm; set weekday L £69 (FP).

Riccardo's SW3 £43 233

126 Fulham Rd 7370 6656 5–3B

"If you have a table on the terrace, the ambience is great" at this "crowded" (and kid-friendly) "local favourite" in Chelsea, where "amiable Riccardo is usually in attendance"; its "simple" staples are regularly "well-prepared", but can also disappoint nowadays.
/ SW3 6HU; www.riccardos-italian-restaurant.co.uk; @riccardoslondon; 11.30 pm.

The Richmond E8 NEW £52 433

316 Queensbridge Rd 7241 1638 1–2D

Bargain bivalves (£1 an oyster at happy hour) are a mainstay of east London's only raw seafood bar – a feature of Brett Redman's new Hackney hang-out (on the site of LMNT, RIP), which also boasts a "superb fish menu" and "good list of wines by the glass". / E8 3NH; therichmondhackney.com; @The Richmond; Mon-Thu 10 pm, Fri & Sat 10.30 pm; closed Sun D.

Riding House Café W1 £56 224

43-51 Great Titchfield St 7927 0840 3–1C

"Capturing the perfect brunch vibe" – this "buzzy", "NYC-style" haunt in Fitzrovia has a "very media" following that adores it, especially at breakfast (or for a business lunch), and it's "always busy"; even fans concede however, that the cooking here generally is "nothing to shout about". / W1W 7PQ; www.ridinghousecafe.co.uk; @ridinghousecafe; 10.30 pm, Sun 9.30 pm.

Rising Sun NW7 £48 343

137 Marsh Ln, Highwood Hill 8959 1357 1–1B

"An interesting Italian menu" helps differentiate this "picturesque", "small", "very friendly" family-run pub in Mill Hill; "prices seem to have edged up" in recent times, but even so "it's the best for miles around". / NW7 4EY; www.therisingsunmillhill.co.uk; @therisingsunpub; 9.30 pm, Sun 8.30 pm; closed Mon L.

Ristorante Frescobaldi W1 NEW £75 344

15 New Burlington Pl 3693 3435 3–2C

"The name is very '70s" – not so the "amazing and modern but comfy" design of this Mayfair newcomer, the first UK venture of a 700-year-old Italian wine dynasty; chef Roberto Reatini's food is well-praised, but, as one would expect, it's the "incredible" cellar that's the real draw here. / W1S 5HX; frescobaldirestaurants.com; @frescobaldi_london; 10.45 pm.

(Palm Court)
The Ritz W1 £69 245

150 Piccadilly 7493 8181 3–4C

Loved by some ("the afternoon tea is unparalleled!"), but this famous and elegant chamber is to many disappointing ("dry, mechanically-cut sandwiches with fillings I had not seen since a wartime Sunday School party, aimed at naive tourists!"); whichever camp you're in, it's not cheap. / W1C 9BR; www.theritzlondon.com; 7.30 pm; jacket & tie required.

The Ritz Restaurant
The Ritz W1 £125 245

150 Piccadilly 7493 8181 3–4C

"The loveliest dining room in London" – this "wonderfully romantic" Louis XVI-style chamber is "a proper, old-school, fine-dining experience"; it's not a reliable one, however, given food that can be "poor", and even ardent fans can find the bill "shocking". / W1J 9BR; www.theritzlondon.com; @theritzlondon; 10 pm; jacket & tie required.

Riva SW13 £65 442

169 Church Rd 8748 0434 10–1A

With its "exceptional" north Italian cooking and "brilliantly knowledgeable" service – much of it from owner Andreas Riva – this "pricey but first-rate" Barnes fixture remains a place of foodie pilgrimage, and it inspired few gripes this year, despite its rather "drab" interior. Top Menu Tip – "the cinnamon ice cream with balsamic sounds weird but is the best dessert in town". / SW13 9HR; 10.30 pm, Sun 9 pm; closed Sat L.

Rivea
Bulgari Hotel SW7 **£70** 2 4 2
171 Knightsbridge 7151 1025 5–1C
"Alain Ducasse is a genius", say fans of his Knightsbridge basement yearling, hailing its "sublime" small plates (prepared by protégé Damien Leroux), and "effortlessly smooth" service; however at its hefty prices, it can be "short on memorable dishes", and what is a "hip" and "magnificent" setting to some is to others plain "vulgar".
/ SW7 1DW; www.bulgarihotels.com; 10.15 pm; set weekday L £44 (FP).

THE RIVER CAFÉ W6 **£100** 3 2 3
Thames Wharf, Rainville Rd 7386 4200 7–2C
"Eye-wateringly expensive, but brilliant", say disciples of this world-famous Italian café (part of a Thames-side wharf in a Hammersmith backwater), for whom the "sophistication" of the "freshest ingredients prepared for maximum flavour" have long put it "in a league of its own" (especially outside on a sunny day). "Cramped" conditions and "brusque" service can "leave a lot to be desired" however, and there are many, many sceptics who – though not disputing that the grub's good – say prices are just "insane for a bit of al dente pasta".
/ W6 9HA; www.rivercafe.co.uk; @RiverCafeLondon; 9 pm, Sat 9.15 pm; closed Sun D.

Rivington Grill **£52** 3 3 3
178 Greenwich High Rd, SE10 8293 9270 1–3D
28-30 Rivington St, EC2 7729 7053 12–1B
"Efficient", somewhat "grown-up" Shoreditch and Greenwich brasseries, whose "straightforward" grills and burgers mean they are "always a safe bet", if an "unexciting" one. / www.rivingtongrill.co.uk; 11 pm, Sun 10 pm; SE10 closed Mon, Tue L & Wed L.

Roast SE1 **£70** 2 2 2
Stoney St 3006 6111 9–4C
A "top notch breakfast" with "sun streaming through those huge windows" is the most reliable attraction in this "light and airy" (but "soulless") dining room, over Borough Market; however at other times its British fare can seem "severely overpriced" given the "unmemorable" results – "I've had better £10 roasts in a pub!".
/ SE1 1TL; www.roast-restaurant.com; @roastrestuarant; 10.45 pm; closed Sun D; set Sun L £60 (FP); SRA-2.*

Rocca Di Papa **£37** 2 3 4
73 Old Brompton Rd, SW7 7225 3413 5–2B
75-79 Dulwich Village, SE21 8299 6333 1–4D
Even if the fare is "fairly standard stuff", these "always very busy" and "noisy" Italians in South Kensington and Dulwich Village win little but praise; a visit is "always fun". / SW7 11.30 pm; SE21 11 pm.

Rochelle Canteen E2 **£50** 4 3 3
Arnold Circus 7729 5677 12–1C
If you're not a "trendy youngster from a Shoreditch start-up" then prepare to "rough it" at Melanie Arnold & Margot Henderson's "almost secret" venture near Spitalfields Market ("you feel like you're eating in a school playground") – those who do are in for "a hidden world of delight", lovely garden and "imaginative" meals; you can even BYO. / E2 7ES; www.arnoldandhenderson.com; L only, closed Sat & Sun; no Amex.

Rocket £46 333

36-38 Kingsway, WC2 7242 8070 2–1D
2 Churchill Pl, E14 3200 2022 11–1C
201 Bishopsgate, EC2 7377 8863 12–2B
6 Adams Ct, EC2 7628 0808 9–2C

For a "cheap and cheerful" meal in areas like Canary Wharf and Bank this chain of "buzzing" diners generally proves an effective standby (even if it doesn't quite convince all reporters) – pizzas are "authentic" and portions "generous". / 10.30 pm, Sun 9.30 pm; W1 closed Sun; EC2 closed Sat & Sun; SW15 Mon-Wed D only, Bishopsgate closed Sun D, E14.

Roka £83 433

30 North Audley St, W1 7305 5644 3–2A
37 Charlotte St, W1 7580 6464 2–1C
Aldwych House, 71-91 Aldwych, WC2 7294 7636 2–2D
Unit 4, Park Pavilion, 40 Canada Sq, E14 7636 5228 11–1C

"Stunning" sushi and "exquisite robatayaki" again win acclaim for this venerated and recently-expanded Japanese-fusion group (whose Charlotte Street original is the best of the bunch). Enthusiasm dipped a little this year, however, with gripes that the newer siblings in particular seem more "noisy" and "corporate". / www.rokarestaurant.com; 11.15 pm, Sun 10.30 pm; booking: max 8.

The Rooftop Café
The Exchange SE1 £47 335

28 London Bridge St 3102 3770 9–4C

Don't be put off by the "very unwelcoming office-building entrance and a climb up some very shabby stairs" – once you emerge onto the terrace you're greeted by "incredible views" of the Shard and "very dependable" cooking at this "light and airy" hidden gem. / SE1 9SG; therooftopcafe.co.uk; @rooftopcafeldn; closed Mon D, Tue D & Sun.

Roots at N1 N1 £48 553

115 Hemingford Rd 7697 4488 8–3D

"Breathtakingly good" cuisine at very "sensible prices" wins rave reviews for this "very interesting" Indian, "tucked away in Islington"; this "candle-lit, high-ceilinged ex-pub" is "a lovely space" too, and the "gracious" staff "always have a smile for guests". / N1 1BZ; www.rootsatn1.com; @rootsatn1; 10 pm, Sun 9 pm; closed Mon, Tue–Sat D only, Sun open L & D.

Rosa's £35 432

23a Ganton St, W1 7287 9617 3–2C
48 Dean St, W1 7494 1638 4–3A
246 Fulham Rd, SW10 7583 9021 5–3B
Westfield Stratford City, E15 8519 1302 1–1D
12 Hanbury St, E1 7247 1093 12–2C

"Zingy", "simple" dishes "with a decent kick" at "reasonable prices" win praise for this high quality chain of straightforward, "busy" Thai cafés; the original near Brick Lane is still the highest rated, and there's a new Islington branch that's "airier than most". / www.rosaslondon.com; 10.30 pm, Fri & Sat 11 pm, Ganton St Sun 10 pm; some booking restrictions apply.

Rossopomodoro £38 2 2 2
50-52 Monmouth St, WC2 7240 9095 4–3B
214 Fulham Rd, SW10 7352 7677 5–3B
1 Rufus St, N1 7739 1899 12–1B
10 Jamestown Rd, NW1 7424 9900 8–3B
46 Garrett Ln, SW18 8877 9903 10–2B
"It's a chain, but it's a good chain" – the consensus on these "buzzing" Italians, particularly praised for their "fantastic pizza"; that said, for a business actually based in Naples, results overall are surprisingly MOR. / www.rossopomodoro.co.uk; 11.30 pm, WC2 Sun 11.30 pm.

Roti Chai W1 £46 4 4 3
3 Portman Mews South 7408 0101 3–1A
"Really authentic" but "not overpowering" flavours characterise the "exciting Indian street food" at this contemporary-style venue near Selfridges, where there's both a no-booking ground floor, and more formal basement. / W1H 6HS; www.rotichai.com; @rotichai; 10.30 pm.

Roti King
Ian Hamilton House NW1 £22 5 1 1
40 Doric Way 07966 093467 8–3C
"Nothing prepares you for the simply wonderful Malaysian rotis" freshly made "in front of your eyes" at the counter of this "tiny", "brusque" and "in-no-way-pretty" basement "dive" in "a grotty bit of Euston". / NW1 1LH; www.facebook.com/rotikinglondon.

Rotorino E8 £48 3 3 3
434 Kingsland Rd 7249 9081 1–1D
"Book a booth, and stay till late", say fans of Stevie Parle's Dalston spin-off, whose "fabulous, stylish interior and seductive low lighting" lends it a "buzzy" and "romantic" aura; it's "slightly pricey" however, and "the food ranges from very good to ordinary". / E8 4AA; www.rotorino.com; @Rotorino; 11 pm.

Rotunda Bar & Restaurant
Kings Place N1 £54 2 2 3
90 York Way 7014 2840 8–3C
With its beautiful canal-side terrace, this "buzzy" arts centre brasserie is ideal in summer, especially on business; realisation of the dishes – meat in particular – can be "wonderful", but can also be "way off-the-mark". / N1 9AG; www.rotundabarandrestaurant.co.uk; @rotundalondon; 11 pm; closed Sun.

Roux at Parliament Square
RICS SW1 £88 5 5 3
12 Great George St 7334 3737 2–3C
The Roux family don't seem to have told Masterchef winner Steve Groves that MPs aren't the most discerning bunch! – his cooking at this elegant dining room near Parliament is "truly noteworthy", with many reports of "absolutely brilliant" meals and "exemplary service". / SW1P 3AD; www.rouxatparliamentsquare.co.uk; @RouxAPS; 10 pm; closed Sat & Sun.

Roux at the Landau
The Langham W1 £100 234

1c Portland Pl 7965 0165 2–1B

"There's a peaceful serenity" to this "beautiful" chamber, over the road from Broadcasting House, suiting it to either a "comfortable" business lunch or "romantic treat"; most reporters praise the "fabulous" cuisine too, although one or two "expected more" of the illustrious Roux brand. / W1B 1JA; www.thelandau.com; @Langham_Hotel; 10.30 pm ; closed Sat L & Sun; no trainers; set weekday L £68 (FP).

Rowley's SW1 £69 222

113 Jermyn St 7930 2707 3–3D

Fans of this St James's veteran (occupying the original Wall's Butchers Shop) hail its Chateaubriand as "among the best in London", and say its "unlimited frites are a joy!"; it's "not cheap" though, and its wine list can seem particularly "ordinary and overpriced". / SW1Y 6HJ; www.rowleys.co.uk; @rowleys_steak; 10.30 pm.

Rox Burger SE13 NEW £26 433

82 Lee High Rd 3372 4631 1–4D

In Lewisham, a tiny burger bar serving "fantastic homemade burgers" and "unusual sides" too; if there's a complaint it's that the "simple" premises are just "too small". / SE13 5PT; www.roxburger.com.

Royal Academy W1 £48 222

Burlington Hs, Piccadilly 7300 5608 3–3D

"They always seem to be trying to improve this barn of a restaurant" – a potentially charming chamber at the heart of the famous galleries; but while fans rate it as a handy West End standby, too often its performance is "lacking". / W1J 0BD; www.royalacademy.org.uk; @khrestaurant; 10.30 pm; L only, ex Fri open L & D; no booking at L.

Royal China £48 412

24-26 Baker St, W1 7487 4688 2–1A
805 Fulham Rd, SW6 7731 0081 10–1B
13 Queensway, W2 7221 2535 6–2C
30 Westferry Circus, E14 7719 0888 11–1B

"If you love Hong Kong, you'll feel right at home" at these "wonderfully garish" Cantonese stalwarts, which attract "overwhelming queues" to enjoy what many fans consider "the best dim sum in London"; service, though, is of the "couldn't-give-a-fig" variety. / www.royalchinagroup.co.uk; 10.45 pm, Fri & Sat 11.15 pm, Sun 9.45 pm; no booking Sat & Sun L.

Royal China Club W1 £74 432

40-42 Baker St 7486 3898 2–1A

"Extremely good Chinese fare is cooked with real class" at the Royal China group's "pricey but superior" Marylebone flagship; no great prizes for decor however, which "lacks warmth". / W1U 7AJ; www.rcguk.co.uk; 11 pm, Sun 10.30 pm.

The Royal Exchange Grand Café
The Royal Exchange EC3 £55 224

The Royal Exchange Bank 7618 2480 9–2C

The "beautiful", ultra-impressive location (a majestic covered courtyard) eclipses all other aspects of this heart-of-the-City seafood operation – "a great venue for business" from breakfast on. / EC3V 3LR; www.royalexchange-grandcafe.co.uk; @rexlondon; 10 pm; closed Sat & Sun; set weekday L £39 (FP).

RSJ SE1 **£50** 3 3 2

33 Coin St 7928 4554 9–4A

"A remarkable and superb Loire wine list" is the crown jewel feature of this "unfailing" old timer near the National Theatre; OK, "the decor is 20 years out of date" (and wasn't great then), but staff are "welcoming", and you get "really good French food at reasonable prices". / SE1 9NR; www.rsj.uk.com; @RSJWaterloo; 11 pm; closed Sat L & Sun; set always available £36 (FP).

Rucoletta EC2 **£47** 4 3 2

6 Foster Lane 7600 7776 9–2C

"A very serviceable Italian, near St Paul's" that's "efficient for hungry bankers and industrialists", and whose "enjoyable and steady" cooking is "a big step-up from the surrounding chains". / EC2V 6HH; www.rucoletta.co.uk; @RucolettaLondon; 9.30 pm, Thu-Sat 10 pm; closed Sat D & Sun; no Amex.

Rugoletta **£38** 3 3 3

59 Church Ln, N2 8815 1743 1–1B

308 Ballards Ln, N12 8445 6742 1–1B

"A traditional, warm Italian welcome" (including to kids) adds to the appeal of these Barnet and East Finchley locals, where the "pizza, pasta and well-presented main dishes" are "for the price, fantastico!" – (and you can BYO). / N2 8DR; www.larugoletta.com; 10.30 pm; closed Sun.

Rules WC2 **£78** 3 2 5

35 Maiden Ln 7836 5314 4–3D

"Even if you would normally avoid tourist spots like the plague", London's oldest restaurant (Covent Garden, 1798) satisfies even sceptical visitors with its "truly historic" interior and "proud-to-be-old-fashioned" menu, majoring in meat, game and "old-school puds"; one caution though – it's getting "oh oh so expensive". / WC2E 7LB; www.rules.co.uk; @RulesRestaurant; 11.30 pm, Sun 10.30 pm; no shorts.

Sackville's W1 NEW **£68**

8a Sackville St 7734 3623 3–3D

Chef/patron Wayne Dixon trained at Ramsay's 'maze Grill' and it certainly shows when it comes to the pricing at this new Mayfair venture; the focus is on posh patties (including the Wagyu Sackville burger at £38), plus expensive cuts of steak with lashings of shaved truffles. / W1S 3DF.

Le Sacré-Coeur N1 **£36** 3 3 4

18 Theberton St 7354 2618 8–3D

"A cheerful piece of Paris, just north of Angel," this well-loved veteran serves "delightful" French fare with "charm and verve"; it is perhaps "a bit tatty" nowadays, but no denying the "brilliant value for money". / N1 0QX; www.lesacrecoeur.co.uk; 11 pm, Sat 11.30 pm, Sun 10.30 pm; set weekday L £24 (FP).

Sacro Cuore NW10 **£36** 4 3 3

45 Chamberlayne Rd 8960 8558 1–2B

"The best pizza in North West London by far" – this "cool" Kensal Rise three-year-old makes "handmade pizza" that's "just like in Naples". / NW10 3NB; www.sacrocuore.co.uk/menu.html; @SacroCuorePizza; 10.15 pm; no Amex; no booking at certain times.

Sagar £35 443

17a Percy St, W1 7631 3319 3–2B
31 Catherine St, WC2 7836 6377 4–3D
157 King St, W6 8741 8563 7–2C

"Delicious" dosas and "excellent breads" are highlights of the "fabulous and very reasonably priced" veggie South Indian dishes at these low-key, but "pleasant and efficient" (and vegan-friendly) cafés. / www.sagarveg.co.uk; Sun-Thu 10.45 pm, Fri & Sat 11.30 pm.

Sager & Wilde E2 £38 344

193 Hackney Rd 8127 7330 12–1C

"The nibbles are fine", but it's the "fabulous and intriguing wine selection", "enthusiastic" staff and "relaxed vibe" which drive the appeal of this Haggerston "jewel". / E2 8JP; www.sagerandwilde.com; 10 pm; closed weekday L.

Saigon Saigon W6 £39 344

313-317 King St 8748 6887 7–2B

"Staff are lovely" and add to the engagingly rickety and "authentic" vibe of this well-established Hammersmith Vietnamese, praised for its "powerful flavours" and "great value". / W6 9NH; www.saigon-saigon.co.uk; @saigonsaigonuk; 11 pm, Sat & Mon 10 pm.

St John EC1 £62 543

26 St John St 7251 0848 9–1B

"Still brilliant after all this time" – Fergus Henderson's white-walled, Smithfield legend continues to produce supremely "honest" offal-heavy dishes based on "awesome ingredients" (most famously the "hugely addictive bone marrow"). Top Tip – the "rowdy" adjacent bar is as good in its way as the main dining room. / EC1M 4AY; www.stjohngroup.uk.com; @SJRestaurant; 11 pm; closed Sat L & Sun D.

St John Bread & Wine E1 £56 533

94-96 Commercial St 7251 0848 12–2C

"The finest bacon butties in the universe" are but one highlight of the "otherworldly" small plates (majoring in "offal-y wonders") served at this marvellously "vibrant" (if "noisy") Shoreditch canteen; "service can be prickly, but hey ho". / E1 6LZ; www.stjohngroup.uk.com/spitalfields; @StJBW; 10.30 pm, Sun 9.30 pm.

St Johns N19 £46 435

91 Junction Rd 7272 1587 8–1C

"A longstanding neighbourhood favourite" in Archway (George Michael's no. 1 pub, apparently), whose huge, "always buzzing" dining room occupies a lovely converted old ballroom; it serves an "intriguing" mix of "traditional-with-a-twist" dishes. / N19 5QU; www.stjohnstavern.com; @stjohnstavern; 11 pm, Sun 9.30 pm; Mon-Thu D only, Fri-Sun open L & D; no Amex; booking: max 12.

St Pancras Grand
St Pancras Int'l Station NW1 £53 123

The Concourse 7870 9900 8–3C

It occupies a "beautiful space", and – if you're waiting for a train – this grand railway brasserie is "a haven from the busy concourse"; the food doesn't live up to the interior however, and "they know how to charge for the experience". / NW1 2QP; www.saintpancrasgrand.co.uk; @SearcyStPancras; 10.30 pm, Sun 8 pm.

Sakana-tei W1 £45 5 2 1
11 Maddox St 7629 3000 3–2C
For "the most authentic Japanese in London", some Asian ex-pats tip this "decrepit" Mayfair basement – "it's the best in the west (and that's not me, but a Japanese CEO with a jaw-dropping expense account!)" / W1S 2QF; 10 pm; closed Sun.

Sake No Hana SW1 £75 3 1 2
23 St James's St 7925 8988 3–4C
You take "a weirdly shopping-centre-esque escalator" to this slickly designed Japanese, in a '60s St James's development next to The Economist; its "Asian-fusion" cuisine can be "very enjoyable", but it's "expensive", service can be "un-welcoming" and too often there's "no atmosphere". / SW1A 1HA; www.sakenohana.com; @sakenonhana; 11 pm, Fri & Sat 11.30 pm; closed Sun.

Salaam Namaste WC1 £36 3 2 2
68 Millman St 7405 3697 2–1D
"Excellent Indian food with a twist" rewards a visit to this "busy", brightly lit Bloomsbury venture. / WC1N 3EF; www.salaam-namaste.co.uk; @SalaamNamasteUK; 11.30 pm, Sun 11 pm.

Sale e Pepe SW1 £66 3 4 3
9-15 Pavilion Rd 7235 0098 5–1D
"It feels like the heydey of the 1980s", at this "always lively" old faithful trattoria, near Harrods; "prices are a bit high", and "it can be so noisy", but the grub's "tasty", service is "with a smile", and it's good "fun". / SW1X 0HD; www.saleepepe.co.uk; 11.30 pm; no shorts.

Salloos SW1 £58 4 4 3
62-64 Kinnerton St 7235 4444 5–1D
"Wonderful, old-style Pakistani", in a posh Belgravia mews – "the marinated lamb chops are to die for", but "it's a shame it's so expensive". / SW1X 8ER; www.salloos.co.uk; 11 pm; closed Sun; need 5+ to book.

Salmontini SW1 NEW £71
1 Pont St 7118 1999 5–1D
On a Belgravia site some still recall as Drones (long RIP), a plush new cocktail bar and restaurant, backed by a Beirut-based brand; early reports are very enthusiastic about its "knowledgeable" staff and "Japanese/European menu" majoring in smoked fish and sushi. / SW1X 9EJ; salmontini.co.uk; @Salmontini_Uk; 10.45pm, Fri & Sat 11.15 pm, Sun 10.30 pm.

The Salon Somerset House WC2 NEW £74
Lancaster Pl 3693 3247 2–2D
A recently added annex to Skye Gyngell's Somerset House dining room (Spring), serving a very pared down menu and drinks to drop-ins only (no reservations); it opened too late for a rating, but it's certainly a relatively affordable option at this beautiful landmark. / WC2R 1LA; www.springrestaurant.co.uk/salon; @Spring_Rest; 10.30 pm; closed Sun D; no booking.

Le Salon Privé TW1 NEW £46 345
43 Crown Rd 8892 0602 1–4A
Hopeful early-days reports on this "newly revitalised" St Margarets bistro (previously Brula, RIP) – under new owners, the small space "is much improved", and the "genuine French cuisine" is at least as good, if not better than before. / TW1 3EJ; 10.30 pm.

Salt & Honey W2 NEW £45
28 Sussex Pl 7706 7900 6–1D
From the duo behind Manuka Kitchen in Fulham, a new, little neighbourhood bistro in Bayswater serving British-Antipodean food – it opened after our survey closed so we look forward to a full review next year. / W2 2TH; www.saltandhoneybistro.com; @Salthoneybistro; 10 pm, Sun 9 pm; closed Mon.

The Salt House NW8 £49 333
63 Abbey Rd 7328 6626 8–3A
Near that famous zebra crossing, an attractive and consistent St John's Wood gastropub with good outdoor seating, that's a "useful" option hereabouts. / NW8 0AE; www.salthouseabbeyroad.com; @thesalthousenw8; 11 pm, Fri & Sat midnight.

Salt Yard W1 £49 323
54 Goodge St 7637 0657 2–1B
Devotees still hail the "sheer deliciousness" of the Italian/Spanish tapas at this convivial Fitzrovia haunt, whose "relaxing" style is fine for a more informal business lunch; compared with its glory days though, it's "lost its edge", and former fans can find it "average" nowadays. / W1T 4NA; www.saltyard.co.uk; @SaltYardLdn; 10.45 pm, Sun 9.45 pm.

Salvation In Noodles £34 322
122 Balls Pond Rd, N1 7254 4534 1–1C
2 Blackstock Rd, N4 7254 4534 8–1D NEW
"The outside bike-parking is a nice touch" at this trendy Dalston yearling, but while fans love its "huge and delicious" pho and other fare, critics say "there are better Vietnamese a short distance away"; they must be doing something right though, as a new branch opened in Finsbury Park in July.

San Carlo Cicchetti £50 333
215 Piccadilly, W1 7494 9435 3–3D
30 Wellington St, WC2 7240 6339 4–3D
Yes, they're a bit "OTT, camp, bright and flashy", but these "efficient" tourist-land outposts of a national Italian chain generally come recommended, thanks to their "fun and bustling style" and "tasty", "relatively well-priced" sharing dishes.

San Daniele del Friuli N5 £44 343
72 Highbury Park 7226 1609 8–1D
The daily specials on the blackboard are a good bet if you visit this engaging, family-run "local favourite", in Highbury Park, with enjoyable, seasonal Italian cooking. / N5 2XE; www.sandanielehighbury.co.uk; 10.30 pm; closed Mon L, Tue L, Wed L & Sun; no Amex.

The Sands End SW6 £51 344
135 Stephendale Rd 7731 7823 10–1B
It's "a bit stereotypically Sloaney" (and pricey), but this popular gastropub in deepest Fulham is "super" – the scoff's "consistently good", and its "lovely interior" helps it feel very "chilled out". / SW6 2PR; www.thesandsend.co.uk; @thesandsend; 10 pm.

Santa Maria W5 £32 533
15 St Mary's Rd 8579 1462 1–3A
"I've seen Italians travel from East London just to get their fix!" – this "superb" Ealing outfit arguably serves "the best pizza in London"; "it's hard to secure a table though, and sometimes they want you out pretty rapido". / W5 5RA; www.santamariapizzeria.com; @SantaMariaPizza; 10.30 pm.

Santini SW1 £75 222
29 Ebury St 7730 4094 2–4B
"Professional" Belgravia stalwart, with a swish, "light and airy" interior, and lovely sunny terrace – the "authentic" Italian cooking is "competent" too; the problem is that it is decidedly "not cheap". / SW1W 0NZ; www.santini-restaurant.com; 10 pm, Sat 11 pm.

Santore EC1 £44 433
59 Exmouth Mkt 7812 1488 9–1A
"Genuine Neapolitan" in Exmouth Market majoring in "winning pizza"; inside is "crowded and noisy", but "outside it's wonderful on a warm evening" – "greet the waiter with a 'Buona Sera' and you might get a better table". / EC1R 4QL; www.santorerestaurant.co.uk; 11 pm.

Sapori Sardi SW6 £48 442
786 Fulham Rd 7731 0755 10–1B
"Simple fresh ingredients, beautifully cooked" inspire rave reviews for this Fulham Sardinian – "a top local", with "friendly" service and a "relaxed" style. / SW6 5SL; www.saporisardi.co.uk; @saporisardi; 11 pm; no Amex.

Sardo W1 £57 322
45 Grafton Way 7387 2521 2–1B
"Really solid, interesting and unfussy" – such are the virtues of this "traditional" Fitzrovia Sardinian, indeed fans of its "authentic" and "copious" cooking, enjoyable wines, and "buzzy" style say it's "underrated"; "slightly cramped in the back room". / W1T 5DQ; www.sardo-restaurant.com; 11 pm; closed Sat L & Sun.

Sarracino NW6 £45 422
186 Broadhurst Gdns 7372 5889 1–1B
"Totally authentic Neapolitan pizza" (served by the metre) is the top draw to this West Hampstead trattoria, although "the Italian chef's pastas and mains are worth a visit in their own right". / NW6 3AY; www.sarracinorestaurant.com; 11 pm; closed weekday L.

Sartoria W1 £69
20 Savile Row 7534 7000 3–2C
Ex L'Anima chef, Francesco Mazzei is – in something of a coup for D&D London – to relaunch this grand, spacious and perennially promising-but-under-performing Mayfair Italian in early November 2015; it's closed till then for a major refit – this should be one to watch. / W1S 3PR; www.sartoria-restaurant.co.uk; @SartoriaRest; 10.45 pm; closed Sat L & Sun; set weekday L £38 (FP).

Satay House W2 £35 322
13 Sale Pl 7723 6763 6–1D
A "cheerful" Malaysian veteran, in a "pleasantly quiet street off Edgware Road", providing a "wide variety of dishes", at a "decent" price. / W2 1PX; www.satay-house.co.uk; 11 pm.

Sauterelle
Royal Exchange EC3 £72 333
Bank 7618 2483 9–2C
"A great view of the Royal Exchange courtyard" (from the right tables) adds to the "surprisingly good" ambience of this mezzanine-level D&D London venture, and "although it's not cheap, prices compare well with places of a similar standard in the City". / EC3V 3LR; www.royalexchange-grandcafe.co.uk/at/sauterelle-bank; @REXLondon; 9.30 pm; closed Sat & Sun; no trainers.

Savoir Faire WC1 £39 332
42 New Oxford St 7436 0707 4–1C
Handy for the British Museum, a budget Gallic spot, where "charming staff serve well-cooked bistro fare to a regular clientele". / WC1A 1EP; www.savoir.co.uk; 10.30 pm, Sun 10 pm.

(Savoy Grill)
The Savoy Hotel WC2 £89 233
Strand 7592 1600 4–3D
This "impressive" panelled chamber – once London's pre-eminent power-dining scene – still looks the part, and can still deliver some "accomplished" traditional British cuisine; prices are "ridiculous" however, especially given the fairly "unimaginative" repertoire. / WC2R 0EU; www.gordonramsay.com/thesavoygrill; @savoygrill; 11 pm, Sun 10.30 pm; set pre-theatre £55 (FP), set weekday L £57 (FP).

Scalini SW3 £75 333
1-3 Walton St 7225 2301 5–2C
"Excellent old-school Italian" buoyed along by its supremely "buzzy", "noisy yet intimate" style; given its ultra-chichi location on the fringes of Knightsbridge it's unsurprisingly no bargain, but on all accounts "worth every penny". / SW3 2JD; www.scalinionline.com; 11.30 pm; no shorts.

Scandinavian Kitchen W1 £14 353
61 Great Titchfield St 7580 7161 2–1B
"Overwhelming friendliness and lack of snootiness" win lots of brownie points for this "charming" (if "cramped") Scandi-"fuel-stop"/grocer, near the Beeb; grab an open sarnie, meatballs, herrings or salad, and check out the Scandi-themed pun of the day on the A-board; spiffing Monmouth coffee too. / W1W 7PP; www.scandikitchen.co.uk; @scanditwitchen; 7 pm, Sat 6 pm, Sun 4 pm; L only; no Maestro; no booking.

The Scarsdale W8 £42 234
23a Edwardes Sq 7937 1811 7–1D
Nestled in the corner of a gorgeous, old Kensington Square, this picturesque tavern (with small garden) is a classic of its genre, with pub grub that's not achingly 'gastro', but perfectly palatable. / W8 6HE; www.scarsdaletavern.co.uk; @onlyatfullers; 10 pm, Sun 9.30 pm.

SCOTT'S W1 **£80** 4 4 4
20 Mount St 7495 7309 3–3A
"For glam, glam, and more glam", it's hard to out-do Richard Caring's "über-slick" Mayfair veteran – a "very grown-up" affair combining "expensive but lovely" fish and seafood and "always professional" service. It does attract the odd cynical report too though – in fact a few more this year than previously. / W1K 2HE; www.scotts-restaurant.com; 10.30 pm, Sun 10 pm; booking: max 6.

Sea Containers Mondrian London SE1 **£67** 2 3 3
20 Upper Ground 3747 1020 9–3A
It looks knockout, and has "wonderful views of the river", but this much-hyped, nautically-themed NYC import, on the South Bank, "is going the same way as the Oxo Tower" – "you pay a lot for average food and nice decor, and overall it's not worth it". / SE1 9PD; www.mondrianlondon.com; @MondrianLDN; 11 pm.

The Sea Cow SE22 **£36** 3 3 2
37 Lordship Ln 8693 3111 1–4D
"The kind of chippy serving grilled tuna, salad, with fries optional... perfect!" – you eat on communal benches at this "upmarket" East Dulwich spot, which provides "a good choice of fish that's very fresh, grilled or fried, with chips or greenery". / SE22 8EW; www.theseacow.co.uk; @seacowcrew; 11 pm, Sun 10 pm; closed Mon; no Amex.

Seafresh SW1 **£37** 4 3 2
80-81 Wilton Rd 7828 0747 2–4B
"Excellent traditional fish 'n' chips" is "efficiently served in an authentic and basic setting", in this veteran Pimlico chippy, whose menu also includes various "upmarket" options ("wonderful fresh lobster at bargain prices and superb Essex oysters"). / SW1V 1DL; www.seafresh-dining.com; 10.30 pm; closed Sun.

The Sea Shell NW1 **£44** 3 2 2
49 Lisson Grove 7224 9000 8–4A
Despite its "dreary" appearance, this sizeable Marylebone café/take-away has some renown as one of London's top chippies; some would say that's over-egging it, but numerous fans do still acclaim it as "one of the best around". / NW1 6UH; www.seashellrestaurant.co.uk; @SeashellRestaur; 10.30 pm; closed Sun.

Season Kitchen N4 **£42** 3 3 3
53 Stroud Green Rd 7263 5500 8–1D
"A stand-out for Finsbury Park" – a "friendly local", where "ever-changing", "always original" dishes from "a well thought-out seasonal menu" are served in "a little, characterful room". / N4 3EF; www.seasonkitchen.co.uk; 10.30 pm, Sun 9 pm; D only.

Señor Ceviche W1 NEW **£42** 3 3 4
Kingly Ct 7842 8540 3–2C
"Funky", new Peruvian pop-up-turned-permanent in Soho's growing Kingly Court; fans extol its "exquisite ceviche", but "creeping" prices spoil the fun for sceptics for whom it's now too "mainstream" and "unremarkable"; still "great frozen Pisco sours". / W1B 5PW; www.senor-ceviche.com; @SenorCevicheLDN; 10.30 pm, Thu-Sat 11 pm.

FSA

Sesame WC2 NEW £21 222

23 Garrick St 7240 4879 4–3C

From the Ottolenghi stable, a new "bench and stool" Covent Garden pitstop offering Middle Eastern street-food; initial reports suggest the overall experience is only "so-so", but it certainly provides "quick, healthy" fare, and is pretty "cheap" too. / WC2E 9BN; www.sesamefood.co.uk; @SesameFood; 11 pm; no booking.

Seven Park Place SW1 £95 334

7-8 Park Pl 7316 1615 3–4C

"To hell with the cost!" – this "charming restaurant attached to a St James's hotel" is often nominated for business entertaining but deserves more attention generally, as William Drabble's "highly accomplished" cuisine is "remarkably good". Top Tip – "excellent value set lunch". / SW1A 1LS; www.stjameshotelandclub.com; @SevenParkPlace; 10 pm; closed Mon & Sun; set weekday L £56 (FP).

Seven Stars WC2 £34 323

53 Carey St 7242 8521 2–2D

Larger-than-life landlady, 'Roxy Beaujolais' and her crew "continue to rustle up above-average pub food" at her quaint, tightly packed tavern, behind the Royal Courts of Justice. / WC2A 2JB; 9 pm; no booking.

Sexy Fish
Berkeley Square House W1 NEW £68

1-4 Berkeley Sq 3764 2000 3–3B

Sitting pretty alongside Bentley and Bugatti showrooms, members' clubs and purveyors of haute couture, Richard Caring's latest venture (on the site of a former Mayfair NatWest bank) adds another seafood specialist to the Caprice empire; it's set to open in October 2015. / W1J 6BR; www.sexyfish.com.

Shackfuyu W1 NEW £34 544

14a, Old Compton St 7734 7492 4–2B

"Small", "US/Asian-fusion" dishes, with "enormous flavours" win rave reviews for this new Bone Daddies pop-up-turned-permanent, on the Soho site that was Made In Italy (RIP); it's "brilliant value" too. Top Menu Tip – "super yummy prawn toast, and also the matcha ice cream – a total revelation of amazing tastes". / W1D 4TH; www.bonedaddies.com; @BoneDaddiesLDN.

Shake Shack £24 322

80 New Oxford St, WC1 awaiting tel 4–1B NEW
24 The Market, WC2 3598 1360 4–3D
The Street, Westfield Stratford, E20 awaiting tel 1–1D NEW

"Yummmmmmmmm" – "lovely burgers", and "the best crinkle chips" win the thumbs-up for Danny Meyer's US-import, which is now in Westfield Stratford as well as Covent Garden; even fans though note it's "quite expensive".

Shampers W1 £49 245

4 Kingly St 7437 1692 3–2D

"Often full of bibulous professional-types", this "noisy and crowded", "'70s time warp" in Soho "always comes up trumps"; longstanding owner Simon is "hands on" and "utterly charming", and presides over the "reliable" fare, "fantastic" atmosphere and "wine list to die for". / W1B 5PE; www.shampers.net; @Shampers_Soho; 10.45 pm; closed Sun.

Shanghai E8 £38 3 2 3
41 Kingsland High St 7254 2878 1–1C
The splendid (listed) tiled front section of this former pie 'n' eel shop is one draw to this Dalston Chinese – the other is its "super dim sum". / E8 2JS; www.shanghaidalston.co.uk; 11 pm; no Amex.

Shanghai Blues WC1 £62 3 3 3
193-197 High Holborn 7404 1668 4–1D
"Pretty, old Shanghainese decor" helps create this Holborn Chinese's "relaxing", rather "sophisticated" ambience (as do the listed surroundings of what was once St Giles Library); lunchtime dim sum is the main event here – "the very high quality and range is the real deal". / WC1V 7BD; www.shanghaiblues.co.uk; 11 pm, Sun 10.30 pm.

The Shed W8 £48 3 3 3
122 Palace Gardens Ter 7229 4024 6–2B
If you like the idea of "slumming it" in what feels like "an actual country shed", this "cute" faux-rustic spot, off Notting Hill Gate, can be "fun", and fans praise its "super-tasty", "farm-to-table British tapas" too; to cynics though, it appears "odd", "over-rated" and "overpriced". / W8 4RT; www.theshed-restaurant.com; @theshed_resto; 11 pm; closed Mon L & Sun.

J SHEEKEY WC2 £75 4 4 4
28-34 St Martin's Ct 7240 2565 4–3B
"Set in the hustle and bustle of Theatreland" – down a cute alleyway – this "star-studded", "old-school" legend (est 1896, but dating its current celebrity to a late '90s relaunch) is yet again London's most talked-about destination. Nowadays owned by Richard Caring, it beat its sibling Scott's to another crown: "the capital's top seafood" (in particular "the world's best fish pie"), which is "immaculately" served in a series of "old-fashioned, panelled rooms" – "noisy and crowded", but superbly "clubby" and "charismatic". / WC2N 4AL; www.j-sheekey.co.uk; @CapriceHoldings; 11.30 pm, Sun 10.30 pm; booking: max 6; set weekday L £51 (FP).

J Sheekey Oyster Bar WC2 £76 4 4 5
28-34 St Martin's Ct 7240 2565 4–3B
"Slurping down quality oysters perched on a stool – is there a better way of spending an evening?" Not according to many devotees of the "brilliant", "friendly" and "glamorous" bar attached to the adjacent "doyenne of seafood restaurants". / WC2N 4AL; www.j-sheekey.co.uk; @CapriceHoldings; 11.30 pm, Sun 10.30 pm; booking: max 3; set weekday L £53 (FP).

Shepherd's SW1 £52 3 4 3
Marsham Ct, Marsham St 7834 9552 2–4C
"It looks as though this Tory watering hole has returned to action just at the right time!" – this archetypal politico bastion near Westminster re-opened after a period of closure this year, and though some "wobbly" meals from its menu of advanced comfort food were reported, most reports say "it's a bonus to have it back". / SW1P 4LA; www.shepherdsrestaurant.co.uk; 10.45 pm; closed Sat & Sun.

Shikumen
Dorsett Hotel W12 NEW £39 5 2 2
58 Shepherd's Bush Grn 8749 9978 7–1C
"A new kid on the block with out-of-this-world dim sum" – this new Chinese in a recently opened W12 boutique hotel "can amaze" with its "exceptional offerings". On the downside, "the atmosphere's a bit stiff and unmistakably hotel-y", but "the so-so ambience isn't all their fault – you are right on Shepherd's Bush Green after all!" / W12 5AA; shikumen.co.uk; @ShikumenUK; 10.45 pm.

Shilpa W6 £31 5 4 2
206 King St 8741 3127 7–2B
An "ordinary façade belies the quality" of this "honest" Hammersmith Indian, which continues to churn out "glorious Keralan food" at "unbelievably low prices". / W6 0RA; www.shilparestaurant.co.uk; 11 pm, Thu-Sat midnight.

The Ship SW18 £52 3 3 4
41 Jews Row 8870 9667 10–2B
Steadfast support for this "must-see" boozer, which benefits from a "great riverside" location (with vast terrace) by Wandsworth Bridge and "good pub food", including a summer BBQ. / SW18 1TB; www.theship.co.uk; @shipwandsworth; 10 pm; no booking, Sun L.

Shoe Shop NW5 NEW £45 5 4 2
122 Fortess Rd 7267 8444 8–2C
"Giaconda is reborn – Hallelujah!" – Paul Merrony and Tracey Petersen are back with a bang at this "tiny", year-old Tuffnell Park shop-conversion; the decor is "basic", but there's "a happy vibe", and the "robust", "intelligent and original cooking" is "a masterclass of what's possible at a reasonable price". / NW5 2HL; www.shoeshoplondon.com; 9 pm; closed Mon & Sun.

Shoryu Ramen £42 4 2 2
9 Regent St, SW1 no tel 3–3D
3 Denman St, W1 no tel 3–2D
5 Kingly Ct, W1 no tel 3–2C
Broadgate Circle, EC2 no tel 12–2B NEW
"Mad popularity creates a rather hectic ambience", at these "crowded and packed-in" Japanese pit-stops; still "you can expect quality food" – "amazing fresh noodles, broth and steamed buns". / Regent St 11.30 pm, Sun 10.30 pm – Soho midnight, Sun 10.30 pm; no booking (except Kingly Ct).

Shotgun W1 NEW
26 Kingly St awaiting tel 3–3C
American chef Brad McDonald (The Lockhart, Marylebone) whose talents divide opinion among our reporters (apart from when it comes to his cornbread) brings more cooking from the Deep South to Soho with a new BBQ, due to open in autumn 2015. / W1B 5QD; www.shotgunbbq.com.

Sichuan Folk E1 £44 4 4 2
32 Hanbury St 7247 4735 12–2C
"An excellent Chinese within a stone's throw of the touristy Brick Lane Indians" – a small, closely packed spot bringing "sensationally good-value", supremely "spicy" Sichuan scoff to this stretch of the East End; staff are "lovely and welcoming" too. / E1 6QR; www.sichuan-folk.co.uk; 10.30 pm; no Amex; set weekday L £18 (FP).

The Sign of The Don Bar & Bistro EC4 **£53** 2 4 4
21 St Swithin's Ln 7626 2606 9–3C
"A more casual version of its elder sibling" next door, the Don's year-old spin-off is "a good alternative", particularly for "more relaxed business lunches", even if the brasserie fare is "not especially notable". / EC4N 8AD; www.thesignofthedon.com; @signofthedon; 10 pm; closed Sat & Sun; set always available £41 (FP).

Signor Sassi SW1 **£65** 3 3 4
14 Knightsbridge Grn 7584 2277 5–1D
"There's never a dull moment", say fans of this "fun", old-school Knightsbridge trattoria – "if you're lost for words on a first date, the waiters are sure to help you out!" / SW1X 7QL; www.signorsassi.co.uk; 11.30 pm, Sun 10.30 pm.

Silk Road SE5 **£24** 5 2 2
49 Camberwell Church St 7703 4832 1–3C
"A whole new take on Chinese food" – the "bold" and "amazingly unusual" Xinjiang dishes shine at this Camberwell café; "it's all a bit spit and sawdust" though, and "the line of hipsters outside the door can be tedious". / SE5 8TR; 10.30 pm; closed Sat L & Sun L; no credit cards.

Simpson's Tavern EC3 **£38** 2 4 5
38 1/2 Ball Ct, Cornhill 7626 9985 9–2C
"The food is almost a side show to the surroundings" at this Dickensian chophouse (fka Simpson's of Cornhill) in a City alleyway, which offers "a real taste of history" in an "unpretentious and thoroughly enjoyable" manner; good breakfasts too. / EC3V 9DR; www.simpsonstavern.co.uk; @SimpsonsTavern; 3 pm; L only, closed Sat & Sun.

Simpsons-in-the-Strand WC2 **£76** 1 1 1
100 Strand 7836 9112 4–3D
"Pity the tourists who go believing it's the home of real English cooking!" – this famous temple to Roast Beef is "a shadow of its former self", with "sloppy" staff serving "school dinners" in a "gloomy" chamber; for a business breakfast, it's just about tolerable. / WC2R 0EW; www.simpsonsinthestrand.co.uk; 10.45 pm, Sun 9 pm; no trainers.

Singapore Garden NW6 **£43** 4 3 3
83a Fairfax Rd 7624 8233 8–2A
"They've maintained quality over three decades" at this "always-packed" north London favourite, which can come as a "surprise" given its off-the-beaten-track location in a Swiss Cottage parade; service is "smiling", and the Chinese/Malaysian/Singaporean fare is "expensive-but-worth-it". / NW6 4DY; www.singaporegarden.co.uk; @SingaporeGarden; 11 pm, Fri & Sat 11.30 pm.

(Gallery)
Sketch W1 **£80** 2 2 4
9 Conduit St 7659 4500 3–2C
Fans of this funky Mayfair fashionista-favourite admit it's "very expensive", but say it's a "cool" joint, with an "always inventive menu, full of surprises"; the less rose-tinted view is that it's "too gimmicky and over-crowded – like a factory processing posh meals for the young and loaded". / W1S 2XG; www.sketch.uk.com; @sketchlondon; 11 pm; booking: max 10.

(Lecture Room)
Sketch W1 **£134** 3 3 5
9 Conduit St 7659 4500 3–2C
"The magnificence of the space" certainly makes for "an experience" at this barmily opulent Mayfair dining room, overseen by Parisian supremo Pierre Gagnaire; fans – particularly of the "steal" of a set lunch – hail its "amazing" and "innovative" cuisine too, but sceptics say it's "so over-priced". / W1S 2XG; www.sketch.uk.com; @sketchlondon; 10.30 pm; closed Mon, Sat L & Sun; no trainers; booking: max 8; set weekday L £65 (FP).

Skipjacks HA3 **£30** 4 4 3
268-270 Streatfield Rd 8204 7554 1–1A
"Fish lovers travel for miles to eat here", at this Harrow chippy, which is "never without a take-away queue and full restaurant"; "you don't come for the ambience" but "everyone is happy knowing that results will be first rate". / HA3 9BY; 10.30 pm; closed Sun; no Amex.

Skylon
South Bank Centre SE1 **£75** 1 2 2
Belvedere Rd 7654 7800 2–3D
"If you have a window table, it ameliorates some of the drawbacks" of this huge, Thames-side chamber; for somewhere so "expensive" however, service can be "chaotic", and the cooking is too often "nothing special". / SE1 8XX; www.skylon-restaurant.co.uk; @skylonsouthbank; 10.30 pm; closed Sun D; no trainers; booking: max 12; set weekday L £53 (FP), set pre-theatre & Sun L £56 (FP).

Skylon Grill SE1 **£61** 1 1 3
Belvedere Rd 7654 7800 2–3D
"Location, location and location" – including the "wonderful" Thames view – are all that "redeems" the cheaper option at D&D London's massive South Bank complex, where service is "indifferent" and the "flair-free food offers much but delivers little". / SE1 8XX; www.skylon-restaurant.co.uk; @skylonsouthbank; 11 pm; closed Sun D.

Smiths Brasserie E1 **£57** 3 3 4
22 Wapping High St 7488 3456 11–1A
"Well worth a visit even though it's a bit off the beaten track" – this Wapping offshoot of a long-established Essex business "has got it all" – "a wide selection of beautiful fish" ("well cooked, but with nothing too clever"), "attentive staff", and "impressive views" of Tower Bridge and the Thames. / E1W 1NJ; smithsrestaurant.com; @Smithsofwapping; 10 pm; closed Sun D.

Smith & Wollensky WC2 NEW **£102**
Adelphi Building, 1-11 John Adam St 7321 6007 4–4D
With a reputed £10m spent on converting the ground floor of The Adelphi, just off The Strand, this hallowed US steakhouse brand's first incursion into the UK market makes a bold statement, with 300 seats, endless leather and brass, and a menu packed with USDA cuts. It opened too late for survey feedback – early press reports suggest it may be heading down the same beserk over-pricing route pursued by other US imports like Palm (RIP) and Cut, but the business-friendly location here could prove a saving grace. / WC2N 6HT.

(Top Floor)
Smiths of Smithfield EC1 **£75** **3 3 4**
67-77 Charterhouse St 7251 7950 9–1A
"Fantastic views of the City" are a highpoint at this business-friendly rooftop destination, whose steak-focussed offerings have seemed "much more up-to-par" of late, and are generally judged "very good, if at a price". / EC1M 6HJ; www.smithsofsmithfield.co.uk; @thisismiths; 10.45 pm; closed Sat L & Sun; booking: max 10.

(Dining Room)
Smiths of Smithfield EC1 **£56** **2 2 2**
67-77 Charterhouse St 7251 7950 9–1A
"Reliable... OK... so very average" – this first-floor Smithfield brasserie is "nothing to write home about" nowadays; its steak-heavy formula is just about serviceable for an informal business lunch, but service is "haphazard" and "the acoustics suck"! / EC1M 6HJ; www.smithsofsmithfield.co.uk; @thisismiths; 10.45 pm; closed Sat L & Sun; booking: max 12.

(Ground Floor)
Smiths of Smithfield EC1 **£32** **2 2 3**
67-77 Charterhouse St 7251 7950 9–1A
Hung over and in need of brunch? – this big and "buzzy" Smithfield venue is a seminal choice for weekend mornings, with "Bloody Mary on hand to remove the cobwebs", and an "SOS English breakfast". / EC1M 6HJ; www.smithsofsmithfield.co.uk; @thisismiths; 5 pm; L only; no booking.

Smokehouse Chiswick W4 NEW **£47** **3 3 3**
12 Sutton Lane North 7354 1144 7–2B
"A bizarre smörgåsbord of smoked meat, Korean spices and whisky – somehow it works!"; this new outer-Chiswick outpost of Ian Rankin's Smokehouse Islington (on the pub site that was the Hole in the Wall, RIP) wins fans both for its "interesting" food and "wonderful garden". By the indifferent standards of W4, "it's a step up for an area desperate for quality". / W4 4LD; www.smokehousechiswick.co.uk; @smokehousen1; 10 pm, Sun Sun 9 pm; Mon-Thu closed L.

The Smokehouse Islington N1 **£53** **3 3 3**
63-69 Canonbury Rd 7354 1144 8–2D
"For an indulgent meat-oriented treat", this "bustling" Canonbury gastropub serves "super-rich", smoked dishes, although the menu is too "limited" for some tastes; see also Smokehouse Chiswick. / N1 2RG; www.smokehouseislington.co.uk; @smokehouseN1; 10 pm, Sun 9 pm; closed weekday L.

Smoking Goat WC2 NEW **£35** **5 2 3**
7 Denmark St no tel 4–1B
"The lights are low, the air is smoky", at Ben Chapman's "tiny", no-bookings, Thai BBQ-newcomer in Soho, whose "short menu" focuses on "hefty chunks of meat, marinated and grilled to perfection"; service though can be a bit "too cool to smile". Top Menu Tip – "the fish sauce wings alone are worth the visit!" / WC2H 8LZ; www.smokinggoatsoho.com; @smokinggoatsoho; no booking.

Snaps & Rye W10 NEW **£40** 4 3 4

93 Golborne Rd 8964 3004 6–1A

"Slightly out of the way, but well worth the trip" – this contemporary, Danish dining room in North Kensington is extolled for its "delicious Scandi food with a modern twist", "light and airy" atmosphere and house-infused Akvavit snaps. / W10 5NL; www.snapsandrye.com; @snapsandrye; 9 pm; closed Mon, Tue D, Wed D, Thu D, Sat D & Sun D.

Social Eating House W1 **£74** 4 4 3

58-59 Poland St 7993 3251 3–2D

"A favourite of the Atherton empire" for many reporters – this "trendy yet superb" Soho two-year-old offers "memorable" cuisine, plus "delightful" cocktails and wines; it has a "lovely loungey vibe" too (but can get "overwhelmingly loud"). Top Tip – "excellent value set lunch". / W1F 7NR; www.socialeatinghouse.com; @blindasapig; 10 pm; closed Sun; set weekday L £50 (FP).

Social Wine & Tapas W1 NEW **£44**

39 James St 7993 3257 3–1A

From the prolific stable of Jason Atherton – a svelte Marylebone newcomer with a heavy focus on wines, sherries and madeiras, plus funky tapas, served from open kitchens in both the tapas bar (ground floor) and cellar bar; it opened too late for the survey, but early press reviews are nothing short of rhapsody. / W1U 1EB; www.socialwineandtapas.com; @socialwinetapas; 10.45 pm; closed Sun.

Soif SW11 **£55** 3 3 3

27 Battersea Rise 7223 1112 10–2C

"The very Gallic staff really know their off-the-beaten-track wines" (the list is "complex", "a bit of a lottery", and can be "excellent value") at this "lively bar-cum-restaurant" in Battersea (a sibling to Terroirs), which serves a "French-accented" menu of "simple and solid" bistro fare. / SW11 1HG; www.soif.co; @soifSW11; 10 pm; closed Mon L & Sun D.

Som Saa
Climpson's Arch E8 NEW **£38** 5 3 3

Arch 374 Helmsley Place 7254 7199 1–2D

"Long may it continue to pop up!" – an "extended residency", in a no frills, no booking, railway arch behind London Fields, where "the cooking is done in a shipping container on the forecourt"; the result? – "some of the best Thai food in the UK" – "if it wasn't so archly hipster it would be perfect!" / E8 3SB; www.climpsonsarch.com; @somsaa_london; 10.30 pm; closed Mon, Tue, Wed, Thu L & Fri L.

Sông Quê E2 **£30** 2 1 2

134 Kingsland Rd 7613 3222 12–1B

"It looks a bit like a Hanoi works canteen", but "if you don't mind full-on and sharing tables", fans say you get "wonderful, no frills" chow at this Shoreditch Vietnamese; critics, though, "expect more" – they say the food's "not as fresh and delicate as it used to be". / E2 8DY; www.sonque.co.uk; 11 pm, Sun 10.30 pm; no Amex.

Sonny's Kitchen SW13 **£56** 2 2 2

94 Church Rd 8748 0393 10–1A

"Everything a local ought to be", claim loyal fans (and "a top spot for weekend brunch"), but compared to its excellence of yesteryear this "airy" Barnes favourite has "lost the plot"; food-wise? – it's "reasonable, but doesn't reflect its links to Phil Howard". / SW13 0DQ; www.sonnyskitchen.co.uk; @SonnysKitchen; Fri-Sat 11 pm, Sun 9.30 pm; set always available £36 (FP), set Sun L £42 (FP).

Sophie's Steakhouse £59 222
29-31 Wellington St, WC2 7836 8836 4–3D
311-313 Fulham Rd, SW10 7352 0088 5–3B
"Good steaks properly cooked – what more do you want of a steakhouse?!"; these Covent Garden and Fulham fixtures also win praise for "amazing" breakfasts and their "family-friendly" approach.
/ www.sophiessteakhouse.com; SW10 11.45 pm, Sun 11.15 pm; WC2 12.45 am, Sun 11 pm; no booking.

Sosharu
Turnmill Building EC1 NEW
63 Clerkenwell Rd awaiting tel 9–1A
Jason Atherton's planned foray into izakaya-style dining (incorporating also teppanyaki, and a robata grill) will need to work well to fill this big Clerkenwell site (formerly Turnmills nightclub, RIP); as this guide goes to press, its debut has been postponed until December 2015.
/ EC1M 5NP; www.jasonatherton.co.uk/restaurants/sosharu.

Sotheby's Café W1 £64 332
34-35 New Bond St 7293 5077 3–2C
"For a people-watching lunch", try this small café off the foyer of the famous Mayfair auction house; "the choice is limited, but the food's always good", and there's "a wide selection of reasonable wines".
/ W1A 2AA; www.sothebys.com; @Sothebys; L only; L only, closed Sat & Sun; booking: max 8; set weekday L £52 (FP).

Source SW11 £51 224
Ransome's Dock, 35-37 Parkgate Rd 7350 0555 5–4C
Opinions divide on this year-old successor to Ransome's Dock (RIP), near the Thames in Battersea; to fans it's a "delightful" local, and "a big improvement on its tired predecessor" – to critics, however, it's "very disappointing", with an "aloof" attitude.
/ SW11 4NP; www.sourcebattersea.com; @SOURCEBattersea; 10 pm, Fri & Sat 10.30 pm; closed Sun D.

Spring
Somerset House WC2 £88 332
Lancaster Pl 3011 0115 2–2D
"A joyful addition to the London dining scene" is how most reporters greet Skye Gyngell's Somerset House yearling – a "magical", "light, bright and airy" new space (with courtyard) where staff "in Boho costumes" deliver her "deliciously balanced" and "wonderfully fragrant" cuisine. "Silly prices" are a big turn-off though, and lead a strident minority to gripe about "not enough ooomph" and "too much hype". / WC2R 1LA; springrestaurant.co.uk; @Spring_Rest; 10.30 pm; closed Sun D; set weekday L & pre-theatre £53 (FP).

Spuntino W1 £44 334
61 Rupert St no tel 3–2D
"The atmosphere's terrific and the cocktails knockout" at Russell Norman's "hipster" Soho bar (where you eat at the counter) – "a perfect spot for a glass of vino and a sharing plate". / W1D 7PW; www.spuntino.co.uk; 11.30 pm, Sun 10.30 pm.

THE SQUARE W1 £126 4 2 2

6-10 Bruton St 7495 7100 3–2C

With its "polished" style, "well-spaced tables" and "one of the Capital's finest wine lists", this Mayfair luminary would be a natural for besuited expense-accounters even without Phil Howard's "complex and highly innovative" cuisine; however, critics of its slightly "sterile" setting and "exorbitant" prices were again more vocal this year. / *W1J 6PU; www.squarerestaurant.com; @square_rest; 9.45 pm, Sat 10.15 pm, Sun 9.30 pm; closed Sun L; booking: max 8; set weekday L £66 (FP).*

Sree Krishna SW17 £25 4 3 2

192-194 Tooting High St 8672 4250 10–2C

"No, it still hasn't changed!" – a Tooting relic, particularly "renowned for its masala dosas" and south Indian specials (although its more "mainstream" fare also "satisfies completely"). / SW17 0SF; www.sreekrishna.co.uk; @SreeKrishnaUk; 10.45 pm, Fri & Sat 11.30 pm.

Star of India SW5 £54 3 2 3

154 Old Brompton Rd 7373 2901 5–2B

"No longer trendy", nor as engagingly camp as in its glory days – this Earl's Court veteran is sometimes accused of "trading on its reputation"; that said, for most reporters it remains an "old favourite", with "original and well-prepared dishes". / SW5 0BE; www.starofindia.eu; 11.45 pm, Sun 11.15 pm.

Sticks'n'Sushi £48 3 3 3

11 Henrietta St, WC2 3141 8810 4–3D

Nelson Rd, SE10 3141 8220 1–3D NEW

58 Wimbledon Hill Rd, SW19 3141 8800 10–2B

Crossrail Pl, E14 3141 8230 11–1C NEW

"Does what it says on the tin pretty well" – this "odd Asian/Scandi concept" (sushi with a Danish twist) wins consistent praise for its "inventive interpretation of dishes" and "gorgeous cocktails"; by the standards of Wimbledon, Greenwich or E14, it's quite "scene-y" too. / www.sticksnsushi.com; Sun-Tue 10 pm, Wed-Sat 11 pm; SRA-1.*

STK Steakhouse ME by Meliá London WC2 £72 1 1 2

336-337 Strand 7395 3450 2–2D

"Like a pulling joint, sponsored by Lycra!" – a "very busy and too noisy" Covent Garden steakhouse, which fans say is "fun for a night out with the girls", but which draws far too much flak for being "overpriced" and with "terrible" food and service too. / WC2R 1HA; www.stkhouse.com; @STKLondon; Mon-Wed 11 pm, Thu-Sat midnight, Sun 10 pm; D only.

Stock Pot £30 2 2 2

38 Panton St, SW1 7839 5142 4–4A

54 James St, W1 7935 6034 3–1A

273 King's Rd, SW3 7823 3175 5–3C

"You certainly don't visit these squished and basic '60s canteens for the ambience"; who cares? – they're "humming from sun-up to sundown with folks who've come for a big plate of tasty fodder" at rock-bottom prices. / SW1 11.30 pm, Wed-Sat midnight, Sun 11 pm SW3 10.15 pm, Sun 9.45 pm; no Amex.

STORY SE1 £103 543
199 Tooley St 7183 2117 9–4D
"Genius!" – "an incredible journey of flavour and excitement" is to be found at Tom Sellers's "Scandi-style" dining room, near Tower Bridge, whose "spectacular and truly exciting" multi-course menus are "akin to a trip to the Fat Duck, but at under half the price".
/ SE1 2UE; www.restaurantstory.co.uk; @Rest_Story; 9.30 pm; closed Mon & Sun; set weekday L £62 (FP).

Strand Dining Rooms WC2 £57
1-3 Grand Buildings, Strand 7930 8855 2–3C
"It has a great location", just off Trafalgar Square, but (aside from its "first-rate breakfast") this big, all-day British brasserie "could be so much better" – let's hope Mark Sargeant's April 2015 appointment (too late for survey feedback) will prove the catalyst for a shake-up.
/ WC2N 4JF; www.thestranddiningrooms.com; @StrandDining; 11 pm; closed Sun D.

Street Kitchen (van) EC2 £17 33-
Finsbury Avenue Sq no tel 12–2B
"Queues are testament" to the "delicious" food ("top burgers" a highlight) from these superior pop-ups, operating from converted Airstream campers, near Broadgate Circle and also from the Battersea 'Hatch'. / EC2 2PG; www.streetkitchen.co.uk; @Streetkitchen; L only.

Suk Saran SW19 £56 332
29 Wimbledon Hill Rd 8947 9199 10–2B
"One of Wimbledon's better restaurants for food" – this Thai "winner" (part of a three-strong southwest London chain) perhaps "isn't cheap", but the style is "un-rushed and relaxed", staff are "an absolute pleasure", and dishes come "packed with flavour".
/ SW19 7NE; www.sukhogroups.com; 10.30 pm; booking: max 25.

Sukho Fine Thai Cuisine SW6 £55 543
855 Fulham Rd 7371 7600 10–1B
Some of "the best Thai food in London" – "beautifully presented, and served with great charm" – compensates for the "packed" conditions at this "fabulous" shop conversion in deepest Fulham.
/ SW6 5HJ; www.sukhogroups.com; 11 pm; set weekday L £38 (FP).

Suksan SW10 £49 443
7 Park Walk 7351 9881 5–3B
The sister restaurant to Fulham's outstanding 'Sukho Fine Thai Cuisine' – feedback on this more casual and family-friendly Chelsea corner café is more limited, but it's consistently highly rated.
/ SW10 0AJ; www.sukhogroups.com; 10.45 pm; set weekday L £30 (FP).

The Summerhouse W9 £57 225
60 Blomfield Rd 7286 6752 8–4A
"Grab a canal-side table" and choose a sunny day, if you visit this "romantic" small spot, in Little Venice; don't go with huge culinary expectations though – while fish is the menu highlight, too often results "could be so much better". / W9 2PA; www.thesummerhouse.co; 10.30 pm, Sun 10 pm; no Amex; set always available £42 (FP).

Sumosan W1 £78 432

26b Albemarle St 7495 5999 3–3C

"It's never been a popular, crowd-pulling destination" like nearby Nobu, but that's what fans love about this "relaxed yet classy" Japanese-fusion spot in Mayfair, where you can "still get a table on a Saturday night". / W1S 4HY; www.sumosan.com; @sumosan_; 11.30 pm, Sun 10.30 pm; closed Sat L & Sun L; set weekday L £48 (FP).

Sunday N1 £44 433

169 Hemingford Rd 7607 3868 8–2D

"The best brunch for miles around" is "recommended at any time of day" (but you queue at weekends), at this "gorgeous" local eatery, on the fringes of Islington; at night, they serve "a small, ever-changing seasonal menu" from the "tiny kitchen". / N1 1DA; @SundayBarnsbury; 10.30 pm; closed Mon, Tue D, Wed D & Sun D; no Amex.

Sushisamba EC2 £79 335

Heron Tower, 110 Bishopsgate 3640 7330 9–2D

"You can't argue with the view from the 39th floor!"; this dazzling City eyrie combines "amazing vistas and outside spaces" with "heavenly" Japanese/South American fusion fare – "incredibly fresh, zingy flavours, blended with panache". And yet… for some reporters "everything is slick, it looks brilliant, but it lacks heart and soul", not helped by the merciless prices. / EC2N 4AY; www.sushisamba.com; @Sushisamba; Sun-Mon 11.30 pm, Tue-Sat 12.30 am.

Sushi Tetsu EC1 £58 553

12 Jerusalem Pas 3217 0090 9–1A

"As close to the Japanese sushi-ya experience as it's possible to get outside Asia"; you sit at the bar, one of only 7 people face-to-face with the chef at this "amazing" Clerkenwell "hole in the wall", run by a "lovely husband and wife team" and serving sushi "like an incredible dream". ("It's akin to the Vienna Philharmonic performing just for you and six others, while explaining every note!") / EC1V 4JP; www.sushitetsu.co.uk; @SushiTetsuUK; 7.30 pm; closed Mon & Sun; set weekday L £37 (FP).

Sushi-Say NW2 £44 542

33b Walm Ln 8459 7512 1–1A

"The best thing in Willesden Green" – well, perhaps even better than that! – this obscure, "no frills", Japanese stalwart is a mecca for sushi lovers thanks to its "always faultless" dishes, and its "congenial and friendly" service; let's hope the owners never retire… / NW2 5SH; 10 pm, Sat 10.30 pm, Sun 9.30 pm; closed Mon, Tue, Wed L, Thu L & Fri L; no Amex.

The Swan W4 £48 455

119 Acton Ln 8994 8262 7–1A

"Strangely rustic in feel for somewhere in deepest Chiswick" – this tucked-away hostelry is "one of the best in West London"; the cooking is "surprisingly interesting and sophisticated", the service is a veritable "charm offensive", and the set-up works well both in winter (wood panels, fire, sofas) and summer ("luscious beer garden"). / W4 5HH; www.theswanchiswick.co.uk; @SwanPubChiswick; 10 pm, Fri & Sat 10.30 pm, Sun 10 pm; closed weekday L.

The Swan at the Globe SE1 £62 212
21 New Globe Walk 7928 9444 9–3B
"Thankfully the wonderful performance made us forget the grief of trying to get fed!" – service has cratered in recent times at this first-floor South Bank venture; the food is "OK" (from a "limited menu") and it has "top views of the North Bank of the Thames", but feels ever-more like a "tourist trap". / SE1 9DT; www.loveswan.co.uk; @swanabout; 10.30 pm, Sun 9 pm; set pre theatre £41 (FP).

Sweet Thursday N1 £40 333
95 Southgate Rd 7226 1727 1–2C
"Cool without trying too hard" – this "chilled" De Beauvoir outfit continues to thrive, "and deservedly so" on its "interesting, proper, thin crust" pizzas, and "a great choice of wines" from the little shop attached. / N1 3JS; www.sweetthursday.co.uk; @Pizza_and_Wine; 10 pm, Mon 9 pm, Sat 10.30 pm, Sun 9 pm.

Sweetings EC4 £75 223
39 Queen Victoria St 7248 3062 9–3B
"If you like an old-style City atmosphere", this "quirky" and "eccentric" Victorian time-warp is a treasured "institution", serving "classic", "plain" fish that's "dependably good, if rather highly priced"; arrive early for a table. / EC4N 4SA; www.sweetingsrestaurant.com; 3 pm; L only, closed Sat & Sun; no booking.

Taberna Do Mercado E1 NEW £44 433
Spitalfields Mkt 7375 0649 12–2B
A surprisingly low-key opening in a unit in Spitalfields Market from celeb chef du jour Nuno Mendes (Chiltern Firehouse, Viajante); clearly a passion-project, the focus is offbeat tapas from the chef's Portuguese homeland, which most (if not quite all) reports say is "superb". Top Menu Tip – "you must try the fish in a tin". / E1 6EW; www.tabernamercado.co.uk; @tabernamercado; 9.30 pm, Sun 7.30 pm; no booking at D.

Taberna Etrusca EC4 £54 244
9 -11 Bow Churchyard 7248 5552 9–2C
"Very slick service" has long been a hallmark of this well-located City Italian, whose tucked-away al-fresco tables are lovely in the sunshine; all this plus "rustic cooking, and good value wine (for the ECs)". / EC4M 9DQ; www.etruscarestaurants.com; 10 pm; closed Sat & Sun.

The Table SE1 £38 333
83 Southwark St 7401 2760 9–4B
"Wonderful brunches" are the top draw to this "entertaining" and stylish café, over the road from Tate Modern; "it's packed out, and you queue round the block, but it's worth it". / SE1 0HX; www.thetablecafe.com; @thetablecafe; 10.30 pm; closed Mon D, Sat D & Sun D.

Taiwan Village SW6 £34 453
85 Lillie Rd 7381 2900 5–3A
"Amazing value, hidden gem off the gritty North End Road", with supremely "helpful" service, and where the "consistently delicious" Chinese cooking comes with "interesting" – and spicy – Taiwanese variations; "go with the superb let-us-feed-you chef's menu". / SW6 1UD; www.taiwanvillage.com; @taiwanvillage85; 11.30 pm, Sun 10.30 pm; closed weekday L; booking: max 20.

Tajima Tei EC1 £36 433

9-11 Leather Ln 7404 9665 9–2A

"Shame that the decor looks a bit cheap" – this busy Japanese hidden near Hatton Gardens has a choice of 19 set lunch menus, and is "very authentic and excellent". / EC1N 7ST; www.tajima-tei.co.uk; 10 pm; closed Sat & Sun; no booking at L.

Talad Thai SW15 £33 431

320 Upper Richmond Rd 8246 5791 10–2A

"A great stalwart for a cheap night out" – a Thai canteen, adjacent to an Asian supermarket in Putney, with "consistently tasty and enjoyable food" at un-scary prices. / SW15 6TL; www.taladthairestaurant.com; 10.30 pm, Sun 9.30 pm; no Amex.

Tamarind W1 £75 332

20 Queen St 7629 3561 3–3B

"Superior cooking with out-of-this-world fragrances and flavours" continues to rank this Mayfair fixture amongst London's top nouvelle Indians; "its basement location is a minus" however, and is it becoming more "corporate"? / W1J 5PR; www.tamarindrestaurant.com; @TamarindMayfair; 10.45 pm, Sun 10.30 pm; closed Sat L; booking: max 20; set weekday L £48 (FP).

Tandoori Nights SE22 £39 433

73 Lordship Ln 8299 4077 1–4D

"Reliably high quality, punchy cooking" keeps south Londoners going back time and again to this stalwart East Dulwich curry house – a "favourite local Indian". / SE22 8EP; www.tandoorinightsdulwich.co.uk; 11.30 pm, Fri & Sat midnight; closed weekday L & Sat L; no Amex.

Tapas Brindisa £45 333

46 Broadwick St, W1 7534 1690 3–2D
18-20 Southwark St, SE1 7357 8880 9–4C
41-43 Atlantic Rd, SW9 7733 0634 10–2D

The "ever-busy", "fun" (but "rushed") Borough Market original is the dominant member of this Spanish group, with wine and tapas that's "superb… but beware it's not cheap"; the Soho and Brixton spin-offs are less known, but in a similar vein. See also Morada Brindisa Asador. / 10.45 pm, Sun 10 pm; W1 booking: max 10.

Taqueria W11 £35 433

141-145 Westbourne Grove 7229 4734 6–1B

"Spot-on", "no frills" Mexican cantina, on the fringe of Notting Hill, with an "interesting" and "authentic" taco-focused menu, not to mention "delicious margaritas", and other Latino tipples; it's "cheap as chips" too. / W11 2RS; www.taqueria.co.uk; @TaqueriaUK; 11 pm, Fri & Sat 11.30 pm, Sun 10.30 pm; no Amex; no booking at weekends.

Taro £36 433

10 Old Compton St, W1 7439 2275 4–2B
61 Brewer St, W1 7734 5826 3–2D

"Delicious, cheap and quick" budget Japanese canteens in Soho, overseen by omnipresent Mr Taro – bento boxes are particularly good value. / www.tarorestaurants.co.uk; 10.30 pm, Sun 9.30 pm; no Amex; Brewer St only small bookings.

F S A

Tartufo SW3 £57 442

11 Cadogan Gdns 7730 6383 5–2D

"Tucked away at the base of a fusty old Chelsea block near Peter Jones", Alexis Gauthier's "surprising" two-year-old makes a "superb" find with its "professional" service and "refined" Italian-ish cooking (with truffles much in evidence); the "dungeon-like" setting is a bit of a downer though. / SW3 2RJ; www.tartufolondon.co.uk; @TartufoLondon; 10 pm; closed Mon & Sun D.

Tas £37 133

Branches throughout London

Is this popular and "well-located" Turkish chain just too "uninspired" nowadays? "For a quick cheap bite" many are still "happy to recommend" the mezze formula, but experiences seemed ever-more "busy and disappointing" this year. / www.tasrestaurant.com; 11.30 pm, Sun 10.30 pm; EC4 Closed Sun.

Tas Pide SE1 £40 233

20-22 New Globe Walk 7928 3300 9–3B

Cosy Anatolian, right by the Globe Theatre, which is "probably the most attractive Tas", and its "fairly traditional mezze and Turkish take on pizza" are similarly "reasonably priced". / SE1 9DR; www.tasrestaurants.co.uk/pide; 11.30 pm, Sun 10.30 pm.

(Whistler Restaurant)
Tate Britain SW1 £54 235

Millbank 7887 8825 2–4C

Whistler's famous murals imbue this serene dining room with a "delightful" ambience, and its other claim to fame is Hamish Anderson's "exceptional" wine list ("from all corners of the globe, with many half-bottles, all at reasonable prices"); food-wise, though, it's "just OK". / SW1 4RG; www.tate.org.uk; @Tate; 3 pm, afternoon tea Sat-Sun 5 pm; L & afternoon tea only; set Sun L £50 (FP).

(Restaurant, Level 6)
Tate Modern SE1 £59 214

Bankside 7887 8888 9–3B

You enjoy "stunning views" (some tables only) in the "airy" top-floor dining room of this South Bank landmark; there's "an exceptional wine list" too, but the "mainly British food is mixed" ("some dishes good, some below par)", and service – though "pleasant" – is "shambolic". / SE1 9TG; www.tate.org.uk; @TateFood; 9 pm; Sun-Thu closed D, Fri & Sat open L & D.

Taylor St Baristas £16 344

Branches throughout London

"Unbelievable coffee" – "their roasts are unsurpassed" – win a big thumbs-up for this Aussie chain, and it does "excellent healthy lunch salads and sandwiches" too; "its artisan-style service means your wait will be long", however. / EC2M 4TP; www.taylor-st.com; all branches 5 pm; Old Broad ST, Clifton St, W1, E14 closed Sat & Sun; New St closed Sat; TW9 closed Sun.

Tayyabs E1 £31 423

83 Fieldgate St 7247 9543 9–2D

"How do they keep it so good, while serving a gazillion people?!" – this "frantic" but "phenomenal" East End Pakistani enjoys "classic" status thanks to its "always fabulous and exceptional value" nosh (not least lamb chops that are "beyond superb"); "massive queues, even if you've booked!" / E1 1JU; www.tayyabs.co.uk; @1tayyabs; 11.30 pm.

Tem Tép W8 NEW £48 333

135 Kensington Church St 7792 7816 6–2B

"A great addition near Notting Hill Gate" – a new Vietnamese 'kitchen', with "wonderful" affordable food. / W8 7LP; temtep.co.uk; Sun-Thu 10 pm, Fri & Sat 10.30 pm; no Amex.

The 10 Cases WC2 £55 243

16 Endell St 7836 6801 4–2C

"Knowledgeable and passionate staff" advise on the "excellent wines by the glass" at this "fabulous and friendly" independent bistro/wine bar in Covent Garden; it serves a "short, simple menu" – "it's proper food, but the place is all about the vino". / WC2H 9BD; www.the10cases.co.uk; @10cases; 11 pm; closed Sun.

10 Greek Street W1 £46 543

10 Greek St 7734 4677 4–2A

"No flim-flam – just pure class!" – this Soho three-year-old may be "simple and basic" (and "a bit cramped" too), but it dishes up "brilliant", "sensitive" seasonal cuisine, and Luke's hand-written list provides "smashing wines at decent prices"; "book at lunch, to avoid the inevitable evening queue". / W1D 4DH; www.10greekstreet.com; @10GreekStreet; 11.30 pm; closed Sun.

Tendido Cero SW5 £52 333

174 Old Brompton Rd 7370 3685 5–2B

"Designer tapas" and "fabulous wine" buoy the "buzz" at this "crowded and noisy" South Kensington bar; it's "not cheap", but fans say "it's worth every penny!" / SW5 0BA; www.cambiodetercio.co.uk; @CambiodTercio; 11 pm.

Tendido Cuatro SW6 £48 232

108-110 New King's Rd 7371 5147 10–1B

Cambio de Tercio's Fulham venture dropped in ratings across the board this year; apologists insist the "cramped, crowded and noisy" tapas bar serves "excellent" food, but detractors feel prices are "totally inauthentic". / SW6 4LY; www.cambiodetercio.co.uk; @CambiodTercio; 11 pm, Sun 10.30 pm.

Tentazioni SE1 £63 223

2 Mill St 7394 5248 11–2A

"Off the beaten track" little Italian, near Shad Thames, which has long been a haven of "surprisingly accomplished" cooking; it has seemed more "impersonal" of late however, and the food "has gone from good to average". / SE1 2BD; www.tentazioni.co.uk; @TentazioniWorld; 10.45 pm, Sun 9 pm; closed Sat L.

Terra Vergine SW10 £53 433

442 King's Rd 7352 0491 5–3B

"Featuring food and wine from the Abruzzo" – a "very authentic" Chelsea operation, where "extremely fresh and unusual ingredients are prepared with great attention to detail"; "you could be in Italy, from the number of Italians who dine there". / SW10 0LQ; www.terravergine.co.uk; closed Mon L, Tue L & Wed L.

The Terrace W8 £67 344

33c Holland St 7937 9252 5–1A

The "cosy interior is complemented by the outside terrace", at this "lovely, tiny and intimate local", in a cute Kensington backwater, well-liked for its "unfussy, modern British cooking". / W8 4LX; www.theterraceonhollandstreet.co.uk; @HollandSt; 10.30 pm; closed Sun; set weekday L £40 (FP).

Terroirs WC2 £49 334
5 William IV St 7036 0660 4–4C
"Bold" and "so, so tasty" Gallic tapas dishes help soak up the many "esoteric" and "fascinating" organic wines at this wildly popular, "casual" bistro, just off Trafalgar Square; both the main room and hidden-away sub-basement are "buzzing" and "great fun". / WC2N 4DW; www.terroirswinebar.com; @terroirswinebar; 11 pm; closed Sun.

Texture W1 £97 442
34 Portman St 7224 0028 2–2A
"Absolutely divine" results from Agnar Sverrisson's "very creative" Icelandic menu, complemented by "stunning" wine matches (with an emphasis on champagnes), inspire raves for this foodie temple near Selfridges, where "charming and solicitous" service helps enliven the slightly "soulless" space. / W1H 7BY; www.texture-restaurant.co.uk; @TextureLondon; 10.30 pm; closed Mon & Sun; set weekday L £54 (FP).

Thali SW5 £48 444
166 Old Brompton Rd 7373 2626 5–2B
"Family recipes make this Indian restaurant special" – a stylish, modern subcontinental in South Kensington (decorated with posters from Bollywood classics) serving slightly offbeat food with "fresh spicing and interesting flavours". / SW5 0BA; www.thali.uk.com; @Thali London; 11.30 pm, Sun 10.30 pm.

Theo Randall
InterContinental Hotel W1 £95 321
1 Hamilton Pl 7318 8747 3–4A
"Ambience has never been a strongpoint" of this "oddly corporate", windowless chamber, in the bowels of this Hyde Park Corner hotel; for fans, its "inspired" Italian cuisine is clear compensation, but a growing band of sceptics fear it's "not all it's cracked up to be" nowadays. / W1J 7QY; www.theorandall.com; @theorandall; 11 pm; closed Sat L & Sun; set weekday L £57 (FP).

34 W1 £75 333
34 Grosvenor Sq 3350 3434 3–3A
Richard Caring's "classy and elegant" operation "feels like it's been around for decades" and its "lively but discreet" quarters, "capable" service and "wide variety" of "excellent" grills make it a natural for business; prices, predictably, are "very Mayfair". / W1K 2HD; www.34-restaurant.co.uk; 10.30 pm.

The Thomas Cubitt SW1 £60 344
44 Elizabeth St 7730 6060 2–4A
"Catering to the well-heeled", this "posh pub" in Belgravia has a "wonderful atmosphere", even if it can be "very crowded" and "terribly noisy"; you can eat "classic pub grub" downstairs, but some prefer to "escape upstairs" to the "classy restaurant". / SW1W 9PA; www.thethomascubitt.co.uk; @TheThomasCubitt; 10 pm, Sun 9.30 pm.

3 South Place
South Place Hotel EC2 £62 323
3 South Pl 3503 0000 12–2A
"Smart, modern bar/restaurant" in D&D London's "funky hotel", by Liverpool Street, which is particularly tipped as "a superb spot for a business breakfast", although it's said to be "a solid choice for lunch" too. / EC2M 2AF; www.southplacehotel.com; @southplacehotel; 10.30 pm; booking: max 22.

tibits W1 £35 3 2 3

12-14 Heddon St 7758 4112 3–2C

"It's self-service, and you pay by weight from the great, wide-ranging, all-veggie buffet" – that's the concept at this very handy (and "family-friendly") Swiss-run operation, which is ideal for a healthy "quick bite" near Piccadilly Circus. / W1B 4DA; www.tibits.co.uk; @tibits_uk; 11.30 pm, Sun 10 pm; no Amex; need 8+ to book.

Tinello SW1 £55 4 4 4

87 Pimlico Rd 7730 3663 5–2D

With its "dark woods and low lighting", this "romantic" Pimlico Tuscan – a stablemate of Mayfair's Locanda Locatelli – is an all-round hit with its "rich" north Italian small dishes matched with "a well-thought-out and unusual wine list". / SW1W 8PH; www.tinello.co.uk; @tinello_london; 10.30 pm; closed Sun.

Ting
Shangri-La Hotel at the Shard SE1 £88 2 2 4

Level 35, 31 St Thomas Street 7234 8108 9–4C

"Astonishing views" of course accompany a trip to this "spacious and luxurious" 35th-floor chamber; as with all this landmark's other elevated eateries however, you pay through the nose for them, especially given the "disjointed" service and food that "verges on boring". / SE1 9RY; www.ting-shangri-la.com; 11.30 pm.

Toasted SE22 £49 2 3 3

38 Lordship Ln 8693 9021 1–4D

"An interesting wine list even if you don't like natural wines" helps win fans for this Caves de Pyène outpost in East Dulwich; the food is no more than "perfectly pleasant" however, and some sceptics would say the same of the whole set-up. / SE22 8HJ; www.toastdulwich.co.uk; @toastdulwich; 9.45 pm; closed Sun D.

Toff's N10 £40 4 3 2

38 Muswell Hill Broadway 8883 8656 1–1B

"Utterly dependable fish 'n' chips" maintains this "always busy and welcoming" Muswell Hill institution as one of north London's most popular chippies. / N10 3RT; www.toffsfish.co.uk; @toffsfish; 10 pm; closed Sun.

Tokyo Diner WC2 £24 3 4 3

2 Newport Pl 7287 8777 4–3B

Battered stalwart Japanese caff that "feels just like Tokyo" (but is actually 'mislocated' in Chinatown); food-wise it's not earth-shattering, but "always reliable" for "freshly prepared" sushi and a good range of other dishes at "rock-bottom" prices. / WC2H 7JJ; www.tokyodiner.com; 11.30 pm; no Amex; no booking, Fri & Sat.

Tokyo Sukiyaji-Tei & Bar SW3 £46

85 Sloane Ave 3583 3797 5–2C

Formerly Sushi des Artistes (but under the same ownership), a Chelsea hideaway serving an eclectic range of fusion dishes as well as Japanese faves like sukiyaki, shabu-shabu and sashimi; feedback is limited, but fans say it's a "must visit". / SW3 3DX; www.tokyosukiyakitei.com.

Tom's Kitchen £63 121

Somerset House, 150 Strand, WC2 7845 4646 2–2D
27 Cale St, SW3 7349 0202 5–2C
11 Westferry Circus, E14 3011 1555 11–1C
1 Commodity Quay, E1 3011 5433 9–3D

"They need to up their game" at Tom Aikens's supposedly upmarket, casual bistro chain – with its "disorganised" service, "hit-and-miss" cooking and "lack of ambience", it's just "all a bit ordinary". / 10 pm - 10.45 pm; WC2 closed Sun D.

Tommi's Burger Joint £20 444

30 Thayer St, W1 7224 3828 3–1A
342 Kings Rd, SW3 7349 0691 5–3C

There's "always a mad rush" for a seat at these "no-frills", order-at-the-counter burger joints in Marylebone and Chelsea, on account of their "impressive steak-burgers and generally chilled-out vibe". / 9 pm.

The Tommy Tucker SW6 NEW £53 334

22 Waterford Rd 7736 1023 5–4A

Fulham's darling Claude Compton (Claude's Kitchen, Amuse Bouche) serves up another hit with his "upbeat and energetic" take on the British gastropub; the slow-cooked fare is "excellent" – particularly Sunday lunch – complemented by an "unusual wine cellar". / SW6 2DR; www.thetommytucker.com; @tommytuckerpub; Mon-Sat 10 pm, Sun 9 pm; set weekday L £30 (FP).

Tonic & Remedy
The M By Montcalm EC1 NEW £55

151-157 City Rd 3837 3102 12–1A

North of Old Street roundabout, a trendy-looking new hotel hang-out, run by Searcys; not enough feedback for a rating, but one early reporter – lauding its "interesting mix of dishes" – says "it's a great place for after work drinks and dinner". / EC1V 1BE; www.tonicandremedy.co.uk; @tonicandremedy; Mon-Thu 10.30 pm, Fri & Sat 11 pm, Sun 10 pm.

Tonkotsu £32 443

Selfridges, 400 Oxford St, W1 7437 0071 3–1A
63 Dean St, W1 7437 0071 4–2A
4 Canvey St, SE1 7928 2228 9–4B
382 Mare St, E8 8533 1840 1–1D NEW
Arch 334 1a Dunston St, E8 7254 2478 1–2D

"Delicious hot and warming bowls of noodles" are the mainstay of these cramped bars in Soho, and now in Bankside, Haggerston and Hackney Central too; there's some dispute however as to whether they're "taking ramen to a new level", or are merely "fine".

Tortilla £17 322

Branches throughout London

For a "fresh and satisfying burrito", these "speedy" operations – neck and neck with rival Chipotle – are "cheap and reasonably authentic". / www.tortilla.co.uk; W1 & N1 11 pm, Sun 9 pm, SE1 & E14 9 pm, EC3 7 pm, E14 Sun 7 pm; SE1 & EC3 closed Sat & Sun, N1 closed sun; no Amex.

Tosa W6 **£35** 3 3 2
332 King St 8748 0002 7–2B
"Freshly cooked over charcoal", the "excellent" yakitori is the speciality of this nondescript but "cosy" Japanese, near Stamford Brook tube, although the sushi and other fare is "very tasty" too. / W6 0RR; www.tosauk.com; 10.30 pm.

Toto's SW3 **£88** 2 3 3
Walton Hs, Lennox Gardens Mews 7589 2062 5–2C
"A beautiful, tucked-away Knightsbridge Italian, whose lovely courtyard is perfect when it's sunny"; "it's good to see it back in operation under its new owners" – "the resurrected incarnation is excellent" (if very expensive). / SW3 2JH; www.totosrestaurant.com; @TotosRestaurant; 11 pm.

Tozi SW1 **£47** 3 3 3
8 Gillingham St 7769 9771 2–4B
"Very useful in the Victoria desert" – this "accommodating" venture may be "pricey" and somewhat hotel-y, but fans love its "scrummy Venetian-inspired tapas", and praise the "flexible and welcoming" staff. / SW1V 1HN; www.tozirestaurant.co.uk; @ToziRestaurant; 10 pm.

The Trading House EC2 **£42**
89-91 Gresham St 7600 5050 9–1A
Newly-opened gastropub in the heart of the City – early days reports say it's "nicely-decorated", serving a wide range of food that's "well-made and well-presented". / EC2V 7NQ; www.thetradinghouse.uk.com; @tradinghouse; 10 pm; closed Sat L & Sun; no Amex.

The Tramshed EC2 **£55** 2 2 3
32 Rivington St 7749 0478 12–1B
"Impressive art including a Damien Hirst number in a tank of formaldehyde" sets the scene at Mark Hix's big Shoreditch shed; but while its "meat-centred" formula (chicken or steak 'n' chips) can be OK on business, it too often seems "all style over substance", delivering "not much flavour for the £££s". / EC2A 3LX; www.chickenandsteak.co.uk; @HIXrestaurants; Mon & Tue 11 pm, Wed-Sat 12.30 am, Sun 9.30 pm.

Trangallan N16 **£44** 5 4 4
61 Newington Grn 7359 4988 1–1C
"None of the plates or cutlery match, but in the quaintest way", at this Stoke Newington Hispanic; all reporters "love everything about the place" – "staff really know their stuff", there's "loads of interesting Spanish wines", and the food's "a revelation". / N16 9PX; www.trangallan.com; @trangallan_N16; 10.30 pm; closed Mon; no Amex; set weekday L £28 (FP).

Tredwell's WC2 **£53** 1 2 1
4 Upper St Martin's Ln 3764 0840 4–3B
"A let-down after such high hopes" – Marcus Wareing's casual West End haunt is "nearly so good… but somehow just isn't"; "is it a gourmet place or a brasserie for theatre-goers?" – "it's not good enough for the former, too expensive for the latter" – too often the service is "amateurish", and the decor strikes too many reporters as "bizarre: not relaxing, not cool, not quirky". / WC2H 9NY; www.tredwells.com; @tredwells; 10 pm, Thu-Sat 11 pm, Sun 9 pm; set weekday L & pre-theatre £35 (FP).

The Tree House SW13 £45 333

73 White Hart Ln 8392 1617 10–1A

"The outside area is a great place to eat in summer", say fans of this cute "pub-style" venue, on the fringes of Barnes, who praise its "reliable" standards generally. / SW13 0PW; www.treehousepeople.com; @TreeHouseBarnes; 11 pm, Fri & Sat midnight, Sun 10.30 pm.

Trinity SW4 £68 554

4 The Polygon 7622 1199 10–2D

"You feel the money's been well-spent" at Adam Byatt's fine-dining "oasis" in Clapham – "a superb all-rounder", where staff are "friendly without being overbearing", the room is "lovely and airy", the cuisine "consistently brilliant" and where "the Chef's Cellar wines are particularly well chosen". In October 2015 it is relaunching after a 3-month closure, with an open kitchen, new outside dining area, and a new 'casual dining' option on the first floor called 'Upstairs', with small plates and communal tables. / SW4 0JG; www.trinityrestaurant.co.uk; @TrinityLondon; 9.45 pm; closed Mon L & Sun D; set weekday L £46 (FP).

Trishna W1 £64 543

15-17 Blandford St 7935 5624 2–1A

Mumbai comes to Marylebone at this London offshoot of its legendary Indian forebear; despite a "trying-to-be-chic" revamp, the interior gets a slightly mixed rep, but the "extraordinarily good" cooking (in particular "memorable seafood and stand-out lamb chops") rivals that of its upstart Mayfair sibling, Gymkhana. / W1U 3DG; www.trishnalondon.com; @TrishnaLondon; 10.45 pm, Sun 9.45 pm; set weekday L & pre-theatre £35 (FP).

LA TROMPETTE W4 £71 444

5-7 Devonshire Rd 8747 1836 7–2A

"A good reason to live in Chiswick!" – this "dream local" is a worthy sibling to Chez Bruce, that's "well worth the trek to W4" for its "exemplary" classic cooking and "quiet wow factor"; a tiny minority, however, quibble that it's "not quite as special as prior to the extension" (a couple of years ago). / W4 2EU; www.latrompette.co.uk; @LaTrompetteUK; 10.30 pm, Sun 9.30 pm; set weekday L £50 (FP), set Sun L £54 (FP).

Troubadour SW5 £46 234

263-267 Old Brompton Rd 7370 1434 5–3A

"Still the same old Troubadour!" – but for how much longer? – this Bohemian relic is up for sale as we go to press; let's hope a buyer can be found, both to preserve the unique "arty" vibe of this "fun" '60s Earl's Court café (and live music venue), and also to improve its basic fodder. / SW5 9JA; www.troubadour.co.uk; @TroubadourLDN; 11 pm.

Trullo N1 £59 443

300-302 St Paul's Rd 7226 2733 8–2D

"A taste of Italy off Highbury Corner" – this "lovely" looking Italian continues to inspire north Londoners with its "simple", "dreamily authentic" cooking and "an amazing wine list that's both clever and good value"; some reports tip the ground floor over the basement. / N1 2LH; www.trullorestaurant.com; @Trullo_LDN; 10.30 pm; closed Sun D; no Amex; booking: max 12.

The Truscott Arms W9 **£56** **434**
55 Shirland Rd 7266 9198 8–2A
"It's transformed the area!"; this "surprise gem" is "just what Maida Vale has been waiting for" – "an exceptional local", whose first-floor dining room provides quite "complex" cuisine, alongside matching wines. Top Menu Tip – an extensive gluten-free menu. / W9 2JD; www.thetruscottarms.com; @TheTruscottArms; 10 pm; SRA-3.*

The Truscott Cellar NW3 NEW **£39**
240 Haverstock Hill 7266 9198 8–3B
On the prominent Belsize Park site that was long Weng Wah House (RIP) – a new wine bar promising a 'British sharing plates' formula from the owners of Maida Vale's popular Truscott Arms; it opened in autumn 2015. / NW3 2AE; www.twitter.com/TruscottCellar; @truscottcellar.

Tsunami **£46** **533**
93 Charlotte St, W1 7637 0050 2–1C
5-7 Voltaire Rd, SW4 7978 1610 10–1D
"Terrific Japanese/Asian cuisine" – not just "spot-on sushi and sashimi" but also many "wonderful grazing options" – continue to win high acclaim for this Clapham outfit (whose more "basic" Fitzrovia spin-off is less well-known); "original cocktails" too, help make for a good night out. / www.tsunamirestaurant.co.uk; @Tsunamirest; SW4 10.30 pm, Fri & Sat 11 pm, Sun 9.30 pm; W1 11 pm; SW4 closed Mon - Fri L, W1 closed Sat L and Sun; no Amex.

Tulse Hill Hotel SE24 NEW **£46** **333**
150 Norwood Rd 8671 7499 1–4D
Between Brixton and Dulwich, this newly-renovated gastropub is proving "a good addition to a rather bereft area"; the food's "a cut above", but "all the hipster beards on show can be a little distracting". / SE24 9AY; www.tulsehillhotel.com; @TulseHillHotel; 10 pm, Sun 9 pm.

28-50 **£54** **334**
15 Maddox St, W1 7495 1505 3–2C
15-17 Marylebone Ln, W1 7486 7922 3–1A
140 Fetter Ln, EC4 7242 8877 9–2A
"Impressively knowledgeable staff make non-wine-buffs feel very comfortable" at these hugely popular bar/bistros, whose "wonderful" list has "many interesting options by the glass and bottle"; the food's "perfect for a business lunch" – "unadventurous but well-prepared". / www.2850.co.uk; EC4 9.30 pm, W1 Mon-Wed 10 pm, Thu-Sat 10.30 pm, Sun 9.30 pm; EC4 closed Sat & Sun.

Twist At Crawford W1 NEW **£59** **444**
42 Crawford St 7723 3377 2–1A
"An innovative take" on tapas (mixing Mediterranean and Asian inspirations) wins praise for this "modest"-looking newcomer, and helps make it "a great new addition" to Marylebone. / W1H 1JW; www.twistkitchen.co.uk; @TwistKitchen; 11 pm, Fri 11.30 pm, Sat midnight; closed Sun; set weekday L £37 (FP).

Two Brothers N3 **£45** **332**
297-303 Regent's Park Rd 8346 0469 1–1B
A recent refurb', with "smart new decor" divides fans of this Finchley fixture – thankfully the "family-friendly charm" is unwavering, and even those who say it's "gone off a bit", still say it's their No. 1 favourite chippie. / N3 1DP; www.twobrothers.co.uk; 10 pm; closed Mon; set weekday L £19 (FP).

2 Veneti W1 £47 343

10 Wigmore St 7637 0789 3–1B

"Interesting Venetian specialities" and "assiduous" service maintain the appeal of this "reliable", "high quality" (if rather "expensive") Italian, which is "very convenient for the Wigmore Hall" (and handy for business too). / W1U 2RD; www.2veneti.com; @2Veneti; 10.30 pm, Sat 11 pm; closed Sat L & Sun.

**Typing Room
Town Hall Hotel E2** £88 543

Patriot Square 7871 0461 1–2D

"Sublime food without snobbery"; Lee Westcott's "meticulous" dishes are delivered by staff who are "friendly, and absolutely on-the-ball" at this ("slightly sterile") Bethnal Green yearling, where "you watch the chefs work in the open kitchen"; it's fully as good as its legendary predecessor (Viajante, RIP). / E2 9NF; www.typingroom.com; @TypingRoom; 10 pm; closed Mon & Tue L; set weekday L £50 (FP).

Umu W1 £120 222

14-16 Bruton Pl 7499 8881 3–2C

"The kaiseki is a revelation, and a confirmation of chef Yoshi's vast talents", say fans of Marlon Abela's Kyoto-style venture in a tucked-away Mayfair mews, for whom this is "the best Japanese food outside of Japan"; almost as many reporters though, just obsess over the bill – "dear, oh dear, oh dear, oh dear…" / W1J 6LX; www.umurestaurant.com; 10.30 pm; closed Sat L & Sun; no trainers; booking: max 14.

Union Street Café SE1 £57 222

47-51 Great Suffolk St 7592 7977 9–4B

Fans of Gordon Ramsay's industrial-chic Italian two-year-old in Borough praise its "interesting and varied menu" and "casual" style; there are a number of sceptics though, who say it's merely "expensive and average", or just plain bad. / SE1 0BS; www.gordonramsay.com/union-street-cafe; @unionstreetcafe; Mon-Sat 10.45 pm; closed Sun D.

Le Vacherin W4 £63 322

76-77 South Pde 8742 2121 7–1A

Malcolm John's "off-the-beaten-track" Gallic classic by Acton Green, is known for its "delicious" bistro fare and "intimate" ambience; its ratings suffered this year though, with quite a number of reports of the "perhaps-they-were-having-a-bad-day" variety. / W4 5LF; www.levacherin.co.uk; @Le_Vacherin; 9.45 pm, Fri & Sat 10.15 pm, Sun 8.30 pm; closed Mon L; set dinner £35 (FP), set weekday L & pre-theatre £41 (FP).

Vanilla Black EC4 £61 432

17-18 Tooks Ct 7242 2622 9–2A

"Wowza!" – even "died-in-the-wool meat eaters" are bowled over by this "little veggie, down a small alley near Chancery Lane", whose "strange combinations" "never cease to surprise with their unimaginable mixture of flavours"; the same could not be said though for its "sombre" interior. / EC4A 1LB; www.vanillablack.co.uk; @vanillablack1; 10 pm; closed Sun; no Amex.

Vapiano £30 322

19-21 Great Portland St, W1 7268 0080 3–1C
90b Southwark St, SE1 7593 2010 9–4B

"For a quick bite at a reasonable price" – pizza, pasta, salads, etc – try this offbeat German-owned food-court concept, in the West End and also Bankside – you serve yourself, but the system of ordering food that's "freshly prepared in front of you to order" gets the thumbs-up. / www.vapiano.co.uk; Mon - Thu 11pm, SE1 Fri & Sat 10.30pm, W1 Fri & Sat 11.30 pm.

Vasco & Piero's Pavilion W1 £59 343

15 Poland St 7437 8774 3–1D

"A real gem for those nostalgic for a more civilised, less trendy past!" – this "unassuming", heart-of-Soho Italian is "untainted by hip decor or noise"; there are sceptics for whom it's too "boring" (and too "closely packed"), but most reports focus on its "friendly and professional" staff, and quality, "traditional" fare. / W1F 8QE; www.vascosfood.com; @Vasco_and_Piero; 10.15 pm; closed Sat L & Sun; set weekday L £41 (FP).

Veeraswamy W1 £77 333

Victory Hs, 99-101 Regent St 7734 1401 3–3D

From its contemporary design, you'd never know this "quiet oasis" near Piccadilly Circus was London's oldest Indian (est 1926); to say, as fans do, that "it's still the best" would over-egg it, but its "inventive and flavourful" food rescues it from any hint of tourist-trap status. / W1B 4RS; www.veeraswamy.com; 10.30 pm, Sun 10 pm; booking: max 14; set Sun L £51 (FP).

Verden E5 £48 444

181 Clarence Rd 8986 4723 1–1D

Rave reviews for this modern wine bar yearling in increasingly gentrified Clapton (once upon a time 'Murder Mile'). There's a good selection of "eclectic wines" ("they even have a 'breakfast wine'!"), served by "knowledgeable staff", alongside a "limited" menu (that's "fairly short on cooked dishes"). / E5 8EE; www.verdene5.com; @VerdenE5; midnight, Sun 10.30 pm; closed Mon, Tue L, Wed L & Thu L.

Verdi's E1 NEW £46 443

237 Mile End Rd 7423 9563 1–2D

"What a brilliant addition to the Whitechapel Road!" – "an excellent and rare trattoria" that would be "well worth a visit in any neighbourhood" thanks to its "delicious, regional Italian food", but is "particularly welcome in under-endowed Stepney!" / E1 4AA; www.gverdi.uk.

El Vergel SE1 £33 444

132 Webber St 7401 2308 9–4B

"Mouthwatering empanadas, and other top authentic South American sarnies and snacks" inspire love – especially at brunch – for this upbeat, budget Latino canteen, near Borough tube. / SE1 0QL; www.elvergel.co.uk; @ElVergel_London; 3 pm, Sat-Sun 4 pm; closed D, closed Sun; no Amex.

Vico WC2 NEW £58

140a Shaftesbury Ave awaiting tel 4–2B

The duo behind Soho's marvellous Bocca di Lupo, Jacob Kenedy and Victor Hugo, branch out into street food with this new 'piazza-eria' in Cambridge Circus (a casual, no-cutlery restaurant offering take-away and Gelupo ice cream counter); it opened in August 2015, too late for our survey. / WC2H 8PA; www.boccadilupo.com; @boccadilupo.

Il Vicolo SW1 £49 344
3-4 Crown Passage 7839 3960 3–4D
Down a cute alley in St James's, a "great little family-run Italian" that's "well worth seeking out" in this über-pricey part of town – "you are always looked after" and the Sicilian cooking is "thoroughly enjoyable". / SW1Y 6PP; 10 pm; closed Sat L & Sun.

The Victoria SW14 £50 344
10 West Temple 8876 4238 10–2A
"A boon if you've got a young family, but adults are well-catered-for too!" – Paul Merrett's "lovely", large gastropub is "hidden away in residential Sheen, near Richmond Park"; "kids get to run around in the enclosed garden" (with playground), while others enjoy the "high quality" cooking. / SW14 7RT; www.thevictoria.net; @thevictoria_pub; winter 10 pm, Sun 8 pm – summer 9 pm; no Amex.

Viet Grill E2 £44 433
58 Kingsland Rd 7739 6686 12–1B
"Spicy and great value for money" – the Vietnamese cooking at this modern Shoreditch café and pho-bar; "it's packed, and no wonder!". / E2 8DP; www.vietnamesekitchen.co.uk; @CayTreVietGrill; 11 pm, Fri & Sat 11.30 pm, Sun 10.30 pm.

Vijay NW6 £32 341
49 Willesden Ln 7328 1087 1–1B
It "could do with a face-lift" (no change for decades there then), but the cooking at this longstanding South Indian in Kilburn is as "reliably delicious" and well priced now, as it has been for many a moon. / NW6 7RF; www.vijayrestaurant.co.uk; 10.45 pm, Fri & Sat 11.45 pm.

Villa Bianca NW3 £58 232
1 Perrins Ct 7435 3131 8–2A
"Well-located off Hampstead High Street in a quaint little alleyway" – "an old school 'silver service' trattoria", where "all the standard Italian dishes are served"; to its very dedicated fan cub it's "not a wow, but a safe bet", but to its detractors "it's shocking and tired". / NW3 1QS; www.villabiancagroup.co.uk; @VBgroupNW3; 11.30 pm, Sun 10.30 pm.

Villa Di Geggiano W4 NEW £63 222
66-68 Chiswick High Rd 3384 9442 7–2B
"Sumptuous Italian newcomer", occupying the Chiswick site that was once Frankie's (long RIP); wines from the Tuscan estate of the same name are a prime feature, as is its outside terrace, but the food can be "disappointing", especially at prices that some find "grabby". / W4 1SY; www.villadigeggiano.com; @VilladiGeggiano; 10 pm; closed Mon.

Village East SE1 £56 333
171-173 Bermondsey St 7357 6082 9–4D
"Too many hipsters" is a hazard at this happening Bermondsey hang-out, tipped for brunch, and also as being "great with a group of friends". / SE1 3UW; www.villageeast.co.uk; @VillageEastSE1; 10 pm, Sun 9.30 pm; set weekday L £35 (FP).

Villandry £55 1 1 2
11-12 Waterloo Pl, SW1 7930 3305 3–3D
170 Gt Portland St, W1 7631 3131 2–1B
Their "elegant" looks and high prices show "pretentions to greatness", but these smart-looking grand cafés – in St James's and Marylebone – "could be so much better", if only they had "more professional" staff and made an effort with their "very disappointing" cooking.

The Vincent Rooms
Westminster Kingsway College SW1 £37 3 3 3
76 Vincent Sq 7802 8391 2–4C
Despite the elegant Westminster location, "low prices reflect that this is a training ground" for one of London's main catering colleges; by nature "it's a bit hit and miss", but typically "you get great food that's good value", and the servers are "charming, and eager for comments and criticism". / SW1P 2PD; www.thevincentrooms.com; @TheVincentRooms; 7 pm; closed Mon D, Tue D, Fri D, Sat & Sun; no Amex.

Vinoteca £46 2 3 4
15 Seymour Pl, W1 7724 7288 2–2A
55 Beak St, W1 3544 7411 3–2D
18 Devonshire Rd, W4 3701 8822 7–2A
One Pancras Sq, N1 3793 7210 8–3C NEW
7 St John St, EC1 7253 8786 9–1B
The "well-curated" list of "fantastic", "eclectic" wines by the glass underpins the major success of these "buzzing" modern wine bars (but its bistro fare is "very sound" too). The new King's Cross branch is "a bit hangar-like" but most reporters give it "three cheers". Top Tip – "Magic Monday, with wines sold at shop prices". / www.vinoteca.co.uk.

Vintage Salt £44 4 4 3
189 Upper St, N1 3227 0979 8–2D
69 Old Broad St, EC2 7920 9103 9–2C NEW
"Quality remains high" at this rebranded chain (from Fish & Chip Shop), where the national staple "can be had grilled or steamed if you prefer"; the "noisy and crowded" Islington branch is still the best-known, and is pepped up by its "charming" staff.

Vivat Bacchus £51 2 2 2
4 Hay's Ln, SE1 7234 0891 9–4C
47 Farringdon St, EC4 7353 2648 9–2A
"A blinding South African wine list", and the "lovely cheeses" ("ask in advance, and they may let you into the cheese room") are the stand-out features of these "packed" ventures, in the City and South Bank; the other simple fare plays second fiddle but is "dependable". / www.vivatbacchus.co.uk; 10.30pm; EC4 closed Sat & Sun, SE1 closed Sat L & Sun.

VQ £46 2 4 3
St Giles Hotel, Great Russell St, WC1 7636 5888 4–1A
325 Fulham Rd, SW10 7376 7224 5–3B
"Just the place for breakfast after a 5am release from hospital... a nightclub... the cells" – these dependable diners (the age-old SW10 original, and newer WC1 spin-off) serve "classic", "simple" fodder, 24/7. / www.vingtquatre.co.uk; open 24 hours.

Vrisaki N22 **£37** 3 3 2

73 Middleton Rd 8889 8760 1–1C

"It's still hard to finish all the food", at this ancient taverna, behind a Bounds Green take-away, whose mezze feasts are, for its devotees, a top "cheap 'n' cheerful" treat. / N22 8LZ; www.vrisaki.uk.com; @vrisakiuk; 11.30 pm, Sun 9 pm; closed Mon; no Amex.

Wagamama **£39** 2 3 2

Branches throughout London

For a "swift", "no-frills", "fuel stop" – particularly "with kids well catered for" – many still recommend these "casual" communal noodle-refectories, even while acknowledging that the food is "nothing special" nowadays. / www.wagamama.com; 10 pm - 11 pm; EC4 & EC2 closed Sat & Sun; no booking.

Wahaca **£33** 2 3 3

Branches throughout London

"Fun, fresh Mexican street food" served by "obliging" staff underpins the "cheap 'n' cheerful" appeal (and "unstoppable expansion") of Thomasina Miers' "colourful and casual" chain; even some who feel "the buzz has gone" since its early days say it's "still decent". / www.wahaca.com; 10 pm - 11 pm; no booking.

The Wallace
The Wallace Collection W1 **£55** 2 2 5

Hertford Hs, Manchester Sq 7563 9505 3–1A

"The magnificent covered atrium" provides a "stunning" and "spacious" setting for this restaurant adjoining the famous 18th-century palazzo and art gallery; the food's usually "decent" enough, but "erratic and lacklustre" service is a hazard. / W1U 3BN; www.peytonandbyrne.co.uk/the-wallace-restaurant/index.html; @PeytonandByrne; Fri & Sat 9.30 pm; Sun-Thu closed D; no Amex.

Waterloo Bar & Kitchen SE1 **£50** 2 2 2

131 Waterloo Rd 7928 5086 9–4A

"A great place to meet fellow Waterloo commuters" or "for the Old Vic" – this "incredibly noisy and packed" venue is a "handy", "reasonably priced" standby in "a hard area for eateries". / SE1 8UR; www.barandkitchen.co.uk; @BarKitchen; 10.30 pm.

The Waterway W9 **£50** 2 3 4

54 Formosa St 7266 3557 8–4A

The hint is in the name – this Little Venice hang-out (same ownership as the nearby Summerhouse) has an unbeatable canal-side terrace that's just the job for a lazy summer day. / W9 2JU; www.thewaterway.co.uk; @thewaterway_; 11 pm, Sun 10.30 pm.

The Wells NW3 **£49** 2 2 4

30 Well Walk 7794 3785 8–1A

"Well-behaved, four-legged customers are welcome to sit under the bench or table", at this hugely popular pub, "superbly located", about 100m from the Heath, serving "solid" nosh (from a rather "unchanging" menu); staff are "smiley" but service "gets wonky at peak times". / NW3 1BX; www.thewellshampstead.london; @WellsHampstead; 10 pm, Sun 9.30 pm.

West Thirty Six W10 NEW £65

36 Golborne Rd 3752 0530 6–1A

Aiming to become a major north Kensington hang-out – a big, three-story newcomer (incorporating grill, lounge, bar, terrace and BBQ), from the owners of Beach Blanket Babylon; perhaps they share the same DNA food-wise? – early feedback is very mixed. / W10 5PR; www.w36.co.uk; @WestThirtySix; 10 pm.

The Wet Fish Café NW6 £47 333

242 West End Ln 7443 9222 1–1B

"Situated in a former fishmongers", this West Hampstead "oasis" is – for its enthusiastic local following – "second to none"; the fish cooking is "delicious", but the place is also "especially good for breakfast and brunch". / NW6 1LG; www.thewetfishcafe.co.uk; @thewetfishcafe; 10 pm, Sun 9.30 pm; no Amex; set always available £25 (FP), set weekday L £27 (FP).

The White Onion SW19 NEW £62 443

67 High St 8947 8278 10–2B

Residents of Wimbledon can't quite believe their luck as Eric and Sarah Guignard, husband and wife behind Surbiton's "charming" French Table, arrive in the heart of the village – with "high quality" Gallic cuisine, "efficient service" and a "good-value set lunch", it's a most "welcome addition". / SW19 5EE; www.thewhiteonion.co.uk; @thewhiteonionSW; 10.30 pm; closed Mon, Tue L, Wed L & Thu L; set weekday L £37 (FP).

White Rabbit N16 £48 434

15-16 Bradbury St 7682 0163 1–1C

"Why isn't this gem loved more?" – so say fans of this Dalston two-year old, who insist its "funky" small-plates cuisine is "some of the cleverest food in London at the moment"; feedback is limited though, and sceptics feel "it's imaginative but overhyped". / N16 8JN; www.whiterabbitdalston.com; @WhiteRabbitEAT; 11 pm ; closed weekday L.

The White Swan EC4 £63 343

108 Fetter Ln 7242 9696 9–2A

"Even when the ground floor is heaving and loud, it's thankfully quiet" in the civilised dining room over this pub, off Fleet Street; the ambitious fare is "perfect for a business lunch", but its value fluctuates as "pricing seems to rely on the frequent 50% off food deals". / EC4A 1ES; www.thewhiteswanlondon.com; @thewhiteswanEC4; 10 pm; closed Sat & Sun.

Wild Honey W1 £73 222

12 St George St 7758 9160 3–2C

This "club-like" Arbutus sibling in Mayfair still wins some praise for its "clever" cooking and "cosy" ambience, but ratings cratered this year amidst encounters with "amateur" service, "average" results and – most notably – silly prices: "they should re-name it Wild Money!" / W1S 2FB; www.wildhoneyrestaurant.co.uk; @whrestaurant; 10.30 pm; closed Sun; set Sun L £50 (FP).

Wiltons SW1 £97 334

55 Jermyn St 7629 9955 3–3C

"Where Lord Grantham would surely have dined when in London!" – this "stuffy" pillar of the St James's Establishment (est 1742, here since 1984) is "as traditional as traditional can be", and its "womb-like comfort" and "wonderful" seafood make for "impressive" entertaining; one snag – "prices verge on robbery!" / SW1Y 6LX; www.wiltons.co.uk; @wiltons1742; 10.15 pm; closed Sat L & Sun; jacket required.

Wimsey's SW6 NEW £46 333
177 New King's Rd 7731 8326 10–1B
An agreeably straightforward Parsons Green newcomer – the first solo venture from Leith's scholar Gwyn Rees-Sheppard, offering seasonal British dishes and English wines; the odd critic says it's "nothing amazing", but prices are generous, and the overall intent very genuine. / SW6 4SW; www.wimseys.co.uk; @Wimseys; 10.30 pm, Sun 10 pm; closed Mon.

The Windmill W1 £41 323
6-8 Mill St 7491 8050 3–2C
"The best pies ever!", and other "good old-fashioned British fare" make this Mayfair gastropub the perfect place to over-indulge in suet pastry and ale – be sure to ask about the Pie Club! / W1S 2AZ; www.windmillmayfair.co.uk; @tweetiepie_w1; 10 pm, Sat 5 pm; closed Sat D & Sun.

The Wine Library EC3 £34 144
43 Trinity Sq 7481 0415 9–3D
"The clue is in the name" when it comes to visiting these "unique", ancient City cellars, where a "superb selection of wines" can be enjoyed "at terrific shop prices, plus corkage"; to accompany, it's "not the finest of dining (a cheese and pâté buffet)" but "adequate". / EC3N 4DJ; www.winelibrary.co.uk; 7.30 pm; closed Mon D, Sat & Sun.

Wolfe's WC2 £48 322
30 Gt Queen St 7831 4442 4–1D
A rather '70s-style family diner in Covent Garden, which feels like "a step back in time"; "excellent burgers" have been the house speciality since time immemorial – the most memorable nowadays is the "brilliant Wagyu/Kobe option". / WC2B 5BB; www.wolfes-grill.net; @wolfesbargrill; 10 pm, Fri & Sat 10.30 pm, Sun 9 pm.

THE WOLSELEY W1 £60 345
160 Piccadilly 7499 6996 3–3C
"It should be a national monument!" – Corbin & King's "tremendously atmospheric" ("mildly cacophonous") European Grand Café by the Ritz has become a "perennial" linchpin of "glamorous" London life ("there's always at least one A-list celeb eating at a nearby table!"). It's the "fun and the buzz" that set it apart, however – the large Mittel-European menu is "very adaptable" but decidedly "not exciting" (even if "it does the best breakfast in town, bar none!") / W1J 9EB; www.thewolseley.com; @TheWolseley; midnight, Sun 11 pm.

Wong Kei W1 £30 222
41-43 Wardour St 7437 8408 4–3A
"You can even now buy a T-shirt saying 'upstairs'!" (the famous rude bark of the waiters to non-Oriental guests) at this Chinatown landmark; under new management of late, service is "more polite than in the old days", but the decor still looks like "it really needs an overhaul" and – though "unbeatably cheap" – "you still come here to eat and go". / W1D 6PY; www.wongkeilondon.com; Mon-Sat 11.15 pm, Sun 10.30 pm ; no credit cards; no booking.

F S A

Woodlands £38 322

37 Panton St, SW1 7839 7258 4–4A
77 Marylebone Ln, W1 7486 3862 2–1A
102 Heath St, NW3 7794 3080 8–1A

"Nutritious, delicious, and very well priced"; these long-established South Indian veggies serve "genuine" dishes, and are "comfy" and "pleasant", if somewhat "bleak" looking.
/ www.woodlandsrestaurant.co.uk; Mon - Sun 10.45 pm ; NW3 no L Mon.

The Woodstock W1 NEW £34

11 Woodstock St 7499 4342 3–2B

A relative newcomer to London's izakaya dining scene, with a plum position just off Oxford Street, and an offering of grilled meat skewers and cocktails, alongside Japanese beers; no survey feedback as yet, hence we've left it un-rated. / W1C 2AE; www.thewoodstocklondon.co.uk; @thewoodstockldn; midnight.

Workshop Coffee £45 344

80a Mortimer St, W1 7253 5754 9–1A NEW
St Christopher's Place, W1 7253 5754 3–1A NEW
27 Clerkenwell Rd, EC1 7253 5754 9–1A
60a Holborn Viaduct, EC1 no tel 9–2A NEW

It's the brilliant blend of coffees ("roasted before your very eyes") which wins nominations for these "friendly and entertaining" independents ("the Cheers of coffee shops!"); brunch is a highlight too though – "a wide variety of delicious sweets and savouries".

Wormwood W11 NEW £65 443

16 All Saints Rd 7854 1808 6–1B

"Delightful", new husband-and-wife project, in the "Notting Hill backwater" site that was once Uli (RIP); fans laud the "cornucopia of tastes" of its "experimental Mediterranean and North African-tinged sharing plates" – a minority of sceptics though, find it "heavily priced" for a "crammed-in" and "loud" experience, whose "over-fussy cooking" has "muddy flavours". / W11 1HH; wormwoodrestaurant.com; 9.30 pm, Fri & Sat 10 pm; closed Mon, Tue, Wed L, Thu L & Sun D.

Wright Brothers £58 443

13 Kingly St, W1 7434 3611 3–2D
56 Old Brompton Rd, SW7 7581 0131 5–2B NEW
11 Stoney St, SE1 7403 9554 9–4C
8 Lamb St, E1 7377 8706 9–2D

"Tanks full of sparkling sea food" showcase the "breathtakingly fresh" oysters, shellfish and other "flavoursome" fare at these "happy and bustling" outfits. Top Menu Tips – "an historic beef and oyster pie", and "blissful oyster Happy Hour". / 10.30 pm, Sun 9 pm; booking: max 8.

XO NW3 £46 222

29 Belsize Ln 7433 0888 8–2A

Will Ricker's "very relaxed" Belsize Park haunt still has fans for its Pan-Asian fusion tapas and cocktails, but seems increasingly "uninspired" – "when it opened it was so fresh and exciting: now it just seems like another boring local". / NW3 5AS; www.rickerrestaurants.com; 10.30 pm, Sun 10pm.

Yalla Yalla £37 334

1 Green's Ct, W1 7287 7663 3–2D
12 Winsley St, W1 7637 4748 3–1C
Greenwich Peninsula Sq, SE10 0772 584 1372 8–3C

A "fresh and filling" feast is to be had at these "buzzy" Lebanese cafés; the "cramped but cosy" original, just off Oxford Street, makes a good respite from shopping, but all locations get the thumbs-up. / www.yalla-yalla.co.uk; Green's Court 11 pm, Sun 10 pm – Winsley Street 11.30 pm, Sat 11 pm; W1 Sun.

Yama Momo SE22 NEW £55 433

72 Lordship Ln 8299 1007 1–4D

"An impressive addition to the East Dulwich food scene" – this "fun" Japanese newcomer (sibling to Clapham's Tsunami) is an instant local hit, thanks to its "fantastic cooking (particularly sushi and sashimi)", and "fab cocktails". / SE22 8HF; www.yamamomo.co.uk; @YamamomoRest; 10 pm, Fri & Sat 10.30 pm, Sun 9.30 pm; closed weekday L.

Yashin W8 £78 532

1a Argyll Rd 7938 1536 5–1A

"Do sit at the bar" – "watch the chefs carefully seasoning or searing the fish" – if you visit this "pricey" Kensington venture; the result is "outstanding modern sushi and sashimi", amongst London's best, with "wonderful and innovative mixes of flavours"; NB the basement can feel a bit "dead". / W8 7DB; www.yashinsushi.com; 10 pm.

Yashin Ocean House SW7 £80 222

117-119 Old Brompton Rd 7373 3990 5–2B

Is Yashin's South Kensington spin-off "just too odd to be a success"? It occupies a potentially characterful site, but feedback remains very limited – even fans concede "the atmosphere could be warmer", and though the Japanese-fusion cuisine can be "very refined", prices are "extortionate". / SW7 3RN; www.yashinocean.com; @YashinLondon; 10 pm, Sun 8 pm; set always available & pre-theatre £46 (FP).

Yasmeen NW8 NEW £46

1 Blenheim Ter 7624 2921 8–3A

On the former site of One Blenheim Terrace (RIP) in St John's Wood, a "sumptuous" new Lebanese where "maitre d' Bashir is a star" – promising initial reports, let's hope for more feedback next year. / NW8 0EH; www.yasmeenrestaurant.com; @yasmeencafe.

Yauatcha £76 523

Broadwick Hs, 15-17 Broadwick St, W1 7494 8888 3–2D
Broadgate Circle, EC2 awaiting tel 12–2B NEW

"Perfectly executed" and "creative" dim sum – probably "the best in London" – have made the "trendy" Soho basement original a "classic" destination, and its new more "airy" sibling in Broadgate fully lives up. W1 also boasts an "HK-style pâtisserie selection – both breathtakingly beautiful and very delicious".

The Yellow House SE16 £45 332

126 Lower Rd 7231 8777 11–2A

If you find yourself near Surrey Quays, check out this "good value local, with plenty of choice" (pizza is the top tip) and "lovely" service. / SE16 2UE; www.theyellowhouse.eu; @Theyellowhouse_; 10 pm, Sun 8 pm; closed Mon, Tue–Sat closed L, Sun open L & D.

Yi-Ban E16 £45 432
London Regatta Centre, Royal Albert Dock 7473 6699 11–1D
An interesting waterside location near City Airport helps justify the trek to this obscure Chinese in deepest Docklands, as does its "solid, very reasonably priced" dim sum and other fare. / E16 2QT; www.yi-ban.co.uk; 11 pm, Sun 10.30 pm.

Yipin China N1 £42 221
70-72 Liverpool Rd 7354 3388 8–3D
Some detect "a fall from grace" at this "stark" Sichuan three-year-old in Islington; fans still hail its "stunning" cooking, but others are "not sure why it's had such raves" given its "slow" service and food they say is "awful and way overpriced". / N1 0QD; www.yipinchina.co.uk; 11 pm.

Yming W1 £41 354
35-36 Greek St 7734 2721 4–2A
"The staff always smile" at Christine Yau's "serene" Soho "haven", "run admirably by the amazing William"; the "interesting" Chinese cuisine is "consistently good" and at times "cracking". / W1D 5DL; www.ymingIondon.com; 11.45 pm; set weekday L & pre-theatre £23 (FP).

York & Albany NW1 £59 223
127-129 Parkway 7592 1227 8–3B
Gordon Ramsay's large, glammed-up tavern on the corner of Regent's Park generates mixed and limited feedback; to fans it's a great all-rounder, but the ambience can also seem "bland", and too often the cooking is "not up to scratch". / NW1 7PS; www.gordonramsay.com; @yorkandalbany; 11 pm, Sun 9 pm.

Yoshi Sushi W6 £35 342
210 King St 8748 5058 7–2B
In a nondescript run of Hammersmith restaurants, this low key stalwart is worth remembering for its "reasonably priced, very decent Japanese and Korean grub, served with a smile". / W6 0RA; www.yoshisushi.co.uk; 11 pm, Sun 10.30 pm; closed Sun L; set weekday L £17 (FP).

Yoshino W1 £44 432
3 Piccadilly Pl 7287 6622 3–3D
"A must for sushi-lovers, expert or novice!" – an "interesting" little Japanese café, tucked down an alley "around a corner near the Royal Academy". / W1J 0DB; www.yoshino.net; @Yoshino_London; 10 pm; closed Sun.

Yum Bun EC1 £15 52–
31 Featherstone St 07919 408221 12–1A
"Great buns!" – the steamed Chinese variety, "cooked with passion and served with a smile" – make Lisa Meyer's pop-up-goes-permanent in Shoreditch (next to the Rotary Bar) "a must-go experience". / EC1Y 2BJ; www.yumbun.co.uk; @yum_bun; 10 pm; closed Mon D, Tue D, Wed D, Sat L & Sun.

Yum Yum N16 £42 344
187 Stoke Newington High St 7254 6751 1–1D
"Lovely cocktails" and dependable tucker has proved a very enduring formula for this large Thai stalwart, in Stoke Newington. / N16 0LH; www.yumyum.co.uk; @yumyum; 11 pm, Fri & Sat midnight.

Zafferano SW1 **£80** 222
15 Lowndes St 7235 5800 5–1D
Once London's top Italian, this "chic" looking Belgravian has fans for whom it's still "somewhere special"; ratings dipped again this year though, and critics feel "its formulaic food is not up to par", and "doesn't justify the prices". / SW1X 9EY; www.zafferanorestaurants.com; 11.30 pm, Sun 11 pm; set weekday L £54 (FP).

Zaffrani N1 **£45** 322
47 Cross St 7226 5522 8–3D
"On a quiet corner away from the hubbub of Upper Street" – a "comfortable" Indian whose "sophisticated" cooking is "much better than you'd expect from a local". / N1 2BB; www.zaffrani-islington.co.uk; 10.30 pm.

Zaibatsu SE10 **£32** 442
96 Trafalgar Rd 8858 9317 1–3D
"Don't judge a book by its cover!" – "it's so hard to get a booking" at this "tiny", "basic", "café-style" Japanese BYO in Greenwich; why? – "the sushi's just amazing" and "very cheap". / SE10 9UW; www.zaibatsufusion.co.uk; @ong_teck; 11 pm; closed Mon.

Zaika
Tamarind Collection W8 **£60** 333
1 Kensington High St 7795 6533 5–1A
"Welcome back Zaika!"; after the briefest flirtation with a British format (as One Kensington, RIP), the Tamarind Collection turned back 180 degrees, "beautifully re-converting" this erstwhile banking hall back to a nouvelle Indian dining room; its authentic cuisine "without all that fusion nonsense" is as popular as ever. / W8 5NP; www.zaikaofkensington.com; @ZaikaLondon; 10.45 pm, Sun 9.45 pm; closed Mon L.

Zayna W1 **£47** 432
25 New Quebec St 7723 2229 2–2A
"Top Punjabi/Pakistani" dishes again score high marks for this handy Marble Arch operation; sit upstairs, as the basement lacks atmosphere. / W1H 7SF; www.zaynarestaurant.co.uk; @zaynarestaurant; Mon-Thu 10.30 pm, Fri & Sat 11 pm, Sun 10.30 pm; closed weekday L.

Zest
JW3 NW3 **£49** 323
341-351 Finchley Rd 7433 8955 1–1B
For a "fresh and modern" take on kosher cooking ("i.e. Middle East not Mittel-European") try this West Hampstead Israeli; you pay "high prices for tiny portions", but results are "healthy" and "tasty", and its contemporary, basement setting "has a real buzz". / NW3 6ET; www.zestatjw3.co.uk; @ZestAtJW3; Sat-Thu 9.45 pm ; closed Fri & Sat L.

Ziani's SW3 **£57** 333
45 Radnor Walk 7351 5297 5–3C
"Always jolly", "traditional" Chelsea Italian, with "such friendly staff"; "much used by the locals", you need to "squash in", but "it's a great place to take the family". / SW3 4BP; www.ziani.co.uk; 11 pm, Sun 10 pm; bank holidays closed on sunday.

Zoilo W1 £54 4 3 3

9 Duke St 7486 9699 3–1A

A "wonderful", little Argentinean tapas spot tucked away near Selfridges, majoring in "wonderfully tasty and moist" meats and burger dishes, and with a "fine selection" of Malbecs too; grab a seat at the downstairs bar, where "watching the chefs at work is an experience". / W1U 3EG; www.zoilo.co.uk; @Zoilo_London; 10.30 pm; closed Sun.

Zucca SE1 £59 4 4 3

184 Bermondsey St 7378 6809 9–4D

"Not as pretty as the River Café, but about as good at a fraction of the price" – Sam Harris's "out-of-the-way", "canteen-like" Bermondsey Italian continues to draw crowds from across town with its "impeccably simple use of first-class ingredients" and "huge range of wines". Top Menu Tip – "fantastic veal chops". / SE1 3TQ; www.zuccalondon.com; @ZuccaSam; 10 pm; closed Mon & Sun D.

Zuma SW7 £80 5 3 4

5 Raphael St 7584 1010 5–1C

"It may be the haunt of hedgies and wealthy Euros", but this "always humming" Japanese-fusion hang-out, near Harrods, is "so goddamn good"! A few critics do feel "it's way too pricey", but most reporters are blown away by its "spectacular" fare and "terrific" vibe. / SW7 1DL; www.zumarestaurant.com; 10.45 pm, Sun 10.15 pm; booking: max 8.

INDEXES

BREAKFAST
(with opening times)

Central

Al Duca *(9)*
Asia de Cuba *(7)*
Athenaeum *(7)*
Babaji Pide *(Sat & Sun 11)*
Bageriet *(9, Sat 10)*
Balans:*W1 (8)*
Balthazar *(7.30 Mon-Fri, Sat & Sun 9)*
Bar Italia *(6.30)*
Bar Termini *(Mon-Fri 7.30, Sat 9, Sun 10.30)*
The Berners Tavern *(7)*
Bonhams Restaurant *(8)*
The Botanist: *SW1 (8, Sat & Sun 9)*
Bouillabaisse *(8)*
Boulestin *(7)*
Browns (Albemarle) *(7, Sun 7.30)*
Café Bohème *(8, Sat & Sun 9)*
Café in the Crypt *(Mon-Sat 8)*
Caffé Vergnano:*WC1 (6.30, Sun 8.30); WC2 (8, Sun 11)*
Carousel *(9)*
The Cavendish *(Sat & Sun 10)*
Cecconi's *(7, Sat & Sun 8)*
The Chiltern Firehouse *(7, Sat & Sun 9)*
Christopher's *(Sat & Sun 11.30)*
The Cinnamon Club *(Mon-Fri 7.30)*
Colbert *(8)*
Cut *(7am, Sat & Sun 7.30)*
Daylesford Organic: *SW1 (8, Sun 10); Oxford St W1 (9)*
Dean Street Townhouse *(Mon-Fri 7, Sat & Sun 8)*
The Delaunay *(7, Sat & Sun 11)*
Dishoom:*WC2 (8, Sat & Sun 10)*
Dorchester Grill *(7, Sat & Sun 8)*
Fernandez & Wells: *Beak St W1 (7.30, Sat & sun 9); Lexington St W1 (7); St Anne's Ct W1 (8, Sat 10);WC2 (8am, Sat & Sun 9am)*
Franco's *(7, Sat 8)*
La Fromagerie Café *(8, Sat 9, Sun 10)*
The Goring Hotel *(7, Sun 7.30)*
The Grazing Goat *(7.30)*
Hélène Darroze *(Sat 11)*
Holborn Dining Room *(Mon-Fri 7, Sat & Sun 8)*
Honey & Co *(Mon-Fri 8, Sat 9.30)*
Hush:*WC1 (8)*
Indigo *(6.30)*
Kaffeine: *Great Titchfield St W1 (7.30, Sat 8.30, Sun 9.30)*
Kaspar's Seafood and Grill *(7)*
Kazan (Café):*Wilton Rd SW1 (8, Sun 9)*
Konditor & Cook:*WC1 (9.30); W1 (9.30, Sun 10.30)*
Kopapa *(8.30, Sat 9, Sun 9.30)*
Koya-Bar *(Mon-Fri 8.30, Sat & Sun 9:30)*
Lantana Café:*W1 (8, Sat & Sun 9)*
Maison Bertaux *(8.30, Sun 9.15)*
maze Grill *(6.45)*
Monmouth Coffee Company:*WC2 (8)*
The National Dining Rooms *(10)*
Nopi *(8, Sat & Sun 10)*
Nordic Bakery: *Dorset St W1 (8, Sat & Sun 9); Golden Sq W1 (Mon-Fri 8, Sat 9, Sun 11)*
The Northall *(6.30, Sat & Sun 7)*
One-O-One *(7)*
The Only Running Footman *(7.30, Sat & Sun 9.30)*
Opso *(Sat & Sun 10)*
The Orange *(8)*
Ottolenghi: *SW1 (8, Sun 9)*
The Pantechnicon *(Sat & Sun 9)*
Pennethorne's Cafe Bar *(8, Sat 10)*
Percy & Founders *(Sat & Sun 7.30)*
The Portrait *(10)*
Princi *(8, Sun 8.30)*
The Providores *(9am)*
Providores (Tapa Room) *(9, Sat & Sun 10)*
Le Restaurant de Paul:*WC2 (7, Sat & Sun 8)*
Rib Room *(7, Sun 8)*
Riding House Café *(7.30, Sat & Sun 9)*
The Ritz Restaurant *(7, Sun 8)*
Roux at the Landau *(7)*
Royal Academy *(8)*
San Carlo Cicchetti:*W1 (8, Sat & Sun 9)*
Scandinavian Kitchen *(8, Sat & Sun 10)*
Sesame *(7, Sat 9, Sun 11)*
Simpsons-in-the-Strand *(Mon-Fri 7.30)*
Sophie's Steakhouse: *all branches (Sat & Sun 11)*
Sotheby's Café *(9)*
Stock Pot: *SW1 (9.30)*
Strand Dining Rooms *(7, Sat 8, Sun 10)*
Tate Britain (Rex Whistler) *(Sat & Sun 10)*
tibits *(9, Sun 11.30)*
Tom's Kitchen:*WC2 (Sat & Sun 10)*
Tredwell's *(8, Sat 9, Sun 9.30)*
Villandry:*W1 (Sat 8, Sun 9)*
The Wallace *(10)*
Wolfe's *(9)*
The Wolseley *(7, Sat & Sun 8)*
The Woodstock *(11)*
Yalla Yalla: *Green's Ct W1 (Sat & Sun 10)*

West

Adams Café *(7.30)*
Angelus *(10)*
Annie's:*W4 (Tue-Thu 10, Fri & Sat 10.30, Sun 10)*
Balans:*W4, W8 (8)*
Best Mangal: *SW6 (10-12)*
La Brasserie *(8)*
Brasserie Gustave *(Sat & Sun 11)*
Bumpkin: *SW7 (11)*
Bush Dining Hall *(Tue-Fri 8.30)*
The Butcher's Hook *(10)*
Clarke's *(8)*
Daylesford Organic:*W11 (8, Sun 11)*
Electric Diner *(8)*
Gallery Mess *(Sat & Sun 10)*
Geales Chelsea Green: *SW3 (9 Sat & Sun)*
Granger & Co:*W11 (7)*
The Hampshire Hog *(8, Sat & Sun 9)*
High Road Brasserie *(7, Sat & Sun 8)*

City Social *(9)*
Coco Di Mama *(6.30)*
Comptoir Gascon *(9 takeaway onl)*
Coq d'Argent *(Mon-Fri 7.30)*
Department of Coffee *(7, Sat & Sun 10)*
Duck & Waffle *(6)*
The Empress *(Sat & Sun 10 pm)*
The Fox and Anchor *(7, Sat & Sun 8.30)*
Hawksmoor: *E1 (Sat & Sun 11)*
Hilliard *(8)*
Hoi Polloi *(7)*
The Hoxton Grill *(7)*
The Jugged Hare *(7)*
Little Georgia Café: *E2 (9, Sun 10)*
Lutyens *(7.30)*
Lyle's *(8)*
Manicomio: *EC2 (Mon-Fri 7)*
The Mercer *(7.30)*
The Modern Pantry: *EC1 (8, Sat 9, Sun 10)*
Nusa Kitchen: *EC2 (7); EC1 (8)*
Obicà: *E14 (9)*
One Canada Square *(7, 9 Sat)*
1 Lombard Street *(7.30)*
Paternoster Chop House *(Mon-Fri 8)*
E Pellicci *(7)*
Resident Of Paradise Row *(11, Sat & Sun 10)*
Rivington Grill: *EC2 (Mon-Fri 8)*
Rochelle Canteen *(9)*
Rocket The City: *Adams Ct EC2 (9); E14 (9.30)*
St John Bread & Wine *(9, Sat & Sun 10)*
The Sign of The Don *(7.30)*
Simpson's Tavern *(Tue-Fri 8)*
Smiths (Ground Floor) *(7, Sat 10, Sun 9.30)*
Street Kitchen (van) *(6.30)*
Taberna Do Mercado *(8)*
Verden *(Sat & Sun 11)*
Vivat Bacchus: *EC4 (Mon-Fri 7)*
Yum Bun *(11.30)*

BRUNCH MENUS

Central

Aurora
Balans: *all branches*
Balthazar
Barnyard
Boisdale
Le Caprice
Cecconi's
Christopher's
Daylesford Organic: *all branches*
Dean Street Townhouse
The Delaunay
Dishoom: *all branches*
La Fromagerie Café
Galvin at Windows
Hardy's Brasserie
Hélène Darroze
Hubbard & Bell
Hush: *W1*
Indigo
The Ivy
Jackson & Rye: *all branches*
Joe Allen
Kopapa
Lantana Café: *all branches*
Nordic Bakery: *Golden Sq W1*
Ottolenghi: *all branches*
La Porte des Indes
The Portrait
The Providores
Providores (Tapa Room)
Quaglino's
Riding House Café
Ristorante Frescobaldi
Scandinavian Kitchen
Sophie's Steakhouse: *all branches*
Strand Dining Rooms
Tom's Kitchen: *all branches*
Villandry: *W1*
VQ: *all branches*
The Wolseley
Workshop Coffee Fitzrovia: *all branches*

West

The Abingdon
Annie's: *all branches*
Balans: *all branches*
Beach Blanket Babylon: *W11*
Bluebird
Bodean's: *SW6*
La Brasserie
The Builders Arms
Bumpkin: *SW7, W11*
Bush Dining Hall
Cheyne Walk Brasserie
The Cross Keys
Daylesford Organic: *all branches*
Eelbrook
Electric Diner
The Enterprise
Ffiona's
The Frontline Club
Granger & Co: *all branches*
High Road Brasserie
Jackson & Rye Chiswick: *all branches*
Joe's Brasserie
Kensington Square Kitchen
Lucky Seven
Megan's Delicatessen: *SW6*
The Oak: *W2*
Ottolenghi: *all branches*
PJ's Bar and Grill
Raoul's Café & Deli: *all branches*
The Sands End
The Shed
Sophie's Steakhouse: *all branches*
Taqueria
Tom's Kitchen: *all branches*
Troubadour
VQ: *all branches*
Zuma

North

Banners
Caravan King's Cross: *all branches*
Dishoom: *all branches*

BUSINESS

The Don
Eyre Brothers
Fish Market
The Fox and Anchor
Galvin La Chapelle
Gatti's: *all branches*
George & Vulture
Goodman: *all branches*
Hawksmoor: *all branches*
Haz: *all branches*
High Timber
The Hoxton Grill
Ibérica: *E14*
José Pizarro
Lutyens
M Grill & M Raw
Manicomio: *all branches*
The Mercer
Merchants Tavern
Moro
New Street Grill
Northbank
One Canada Square
1 Lombard Street
Paternoster Chop House
Plateau
Roka: *E14*
The Royal Exchange Grand Café
St John
Sauterelle
The Sign of The Don
Smith's Of Ongar
Smiths (Top Floor)
Smiths (Dining Rm)
Sushisamba
Sweetings
Taberna Etrusca
3 South Place
The Trading House
The Tramshed
28-50: *all branches*
Vivat Bacchus: *all branches*
The White Swan

BYO

(Bring your own wine at no or low – less than £3 – corkage. Note for £5-£15 per bottle, you can normally negotiate to take your own wine to many, if not most, places.)

Central

Golden Hind
India Club
Patogh
Ragam

West

Adams Café
Alounak: *all branches*
Café 209
Faanoos: *W4*
Fez Mangal
Outlaw's Seafood and Grill
Pappa Ciccia: *all branches*

North

Ali Baba
Ariana II
Chutneys
Diwana Bhel-Poori House
Roti King
Rugoletta: *all branches*
Toff's
Vijay

South

Apollo Banana Leaf
Cah-Chi: *all branches*
Faanoos: *SW14*
Hot Stuff
Kaosarn: *all branches*
Lahore Karahi
Lahore Kebab House: *all branches*
Mien Tay: *all branches*
Mirch Masala
Sree Krishna
Zaibatsu

East

Lahore Kebab House: *all branches*
Little Georgia Café: *E2*
Mangal 1
Mien Tay: *all branches*
Needoo
Rochelle Canteen
Tayyabs
Viet Grill

ENTERTAINMENT

(Check times before you go)

Central

Bentley's
(pianist, Thu-Sat)
Blanchette
(DJ every second Sun)
Boisdale
(jazz, soul, blues, Mon-Sat)
Café in the Crypt
(jazz, Wed night)
Le Caprice
(jazz brunch, Sat & last Sun D of each month)
Ciao Bella
(pianist, nightly)
Crazy Bear
(DJ, Sat)
The Diamond Jub' Salon (Fortnum's)
(Pianist daily)
Hakkasan: *Hanway Pl W1*
(DJ, nightly)
Ham Yard Restaurant
(theatre, movies)
Hard Rock Café
(regular live music)
Ishtar
(live music, Tue-Sat; belly dancer, Fri & Sat)
Joe Allen
(pianist, Mon-Fri & Sun L)
Maroush: *W1*
(music & dancing, nightly)
Mint Leaf: *SW1*
(DJ, Fri D)
Momo
(live music on various days)

The Northall
(Jazz on Sun Brunch)
Quaglino's
(live music, Fri & Sat)
Quattro Passi
(member's club)
Rainforest Café
(nightclub, Thu-Sat)
Red Fort
(DJ, Fri & Sat)
The Ritz Restaurant
(live music, Sat)
Roka: *Charlotte St W1*
(DJ, Thu-Sat)
Royal Academy
(jazz, Fri)
Shanghai Blues
(jazz, Fri & Sat)
Simpsons-in-the-Strand
(pianist, nightly)
Sketch (Gallery)
(DJ, Thu-Sat)
STK Steakhouse
(DJ, Tue-Sat from 8.00 pm)
Tom's Kitchen: *WC2*
(DJ, Fri)
The Windmill
(live music, Mon)

West

The Andover Arms
(jazz, first Thu of each month, opera last Thu)
Babylon
(nightclub, Fri & Sat; magician, Sun; jazz, Tue)
Beach Blanket Babylon: *all branches*
(DJ, Fri & Sat)
Bel Canto
(opera, nightly)
Belvedere
(pianist, nightly Sat & Sun all day)
Big Easy: *SW3*
(live music, nightly)
The Builders Arms
(jazz, Tue D)
Da Mario
(disco and dancing in basement)
Harwood Arms
(quiz night, first Tue of every month)
Maroush: *I) 21 Edgware Rd W2*
(music & dancing, nightly)
Paradise by Way of Kensal Green
(comedy, Wed; Jazz, Fri)
Troubadour
(live music, most nights)
The Waterway
(live music, Thu)

North

Bull & Last
(quiz night, Sun)
Camino: *N1*
(DJ, Thu-Sat)
Gilgamesh
(DJ, Fri & Sat)
Landmark (Winter Gdn)
(pianist & musicians, daily)
The North London Tavern
(jazz, Sun; quiz night, Mon; open mic, Tue; Every third Thu comedy)
Rotunda Bar & Restaurant
(jazz, some Fri)
Villa Bianca
(guitarist, Mon-Wed; pianist, Thu, Fri, Sat & Sun L)

The Wet Fish Café
(Spanish soul, occasionally)
York & Albany
(live music, Tue D)
Zest
(outdoor beach and screens during sporting events)

South

Al Forno: *SW15*
(live music, Sat)
Archduke Wine Bar
(jazz, Mon-Sun)
Bengal Clipper
(pianist, Tue-Sat)
Brasserie Toulouse-Lautrec
(live music, nightly)
The Crooked Well
(jazz, Sun D)
Garrison
(cinema on Sun)
The Gowlett
(DJ, Sun; BYO 7 inch monthly; eccentric disco, last Fri of every month)
Meson don Felipe
(guitarist, nightly)
Olympic Café
(live music)
Oxo Tower (Brass')
(jazz, Sat & Sun L, Sun & Mon D)
Le Pont de la Tour
(pianist, every D & Sun L)
The Prince Of Wales
(quiz night, Sun)
Roast
(live music D)
The Ship
(live music, Sun; quiz, Wed)
Tas Pide
(live music, daily D)
Tentazioni
(opera, monthly)

East

Beach Blanket Babylon: *all branches*
(DJ, Fri & Sat)
Boisdale of Canary Wharf
(live music, daily)
Café du Marché
(pianist & bass, Mon-Thu; pianist, Fri & Sat)
Cinnamon Kitchen
(DJ, Wed-Fri)
Hix Oyster & Chop House
(jazz, Sun L)
Hoi Polloi
(live music including string quartet Sun)
The Hoxton Grill
(DJ, Fri & Sat)
The Little Bay: *EC1*
(opera, Thu-Sat)
Mint Leaf: *EC2*
(Jazz, Fri D; DJ, weekends)
One Canada Square
(pianist, Fri & Sat)
1 Lombard Street
(DJ, Fri)
Pizza East: *E1*
(DJ, live music, quiz nights, Tue, Thu, Sat)
Shanghai
(karaoke)
Smith's Of Ongar
(pianist every evening)
Smiths (Ground Floor)
(DJ, Wed-Sat (summer))
3 South Place
(pianist, brunch last Sun of month)

Vivat Bacchus: *EC4 (jazz, Fri D)*
Yi-Ban *(live smooth jazz, Fri & Sat)*

LATE

(open till midnight or later as shown; may be earlier Sunday)

Central

Asia de Cuba *(1)*
L'Atelier de Joel Robuchon *(1)*
Balans: *W1 (5 am, Sun 1 am)*
Bar Italia *(open 24 hours, Sun 4 am)*
Bistro 1: *all branches (1)*
Bob Bob Ricard *(Sat only)*
La Bodega Negra *(1 am, not Sun)*
Café Bohème *(2.45 am, Sun midnight)*
Cantina Laredo *(Fri & Sat midnight)*
Chotto Matte *(Mon-Sat 1 am)*
Dean Street Townhouse *(Fri & Sat midnight)*
The Delaunay *(1)*
Dishoom: *WC2 (Fri & Sat midnight)*
Gaby's *(1)*
Gelupo *(Fri & Sat midnight)*
Hakkasan Mayfair: *Bruton St W1 (12.30 am); Hanway Pl W1 (Thu-Sat 12.30 am)*
Harbour City *(Fri & Sat midnight)*
Hard Rock Café *(1)*
Inamo: *SW1 (Fri & Sat 12.30 am)*
Joe Allen *(Fri & Sat 12.45 am)*
Maroush: *W1 (12.30 am)*
MEATLiquor: *W1 (Fri & Sat 1 am)*
New Mayflower *(4 am)*
La Porchetta Pizzeria: *WC1 (Sat & Sun midnight)*
Princi *(1)*
Randall & Aubin *(Sat midnight)*
Rossopomodoro: *WC2 (1)*
Shoryu Ramen: *Denman St W1 (1)*
Sophie's Steakhouse: *all branches (12.45 am, not Sun)*
STK Steakhouse *(Thu-Sat mignight)*
VQ: *all branches (24 hours)*
The Wolseley *(1)*

West

Anarkali *(1)*
Balans: *W8 (1)*
Best Mangal: *SW6 (1); North End Rd W14 (midnight, Sat 1 am)*
Buona Sera: *all branches (1)*
The Cross Keys *(1)*
Gifto's *(Sat & Sun midnight)*
Khan's *(Sat & Sun midnight)*
Maroush: *I) 21 Edgware Rd W2 (1.45 am); VI) 68 Edgware Rd W2 (12.30 am); SW3 (3.30 am)*
Pizza East Portobello: *W10 (Fri & Sat midnight)*
Rossopomodoro: *SW10 (1)*
Shilpa *(Thu-Sat midnight)*
Sophie's Steakhouse: *all branches (12.45 am, not Sun)*
VQ: *all branches (24 hours)*

North

Ali Baba *(1)*
Banners *(Fri & Sat midnight)*
Chilango: *N1 (Fri & Sat midnight)*
Dirty Burger: *NW5 (Mon-Thu midnight, Fri & Sat 1 am)*
Gallipoli: *all branches (Fri & Sat midnight)*
Gem *(Fri & Sat midnight)*
Mangal II *(1 am)*
Meat Mission *(1)*
Le Mercury *(1)*
Pizzeria Pappagone *(1)*
La Porchetta Pizzeria: *NW1 (Fri & Sat midnight); N1, N4 (Sat & Sun midnight)*
The Salt House *(Fri & Sat midnight)*
Yum Yum *(Fri & Sat midnight)*

South

Boqueria *(Fri & Sat midnight)*
Buona Sera: *all branches (1)*
Caffé Vergnano: *SE1 (1)*
Cah-Chi: *SW18 (not Sat & Sun)*
Dirty Burger: *SW8 (Fri & Sat 2 am)*
Everest Inn *(1)*
Fish in a Tie *(1)*
Indian Moment *(Fri & Sat midnight)*
Lahore Karahi *(1)*
Lahore Kebab House: *all branches (1)*
Mirch Masala *(1)*
Tandoori Nights *(Fri & Sat midnight)*
The Tree House *(Fri & Sat midnight)*
Tsunami: *SW4 (Fri-Sun midnight)*

East

Brick Lane Beigel Bake *(24 hours)*
Cellar Gascon *(1)*
Hoi Polloi *(Thu-Sat 1 am)*
The Jugged Hare *(Thu-Sat midnight)*
Lahore Kebab House: *all branches (1)*
Mangal 1 *(midnight, Sat & Sun 1 am)*
Pizza East: *E1 (Thu midnight, Fri & Sat 1 am)*
La Porchetta Pizzeria: *EC1 (Sat & Sun midnight)*
Rocket Canary Wharf: *E14 (1)*
Sushisamba *(Tue-Sat 12.30 am)*
Verden *(1)*

OUTSIDE TABLES

(* particularly recommended)

Central

A Wong
Al Duca
Andrew Edmunds
Antidote
aqua nueva
L'Artiste Musclé
Atari-Ya: *W1*
Aurora
L'Autre Pied
Bank Westminster
Bar Italia
Il Baretto
Barrafina: *W1*
Barrica
Bea's Of Bloomsbury
Bentley's
Bistro 1: *all branches*

West

North

ROMANTIC

Central

West

ROOMS WITH A VIEW

The Ship
Skylon
Skylon Grill
The Swan at the Globe
Tate Modern (Level 7)
Ting

East
Angler
Barbecoa: *EC4*
Boisdale of Canary Wharf
City Social
Coq d'Argent
Darwin Brasserie
Duck & Waffle
Gin Joint
The Grapes
The Gun
High Timber
The Narrow
Northbank
Plateau
Rocket Canary Wharf: *E14*
Smiths (Top Floor)
Sushisamba
Yi-Ban

NOTABLE WINE LISTS

Central
Alyn Williams
Andrew Edmunds
Antidote
Arbutus
L'Autre Pied
Barrica
Boisdale
Bonhams Restaurant
Cigala
Clos Maggiore
Compagnie des Vins S.
Cork & Bottle
Dehesa
Ebury Rest' & Wine Bar
L'Escargot
Fera at Claridge's
The Fifth Floor Restaurant
1707
La Fromagerie Café
Galvin Bistrot de Luxe
Gauthier Soho
Le Gavroche
Goodman: *all branches*
Gordon's Wine Bar
The Greenhouse
Hardy's Brasserie
Hibiscus
The Ivy
Kai Mayfair
Latium
Locanda Locatelli
Marcus
Olivo
Olivomare
Les 110 de Taillevent
Opera Tavern
Orrery
Otto's
Pétrus
Pied à Terre
The Providores
Providores (Tapa Room)
Quattro Passi
Quo Vadis
Ristorante Frescobaldi
The Ritz Restaurant
Salt Yard
Sardo
Sartoria
Savoy Grill
Shampers
Social Eating House
Social Wine & Tapas
Sotheby's Café
The Square
Tapas Brindisa Soho: *W1*
Tate Britain (Rex Whistler)
The 10 Cases
10 Greek Street
Terroirs
Texture
Tinello
28-50: *all branches*
Vinoteca Seymour Place: *all branches*
Wild Honey
Zafferano

West
Albertine
L'Amorosa
Angelus
Bibendum
Brinkley's
Cambio de Tercio
Capote Y Toros
Clarke's
Le Colombier
L'Etranger
The Frontline Club
Garnier
Gordon Ramsay
Hedone
Joe's Brasserie
The Kensington Wine Rooms
The Ledbury
Locanda Ottomezzo
Margaux
Medlar
Popeseye: *W14*
Princess Victoria
The River Café
Tendido Cero
Tendido Cuatro
La Trompette
The Truscott Arms
Villa Di Geggiano
Vinoteca: *all branches*

North
La Collina
8 Hoxton Square
Prawn On The Lawn
Primeur

CUISINES

An asterisk (*) after an entry indicates exceptional or very good cooking

AMERICAN

Central

The Avenue *(SW1)*
Big Easy *(WC2)*
Bodean's *(W1)*
Bubbledogs *(W1)*
The Chiltern Firehouse *(W1)*
Christopher's *(WC2)*
Delancey & Co. *(W1)**
Hard Rock Café *(W1)*
Hubbard & Bell *(WC1)*
Jackson & Rye *(W1)*
Jamie's Diner *(W1)*
Joe Allen *(WC2)*
The Joint Marylebone *(W1)**
The Lockhart *(W1)*
Mishkin's *(WC2)*
Pitt Cue Co *(W1)**
Rainforest Café *(W1)*
Shake Shack *(WC1,WC2)*
Shotgun *(W1)*
Spuntino *(W1)*
Wolfe's *(WC2)*

West

Big Easy *(SW3)*
Bodean's *(SW6)*
Electric Diner *(W11)*
Jackson & Rye Chiswick *(W4)*
Lucky Seven *(W2)*

North

One Sixty Smokehouse *(NW6)**
Red Dog Saloon *(N1)*

South

Bodean's *(SW4)*
Jackson & Rye Richmond *(TW9)*
The Joint *(SW9)**
Oblix *(SE1)*
Red Dog South *(SW4)*

East

Big Easy *(E14)*
Bodean's *(EC1, EC3)*
The Hoxton Grill *(EC2)*
One Sixty Smokehouse *(E1)**
Shake Shack *(E20)*

AUSTRALIAN

Central

Lantana Café *(W1)*

West

Granger & Co *(W11)*

North

Friends of Ours *(N1)**
Granger & Co *(N1)*
Lantana Cafe *(NW1)*
Sunday *(N1)**

South

Brew *(SW11, SW18, SW19)*
Flotsam and Jetsam *(SW17)**

East

Granger & Co *(EC1)*
Lantana Café *(EC1)*

BELGIAN

Central

Belgo *(WC2)*
Belgo Soho *(W1)*

North

Belgo Noord *(NW1)*

BRITISH, MODERN

Central

Adam Handling at Caxton *(SW1)*
Alyn Williams *(W1)**
Andrew Edmunds *(W1)**
Arbutus *(W1)*
Athenaeum *(W1)*
Aurora *(W1)*
Balthazar *(WC2)*
Bank Westminster *(SW1)*
Barnyard *(W1)*
Bellamy's *(W1)*
The Berners Tavern *(W1)*
Blacklock *(W1)**
Bob Bob Ricard *(W1)*
Bonhams Restaurant *(W1)**
The Botanist *(SW1)*
Le Caprice *(SW1)*
The Cavendish *(W1)*
Coopers Restaurant & Bar *(WC2)*
Daylesford Organic *(SW1,W1)*
Dean Street Townhouse *(W1)*
Dorchester Grill *(W1)*
Ducksoup *(W1)*
Ebury Rest' & Wine Bar *(SW1)*
Fera at Claridge's *(W1)*
The Fifth Floor Restaurant *(SW1)*
45 Jermyn St *(W1)*
Gordon's Wine Bar *(WC2)*
The Goring Hotel *(SW1)*
The Grazing Goat *(W1)*
Ham Yard Restaurant *(W1)*
Hardy's Brasserie *(W1)*
Heddon Street Kitchen *(W1)*
Hix *(W1)*
Hush *(W1,WC1)*
Indigo *(WC2)*
The Ivy *(WC2)*
The Ivy Café *(W1)*
The Ivy Market Grill *(WC2)*
Jar Kitchen *(WC2)*
Kettners *(W1)*
Kitty Fisher's *(W1)**
Langan's Brasserie *(W1)*
Little Social *(W1)*
Mews of Mayfair *(W1)*
Morden & Lea *(W1)*
The Newman Arms *(W1)*
Newman Street Tavern *(W1)*
The Norfolk Arms *(WC1)**
The Northall *(SW1)*

Old Tom & English *(W1)*
The Only Running Footman *(W1)*
The Orange *(SW1)*
The Pantechnicon *(SW1)*
Pennethorne's Cafe Bar *(WC2)*
Percy & Founders *(W1)*
Picture *(W1)*
Pollen Street Social *(W1)*
Polpo at Ape & Bird *(WC2)*
Portland *(W1)**
The Portrait *(WC2)*
The Punchbowl *(W1)*
Quaglino's *(SW1)*
The Queens Arms *(SW1)*
Quo Vadis *(W1)*
Roux at Parliament Square *(SW1)**
Roux at the Landau *(W1)*
Seven Park Place *(SW1)*
Seven Stars *(WC2)*
1707 *(W1)*
Shampers *(W1)*
Social Eating House *(W1)**
Sotheby's Café *(W1)*
Spring *(WC2)*
Tate Britain (Rex Whistler) *(SW1)*
10 Greek Street *(W1)**
The Thomas Cubitt *(SW1)*
Tom's Kitchen *(WC2)*
Tredwell's *(WC2)*
Villandry *(W1)*
The Vincent Rooms *(SW1)*
Vinoteca *(W1)*
VQ *(WC1)*
Wild Honey *(W1)*
The Wolseley *(W1)*

West

The Abingdon *(W8)*
The Anglesea Arms *(W6)*
Babylon *(W8)*
Beach Blanket Babylon *(W11)*
Belvedere *(W8)*
Bluebird *(SW3)*
The Brackenbury *(W6)*
Brinkley's *(SW10)*
The Builders Arms *(SW3)*
Bush Dining Hall *(W12)*
The Butcher's Hook *(SW6)*
The Carpenter's Arms *(W6)*
Charlotte's W5 *(W5)*
City Barge *(W4)*
Clarke's *(W8)**
The Dartmouth Castle *(W6)*
Daylesford Organic *(W11)*
The Dock Kitchen *(W10)*
The Dove *(W6)*
Duke of Sussex *(W4)*
Ealing Park Tavern *(W5)*
The Enterprise *(SW3)*
The Five Fields *(SW3)**
The Frontline Club *(W2)*
Harwood Arms *(SW6)**
The Havelock Tavern *(W14)*
Hedone *(W4)**
High Road Brasserie *(W4)*
The Ivy Chelsea Garden *(SW3)*
The Ivy Kensington Bras' *(W8)*
Joe's Brasserie *(SW6)*
Julie's *(W11)*
Kensington Place *(W8)*
Kensington Square Kitchen *(W8)*
Kitchen W8 *(W8)**
The Ladbroke Arms *(W11)**
Launceston Place *(W8)**
The Ledbury *(W11)**
The Magazine Restaurant *(W2)*
Marianne *(W2)**
maze Grill *(SW10)*
Medlar *(SW10)**
Megan's Delicatessen *(SW6)*
Paradise by Way of Kensal Gn *(W10)*
The Pear Tree *(W6)*
The Phoenix *(SW3)*
Princess Victoria *(W12)*
Rabbit *(SW3)**
Salt & Honey *(W2)*
The Sands End *(SW6)*
The Shed *(W8)*
The Terrace *(W8)*
Tom's Kitchen *(SW3)*
The Truscott Arms *(W9)**
Vinoteca *(W4)*
VQ *(SW10)*
The Waterway *(W9)*

North

The Albion *(N1)*
Bald Faced Stag *(N2)*
The Booking Office *(NW1)*
Bradley's *(NW3)*
The Bull *(N6)*
Caravan King's Cross *(N1)*
Chriskitch *(N10)**
Crocker's Folly *(NW8)*
The Drapers Arms *(N1)*
Frederick's *(N1)*
Grain Store *(N1)*
The Haven *(N20)*
Heirloom *(N8)*
The Horseshoe *(NW3)*
The Junction Tavern *(NW5)*
Landmark (Winter Gdn) *(NW1)*
Made In Camden *(NW1)*
Market *(NW1)*
Megan's *(NW8)*
The North London Tavern *(NW6)*
Odette's *(NW1)*
Oldroyd *(N1)*
Parlour *(NW10)**
Pig & Butcher *(N1)**
Plum + Spilt Milk *(N1)*
The Refinery *(NW1)*
Rising Sun *(NW7)*
Rotunda Bar & Restaurant *(N1)*
St Pancras Grand *(NW1)*
Season Kitchen *(N4)*
Shoe Shop *(NW5)**
The Wells *(NW3)*
The Wet Fish Café *(NW6)*
White Rabbit *(N16)**

South

Abbeville Kitchen *(SW4)*

Albion *(SE1)*
Aqua Shard *(SE1)*
The Bingham *(TW10)*
Bistro Union *(SW4)*
Blueprint Café *(SE1)*
The Brown Dog *(SW13)*
Brunswick House Café *(SW8)*
The Camberwell Arms *(SE5)**
Hotel du Vin *(SW19)*
Chapters *(SE3)*
Chez Bruce *(SW17)**
Claude's Kitchen *(SW6)**
Counter *(SW8)*
Craft London *(SE10)*
The Crooked Well *(SE5)*
The Dairy *(SW4)**
The Depot *(SW14)*
The Dysart Petersham *(TW10)**
Earl Spencer *(SW18)**
Edwins *(SE1)*
Elliot's Café *(SE1)*
Emile's *(SW15)*
Fields *(SW4)*
40 Maltby Street *(SE1)**
Franklins *(SE22)**
The Garrison *(SE1)*
The Glasshouse *(TW9)**
The Green Room *(SE1)*
Hood *(SW2)**
House Restaurant *(SE1)*
Inside *(SE10)**
Lamberts *(SW12)**
The Lido Café *(SE24)*
Linnea *(TW9)**
The Lucky Pig Fulham *(SW6)*
Magdalen *(SE1)**
The Manor *(SW4)**
Manuka Kitchen *(SW6)**
Menier Chocolate Factory *(SE1)*
Olympic Café *(SW13)*
Oxo Tower (Rest') *(SE1)*
The Palmerston *(SE22)**
Peckham Refreshment Rms *(SE15)*
Petersham Hotel *(TW10)*
Petersham Nurseries *(TW10)*
Le Pont de la Tour *(SE1)*
The Prince Of Wales *(SW15)**
Rivington Grill *(SE10)*
RSJ *(SE1)*
Sea Containers *(SE1)*
Skylon *(SE1)*
Skylon Grill *(SE1)*
Sonny's Kitchen *(SW13)*
Source *(SW11)*
Story *(SE1)**
The Swan at the Globe *(SE1)*
The Table *(SE1)*
Tate Modern (Level 7) *(SE1)*
The Tommy Tucker *(SW6)*
The Tree House *(SW13)*
Trinity *(SW4)**
Union Street Café *(SE1)*
The Victoria *(SW14)*
Waterloo Bar & Kitchen *(SE1)*
Wimsey's *(SW6)*

East
The Anthologist *(EC2)*
Bad Egg *(EC2)**
Balans *(E20)*
Beach Blanket Babylon *(E1)*
Beagle *(E2)**
Bird of Smithfield *(EC1)*
Blackfoot *(EC1)*
The Botanist *(EC2)*
The Boundary *(E2)*
Bread Street Kitchen *(EC4)*
Café Below *(EC2)*
Cafe Football *(E20)*
Caravan *(EC1)*
The Chancery *(EC4)**
Chiswell Street Dining Rms *(EC1)*
City Social *(EC2)*
The Clove Club *(EC1)**
The Culpepper *(E1)**
Darwin Brasserie *(EC3)*
The Don *(EC4)*
Duck & Waffle *(EC2)*
Eat 17 *(E17)*
Ellory *(E8)*
The Empress *(E9)**
Gin Joint *(EC2)*
The Gun *(E14)*
High Timber *(EC4)*
Hilliard *(EC4)**
Hoi Polloi *(E1)*
Jones & Sons *(E8)**
The Jugged Hare *(EC1)*
Lyle's *(E1)**
The Mercer *(EC2)*
Merchants Tavern *(EC2)*
The Modern Pantry *(EC1, EC2)*
The Morgan Arms *(E3)**
The Narrow *(E14)*
Northbank *(EC4)*
One Canada Square *(E14)*
1 Lombard Street *(EC3)*
Paradise Garage *(E2)*
Princess of Shoreditch *(EC2)*
Resident Of Paradise Row *(E2)*
The Richmond *(E8)**
Rivington Grill *(EC2)*
Rochelle Canteen *(E2)**
Sager & Wilde *(E2)*
The Sign of The Don *(EC4)*
Smith's Of Ongar *(E1)*
Smiths (Ground Floor) *(EC1)*
Street Kitchen (van) *(EC2)*
3 South Place *(EC2)*
Tom's Kitchen *(E1, E14)*
Tonic & Remedy *(EC1)*
The Trading House *(EC2)*
Vinoteca *(EC1)*
The White Swan *(EC4)*

BRITISH, TRADITIONAL

Central
Boisdale *(SW1)*
Browns (Albemarle) *(W1)*
Corrigan's Mayfair *(W1)*
Dinner *(SW1)*
Great Queen Street *(WC2)*
Green's *(SW1)*

The Guinea Grill *(W1)*
Hardy's Brasserie *(W1)*
Holborn Dining Room *(WC1)*
The Keeper's House *(W1)*
The Lady Ottoline *(WC1)*
National Dining Rooms *(WC2)*
Rib Room *(SW1)*
Rules *(WC2)*
Savoy Grill *(WC2)*
Scott's *(W1)**
Shepherd's *(SW1)*
Simpsons-in-the-Strand *(WC2)*
Strand Dining Rooms *(WC2)*
Wiltons *(SW1)*
The Windmill *(W1)*

West
The Admiral Codrington *(SW3)*
The Brown Cow *(SW6)*
Bumpkin *(SW3, SW7, W11)*
Ffiona's *(W8)*
The Hampshire Hog *(W6)*
Hereford Road *(W2)**
Maggie Jones's *(W8)*

North
Gilbert Scott *(NW1)*
Piebury Corner *(N7)**
St Johns *(N19)**

South
The Anchor & Hope *(SE1)**
Butlers Wharf Chop House *(SE1)*
Canteen *(SE1)*
Canton Arms *(SW8)*
The Lord Northbrook *(SE12)**
Roast *(SE1)*

East
Albion *(E2)*
Boisdale of Bishopsgate *(EC2)*
Bumpkin *(E20)*
Canteen *(E1, E14)*
The Fox and Anchor *(EC1)*
George & Vulture *(EC3)*
Hix Oyster & Chop House *(EC1)*
The Marksman *(E2)*
Paternoster Chop House *(EC4)*
E Pellicci *(E2)*
The Quality Chop House *(EC1)*
St John *(EC1)**
St John Bread & Wine *(E1)**
Simpson's Tavern *(EC3)*
Sweetings *(EC4)*

DANISH

Central
Sticks'n'Sushi *(WC2)*

West
Snaps & Rye *(W10)**

South
Sticks'n'Sushi *(SE10, SW19)*

East
Sticks'n'Sushi *(E14)*

EAST & CENT. EUROPEAN

Central
Boopshis *(W1)*
The Delaunay *(WC2)*
Fischer's *(W1)*
Gay Hussar *(W1)*
The Wolseley *(W1)*

North
Bellanger *(N1)*
German Gymnasium *(N1)*
Kipferl *(N1)*

FRENCH

Central
Alain Ducasse *(W1)*
Antidote *(W1)**
L'Artiste Musclé *(W1)*
L'Atelier de Joel Robuchon *(WC2)*
L'Autre Pied *(W1)**
The Balcon *(SW1)*
Bar Boulud *(SW1)*
Bellamy's *(W1)*
Blanchette *(W1)*
Boudin Blanc *(W1)*
Boulestin *(SW1)*
Brasserie Chavot *(W1)*
Brasserie Zédel *(W1)*
Café Bohème *(W1)*
Chez Antoinette *(WC2)*
Cigalon *(WC2)*
Clos Maggiore *(WC2)**
Colbert *(SW1)*
Compagnie des Vins S. *(WC2)*
Les Deux Salons *(WC2)*
Elena's L'Etoile *(W1)*
L'Escargot *(W1)*
Galvin at Windows *(W1)*
Galvin Bistrot de Luxe *(W1)**
Le Garrick *(WC2)*
Gauthier Soho *(W1)**
Le Gavroche *(W1)**
Les Gourmets des Ternes *(SW1)*
The Greenhouse *(W1)*
Hélène Darroze *(W1)*
Hibiscus *(W1)**
Koffmann's *(SW1)**
Marcus *(SW1)*
maze *(W1)*
Mon Plaisir *(WC2)*
Les 110 de Taillevent *(W1)*
Orrery *(W1)*
Otto's *(WC1)**
La Petite Maison *(W1)**
Pétrus *(SW1)*
Pied à Terre *(W1)**
Piquet *(W1)*
La Poule au Pot *(SW1)*
Prix Fixe *(W1)*
Le Relais de Venise *(W1)*
Le Restaurant de Paul *(WC2)**
The Ritz Restaurant *(W1)*
Savoir Faire *(WC1)*
Savoy Grill *(WC2)*
Sketch (Lecture Rm) *(W1)*
Sketch (Gallery) *(W1)*
The Square *(W1)**

Terroirs (WC2)
28-50 (W1)
Villandry (W1)
Villandry St James's (SW1)
The Wallace (W1)

West
Albertine (W12)
Angelus (W2)
Bandol (SW10)
Bel Canto (W2)
Belvedere (W8)
Bibendum (SW3)
La Brasserie (SW3)
Brasserie Gustave (SW3)*
Charlotte's Place (W5)
Charlotte's W4 (W4)
Cheyne Walk Brasserie (SW3)
Chez Patrick (W8)
Le Colombier (SW3)
L'Etranger (SW7)
Garnier (SW5)*
Gordon Ramsay (SW3)
Les Gourmets des Ternes (W9)
Michael Nadra (W4)*
Poissonnerie de l'Avenue (SW3)
Quantus (W4)*
La Trompette (W4)*
Le Vacherin (W4)

North
L'Absinthe (NW1)
The Almeida (N1)
L'Aventure (NW8)*
Bistro Aix (N8)*
Bradley's (NW3)
La Cage Imaginaire (NW3)
Le Mercury (N1)
Michael Nadra (NW1)*
Mill Lane Bistro (NW6)
Oslo Court (NW8)
Patron (NW5)
Le Sacré-Coeur (N1)
The Wells (NW3)

South
Augustine Kitchen (SW11)
Bellevue Rendez-Vous (SW17)
Boro Bistro (SE1)
Brasserie Toulouse-Lautrec (SE11)
La Buvette (TW9)
Casse-Croute (SE1)*
Gazette (SW11, SW12, SW15)
Lobster Pot (SE11)*
Ma Cuisine (TW9)
Le Salon Privé (TW1)
Soif (SW11)
Toasted (SE22)
The White Onion (SW19)*

East
Bleeding Heart Restaurant (EC1)
Brawn (E2)*
Café du Marché (EC1)
Café Pistou (EC1)
Cellar Gascon (EC1)
Club Gascon (EC1)
Comptoir Gascon (EC1)
Coq d'Argent (EC2)
The Don (EC4)
Galvin La Chapelle (E1)*
Lutyens (EC4)
Plateau (E14)
Provender (E11)*
Relais de Venise (E14, EC2)
Restaurant de Paul (EC2)*
Royal Exchange (EC3)
Sauterelle (EC3)
The Trading House (EC2)
28-50 (EC4)

FUSION

Central
Asia de Cuba (WC2)
Bubbledogs (Kitchen Table) (W1)*
Carousel (W1)*
Dabbous (W1)
Kopapa (WC2)
Providores (Tapa Room) (W1)
The Providores (W1)
The Salon (WC2)
Twist At Crawford (W1)*

West
E&O (W11)
Eight Over Eight (SW3)
L'Etranger (SW7)

North
XO (NW3)

South
Bistrò by Shot (SW6)
Champor-Champor (SE1)
MOMMI (SW4)
Pedler (SE15)
Queenswood (SW11)
Tsunami (SW4)*
Village East (SE1)

East
Amaru (E1)
Caravan (EC1)
Jago (E1)

GREEK

Central
Opso (W1)

West
Mazi (W8)

North
Carob Tree (NW5)*
The Greek Larder (N1)
Lemonia (NW1)
Vrisaki (N22)

East
Hungry Donkey (E1)
Kolossi Grill (EC1)

HUNGARIAN

Central

Gay Hussar *(W1)*

INTERNATIONAL

Central

Balans *(W1)*
Café in the Crypt *(WC2)*
Canvas *(SW1)*
Colony Grill Room *(W1)*
Cork & Bottle *(WC2)*
Ember Yard *(W1)*
Gordon's Wine Bar *(WC2)*
Grumbles *(SW1)*
Motcombs *(SW1)*
Rextail *(W1)*
Rocket Holborn *(WC2)*
Stock Pot *(SW1,W1)*
The 10 Cases *(WC2)*

West

The Andover Arms *(W6)*
Annie's *(W4)*
Balans *(W12,W4,W8)*
Eelbrook *(SW6)*
Gallery Mess *(SW3)*
The Kensington Wine Rooms *(W8)*
Margaux *(SW5)*
Mona Lisa *(SW10)*
Rivea *(SW7)*
The Scarsdale *(W8)*
Stock Pot *(SW3)*
Troubadour *(SW5)*

North

Banners *(N8)*
8 Hoxton Square *(N1)**
The Haven *(N20)*
The Orange Tree *(N20)*
Primeur *(N5)**

South

Annie's *(SW13)*
Brew *(SW15)*
Brigade *(SE1)*
Joanna's *(SE19)*
The Light House *(SW19)*
London House *(SW11)*
The Plough *(SW14)*
Rabot 1745 *(SE1)*
The Rooftop Café *(SE1)*
The Ship *(SW18)*
Ting *(SE1)*
Tulse Hill Hotel *(SE24)*
Vivat Bacchus *(SE1)*
The Yellow House *(SE16)*

East

Blixen *(E1)*
Eat 17 *(E9)*
Mission *(E2)*
Typing Room *(E2)**
Verden *(E5)**
Vivat Bacchus *(EC4)*
The Wine Library *(EC3)*

IRISH

West

The Cow *(W2)**

ITALIAN

Central

Al Duca *(SW1)*
Amico Bio *(WC1)*
Assunta Madre *(W1)*
Babbo *(W1)*
Bar Termini *(W1)**
Il Baretto *(W1)*
Bocca Di Lupo *(W1)**
Briciole *(W1)*
C London *(W1)*
Café Murano *(SW1,WC2)**
Caffè Caldesi *(W1)*
Caffé Vergnano *(WC2)*
Caraffini *(SW1)*
Cecconi's *(W1)*
Ciao Bella *(WC1)*
Como Lario *(SW1)*
Il Convivio *(SW1)*
Da Mario *(WC2)*
Dehesa *(W1)*
Delfino *(W1)*
Franco's *(SW1)*
La Genova *(W1)*
Gustoso *(SW1)*
Latium *(W1)**
Locanda Locatelli *(W1)*
Luce e Limoni *(WC1)**
Made in Italy *(W1)*
Mele e Pere *(W1)*
Morelli's Gelato *(WC2)*
Murano *(W1)*
Novikov (Italian restaurant) *(W1)*
Obicà *(W1)*
Oliveto *(SW1)**
Olivo *(SW1)*
Olivocarne *(SW1)**
Olivomare *(SW1)**
Opera Tavern *(WC2)**
Orso *(WC2)*
Ottolenghi *(SW1)**
Pescatori *(W1)*
Polpetto *(W1)*
Polpo *(W1,WC2)*
La Porchetta Pizzeria *(WC1)*
Princi *(W1)*
Quattro Passi *(W1)*
Quirinale *(SW1)*
Rex & Mariano *(W1)**
Ristorante Frescobaldi *(W1)*
Rossopomodoro *(WC2)*
Sale e Pepe *(SW1)*
Salt Yard *(W1)*
San Carlo Cicchetti *(W1,WC2)*
Santini *(SW1)*
Sardo *(W1)*
Sartoria *(W1)*
Signor Sassi *(SW1)*
Theo Randall *(W1)*
Tinello *(SW1)**
Tozi *(SW1)*
2 Veneti *(W1)*
Vapiano *(W1)*

Vasco & Piero's Pavilion *(W1)*
Vico *(WC2)*
Il Vicolo *(SW1)*
Zafferano *(SW1)*

West
Aglio e Olio *(SW10)*
L'Amorosa *(W6)**
Bird in Hand *(W14)*
Buona Sera *(SW3)*
Canta Napoli *(W4)*
Cibo *(W14)**
Da Mario *(SW7)*
Daphne's *(SW3)*
La Delizia Limbara *(SW3)*
Edera *(W11)*
Essenza *(W11)*
La Famiglia *(SW10)*
Frantoio *(SW10)*
Iddu *(SW7)*
The Italian Job *(W4)*
Locanda Ottomezzo *(W8)*
Lucio *(SW3)*
Made in Italy *(SW3)*
Manicomio *(SW3)*
Mediterraneo *(W11)*
Mona Lisa *(SW10)*
Nuovi Sapori *(SW6)*
The Oak W12 *(W12, W2)**
Obicà *(SW3)*
Osteria Basilico *(W11)*
Ottolenghi *(W11, W8)**
Pappa Ciccia *(SW6)**
Pellicanino *(SW3)*
Pentolina *(W14)**
Polpo *(SW3, W11)*
Il Portico *(W8)*
Portobello Ristorante *(W11)*
The Red Pepper *(W9)*
Riccardo's *(SW3)*
The River Café *(W6)*
Rossopomodoro *(SW10)*
Scalini *(SW3)*
Tartufo *(SW3)**
Terra Vergine *(SW10)**
Toto's *(SW3)*
Villa Di Geggiano *(W4)*
Ziani's *(SW3)*

North
Anima e Cuore *(NW1)**
Artigiano *(NW3)*
L'Artista *(NW11)*
Il Bacio *(N16, N5)*
La Collina *(NW1)*
Fabrizio *(N19)*
Fifteen *(N1)*
500 *(N19)*
Giacomo's *(NW2)**
Osteria Tufo *(N4)**
Ostuni *(NW6)*
Ottolenghi *(N1)**
Pizzeria Oregano *(N1)**
Pizzeria Pappagone *(N4)*
Porchetta Pizzeria *(N1, N4, NW1)*
Rugoletta *(N2)*
The Salt House *(NW8)*
San Daniele del Friuli *(N5)*
Sarracino *(NW6)**
Trullo *(N1)**
Villa Bianca *(NW3)*
York & Albany *(NW1)*

South
A Cena *(TW1)**
Al Forno *(SW15, SW19)*
Antico *(SE1)*
Artusi *(SE15)**
Bacco *(TW9)*
La Barca *(SE1)*
Bibo *(SW15)**
Al Boccon di'vino *(TW9)**
Buona Sera *(SW11)*
Canta Napoli *(TW11)*
Donna Margherita *(SW11)**
Enoteca Turi *(SW15)**
Lorenzo *(SE19)*
Numero Uno *(SW11)**
Osteria Antica Bologna *(SW11)**
Pizza Metro *(SW11)**
Pulia *(SE1)*
Le Querce *(SE23)**
Riva *(SW13)**
Sapori Sardi *(SW6)**
The Table *(SE1)*
Tentazioni *(SE1)*
Vapiano *(SE1)*
Zucca *(SE1)**

East
Amico Bio *(EC1)*
L'Anima *(EC2)*
L'Anima Café *(EC2)**
Apulia *(EC1)*
Il Bordello *(E1)*
Caravaggio *(EC3)*
Coco Di Mama *(EC4)*
Enoteca Rabezzana *(EC1)*
Fabrizio *(EC1)**
Gatti's City Point *(EC2)*
Lardo & Lardo Bebè *(E8)*
Luppolo *(E11)*
Manicomio *(EC2)*
Obicà *(E14)*
E Pellicci *(E2)*
Polpo *(EC1)*
La Porchetta Pizzeria *(EC1)*
Rotorino *(E8)*
Rucoletta *(EC2)**
Santore *(EC1)**
Taberna Etrusca *(EC4)*
Verdi's *(E1)**

MEDITERRANEAN

Central
About Thyme *(SW1)*
Bistro 1 *(W1, WC2)*
Massimo *(WC2)*
Nopi *(W1)*
The Norfolk Arms *(WC1)**
Riding House Café *(W1)*

West
The Atlas *(SW6)**

The Cross Keys *(SW3)*
Cumberland Arms *(W14)**
Locanda Ottomezzo *(W8)*
Made in Italy *(SW3)*
Mediterraneo *(W11)*
Raoul's Café *(W9)*
Raoul's Café & Deli *(W11)*
The Swan *(W4)**
Troubadour *(SW5)*
Wormwood *(W11)**

North
The Little Bay *(NW6)*
Vinoteca *(N1)*

South
The Bobbin *(SW4)*
Ceru *(SE1)*
Fish in a Tie *(SW11)*
The Fox & Hounds *(SW11)**
Oxo Tower (Brass') *(SE1)*
Peckham Bazaar *(SE15)**

East
The Eagle *(EC1)**
The Little Bay *(EC1)*
Morito *(EC1)**
Rocket Bishopgate *(EC2)*
Rocket Canary Wharf *(E14)*
Vinoteca *(EC1)*

POLISH

West
Daquise *(SW7)*
Polish Club *(SW7)*
Patio *(W12)*

South
Baltic *(SE1)*

PORTUGUESE

West
Lisboa Pâtisserie *(W10)*

East
Corner Room *(E2)*
Eyre Brothers *(EC2)**
The Gun *(E14)*
Taberna Do Mercado *(E1)**

RUSSIAN

Central
Bob Bob Ricard *(W1)*
Mari Vanna *(SW1)*

SCANDINAVIAN

Central
Bageriet *(WC2)**
Nordic Bakery *(W1)*
Scandinavian Kitchen *(W1)*
Texture *(W1)**

West
Flat Three *(W11)*

SCOTTISH

Central
Boisdale *(SW1)*

East
Boisdale of Bishopsgate *(EC2)*
Boisdale of Canary Wharf *(E14)*

SPANISH

Central
Ametsa *(SW1)**
aqua nueva *(W1)*
Barrafina *(W1)**
Barrafina Drury Lane *(WC2)**
Barrica *(W1)*
Bilbao Berria *(SW1)*
Cigala *(WC1)*
Dehesa *(W1)*
Donostia *(W1)**
Drakes Tabanco *(W1)*
Goya *(SW1)*
Ibérica *(SW1, W1)*
Lurra *(W1)*
Morada Brindisa Asador *(W1)*
Opera Tavern *(WC2)**
El Pirata *(W1)*
Salt Yard *(W1)*
Social Wine & Tapas *(W1)*
Tapas Brindisa Soho *(W1)*

West
Cambio de Tercio *(SW5)*
Capote Y Toros *(SW5)*
Casa Brindisa *(SW7)*
Duke of Sussex *(W4)*
Tendido Cero *(SW5)*
Tendido Cuatro *(SW6)*

North
Bar Esteban *(N8)**
La Bota *(N8)*
Café del Parc *(N19)**
Camino *(N1)*
El Parador *(NW1)**
Trangallan *(N16)**

South
Alquimia *(SW15)*
Angels & Gypsies *(SE5)*
Boqueria *(SW2)*
Brindisa Food Rooms *(SW9)*
Camino *(SE1)*
Gremio de Brixton *(SW2)*
José *(SE1)**
Lola Rojo *(SW11)**
Mar I Terra *(SE1)*
Meson don Felipe *(SE1)*
Pizarro *(SE1)*
Tapas Brindisa *(SE1)*

East
Bravas *(E1)*
Camino Blackfriars *(EC4)*
Camino Monument *(EC3)*
Copita Del Mercado *(E1)**
Eyre Brothers *(EC2)**
Ibérica *(E14, EC1)*

José Pizarro *(EC2)**
Morito *(EC1)**
Moro *(EC1)**

AFTERNOON TEA

Central

Athenaeum *(W1)*
The Delaunay *(WC2)*
Diamond Jub' Salon (Fortnum's) *(W1)*
La Fromagerie Café *(W1)*
The Goring Hotel *(SW1)*
Maison Bertaux *(W1)**
Ritz (Palm Court) *(W1)*
Royal Academy *(W1)*
Villandry *(W1)*
Villandry St James's *(SW1)*
The Wallace *(W1)*
The Wolseley *(W1)*
Yauatcha *(W1)**

North

Kenwood (Brew House) *(NW3)*
Landmark (Winter Gdn) *(NW1)*

South

Hotel du Vin *(SW19)*

BURGERS, ETC

Central

Balls & Company *(W1)*
Bar Boulud *(SW1)*
Bobo Social *(W1)**
Bodean's *(W1)*
Burger & Lobster *(W1)*
Dub Jam *(WC2)**
Five Guys *(WC2)*
Goodman *(W1)**
Hard Rock Café *(W1)*
Hawksmoor *(W1, WC2)*
Joe Allen *(WC2)*
Kettners *(W1)*
MEATLiquor *(W1)*
MEATmarket *(WC2)**
Opera Tavern *(WC2)**
Patty and Bun *(W1)**
The Queens Arms *(SW1)*
Rainforest Café *(W1)*
Sackville's *(W1)*
Shake Shack *(WC1, WC2)*
Tommi's Burger Joint *(W1)**
Wolfe's *(WC2)*
Zoilo *(W1)**

West

The Admiral Codrington *(SW3)*
Big Easy *(SW3)*
Bodean's *(SW6)*
Boom Burger *(W10)*
Electric Diner *(W11)*
Haché *(SW10)*
Lucky Seven *(W2)*
Tommi's Burger Joint *(SW3)**
Troubadour *(SW5)*

lorth

'rty Burger *(NW5)*
ke's Brew & Que *(N1)*
Five Guys Islington *(N1)*
Haché *(NW1)*
Harry Morgan's *(NW8)*
Meat Mission *(N1)*
MEATLiquor Islington *(N1)*
One Sixty Smokehouse *(NW6)**
Red Dog Saloon *(N1)*

South

Bodean's *(SW4)*
Boom Burger *(SW9)*
Dip & Flip *(SW11, SW19)**
Dirty Burger *(SW8)*
Haché *(SW12, SW4)*
Red Dog South *(SW4)*
Rivington Grill *(SE10)*
Rox Burger *(SE13)**
Village East *(SE1)*

East

Bleecker Street Burger *(E1)**
Bodean's *(EC1, EC3)*
Burger & Lobster *(EC1, EC4)*
Caboose *(E1)*
Chicken Shop & Dirty Burger *(E1)*
Comptoir Gascon *(EC1)*
Dirty Burger Shoreditch *(E1)*
Goodman *(E14)**
Goodman City *(EC2)**
Haché *(EC2)*
Hawksmoor *(E1, EC2)*
One Sixty Smokehouse *(E1)**
Patty and Bun *(EC2)**
The Rib Man *(E1)**
Rivington Grill *(EC2)*
Shake Shack *(E20)*
Smiths (Dining Rm) *(EC1)*
Street Kitchen (van) *(EC2)*

CHICKEN

Central

Bao *(W1)**
Chicken Shop *(WC1)*
Clockjack Oven *(W1)*
Randall & Aubin *(W1)**

North

Bird Islington *(N7)*
Chicken Shop *(NW5)*
Chicken Town *(N15)*
Le Coq *(N1)*

South

Chicken & Egg Shop *(SW12)*
Chicken Shop *(SW17)*

East

Bird *(E2)*
Chick 'n' Sours *(E8)**
Chicken Shop & Dirty Burger *(E1)*
The Tramshed *(EC2)*

FISH & CHIPS

Central

Golden Hind *(W1)**

North Sea Fish *(WC1)*
Seafresh *(SW1)**

West
Geales *(W8)*
Geales Chelsea Green *(SW3)*
Kerbisher & Malt *(W5,W6)*

North
Nautilus *(NW6)**
Olympus Fish *(N3)**
Poppies Camden *(NW1)**
The Sea Shell *(NW1)*
Skipjacks *(HA3)**
Toff's *(N10)**
Two Brothers *(N3)*
Vintage Salt *(N1)**

South
Brady's *(SW18)*
Fish Club *(SW11, SW4)**
fish! *(SE1)*
Kerbisher & Malt *(SW14, SW4)*
Masters Super Fish *(SE1)**
The Sea Cow *(SE22)*

East
Ark Fish *(E18)**
The Grapes *(E14)*
Kerbisher & Malt *(EC1)*
Poppies *(E1)**
Vintage Salt *(EC2)**

FISH & SEAFOOD

Central
Belgo Centraal *(WC2)*
Bellamy's *(W1)*
Bentley's *(W1)**
Bonnie Gull *(W1)**
Bouillabaisse *(W1)*
Burger & Lobster *(W1)*
Fishworks *(W1)*
Green's *(SW1)*
Kaspar's Seafood and Grill *(WC2)*
Olivomare *(SW1)**
One-O-One *(SW1)**
The Pantechnicon *(SW1)*
Pescatori *(W1)*
Quaglino's *(SW1)*
Randall & Aubin *(W1)**
Rib Room *(SW1)*
Royal China Club *(W1)**
Salmontini *(SW1)*
Scott's *(W1)**
Sexy Fish *(W1)*
J Sheekey *(WC2)**
J Sheekey Oyster Bar *(WC2)**
Wiltons *(SW1)*
Wright Brothers *(W1)**

West
Bibendum Oyster Bar *(SW3)*
Big Easy *(SW3)*
Chez Patrick *(W8)*
The Cow *(W2)**
Geales *(W8)*
Kensington Place *(W8)*
Mandarin Kitchen *(W2)**
Outlaw's Seafood *(SW3)**
Poissonnerie de l'Avenue *(SW3)*
The Summerhouse *(W9)*
Wright Brothers *(SW7)**

North
Belgo Noord *(NW1)*
Bradley's *(NW3)*
Carob Tree *(NW5)**
Lure *(NW5)**
Olympus Fish *(N3)**
Prawn On The Lawn *(N1)**
Toff's *(N10)**

South
Applebee's Café *(SE1)**
Cornish Tiger *(SW11)*
fish! *(SE1)*
Lobster Pot *(SE11)**
Le Querce *(SE23)**
Wright Brothers *(SE1)**

East
Angler *(EC2)**
Bonnie Gull Seafood Bar *(EC1)*
Burger & Lobster *(EC1, EC4)*
Chamberlain's *(EC3)*
Fish Central *(EC1)*
Fish Market *(EC2)*
The Grapes *(E14)*
Hix Oyster & Chop House *(EC1)*
M Raw *(EC2)**
Orpheus *(EC3)**
Royal Exchange *(EC3)*
Sweetings *(EC4)*
Wright Brothers *(E1)**

GAME

Central
Bocca Di Lupo *(W1)**
Boisdale *(SW1)*
Rules *(WC2)*
Wiltons *(SW1)*

West
Harwood Arms *(SW6)**
John Doe *(W10)**

North
San Daniele del Friuli *(N5)*

South
The Anchor & Hope *(SE1)**

East
Boisdale of Bishopsgate *(EC2)*
The Jugged Hare *(EC1)*

ICE CREAM

Central
Gelupo *(W1)**
Morelli's Gelato *(WC2)*

ORGANIC

Central
Daylesford Organic *(SW1,W1)*

West
Daylesford Organic *(W11)*

East
Smiths (Dining Rm) *(EC1)*

PIZZA

Central
Il Baretto *(W1)*
Bianco43 *(WC2)*
Delfino *(W1)*
Fire & Stone *(WC2)*
Homeslice *(W1, WC2)**
Kettners *(W1)*
Mayfair Pizza Company *(W1)*
Oliveto *(SW1)**
The Orange *(SW1)*
Pizza Pilgrims *(W1)*
La Porchetta Pizzeria *(WC1)*
Princi *(W1)*
Rossopomodoro *(WC2)*

West
Bird in Hand *(W14)*
Buona Sera *(SW3)*
Canta Napoli *(W4)*
Da Mario *(SW7)*
La Delizia Limbara *(SW3)*
Fire & Stone *(W12)*
Made in Italy *(SW3)*
The Oak W12 *(W12, W2)**
Osteria Basilico *(W11)*
Pappa Ciccia *(SW6)**
Pizza East Portobello *(W10)**
Portobello Ristorante *(W11)*
The Red Pepper *(W9)*
Rocca Di Papa *(SW7)*
Rossopomodoro *(SW10)*
Santa Maria *(W5)**

North
L' Antica Pizzeria *(NW3)**
Il Bacio *(N16, N5)*
Fabrizio *(N19)*
Pizza East *(NW5)**
Pizzeria Oregano *(N1)**
Pizzeria Pappagone *(N4)*
La Porchetta Pizzeria *(N1, N4, NW1)*
Rossopomodoro *(N1, NW1)*
Sacro Cuore *(NW10)**
Sweet Thursday *(N1)*

South
Al Forno *(SW15, SW19)*
Bianco43 *(SE10, SE3)*
Buona Sera *(SW11)*
Donna Margherita *(SW11)**
Eco *(SW4)*
Gourmet Pizza Company *(SE1)*
The Gowlett *(SE15)**
Lorenzo *(SE19)*
Mamma Dough *(SE23, SW9)*
Pizza Metro *(SW11)**
Pizzeria Rustica *(TW9)**
Rocca Di Papa *(SE21)*
Rossopomodoro *(SW18)*
The Yellow House *(SE16)*

East
Il Bordello *(E1)*
Pizza East *(E1)**
La Porchetta Pizzeria *(EC1)*
Rocket Bishopgate *(EC2)*
Rocket Canary Wharf *(E14)*

SANDWICHES, CAKES, ETC

Central
Bageriet *(WC2)**
Bar Italia *(W1)*
Bea's Of Bloomsbury *(WC1)**
Caffé Vergnano *(WC1)*
Crosstown Doughnuts *(W1)*
Daylesford Organic *(W1)*
Fernandez & Wells *(W1, WC2)*
La Fromagerie Café *(W1)*
Kaffeine *(W1)**
Konditor & Cook *(W1, WC1)*
Maison Bertaux *(W1)**
The Melt Room *(W1)*
Monmouth Coffee Company *(WC2)**
Nordic Bakery *(W1)*
Royal Academy *(W1)*
Scandinavian Kitchen *(W1)*
Workshop Coffee Fitzrovia *(W1)*

West
Lisboa Pâtisserie *(W10)*

North
Ginger & White *(NW3)*
Greenberry Café *(NW1)*
Kenwood (Brew House) *(NW3)*
Max's Sandwich Shop *(N4)**

South
Caffé Vergnano *(SE1)*
Fulham Wine Rooms *(SW6)*
Grind Coffee Bar *(SW15)**
Kappacasein *(SE16)**
Kitchen *(SE1)*
Konditor & Cook *(SE1)*
Milk *(SW12)**
Monmouth Coffee Company *(SE1, SE16)**
Orange Pekoe *(SW13)*

East
Brick Lane Beigel Bake *(E1)**
Caffé Vergnano *(EC4)*
Department of Coffee *(EC1)**
Konditor & Cook *(EC3)*
Nusa Kitchen *(EC1, EC2)**
Prufrock Coffee *(EC1)*
Workshop Coffee Holborn *(EC1)*

SALADS

Central
Kaffeine *(W1)**

STEAKS & GRILLS

Central
Barbecoa Piccadilly *(W1)*
Beast *(W1)*
Bodean's *(W1)*

Christopher's *(WC2)*
Cut *(W1)*
Flat Iron *(W1,WC2)**
Goodman *(W1)**
The Guinea Grill *(W1)*
Hawksmoor *(W1,WC2)*
M Restaurant Victoria Street *(SW1)**
MASH Steakhouse *(W1)*
maze Grill *(W1)*
Le Relais de Venise L'Entrecôte *(W1)*
Rib Room *(SW1)*
Rowley's *(SW1)*
Sackville's *(W1)*
Sophie's Steakhouse *(WC2)*
STK Steakhouse *(WC2)*
34 *(W1)*
Wolfe's *(WC2)*
Zoilo *(W1)**

West
Bodean's *(SW6)*
Casa Malevo *(W2)*
Haché *(SW10)*
Hawksmoor Knightsbridge *(SW3)*
John Doe *(W10)**
MacellaioRC *(SW7)**
PJ's Bar and Grill *(SW3)*
Popeseye *(W14)*
Smokehouse Chiswick *(W4)*
Sophie's Steakhouse *(SW10)*
West Thirty Six *(W10)*

North
Foxlow *(N16)*
Haché *(NW1)*
Popeseye *(N19)*
The Smokehouse Islington *(N1)*

South
Archduke Wine Bar *(SE1)*
Bodean's *(SW4)*
Buenos Aires Café *(SE10, SE3)*
Butcher & Grill *(SW11)*
Cau *(SE3, SW19)**
Cornish Tiger *(SW11)*
Naughty Piglets *(SW2)**
Popeseye *(SW15)*

East
Barbecoa *(EC4)*
Bodean's *(EC1, EC3)*
Buen Ayre *(E8)**
Cau *(E1)**
Foxlow *(EC1)*
Goodman *(E14)**
Goodman City *(EC2)**
Hawksmoor *(E1, EC2)*
Hill & Szrok *(E8)**
Hix Oyster & Chop House *(EC1)*
Jones & Sons *(E8)**
The Jones Family Project *(EC2)*
M Grill *(EC2)**
New Street Grill *(EC2)*
Paternoster Chop House *(EC4)*
Relais de Venise *(E14, EC2)*
Simpson's Tavern *(EC3)*
Smiths (Top Floor) *(EC1)*
Smiths (Dining Rm) *(EC1)*
Smiths (Ground Floor) *(EC1)*
The Tramshed *(EC2)*

VEGETARIAN

Central
Amico Bio *(WC1)*
Chettinad *(W1)**
Ethos *(W1)**
Malabar Junction *(WC1)*
Mildreds *(W1)*
Ragam *(W1)**
Rasa *(W1)**
Rasa Maricham *(WC1)**
Sagar *(W1)**
tibits *(W1)*
Woodlands *(SW1,W1)*

West
The Gate *(W6)**
Sagar *(W6)**

North
Chutneys *(NW1)*
Diwana Bhel-Poori House *(NW1)*
Jashan *(N8)**
Manna *(NW3)*
Rani *(N3)*
Rasa Travancore *(N16)**
Vijay *(NW6)*
Woodlands *(NW3)*

South
Blue Elephant *(SW6)*
Ganapati *(SE15)**
Le Pont de la Tour *(SE1)*
Sree Krishna *(SW17)**

East
Amico Bio *(EC1)*
The Gate *(EC1)**
Vanilla Black *(EC4)**

ARGENTINIAN

Central
Zoilo *(W1)**

West
Casa Malevo *(W2)*
Quantus *(W4)**

South
Buenos Aires Café *(SE10, SE3)*

East
Buen Ayre *(E8)**

BRAZILIAN

East
Sushisamba *(EC2)*

MEXICAN/TEXMEX

Central
La Bodega Negra *(W1)*
Cantina Laredo *(WC2)**

Chilango *(WC2)*
DF Mexico *(W1)**
Lupita *(WC2)*
Peyote *(W1)*

West
Habanera *(W12)*
Taqueria *(W11)**

North
Chilango *(N1)*

East
Chilango *(E1, EC2, EC4)*
Daddy Donkey *(EC1)**
DF Mexico *(E1)**

PERUVIAN

Central
Ceviche Soho *(W1)*
Coya *(W1)*
Lima *(W1)*
Lima Floral *(WC2)*
Pachamama *(W1)*
Señor Ceviche *(W1)*

East
Andina *(E2)*
Ceviche Old St *(EC1)*
Sushisamba *(EC2)*

SOUTH AMERICAN

West
Casa Cruz *(W11)*
Quantus *(W4)**

South
El Vergel *(SE1)**

AFRO-CARIBBEAN

Central
Jamaica Patty Co. *(WC2)*

MOROCCAN

West
Adams Café *(W12)*

NORTH AFRICAN

Central
Momo *(W1)*

West
Azou *(W6)*

SOUTH AFRICAN

Central
Bunnychow *(W1)*

TUNISIAN

West
Adams Café *(W12)*

EGYPTIAN

North
Ali Baba *(NW1)*

ISRAELI

Central
Gaby's *(WC2)*
The Palomar *(W1)**

East
Ottolenghi *(E1)**

KOSHER

Central
Reubens *(W1)*

North
Kaifeng *(NW4)*
Zest *(NW3)*

East
Brick Lane Beigel Bake *(E1)**

LEBANESE

Central
Fairuz *(W1)*
Maroush *(W1)*
Yalla Yalla *(W1)*

West
Chez Abir *(W14)**
Maroush *(SW3)*
Maroush Gardens *(W2)*

South
Arabica Bar and Kitchen *(SE1)*
Meza Trinity Road *(SW17)**
Yalla Yalla *(SE10)*

MIDDLE EASTERN

Central
Honey & Co *(W1)**
Patogh *(W1)**
Sesame *(WC2)*

North
Yasmeen *(NW8)*

East
Berber & Q *(E8)**
Morito *(EC1)**
Nusa Kitchen *(EC4)**
Pilpel *(E1, EC4)**

PERSIAN

Central
Kateh Knightsbridge *(SW1)**

West
Alounak *(W14, W2)*
Faanoos *(W4, W5)*
Kateh *(W9)**

South
Faanoos *(SW14)*

SYRIAN

West
Abu Zaad *(W12)*

TURKISH

Central

Babaji Pide *(W1)*
Ishtar *(W1)*
Kazan (Café) *(SW1)*

West

Best Mangal *(SW6,W14)**
Fez Mangal *(W11)**

North

Durum Ocakbasi *(N3)*
Gallipoli *(N1)*
Gem *(N1)**
Gökyüzü *(N4)**
Izgara *(N3)*
Mangal II *(N16)**

South

FM Mangal *(SE5)*
Tas Pide *(SE1)*

East

Chifafa *(EC1)**
Haz *(E1, EC2, EC3)*
Mangal 1 *(E8)**

AFGHANI

North

Afghan Kitchen *(N1)**
Ariana II *(NW6)**

BURMESE

West

Mandalay *(W2)*

CHINESE

Central

A Wong *(SW1)**
Baozi Inn *(WC2)**
Barshu *(W1)**
The Bright Courtyard *(W1)**
Chilli Cool *(WC1)*
China Tang *(W1)*
The Duck & Rice *(W1)*
The Four Seasons *(W1)**
Golden Dragon *(W1)*
The Grand Imperial *(SW1)*
Hakkasan Mayfair *(W1)**
Harbour City *(W1)*
Hunan *(SW1)**
Joy King Lau *(WC2)*
Kai Mayfair *(W1)*
Ken Lo's Memories *(SW1)*
Leong's Legends *(W1)**
Mr Chow *(SW1)*
New Mayflower *(W1)*
New World *(W1)*
Plum Valley *(W1)*
Princess Garden *(W1)*
Royal China *(W1)**
Royal China Club *(W1)**
Shanghai Blues *(WC1)*
Wong Kei *(W1)*
Yauatcha *(W1)**
Yming *(W1)*

West

The Four Seasons *(W2)**
Gold Mine *(W2)**
Good Earth *(SW3)*
Mandarin Kitchen *(W2)**
Min Jiang *(W8)**
North China *(W3)**
Pearl Liang *(W2)**
Royal China *(SW6,W2)**
Shikumen *(W12)**
Taiwan Village *(SW6)**

North

Good Earth *(NW7)*
Green Cottage *(NW3)*
Gung-Ho *(NW6)*
Kaifeng *(NW4)*
Phoenix Palace *(NW1)*
Singapore Garden *(NW6)**
Yipin China *(N1)*

South

Dalchini *(SW19)*
Dragon Castle *(SE17)*
Good Earth *(SW17)*
Hutong *(SE1)*
Silk Road *(SE5)**

East

Chinese Cricket Club *(EC4)**
Gourmet San *(E2)**
HKK *(EC2)**
Royal China *(E14)**
Shanghai *(E8)*
Sichuan Folk *(E1)**
Yauatcha City *(EC2)**
Yi-Ban *(E16)**

CHINESE, DIM SUM

Central

The Bright Courtyard *(W1)**
Dumplings' Legend *(W1)**
Golden Dragon *(W1)*
The Grand Imperial *(SW1)*
Hakkasan Mayfair *(W1)**
Harbour City *(W1)*
Joy King Lau *(WC2)*
New World *(W1)*
Princess Garden *(W1)*
Royal China *(W1)**
Royal China Club *(W1)**
Shanghai Blues *(WC1)*
Yauatcha *(W1)**

West

Min Jiang *(W8)**
Pearl Liang *(W2)**
Royal China *(SW6,W2)**
Shikumen *(W12)**

North

Jun Ming Xuan *(NW9)**
Phoenix Palace *(NW1)*

South

Dragon Castle *(SE17)*

East
Royal China *(E14)**
Shanghai *(E8)*
Yauatcha City *(EC2)**
Yi-Ban *(E16)**

GEORGIAN

North
Little Georgia Café *(N1)*

East
Little Georgia Café *(E2)*

INDIAN

Central
Amaya *(SW1)**
Benares *(W1)*
Carom at Meza *(W1)*
Chettinad *(W1)**
Chor Bizarre *(W1)*
Chutney Mary *(SW1)**
The Cinnamon Club *(SW1)*
Cinnamon Soho *(W1)**
Dishoom *(W1,WC2)**
Gaylord *(W1)*
Gymkhana *(W1)**
Imli Street *(W1)*
India Club *(WC2)*
Malabar Junction *(WC1)*
Mint Leaf *(SW1)*
Moti Mahal *(WC2)*
La Porte des Indes *(W1)*
Punjab *(WC2)*
Ragam *(W1)**
Red Fort *(W1)*
Roti Chai *(W1)**
Sagar *(W1,WC2)**
Salaam Namaste *(WC1)*
Salloos *(SW1)**
Tamarind *(W1)*
Trishna *(W1)**
Veeraswamy *(W1)*
Woodlands *(SW1,W1)*
Zayna *(W1)**

West
Anarkali *(W6)*
Bombay Brasserie *(SW7)*
Bombay Palace *(W2)**
Brilliant *(UB2)**
Chakra *(W11)*
Gifto's *(UB1)**
The Greedy Buddha *(SW6)*
Indian Zing *(W6)**
Karma *(W14)**
Khan's *(W2)*
Madhu's *(UB1)**
Malabar *(W8)**
Masala Grill *(SW10)**
Nayaab *(SW6)**
Noor Jahan *(SW5,W2)**
The Painted Heron *(SW10)**
Potli *(W6)**
Rasoi *(SW3)**
Sagar *(W6)**
Star of India *(SW5)*
Thali *(SW5)**
Zaika *(W8)*

North
Abi Ruchi *(N16)**
Chutneys *(NW1)*
Delhi Grill *(N1)**
Dishoom *(N1)**
Diwana Bhel-Poori House *(NW1)*
Great Nepalese *(NW1)*
Guglee *(NW3, NW6)*
Indian Rasoi *(N2)**
Indian Veg *(N1)**
Jashan *(N8)**
Kadiri's *(NW10)**
Namaaste Kitchen *(NW1)**
Paradise Hampstead *(NW3)**
Rani *(N3)*
Ravi Shankar *(NW1)*
Roots at N1 *(N1)**
Vijay *(NW6)*
Woodlands *(NW3)*
Zaffrani *(N1)*

South
Apollo Banana Leaf *(SW17)**
Babur *(SE23)**
Bengal Clipper *(SE1)*
Dalchini *(SW19)*
Everest Inn *(SE3)**
Ganapati *(SE15)**
Hot Stuff *(SW8)**
Indian Moment *(SW11)*
Indian Ocean *(SW17)**
Indian Zilla *(SW13)*
Jaffna House *(SW17)**
Kennington Tandoori *(SE11)*
Kishmish *(SW6)**
Kricket *(SW9)*
Lahore Karahi *(SW17)**
Lahore Kebab House *(SW16)**
Ma Goa *(SW15)**
Mirch Masala *(SW17)**
Radha Krishna Bhaven *(SW17)*
Sree Krishna *(SW17)**
Tandoori Nights *(SE22)**

East
Café Spice Namaste *(E1)**
Cinnamon Kitchen *(EC2)**
Dishoom *(E2)**
Lahore Kebab House *(E1)**
Mint Leaf *(EC2)*
Needoo *(E1)**
Tayyabs *(E1)**

INDIAN, SOUTHERN

Central
Hoppers *(W1)*
India Club *(WC2)*
Malabar Junction *(WC1)*
Quilon *(SW1)**
Ragam *(W1)**
Rasa *(W1)**
Rasa Maricham *(WC1)**
Sagar *(W1,WC2)**
Woodlands *(SW1,W1)*

West
Sagar *(W6)**
Shilpa *(W6)**

North
Chutneys *(NW1)*
Rani *(N3)*
Rasa Travancore *(N16)**
Vijay *(NW6)*
Woodlands *(NW3)*

South
Ganapati *(SE15)**
Sree Krishna *(SW17)**

JAPANESE

Central
Abeno *(WC1,WC2)*
aqua kyoto *(W1)*
The Araki *(W1)**
Atari-Ya *(W1)**
Bone Daddies *(W1)**
Chisou *(W1)**
Chotto Matte *(W1)**
Defune *(W1)**
Dinings *(W1)**
Eat Tokyo *(WC1,WC2)**
Engawa *(W1)*
Flesh and Buns *(WC2)*
Ippudo London *(WC2)*
Kanada-Ya *(SW1,WC2)**
Kiku *(W1)**
Kikuchi *(W1)**
Kintan *(WC1)**
Koya-Bar *(W1)**
Kulu Kulu *(W1,WC2)*
Kurobuta Harvey Nics *(SW1)**
Matsuri *(SW1)*
Murakami *(WC2)*
Nobu *(W1)*
Nobu Berkeley *(W1)*
Oka *(W1)**
Roka *(W1,WC2)**
Sakana-tei *(W1)**
Sake No Hana *(SW1)*
Salmontini *(SW1)*
Shackfuyu *(W1)**
Shoryu Ramen *(SW1,W1)**
Sticks'n'Sushi *(WC2)*
Sumosan *(W1)**
Taro *(W1)**
Tokyo Diner *(WC2)*
Tonkotsu *(W1)**
Tsunami *(W1)**
Umu *(W1)*
The Woodstock *(W1)*
Yoshino *(W1)**

West
Atari-Ya *(W3,W5)**
Bone Daddies *(W8)**
Chisou *(SW3)**
Eat Tokyo *(W6,W8)**
Flat Three *(W11)*
Hare & Tortoise *(W4)*
Inaho *(W2)**
Kiraku *(W5)**
Kulu Kulu *(SW7)*
Kurobuta *(SW3,W2)**
Maguro *(W9)*
Tokyo Sukiyaji-Tei & Bar *(SW3)*
Tosa *(W6)*
Yashin *(W8)**
Yashin Ocean House *(SW7)*
Yoshi Sushi *(W6)*
Zuma *(SW7)**

North
Asakusa *(NW1)**
Atari-Ya *(N12, NW4, NW6)**
Dotori *(N4)**
Eat Tokyo *(NW11)**
Jin Kichi *(NW3)**
Sushi-Say *(NW2)**

South
Hashi *(SW20)**
Matsuba *(TW9)**
Sticks'n'Sushi *(SE10, SW19)*
Tonkotsu Bankside *(SE1)**
Tsunami *(SW4)**
Yama Momo *(SE22)**
Zaibatsu *(SE10)**

East
Beer and Buns *(EC2)*
Bone Daddies *(EC1)**
City Miyama *(EC4)*
Ippudo London *(E14)*
K10, Appold Street *(EC2, EC3)*
Pham Sushi *(EC1)**
Roka *(E14)**
Shoryu Ramen *(EC2)**
Sosharu *(EC1)*
Sticks'n'Sushi *(E14)*
Sushisamba *(EC2)*
Sushi Tetsu *(EC1)**
Tajima Tei *(EC1)**
Tonkotsu East *(E8)**
Yum Bun *(EC1)**

KOREAN

Central
Bibimbap Soho *(W1)*
Bó Drake *(W1)*
Jinjuu *(W1)*
Kimchee *(WC1)*
Kintan *(WC1)**
Koba *(W1)*
On The Bab *(WC2)**
On The Bab Express *(W1)**

West
Yoshi Sushi *(W6)*

North
Dotori *(N4)**
The Petite Coree *(NW6)**

South
Cah-Chi *(SW18, SW20)*
Matsuba *(TW9)**

East
Bibimbap *(EC3)*

On The Bab *(EC1)**

MALAYSIAN

Central

C&R Café *(W1)**

West

C&R Café *(W2)**
Satay House *(W2)*

North

Roti King *(NW1)**
Singapore Garden *(NW6)**

South

Champor-Champor *(SE1)*

PAKISTANI

Central

Salloos *(SW1)**

West

Nayaab *(SW6)**

South

Lahore Karahi *(SW17)**
Lahore Kebab House *(SW16)**
Mirch Masala *(SW17)**

East

Lahore Kebab House *(E1)**
Needoo *(E1)**
Tayyabs *(E1)**

PAN-ASIAN

Central

Banana Tree Canteen *(W1)*
Buddha-Bar London *(SW1)*
Cocochan *(W1)*
Hare & Tortoise *(WC1)*
Inamo *(SW1,W1)*
Novikov (Asian restaurant) *(W1)*

West

Banana Tree Canteen *(W2,W9)*
E&O *(W11)*
Eight Over Eight *(SW3)*
Hare & Tortoise *(W14,W5)*

North

The Banana Tree Canteen *(NW6)*
Gilgamesh *(NW1)*
XO *(NW3)*

South

The Banana Tree Canteen *(SW11)*
Hare & Tortoise *(SW15)*

East

Banana Tree Canteen *(EC1)*
Hare & Tortoise *(EC4)*

THAI

Central

Crazy Bear *(W1)*
Patara Fitzrovia *(W1)*
Rosa's Soho *(W1)**
Smoking Goat *(WC2)**

West

Addie's Thai Café *(SW5)**
Bangkok *(SW7)*
Café 209 *(SW6)*
Churchill Arms *(W8)*
Esarn Kheaw *(W12)**
The Heron *(W2)**
101 Thai Kitchen *(W6)**
Patara South Kensington *(SW3)*
Rosa's Fulham *(SW10)**
Sukho Fine Thai Cuisine *(SW6)**
Suksan *(SW10)**

North

Isarn *(N1)**
Yum Yum *(N16)*

South

Awesome Thai *(SW13)*
The Begging Bowl *(SE15)*
Blue Elephant *(SW6)*
Kaosarn *(SW11, SW9)*
The Pepper Tree *(SW4)*
Suk Saran *(SW19)*
Talad Thai *(SW15)**

East

Rosa's *(E1)**
Rosa's Soho *(E15)**
Som Saa *(E8)**

VIETNAMESE

Central

Cây Tre *(W1)*
House of Ho *(W1)*

West

Saigon Saigon *(W6)*
Tem Tép *(W8)*

North

Salvation In Noodles *(N1, N4)*

South

Café East *(SE16)**
Mien Tay *(SW11)*

East

Cây Tre *(EC1)*
City Càphê *(EC2)**
Mien Tay *(E2)*
Sông Quê *(E2)*
Viet Grill *(E2)**

TAIWANESE

Central

Bao *(W1)**
Leong's Legends *(W1)**

West

Taiwan Village *(SW6)**

AREA OVERVIEWS

CENTRAL

Soho, Covent Garden & Bloomsbury (Parts of W1, all WC2 and WC1)

Price	Restaurant	Cuisine	Ratings
£100+	Smith & Wollensky	*Steak & grills*	
£90+	L'Atelier de Joel Robuchon	*French*	333
£80+	Spring	*British, Modern*	332
	Savoy Grill	*British, Traditional*	233
	Asia de Cuba	*Fusion*	222
	MASH Steakhouse	*Steaks & grills*	221
	Engawa	*Japanese*	343
	Roka	"	433
£70+	Christopher's	*American*	223
	Social Eating House	*British, Modern*	443
	Rules	*British, Traditional*	325
	Simpsons-in-the-Strand	"	111
	Kaspar's Seafood and Grill	*Fish & seafood*	333
	J Sheekey	"	444
	J Sheekey Oyster Bar	"	445
	The Salon	*Fusion*	– – –
	Massimo	*Mediterranean*	243
	Nopi	"	322
	STK Steakhouse	*Steaks & grills*	112
	Yauatcha	*Chinese*	523
	aqua kyoto	*Japanese*	223
£60+	Balthazar	*British, Modern*	223
	Bob Bob Ricard	"	345
	Hix	"	222
	Hush	"	233
	Indigo	"	243
	The Ivy	"	– – –
	Tom's Kitchen	"	121
	Holborn Dining Room	*British, Traditional*	234
	Antidote	*French*	433
	Clos Maggiore	"	455
	L'Escargot	"	333
	Gauthier Soho	"	554
	Otto's	"	454
	Kopapa	*Fusion*	222
	aqua nueva	*Spanish*	334
	Hawksmoor	*Steaks & grills*	333
	Lima Floral	*Peruvian*	332
	Shanghai Blues	*Chinese*	333
	Moti Mahal	*Indian*	332
	Red Fort	"	222

 FSA Ratings: from 1 (Poor) to 5 (Exceptional)

£50+	Big Easy	*American*	223
	Hubbard & Bell	*"*	334
	Joe Allen	*"*	124
	Arbutus	*British, Modern*	332
	Aurora	*"*	345
	Coopers	*"*	223
	Dean Street Townhouse	*"*	234
	Ducksoup	*"*	344
	Ham Yard Restaurant	*"*	114
	The Ivy Market Grill	*"*	223
	Kettners	*"*	– – –
	The Portrait	*"*	234
	Quo Vadis	*"*	354
	Tredwell's	*"*	121
	The Lady Ottoline	*British, Traditional*	333
	The National Dining Rms	*"*	113
	Strand Dining Rooms	*"*	– – –
	The Delaunay	*Mittel-European*	345
	Randall & Aubin	*Fish & seafood*	444
	Wright Brothers	*"*	443
	Cigalon	*French*	332
	Compagnie des Vins S.	*"*	334
	Les Deux Salons	*"*	– – –
	Mon Plaisir	*"*	224
	Gay Hussar	*Hungarian*	225
	The 10 Cases	*International*	243
	Bocca Di Lupo	*Italian*	544
	Café Murano	*"*	444
	Dehesa	*"*	334
	Luce e Limoni	*"*	444
	Mele e Pere	*"*	333
	Orso	*"*	222
	San Carlo Cicchetti	*"*	333
	Vasco & Piero's Pavilion	*"*	343
	Vico	*"*	– – –
	Cigala	*Spanish*	222
	Sophie's Steakhouse	*Steaks & grills*	222
	Rainforest Café	*Burgers, etc*	123
	La Bodega Negra	*Mexican/TexMex*	224
	Cantina Laredo	*"*	444
	Barshu	*Chinese*	412
	The Duck & Rice	*"*	235
	Plum Valley	*"*	323
	Chotto Matte	*Japanese*	434
	Flesh and Buns	*"*	333
	Patara Soho	*Thai*	333
	House of Ho	*Vietnamese*	322
£40+	Bodean's	*American*	223
	Jackson & Rye	*"*	123
	Jamie's Diner	*"*	222
	Mishkin's	*"*	123

Spuntino	"	334
Belgo Soho	*Belgian*	222
Andrew Edmunds	*British, Modern*	445
Jar Kitchen	"	333
Morden & Lea	"	– – –
The Norfolk Arms	"	433
Old Tom & English	"	– – –
Polpo at Ape & Bird	"	223
Shampers	"	245
10 Greek Street	"	543
Vinoteca	"	234
VQ	"	243
Great Queen Street	*British, Traditional*	223
Brasserie Zédel	*French*	245
Café Bohème	"	244
Chez Antoinette	"	– – –
Le Garrick	"	233
Terroirs	"	334
Balans	*International*	233
Cork & Bottle	"	235
Ember Yard	"	333
Rocket Holborn	"	333
Ciao Bella	*Italian*	244
Da Mario	"	344
Obicà	"	332
Polpetto	"	333
Polpo	"	223
Rex & Mariano	"	543
Barrafina Drury Lane	*Spanish*	555
Opera Tavern	"	444
Tapas Brindisa Soho	"	333
Mildreds	*Vegetarian*	332
Burger & Lobster	*Burgers, etc*	323
Wolfe's	"	322
Bianco43	*Pizza*	322
Fire & Stone	"	222
Lupita	*Mexican/TexMex*	332
Ceviche Soho	*Peruvian*	344
Señor Ceviche	"	334
The Palomar	*Israeli*	444
New Mayflower	*Chinese*	322
Yming	"	354
Cinnamon Soho	*Indian*	422
Dishoom	"	434
Imli Street	"	322
Malabar Junction	"	343
Abeno	*Japanese*	341
Kintan	"	433
Murakami	"	– – –
Oka	"	433
Shoryu Ramen	"	422
Sticks'n'Sushi	"	333
Bó Drake	*Korean*	223

 FSA Ratings: from 1 (Poor) to 5 (Exceptional)

	Jinjuu	"	333
	Kimchee	"	322
	Inamo	*Pan-Asian*	222
£35+	Blacklock	*British, Modern*	443
	Pennethorne's Cafe Bar	"	– – –
	Blanchette	*French*	345
	Prix Fixe	"	323
	Le Restaurant de Paul	"	443
	Savoir Faire	"	332
	Bar Termini	*Italian*	444
	Caffé Vergnano	"	223
	Princi	"	324
	Amico Bio	*Vegetarian*	232
	Balls & Company	*Burgers, etc*	– – –
	North Sea Fish	*Fish & chips*	332
	Rossopomodoro	*Pizza*	222
	Bea's Of Bloomsbury	*Sandwiches, cakes, etc*	433
	Caffé Vergnano	"	223
	Yalla Yalla	*Lebanese*	334
	Harbour City	*Chinese*	211
	Joy King Lau	"	322
	New World	"	323
	Dumplings' Legend	*Chinese, Dim sum*	423
	Carom at Meza	*Indian*	233
	Sagar	"	443
	Salaam Namaste	"	322
	Rasa Maricham	*Indian, Southern*	433
	Ippudo London	*Japanese*	232
	Taro	"	433
	On The Bab	*Korean*	432
	C&R Café	*Malaysian*	422
	Banana Tree Canteen	*Pan-Asian*	222
	Rosa's Soho	*Thai*	432
	Smoking Goat	"	523
	Cây Tre	*Vietnamese*	323
	Leong's Legends	*Taiwanese*	422
£30+	Seven Stars	*British, Modern*	323
	Café in the Crypt	*International*	223
	Gordon's Wine Bar	"	235
	La Porchetta Pizzeria	*Italian*	233
	MEATmarket	*Burgers, etc*	422
	Pizza Pilgrims	*Pizza*	334
	Fernandez & Wells	*Sandwiches, cakes, etc*	224
	Chicken Shop	*Chicken*	344
	Clockjack Oven	"	333
	Chilli Cool	*Chinese*	311
	The Four Seasons	"	411
	Golden Dragon	"	322
	Wong Kei	"	222
	Punjab	*Indian*	333

	Bone Daddies	*Japanese*	444
	Koya-Bar	*"*	444
	Kulu Kulu	*"*	312
	Shackfuyu	*"*	544
	Tonkotsu	*"*	443
	Hare & Tortoise	*Pan-Asian*	323
£25+	Pitt Cue Co	*American*	533
	Bistro 1	*Mediterranean*	232
	Bar Italia	*Sandwiches, cakes, etc*	345
	Gaby's	*Israeli*	333
	India Club	*Indian*	321
	Bibimbap Soho	*Korean*	322
	Bao	*Taiwanese*	542
£20+	Flat Iron Henrietta Street	*Steaks & grills*	444
	Dub Jam	*Burgers, etc*	443
	Shake Shack	*"*	322
	Morelli's Gelato	*Ice cream*	— — —
	Homeslice	*Pizza*	544
	Konditor & Cook	*Sandwiches, cakes, etc*	332
	Sesame	*Middle Eastern*	222
	Baozi Inn	*Chinese*	432
	Eat Tokyo	*Japanese*	422
	Tokyo Diner	*"*	343
£15+	Nordic Bakery	*Scandinavian*	333
	Maison Bertaux	*Afternoon tea*	423
	The Melt Room	*Sandwiches, cakes, etc*	— — —
	Chilango	*Mexican/TexMex*	332
	Kanada-Ya	*Japanese*	532
£10+	Five Guys	*Burgers, etc*	222
	Bageriet	*Sandwiches, cakes, etc*	444
	Monmouth Coffee Co	*"*	554
	Jamaica Patty Co.	*Afro-Caribbean*	332
	Bunnychow	*South African*	322
£5+	Gelupo	*Ice cream*	433
	Crosstown Doughnuts	*Sandwiches, cakes, etc*	342

Mayfair & St James's (Parts of W1 and SW1)

Price	Restaurant	Cuisine	Rating
£360+	The Araki	*Japanese*	544
£140+	Fera at Claridge's	*British, Modern*	344
£130+	Le Gavroche	*French*	554
	The Greenhouse	"	344
	Sketch (Lecture Rm)	"	335
£120+	Alain Ducasse	*French*	222
	Hélène Darroze	"	233
	Hibiscus	"	443
	The Ritz Restaurant	"	245
	The Square	"	422
	Umu	*Japanese*	222
£110+	Novikov (Italian restaurant)	*Italian*	222
	Cut	*Steaks & grills*	222
£100+	Dorchester Grill	*British, Modern*	232
	Galvin at Windows	*French*	224
	Assunta Madre	*Italian*	332
	C London	"	123
	Novikov (Asian restaurant)	*Pan-Asian*	112
£90+	Pollen Street Social	*British, Modern*	222
	Seven Park Place	"	334
	Corrigan's Mayfair	*British, Traditional*	344
	Wiltons	"	334
	Murano	*Italian*	333
	Quattro Passi	"	232
	Theo Randall	"	321
	Kai Mayfair	*Chinese*	322
	Benares	*Indian*	322
	Nobu, Park Ln	*Japanese*	332
	Nobu, Berkeley St	"	322
£80+	Alyn Williams	*British, Modern*	453
	Bentley's	*Fish & seafood*	443
	Bouillabaisse	"	– – –
	Scott's	"	444
	maze	*French*	222
	La Petite Maison	"	434
	Sketch (Gallery)	"	224
	Rextail	*International*	333
	Babbo	*Italian*	333
	Hakkasan Mayfair	*Chinese*	434
	Matsuri	*Japanese*	331
	Roka	"	433

Price	Restaurant	Cuisine	Ratings
£70+	The Berners Tavern	*British, Modern*	2 2 4
	Le Caprice	"	3 4 4
	Little Social	"	3 3 3
	Wild Honey	"	2 2 2
	Browns (Albemarle)	*British, Traditional*	2 2 2
	Green's	"	3 3 3
	Boulestin	*French*	2 3 2
	Brasserie Chavot	"	3 4 4
	Cecconi's	*Italian*	3 3 5
	Franco's	"	3 4 3
	Ristorante Frescobaldi	"	3 4 4
	The Guinea Grill	*Steaks & grills*	2 3 3
	maze Grill	"	2 2 2
	34	"	3 3 3
	Peyote	*Mexican/TexMex*	2 2 3
	Coya	*Peruvian*	3 2 3
	China Tang	*Chinese*	2 1 3
	Tamarind	*Indian*	3 3 2
	Veeraswamy	"	3 3 3
	Sake No Hana	*Japanese*	3 1 2
	Sumosan	"	4 3 2
£60+	Athenaeum	*British, Modern*	3 3 3
	Bellamy's	"	3 4 4
	Bonhams Restaurant	"	4 3 3
	Hush	"	2 3 3
	Kitty Fisher's	"	4 4 4
	Langan's Brasserie	"	2 2 4
	Mews of Mayfair	"	2 3 4
	The Only Running Footman	"	3 3 3
	Quaglino's	"	2 2 3
	Sotheby's Café	"	3 3 2
	The Wolseley	"	3 4 5
	The Keeper's House	*British, Traditional*	2 2 2
	Sexy Fish	*Fish & seafood*	– – –
	La Genova	*Italian*	3 3 3
	Sartoria	"	– – –
	Barbecoa Piccadilly	*Steaks & grills*	1 2 1
	Goodman	"	4 4 3
	Hawksmoor	"	3 3 3
	Rowley's	"	2 2 2
	Sackville's	"	– – –
	Diamond Jub' Salon	*Afternoon tea*	3 3 3
	Ritz (Palm Court)	"	2 4 5
	Momo	*North African*	2 2 3
	Chor Bizarre	*Indian*	3 2 3
	Gymkhana	"	5 4 4
£50+	The Avenue	*American*	2 3 3
	Hard Rock Café	"	2 2 4
	Heddon Street Kitchen	*British, Modern*	2 3 3
	1707	"	2 2 3

	Fishworks	*Fish & seafood*	322
	Pescatori	*"*	322
	The Balcon	*French*	232
	Boudin Blanc	*"*	224
	28-50	*"*	334
	Colony Grill Room	*International*	322
	Café Murano	*Italian*	444
	Princess Garden	*Chinese*	333
	Chutney Mary	*Indian*	444
	Mint Leaf	*"*	332
	Chisou	*Japanese*	442
	Kiku	*"*	432
	Patara Mayfair	*Thai*	333
£40+	The Punchbowl	*British, Modern*	334
	The Windmill	*British, Traditional*	323
	L'Artiste Musclé	*French*	224
	Al Duca	*Italian*	332
	Il Vicolo	*"*	344
	Burger & Lobster	*Burgers, etc*	323
	Delfino	*Pizza*	322
	Mayfair Pizza Company	*"*	334
	Royal Academy	*Sandwiches, cakes, etc*	222
	Sakana-tei	*Japanese*	521
	Shoryu Ramen	*"*	422
	Yoshino	*"*	432
	Inamo	*Pan-Asian*	222
£35+	El Pirata	*Spanish*	344
	tibits	*Vegetarian*	323
	Woodlands	*Indian*	322
	Rasa	*Indian, Southern*	433
£30+	Stock Pot	*International*	222
	The Woodstock	*Japanese*	– – –

Fitzrovia & Marylebone (Part of W1)

£110+	Pied à Terre	*French*	553
	Beast	*Steaks & grills*	222
£100+	Roux at the Landau	*British, Modern*	234
	Bubbledogs (Kitchen Table)	*Fusion*	444
£90+	Texture	*Scandinavian*	442
£80+	The Chiltern Firehouse	*American*	124
	L'Autre Pied	*French*	443
	Orrery	*"*	343

	Dabbous	*Fusion*	332
	Hakkasan	*Chinese*	434
	Roka	*Japanese*	433
£70+	The Cavendish	*British, Modern*	344
	The Providores	*Fusion*	332
	Locanda Locatelli	*Italian*	333
	Royal China Club	*Chinese*	432
£60+	Galvin Bistrot de Luxe	*French*	444
	Il Baretto	*Italian*	322
	Caffè Caldesi	*"*	343
	Lima	*Peruvian*	332
	La Porte des Indes	*Indian*	334
	Trishna	*"*	543
	Defune	*Japanese*	432
	Crazy Bear	*Thai*	334
£50+	The Lockhart	*American*	222
	The Grazing Goat	*British, Modern*	333
	Percy & Founders	*"*	333
	Portland	*"*	553
	Fischer's	*Mittel-European*	344
	Bonnie Gull	*Fish & seafood*	443
	Fishworks	*"*	322
	Pescatori	*"*	322
	Elena's L'Etoile	*French*	111
	Piquet	*"*	– – –
	28-50	*"*	334
	Villandry	*"*	112
	The Wallace	*"*	225
	Carousel	*Fusion*	433
	Providores (Tapa Room)	*"*	333
	Twist At Crawford	*"*	444
	Latium	*Italian*	453
	Sardo	*"*	322
	Riding House Café	*Mediterranean*	224
	Lurra	*Spanish*	– – –
	Zoilo	*Argentinian*	433
	Pachamama	*Peruvian*	332
	Reubens	*Kosher*	332
	Maroush	*Lebanese*	322
	The Bright Courtyard	*Chinese*	434
	Gaylord	*Indian*	333
	Dinings	*Japanese*	541
	Kikuchi	*"*	532
	Cocochan	*Pan-Asian*	333
	Patara Fitzrovia	*Thai*	333
	House of Ho	*Vietnamese*	322
£40+	Barnyard	*British, Modern*	222
	Daylesford Organic	*"*	213

	Hardy's Brasserie	"	233
	The Newman Arms	"	– – –
	Newman Street Tavern	"	334
	Picture	"	343
	Vinoteca Seymour Place	"	234
	Boopshis	*Mittel-European*	333
	Opso	*Greek*	224
	Briciole	*Italian*	343
	Made in Italy	"	333
	Obicà	"	332
	2 Veneti	"	343
	Barrica	*Spanish*	333
	Donostia	"	544
	Drakes Tabanco	"	323
	Ibérica	"	334
	Salt Yard	"	323
	Social Wine & Tapas	"	– – –
	Le Relais de Venise	*Steaks & grills*	322
	Bobo Social	*Burgers, etc*	443
	Burger & Lobster	"	323
	Daylesford Organic	*Sandwiches, cakes, etc*	213
	Workshop Coffee Fitzrovia	"	344
	Fairuz	*Lebanese*	343
	Honey & Co	*Middle Eastern*	542
	Ishtar	*Turkish*	332
	Royal China	*Chinese*	412
	Roti Chai	*Indian*	443
	Zayna	"	432
	Tsunami	*Japanese*	533
	Koba	*Korean*	333
£35+	Lantana Café	*Australian*	333
	Ethos	*Vegetarian*	423
	MEATLiquor	*Burgers, etc*	324
	La Fromagerie Café	*Sandwiches, cakes, etc*	323
	Yalla Yalla	*Lebanese*	334
	Babaji Pide	*Turkish*	343
	Chettinad	*Indian*	433
	Sagar	"	443
	Woodlands	"	322
	On The Bab Express	*Korean*	432
£30+	Bubbledogs	*American*	123
	Stock Pot	*International*	222
	Vapiano	*Italian*	322
	DF Mexico	*Mexican/TexMex*	433
	Atari-Ya	*Japanese*	532
	Tonkotsu	"	443
£25+	The Joint Marylebone	*American*	532
	Golden Hind	*Fish & chips*	443
	Ragam	*Indian*	542

	Bibimbap Soho	*Korean*	322
£20+	Patty and Bun	*Burgers, etc*	433
	Tommi's Burger Joint	*"*	444
	Homeslice	*Pizza*	544
	Patogh	*Middle Eastern*	444
£15+	Delancey & Co.	*American*	433
	Nordic Bakery	*Scandinavian*	333
£10+	Scandinavian Kitchen	*Scandinavian*	353
	Kaffeine	*Sandwiches, cakes, etc*	455

Belgravia, Pimlico, Victoria & Westminster (SW1, except St James's)

£110+	Marcus	*French*	232
£100+	Dinner	*British, Traditional*	333
	One-O-One	*Fish & seafood*	521
	Pétrus	*French*	343
	Rib Room	*Steaks & grills*	342
£80+	The Goring Hotel	*British, Modern*	355
	The Northall	*"*	344
	Roux at Parliament Square	*"*	553
	Koffmann's	*French*	553
	Zafferano	*Italian*	222
	Ametsa	*Spanish*	442
	Mr Chow	*Chinese*	333
£70+	Adam Handling at Caxton	*British, Modern*	332
	Salmontini	*Fish & seafood*	– – –
	Bar Boulud	*French*	333
	Canvas	*International*	– – –
	Santini	*Italian*	222
	Mari Vanna	*Russian*	234
	M Restaurant Victoria Street	*Steaks & grills*	433
	Hunan	*Chinese*	521
	Amaya	*Indian*	534
	The Cinnamon Club	*"*	334
	Quilon	*Indian, Southern*	442
£60+	Bank Westminster	*British, Modern*	222
	The Botanist	*"*	223
	The Fifth Floor Restaurant	*"*	333
	The Thomas Cubitt	*"*	344
	Olivomare	*Fish & seafood*	432
	Les Gourmets des Ternes	*French*	223

	La Poule au Pot	"	335
	Motcombs	*International*	233
	Olivocarne	*Italian*	442
	Quirinale	"	332
	Sale e Pepe	"	343
	Signor Sassi	"	334
	Boisdale	*Scottish*	223
	Oliveto	*Pizza*	422
	The Grand Imperial	*Chinese*	332
	Ken Lo's Memories	"	342
	Buddha-Bar London	*Pan-Asian*	333
£50+	Ebury Rest' & Wine Bar	*British, Modern*	233
	The Orange	"	334
	The Pantechnicon	"	334
	Tate Britain (Rex Whistler)	"	235
	Shepherd's	*British, Traditional*	343
	Colbert	*French*	123
	Villandry St James's	"	112
	Caraffini	*Italian*	354
	Il Convivio	"	333
	Olivo	"	342
	Ottolenghi	"	422
	Tinello	"	444
	About Thyme	*Mediterranean*	344
	Bilbao Berria	*Spanish*	223
	Kurobuta Harvey Nics	*Japanese*	423
	Salloos	*Pakistani*	443
£40+	Daylesford Organic	*British, Modern*	213
	The Queens Arms	"	344
	Grumbles	*International*	233
	Como Lario	*Italian*	244
	Gustoso	"	353
	Tozi	"	333
	Goya	*Spanish*	333
	Ibérica	"	334
	Kateh Knightsbridge	*Persian*	542
	Kazan (Café)	*Turkish*	342
£35+	The Vincent Rooms	*British, Modern*	333
	Seafresh	*Fish & chips*	432
	A Wong	*Chinese*	543
£15+	Kanada-Ya	*Japanese*	532

WEST

Chelsea, South Kensington, Kensington, Earl's Court & Fulham (SW3, SW5, SW6, SW7, SW10 & W8)

£120+	Gordon Ramsay	*French*	3 4 3
£90+	Rasoi	*Indian*	4 2 3
£80+	Outlaw's Seafood and Grill	*Fish & seafood*	4 4 2
	Toto's	*Italian*	2 3 3
	Yashin Ocean House	*Japanese*	2 2 2
	Zuma	*"*	5 3 4
£70+	Babylon	*British, Modern*	2 3 4
	The Five Fields	*"*	5 5 5
	Launceston Place	*"*	4 5 4
	maze Grill	*"*	2 2 2
	Medlar	*"*	4 4 3
	Poissonnerie de l'Av.	*Fish & seafood*	3 3 3
	Bibendum	*French*	2 3 3
	Cheyne Walk Bras'	*"*	3 3 3
	L'Etranger	*"*	3 4 2
	Rivea	*International*	2 4 2
	Daphne's	*Italian*	2 3 2
	Scalini	*"*	3 3 3
	Min Jiang	*Chinese*	4 3 5
	Yashin	*Japanese*	5 3 2
£60+	The Abingdon	*British, Modern*	3 4 4
	Bluebird	*"*	1 2 3
	Clarke's	*"*	4 4 3
	Harwood Arms	*"*	5 3 3
	Kensington Place	*"*	3 3 3
	Kitchen W8	*"*	5 4 3
	The Terrace	*"*	3 4 4
	Tom's Kitchen	*"*	1 2 1
	Belvedere	*French*	2 2 4
	Le Colombier	*"*	3 3 4
	Mazi	*Greek*	3 3 4
	Margaux	*International*	3 2 3
	Lucio	*Italian*	3 3 3
	Manicomio	*"*	2 2 3
	Locanda Ottomezzo	*Mediterranean*	3 4 3
	Cambio de Tercio	*Spanish*	3 3 3
	Hawksmoor Knightsbridge	*Steaks & grills*	3 3 3
	Zaika	*Indian*	3 3 3
£50+	Big Easy	*American*	2 2 3
	Brinkley's	*British, Modern*	2 2 4

	The Enterprise	"	233
	The Ivy Chelsea Garden	"	225
	The Sands End	"	344
	The Admiral Codrington	*British, Traditional*	224
	Bumpkin	"	222
	Ffiona's	"	344
	Maggie Jones's	"	235
	Bibendum Oyster Bar	*Fish & seafood*	242
	Wright Brothers	"	443
	La Brasserie	*French*	224
	Chez Patrick	"	353
	Garnier	"	441
	Eelbrook	*International*	343
	Gallery Mess	"	223
	The Kensington Wine Rms	"	223
	La Famiglia	*Italian*	222
	Frantoio	"	233
	Ottolenghi	"	422
	Pellicanino	"	343
	Il Portico	"	354
	Tartufo	"	442
	Terra Vergine	"	433
	Ziani's	"	333
	The Cross Keys	*Mediterranean*	334
	Polish Club	*Polish*	334
	Tendido Cero	*Spanish*	333
	MacellaioRC	*Steaks & grills*	534
	PJ's Bar and Grill	"	344
	Sophie's Steakhouse	"	222
	Geales Chelsea Green	*Fish & chips*	233
	Maroush	*Lebanese*	322
	Good Earth	*Chinese*	332
	Bombay Brasserie	*Indian*	333
	Masala Grill	"	444
	The Painted Heron	"	443
	Star of India	"	323
	Chisou	*Japanese*	442
	Kurobuta	"	423
	Eight Over Eight	*Pan-Asian*	324
	Patara South Kensington	*Thai*	333
	Sukho Fine Thai Cuisine	"	543
£40+	Bodean's	*American*	223
	The Builders Arms	*British, Modern*	234
	The Butcher's Hook	"	343
	Joe's Brasserie	"	233
	Megan's Delicatessen	"	224
	The Phoenix	"	233
	Rabbit	"	444
	The Shed	"	333
	VQ	"	243
	The Brown Cow	*British, Traditional*	333
	Brasserie Gustave	*French*	453

	Balans	*International*	233
	The Scarsdale	*"*	234
	Troubadour	*"*	234
	Aglio e Olio	*Italian*	332
	Buona Sera	*"*	333
	Da Mario	*"*	233
	Iddu	*"*	212
	Made in Italy	*"*	333
	Nuovi Sapori	*"*	343
	Obicà	*"*	332
	Polpo	*"*	223
	Riccardo's	*"*	233
	The Atlas	*Mediterranean*	444
	Daquise	*Polish*	222
	Capote Y Toros	*Spanish*	344
	Casa Brindisa	*"*	232
	Tendido Cuatro	*"*	232
	La Delizia Limbara	*Pizza*	323
	Royal China	*Chinese*	412
	Malabar	*Indian*	442
	Noor Jahan	*"*	433
	Thali	*"*	444
	Tokyo Sukiyaji-Tei & Bar	*Japanese*	– – –
	Bangkok	*Thai*	332
	Suksan	*"*	443
	Tem Tép	*Vietnamese*	333
£35+	Haché	*Steaks & grills*	334
	Rocca Di Papa	*Pizza*	234
	Rossopomodoro	*"*	222
	Best Mangal	*Turkish*	432
	Nayaab	*Indian*	432
	Churchill Arms	*Thai*	345
	Rosa's Fulham	*"*	432
£30+	Kensington Square Kitchen	*British, Modern*	343
	Stock Pot	*International*	222
	Pappa Ciccia	*Italian*	444
	The Greedy Buddha	*Indian*	322
	Bone Daddies	*Japanese*	444
	Kulu Kulu	*"*	312
	Addie's Thai Café	*Thai*	442
	Taiwan Village	*Taiwanese*	453
£25+	Mona Lisa	*International*	332
	Café 209	*Thai*	233
£20+	Tommi's Burger Joint	*Burgers, etc*	444
	Eat Tokyo	*Japanese*	422

Notting Hill, Holland Park, Bayswater, North Kensington & Maida Vale (W2, W9, W10, W11)

£130+	The Ledbury	*British, Modern*	555
£120+	Marianne	*British, Modern*	454
£70+	Angelus	*French*	353
	Flat Three	*Japanese*	233
£60+	Beach Blanket Babylon	*British, Modern*	113
	The Dock Kitchen	"	345
	Julie's	"	– – –
	Les Gourmets des Ternes	*French*	223
	Edera	*Italian*	353
	Essenza	"	323
	Mediterraneo	"	334
	Wormwood	*Mediterranean*	443
	West Thirty Six	*Steaks & grills*	– – –
	E&O	*Pan-Asian*	334
£50+	The Frontline Club	*British, Modern*	333
	The Ladbroke Arms	"	434
	The Magazine Restaurant	"	345
	Paradise, Kensal Green	"	225
	The Truscott Arms	"	434
	The Waterway	"	234
	Bumpkin	*British, Traditional*	222
	The Summerhouse	*Fish & seafood*	225
	Bel Canto	*French*	244
	The Cow	*Irish*	444
	The Oak	*Italian*	424
	Osteria Basilico	"	324
	Ottolenghi	"	422
	Portobello Ristorante	"	333
	Casa Malevo	*Argentinian*	323
	Maroush Gardens	*Lebanese*	322
	Chakra	*Indian*	312
	Kurobuta	*Japanese*	423
£40+	Pizza Metro	"	432
	Electric Diner	*American*	244
	Granger & Co	*Australian*	324
	Daylesford Organic	*British, Modern*	213
	Salt & Honey	"	– – –
	Hereford Road	*British, Traditional*	423
	Snaps & Rye	*Danish*	434
	Polpo	*Italian*	223
	Raoul's Café & Deli	*Mediterranean*	223
	John Doe	*Steaks & grills*	433
	Pizza East Portobello	*Pizza*	434

	The Red Pepper	"	322
	Casa Cruz	South American	---
	Kateh	Persian	542
	Mandarin Kitchen	Chinese	422
	Pearl Liang	"	432
	Royal China	"	412
	Bombay Palace	Indian	542
	Noor Jahan	"	433
	Inaho	Japanese	515
£35+	Lucky Seven	American	333
	Taqueria	Mexican/TexMex	433
	Maguro	Japanese	343
	C&R Café	Malaysian	422
	Satay House	"	322
	Banana Tree Canteen	Pan-Asian	222
£30+	Alounak	Persian	323
	Mandalay	Burmese	221
	The Four Seasons	Chinese	411
	Gold Mine	"	521
	The Heron	Thai	521
£25+	Fez Mangal	Turkish	543
£20+	Boom Burger	Burgers, etc	332
	Khan's	Indian	332
£10+	Lisboa Pâtisserie	Sandwiches, cakes, etc	335

Hammersmith, Shepherd's Bush, Olympia, Chiswick, Brentford & Ealing (W4, W5, W6, W12, W13, W14, TW8)

£100+	Hedone	British, Modern	433
	The River Café	Italian	323
£70+	La Trompette	French	444
£60+	Le Vacherin	French	322
	Villa Di Geggiano	Italian	222
£50+	The Anglesea Arms	British, Modern	334
	The Brackenbury	"	343
	Charlotte's W5	"	344
	High Road Brasserie	"	113
	The Hampshire Hog	British, Traditional	223
	Charlotte's Place	French	343
	Charlotte's W4	"	344

	Michael Nadra	"	432
	Cibo	*Italian*	454
	The Oak W12	"	424
£40+	Jackson & Rye Chiswick	*American*	123
	Bush Dining Hall	*British, Modern*	222
	The Carpenter's Arms	"	333
	City Barge	"	333
	The Dartmouth Castle	"	344
	The Dove	"	225
	Duke of Sussex	"	334
	Ealing Park Tavern	"	334
	The Havelock Tavern	"	324
	The Pear Tree	"	334
	Princess Victoria	"	333
	Vinoteca	"	234
	The Andover Arms	*International*	344
	Annie's	"	235
	Balans	"	233
	L'Amorosa	*Italian*	543
	Pentolina	"	454
	Cumberland Arms	*Mediterranean*	443
	The Swan	"	455
	Popeseye	*Steaks & grills*	342
	Smokehouse Chiswick	"	333
	The Gate	*Vegetarian*	423
	Bird in Hand	*Pizza*	333
	Fire & Stone	"	222
	Quantus	*South American*	454
	Azou	*North African*	333
	North China	*Chinese*	432
	Indian Zing	*Indian*	532
	Karma	"	432
	Potli	"	433
£35+	Albertine	*French*	234
	Canta Napoli	*Italian*	332
	Patio	*Polish*	355
	Habanera	*Mexican/TexMex*	323
	Chez Abir	*Lebanese*	432
	Best Mangal	*Turkish*	432
	Shikumen	*Chinese*	522
	Anarkali	*Indian*	342
	Brilliant	"	443
	Madhu's	"	433
	Sagar	"	443
	Kiraku	*Japanese*	532
	Tosa	"	332
	Yoshi Sushi	"	342
	Saigon Saigon	*Vietnamese*	344

Price	Restaurant	Cuisine	Ratings
£30+	The Italian Job	*Italian*	2 2 4
	Santa Maria	*Pizza*	5 3 3
	Adams Café	*Moroccan*	3 5 3
	Alounak	*Persian*	3 2 3
	Shilpa	*Indian, Southern*	5 4 2
	Atari-Ya	*Japanese*	5 3 2
	Hare & Tortoise	*Pan-Asian*	3 2 3
	Esarn Kheaw	*Thai*	4 4 1
	101 Thai Kitchen	*"*	4 2 1
£25+	Faanoos	*Persian*	2 2 3
£20+	Kerbisher & Malt	*Fish & chips*	3 3 2
	Abu Zaad	*Syrian*	3 3 2
	Gifto's	*Indian*	4 3 2
	Eat Tokyo	*Japanese*	4 2 2

NORTH

Hampstead, West Hampstead, St John's Wood, Regent's Park, Kilburn & Camden Town (NW postcodes)

Price	Restaurant	Cuisine	Ratings
£70+	Landmark (Winter Gdn)	*British, Modern*	234
£60+	The Booking Office	*British, Modern*	224
	Odette's	*"*	333
	Bull & Last	*British, Traditional*	433
	Gilbert Scott	*"*	223
	L'Aventure	*French*	455
	Oslo Court	*"*	354
	Kaifeng	*Chinese*	323
	Gilgamesh	*Pan-Asian*	223
£50+	One Sixty Smokehouse	*American*	443
	Bradley's	*British, Modern*	332
	Crocker's Folly	*"*	223
	Market	*"*	332
	St Pancras Grand	*"*	123
	Michael Nadra	*French*	432
	Mill Lane Bistro	*"*	232
	La Collina	*Italian*	322
	Villa Bianca	*"*	232
	York & Albany	*"*	223
	Manna	*Vegetarian*	332
	Greenberry Café	*Sandwiches, cakes, etc*	223
	Good Earth	*Chinese*	332
	Phoenix Palace	*"*	322
£40+	Belgo Noord	*Belgian*	222
	The Horseshoe	*British, Modern*	323
	The Junction Tavern	*"*	333
	Made In Camden	*"*	222
	Megan's	*"*	224
	The North London Tavern	*"*	333
	Parlour	*"*	444
	The Refinery	*"*	233
	Rising Sun	*"*	343
	Shoe Shop	*"*	542
	The Wells	*"*	224
	The Wet Fish Café	*"*	333
	The Bull & Gate	*British, Traditional*	323
	Lure	*Fish & seafood*	433
	L'Absinthe	*French*	233
	La Cage Imaginaire	*"*	344
	Patron	*"*	334
	Lemonia	*Greek*	245
	Anima e Cuore	*Italian*	432
	Artigiano	*"*	333

	Ostuni	"	334
	The Salt House	"	333
	Sarracino	"	422
	Harry Morgan's	*Burgers, etc*	221
	Nautilus	*Fish & chips*	441
	The Sea Shell	"	322
	Pizza East	*Pizza*	434
	Zest	*Kosher*	323
	Yasmeen	*Middle Eastern*	– – –
	Gung-Ho	*Chinese*	232
	Jun Ming Xuan	*Chinese, Dim sum*	442
	Namaaste Kitchen	*Indian*	442
	Jin Kichi	*Japanese*	543
	Sushi-Say	"	542
	Singapore Garden	*Malaysian*	433
	XO	*Pan-Asian*	222
£35+	Lantana Cafe	*Australian*	333
	The Truscott Cellar	*British, Traditional*	– – –
	Carob Tree	*Greek*	454
	Giacomo's	*Italian*	453
	El Parador	*Spanish*	454
	Haché	*Steaks & grills*	334
	L' Antica Pizzeria	*Pizza*	433
	Rossopomodoro	"	222
	Sacro Cuore	"	433
	Green Cottage	*Chinese*	322
	Great Nepalese	*Indian*	332
	Woodlands	"	322
	Asakusa	*Japanese*	532
	The Petite Coree	*Korean*	542
	The Banana Tree Canteen	*Pan-Asian*	222
£30+	L'Artista	*Italian*	244
	La Porchetta Pizzeria	"	233
	Skipjacks	*Fish & chips*	443
	Kenwood (Brew House)	*Sandwiches, cakes, etc*	224
	Chicken Shop	*Chicken*	344
	Ariana II	*Afghani*	432
	Chutneys	*Indian*	222
	Guglee	"	333
	Paradise Hampstead	"	454
	Ravi Shankar	"	322
	Vijay	"	341
	Atari-Ya	*Japanese*	532
£25+	The Little Bay	*Mediterranean*	235
	Poppies Camden	*Fish & chips*	434
	Diwana B-P House	*Indian*	321
£20+	Ali Baba	*Egyptian*	323
	Kadiri's	*Indian*	432

	Eat Tokyo	*Japanese*	422
	Roti King	*Malaysian*	511
£15+	Ginger & White	*Sandwiches, cakes, etc*	333
£10+	Dirty Burger	*Burgers, etc*	322

Hoxton, Islington, Highgate, Crouch End, Stoke Newington, Finsbury Park, Muswell Hill & Finchley (N postcodes)

£60+	Frederick's	*British, Modern*	224
	Plum + Spilt Milk	*"*	233
	The Almeida	*French*	222
	Fifteen Restaurant	*Italian*	122
£50+	The Drapers Arms	*British, Modern*	223
	Grain Store	*"*	223
	The Haven	*"*	222
	Pig & Butcher	*"*	444
	Rotunda Bar & Restaurant	*"*	223
	Bistro Aix	*French*	442
	The Greek Larder	*Greek*	332
	Ottolenghi	*Italian*	422
	Trullo	*"*	443
	Foxlow	*Steaks & grills*	333
	The Smokehouse Islington	*"*	333
	Duke's Brew & Que	*"*	323
£40+	Red Dog Saloon	*American*	323
	Granger & Co	*Australian*	324
	Sunday	*"*	433
	The Albion	*British, Modern*	213
	Bald Faced Stag	*"*	333
	The Bull	*"*	234
	Caravan King's Cross	*"*	323
	Heirloom	*"*	343
	Oldroyd	*"*	– – –
	Season Kitchen	*"*	333
	White Rabbit	*"*	434
	St Johns	*British, Traditional*	435
	Kipferl	*Mittel-European*	333
	Prawn On The Lawn	*Fish & seafood*	443
	Banners	*International*	345
	8 Hoxton Square	*"*	443
	The Orange Tree	*"*	223
	Primeur	*"*	433
	500	*Italian*	342
	Osteria Tufo	*"*	453
	Pizzeria Oregano	*"*	443

	San Daniele	"	343
	Vinoteca	*Mediterranean*	234
	Café del Parc	*Spanish*	543
	Camino	"	333
	Trangallan	"	544
	Popeseye	*Steaks & grills*	342
	Toff's	*Fish & chips*	432
	Two Brothers	"	332
	Vintage Salt	"	443
	Sweet Thursday	*Pizza*	333
	Le Coq	*Chicken*	232
	Yipin China	*Chinese*	221
	Dishoom	*Indian*	434
	Roots at N1	"	553
	Zaffrani	"	322
	Isarn	*Thai*	432
	Yum Yum	"	344
£35+	Le Sacré-Coeur	*French*	334
	Vrisaki	*Greek*	332
	Pizzeria Pappagone	*Italian*	344
	Rugoletta	"	333
	Bar Esteban	*Spanish*	534
	La Bota	"	334
	MEATLiquor Islington	*Burgers, etc*	324
	Il Bacio	*Pizza*	333
	Fabrizio	"	242
	Rossopomodoro	"	222
	Bird Islington	*Chicken*	332
	Gallipoli	*Turkish*	343
	Mangal II	"	432
	Little Georgia Café	*Georgian*	334
	Delhi Grill	*Indian*	443
	Indian Rasoi	"	433
	Rasa Travancore	*Indian, Southern*	433
£30+	Le Mercury	*French*	234
	La Porchetta Pizzeria	*Italian*	233
	Meat Mission	*Burgers, etc*	334
	Olympus Fish	*Fish & chips*	452
	Durum Ocakbasi	*Turkish*	322
	Gem	"	444
	Gökyüzü	"	433
	Izgara	"	322
	Jashan	*Indian*	542
	Atari-Ya	*Japanese*	532
	Salvation In Noodles	*Vietnamese*	322
£25+	Chriskitch	*British, Modern*	442
	Afghan Kitchen	*Afghani*	421
	Abi Ruchi	*Indian*	442
	Rani	"	322

	Dotori	*Korean*	432
£20+	Max's Sandwich Shop	*Sandwiches, cakes, etc*	422
£15+	Friends of Ours	*Australian*	442
	Piebury Corner	*British, Traditional*	433
	Chilango	*Mexican/TexMex*	332
£10+	Five Guys Islington	*Burgers, etc*	222
	Indian Veg	*Indian*	433

SOUTH

South Bank (SE1)

Price	Restaurant	Cuisine	Ratings
£100+	Story	British, Modern	543
£80+	Oblix	American	224
	Aqua Shard	British, Modern	114
	Oxo Tower (Rest')	"	111
	Le Pont de la Tour	"	224
	Ting	International	224
	Hutong	Chinese	224
£70+	Skylon	British, Modern	122
	Roast	British, Traditional	222
	La Barca	Italian	232
	Oxo Tower (Brass')	Mediterranean	112
£60+	Sea Containers	British, Modern	233
	Skylon Grill	"	113
	The Swan at the Globe	"	212
	Tentazioni	Italian	223
£50+	Albion	British, Modern	122
	Elliot's Café	"	223
	The Garrison	"	333
	House Restaurant	"	232
	Magdalen	"	443
	Menier Chocolate Factory	"	123
	RSJ	"	332
	Tate Modern (Level 7)	"	214
	Union Street Café	"	222
	Waterloo Bar & Kitchen	"	222
	The Anchor & Hope	British, Traditional	433
	Butlers W'f Chop-house	"	233
	fish!	Fish & seafood	322
	Wright Brothers	"	443
	Champor-Champor	Fusion	334
	Village East	"	333
	Brigade	International	233
	Rabot 1745	"	223
	Vivat Bacchus	"	222
	Zucca	Italian	443
	Baltic	Polish	333
	Pizarro	Spanish	344
	Archduke Wine Bar	Steaks & grills	222
£40+	Blueprint Café	British, Modern	235
	Edwins	"	333
	40 Maltby Street	"	434
	The Green Room	"	222

 FSA Ratings: from 1 (Poor) to 5 (Exceptional)

	Canteen	*British, Traditional*	221
	Applebee's Café	*Fish & seafood*	443
	Boro Bistro	*French*	333
	Casse-Croute	*"*	444
	The Rooftop Café	*International*	335
	Antico	*Italian*	343
	Camino	*Spanish*	333
	José	*"*	555
	Meson don Felipe	*"*	223
	Tapas Brindisa	*"*	333
	Arabica Bar and Kitchen	*Lebanese*	323
	Tas Pide	*Turkish*	233
	Bengal Clipper	*Indian*	322
£35+	The Table	*British, Modern*	333
	Pulia	*Italian*	– – –
	Ceru	*Mediterranean*	333
	Gourmet Pizza Co.	*Pizza*	333
	Caffé Vergnano	*Sandwiches, cakes, etc*	223
£30+	Vapiano	*Italian*	322
	Mar I Terra	*Spanish*	232
	El Vergel	*South American*	444
	Tonkotsu Bankside	*Japanese*	443
£25+	Masters Super Fish	*Fish & chips*	422
	Kitchen	*Sandwiches, cakes, etc*	222
£20+	Konditor & Cook	*Sandwiches, cakes, etc*	332
£10+	Monmouth Coffee Co	*Sandwiches, cakes, etc*	554

Greenwich, Lewisham, Dulwich & Blackheath (All SE postcodes, except SE1)

£60+	Craft London	*British, Modern*	224
	Lobster Pot	*Fish & seafood*	433
£50+	The Camberwell Arms	*British, Modern*	433
	Chapters	*"*	332
	Franklins	*"*	434
	The Palmerston	*"*	433
	Rivington Grill	*"*	333
	Buenos Aires Café	*Argentinian*	343
	Babur	*Indian*	554
	Yama Momo	*Japanese*	433
£40+	The Crooked Well	*British, Modern*	344
	Inside	*"*	441

Price	Restaurant	Cuisine	Ratings
	The Lido Café	"	3 3 4
	Peckham Refreshment Rms	"	3 2 3
	Brasserie Toulouse-Lautrec	*French*	3 3 3
	Toasted	"	2 3 3
	Joanna's	*International*	3 3 4
	Tulse Hill Hotel	"	3 3 3
	The Yellow House	"	3 3 2
	Artusi	*Italian*	4 3 2
	Lorenzo	"	2 2 3
	Peckham Bazaar	*Mediterranean*	4 4 4
	Angels & Gypsies	*Spanish*	3 3 3
	Cau	*Steaks & grills*	4 3 3
	Bianco43	*Pizza*	3 2 2
	Ganapati	*Indian*	5 4 4
	Kennington Tandoori	"	3 3 3
	Sticks'n'Sushi	*Japanese*	3 3 3
£35+	The Lord Northbrook	*British, Traditional*	4 4 4
	Pedler	*Fusion*	3 2 4
	Le Querce	*Italian*	4 4 3
	The Sea Cow	*Fish & chips*	3 3 2
	Rocca Di Papa	*Pizza*	2 3 4
	Yalla Yalla	*Lebanese*	3 3 4
	Dragon Castle	*Chinese*	3 3 2
	Everest Inn	*Indian*	4 5 3
	Tandoori Nights	"	4 3 3
	The Begging Bowl	*Thai*	3 3 3
£30+	The Gowlett	*Pizza*	4 3 4
	Zaibatsu	*Japanese*	4 4 2
£25+	Rox Burger	*Burgers, etc*	4 3 3
	Mamma Dough	*Pizza*	3 3 3
	FM Mangal	*Turkish*	3 2 2
£20+	Silk Road	*Chinese*	5 2 2
	Café East	*Vietnamese*	4 2 2
£10+	Monmouth Coffee Company	*Sandwiches, cakes, etc*	5 5 4
£5+	Kappacasein	*Sandwiches, cakes, etc*	5 3 2

Battersea, Brixton, Clapham, Wandsworth Barnes, Putney & Wimbledon (All SW postcodes south of the river)

Price	Restaurant	Cuisine	Ratings
£60+	Hotel du Vin	*British, Modern*	2 3 3
	Chez Bruce	"	5 5 4
	Trinity	"	5 5 4
	The White Onion	*French*	4 4 3

	London House	*International*	332
	Enoteca Turi	*Italian*	443
	Riva	*"*	442
£50+	Abbeville Kitchen	*British, Modern*	333
	The Brown Dog	*"*	334
	Claude's Kitchen	*"*	444
	Lamberts	*"*	554
	The Lucky Pig Fulham	*"*	– – –
	The Manor	*"*	543
	Olympic Café	*"*	224
	Sonny's Kitchen	*"*	222
	Source	*"*	224
	The Tommy Tucker	*"*	334
	The Victoria	*"*	344
	Fox & Grapes	*British, Traditional*	222
	Soif	*French*	333
	The Light House	*International*	222
	The Ship	*"*	334
	Bibo	*Italian*	443
	Numero Uno	*"*	444
	Alquimia	*Spanish*	342
	Cornish Tiger	*Steaks & grills*	333
	Fulham Wine Rooms	*Sandwiches, cakes, etc*	334
	Good Earth	*Chinese*	332
	Kishmish	*Indian*	443
	Blue Elephant	*Thai*	223
	Suk Saran	*"*	332
£40+	Bodean's	*American*	223
	Red Dog South	*"*	323
	Bistro Union	*British, Modern*	343
	Brunswick House Café	*"*	225
	Counter	*"*	222
	The Dairy	*"*	543
	The Depot	*"*	225
	Earl Spencer	*"*	423
	Emile's	*"*	342
	Hood	*"*	442
	Manuka Kitchen	*"*	444
	The Prince Of Wales	*"*	434
	The Tree House	*"*	333
	Wimsey's	*"*	333
	Canton Arms	*British, Traditional*	324
	Jolly Gardners	*"*	433
	Augustine Kitchen	*French*	341
	Bellevue Rendez-Vous	*"*	333
	Bistrò by Shot	*Fusion*	343
	Queenswood	*"*	223
	Annie's	*International*	235
	The Plough	*"*	344
	Buona Sera	*Italian*	333

	Donna Margherita	"	433
	Ost. Antica Bologna	"	433
	Pizza Metro	"	432
	Sapori Sardi	"	442
	The Bobbin	*Mediterranean*	343
	The Fox & Hounds	"	444
	Brindisa Food Rooms	*Spanish*	333
	Gremio de Brixton	"	324
	Lola Rojo	"	434
	Butcher & Grill	*Steaks & grills*	223
	Cau	"	433
	Naughty Piglets	"	452
	Popeseye	"	342
	Fish Club	*Fish & chips*	422
	Indian Zilla	*Indian*	332
	Kricket	"	– – –
	Ma Goa	"	442
	Sticks'n'Sushi	*Japanese*	333
	Tsunami	"	533
£35+	Gazette	*French*	244
	MOMMI	*Fusion*	– – –
	Brew	*International*	223
	Fish in a Tie	*Mediterranean*	243
	Haché	*Burgers, etc*	334
	Eco	*Pizza*	224
	Rossopomodoro	"	222
	Dalchini	*Chinese*	342
	Indian Moment	*Indian*	343
	Hashi	*Japanese*	443
	Cah-Chi	*Korean*	332
	The Banana Tree Canteen	*Pan-Asian*	222
£30+	Fields	*British, Modern*	– – –
	Boqueria	*Spanish*	344
	Brady's	*Fish & chips*	333
	Al Forno	*Pizza*	244
	Chicken & Egg Shop	*Chicken*	344
	Meza Trinity Road	*Lebanese*	532
	Indian Ocean	*Indian*	453
	Hare & Tortoise	*Pan-Asian*	323
	The Pepper Tree	*Thai*	333
	Talad Thai	"	431
	Mien Tay	*Vietnamese*	311
£25+	The Joint	*American*	532
	Dip & Flip	*Burgers, etc*	422
	Mamma Dough	*Pizza*	333
	Orange Pekoe	*Sandwiches, cakes, etc*	344
	Faanoos	*Persian*	223
	Radha Krishna Bhaven	*Indian*	332
	Sree Krishna	"	432

	Mirch Masala SW17	*Pakistani*	521
	Awesome Thai	*Thai*	342
	Kaosarn	*"*	343
£20+	Boom Burger	*Burgers, etc*	332
	Kerbisher & Malt	*Fish & chips*	332
	Apollo Banana Leaf	*Indian*	421
	Hot Stuff	*"*	442
	Lahore Karahi	*Pakistani*	412
	Lahore Kebab House	*"*	412
£15+	Grind Coffee Bar	*Sandwiches, cakes, etc*	424
	Jaffna House	*Indian*	542
£10+	Flotsam and Jetsam	*Australian*	434
	Dirty Burger	*Burgers, etc*	322
	Milk	*Sandwiches, cakes, etc*	444

Outer western suburbs
Kew, Richmond, Twickenham, Teddington

£70+	The Glasshouse	*British, Modern*	443
	Petersham Nurseries	*"*	224
£60+	The Bingham	*British, Modern*	324
	The Dysart Petersham	*"*	443
	Petersham Hotel	*"*	345
	Al Boccon di'vino	*Italian*	445
£50+	Linnea	*British, Modern*	443
	A Cena	*Italian*	444
£40+	Jackson & Rye Richmond	*American*	123
	La Buvette	*French*	334
	Ma Cuisine	*"*	222
	Le Salon Privé	*"*	345
	Bacco	*Italian*	343
	Pizzeria Rustica	*Pizza*	443
	Matsuba	*Japanese*	443
£35+	Canta Napoli	*Italian*	332

EAST

Smithfield & Farringdon (EC1)

Price	Restaurant	Cuisine	Ratings
£90+	The Clove Club	*British, Modern*	433
£70+	Club Gascon	*French*	333
	Smiths (Top Floor)	*Steaks & grills*	334
£60+	Bird of Smithfield	*British, Modern*	223
	Chiswell Street Dining Rms	"	222
	The Jugged Hare	"	323
	St John	*British, Traditional*	543
	Bleeding Heart Restaurant	*French*	335
	Moro	*Spanish*	543
£50+	The Modern Pantry	*British, Modern*	334
	Tonic & Remedy	"	– – –
	Bonnie Gull Seafood Bar	*Fish & seafood*	332
	Café du Marché	*French*	334
	Fabrizio	*Italian*	442
	Foxlow	*Steaks & grills*	333
	Hix	"	333
	Smiths (Dining Rm)	"	222
	Sushi Tetsu	*Japanese*	553
£40+	Bodean's	*American*	223
	Granger & Co	*Australian*	324
	Blackfoot	*British, Modern*	333
	Caravan	"	323
	Vinoteca	"	234
	The Fox and Anchor	*British, Traditional*	334
	The Quality Chop House	"	353
	Café Pistou	*French*	323
	Comptoir Gascon	"	333
	Enoteca Rabezzana	*Italian*	223
	Polpo	"	223
	Santore	"	433
	Ibérica	*Spanish*	334
	The Gate	*Vegetarian*	423
	Burger & Lobster	*Burgers, etc*	323
	Workshop Coffee Holborn	*Sandwiches, cakes, etc*	344
	Ceviche Old St	*Peruvian*	344
£35+	Lantana Café	*Australian*	333
	Apulia	*Italian*	332
	Morito	*Spanish*	432
	Amico Bio	*Vegetarian*	232
	Pham Sushi	*Japanese*	531
	Tajima Tei	"	433
	On The Bab	*Korean*	432

 FSA Ratings: from 1 (Poor) to 5 (Exceptional)

	Restaurant	Cuisine	Ratings
	Banana Tree Canteen	*Pan-Asian*	222
	Cây Tre	*Vietnamese*	323
£30+	Smiths (Ground Floor)	*British, Modern*	223
	Fish Central	*Fish & seafood*	332
	Cellar Gascon	*French*	333
	Kolossi Grill	*Greek*	343
	La Porchetta Pizzeria	*Italian*	233
	The Eagle	*Mediterranean*	435
	Bone Daddies	*Japanese*	444
£25+	The Little Bay	*Mediterranean*	235
£20+	Kerbisher & Malt	*Fish & chips*	332
£15+	Department of Coffee	*Sandwiches, cakes, etc*	445
	Daddy Donkey	*Mexican/TexMex*	432
	Yum Bun	*Japanese*	52–
£10+	Nusa Kitchen	*Sandwiches, cakes, etc*	443
	Prufrock Coffee	"	344
	Chifafa	*Turkish*	433

The City (EC2, EC3, EC4)

	Restaurant	Cuisine	Ratings
£70+	City Social	*British, Modern*	335
	Angler	*Fish & seafood*	444
	M Raw Threadneedle Street	"	433
	Sweetings	"	223
	Coq d'Argent	*French*	233
	Lutyens	"	222
	Sauterelle	"	333
	L'Anima	*Italian*	333
	M Grill Threadneedle Street	*Steaks & grills*	433
	HKK	*Chinese*	543
	Yauatcha City	"	523
	Sushisamba	*Japanese*	335
£60+	The Botanist	*British, Modern*	223
	Bread Street Kitchen	"	111
	The Chancery	"	443
	Darwin Brasserie	"	223
	The Don	"	333
	Duck & Waffle	"	225
	High Timber	"	223
	The Mercer	"	222
	I Lombard Street	"	233
	3 South Place	"	323
	The White Swan	"	343

Price	Restaurant	Cuisine	Ratings
	Chamberlain's	*Fish & seafood*	343
	Caravaggio	*Italian*	332
	Gatti's City Point	*"*	343
	Manicomio	*"*	223
	Boisdale of Bishopsgate	*Scottish*	222
	Eyre Brothers	*Spanish*	533
	Barbecoa	*Steaks & grills*	121
	Goodman City	*"*	443
	Hawksmoor	*"*	333
	Vanilla Black	*Vegetarian*	432
	Chinese Cricket Club	*Chinese*	431
£50+	The Hoxton Grill	*American*	234
	Gin Joint	*British, Modern*	233
	Merchants Tavern	*"*	334
	Modern Pantry	*"*	334
	Northbank	*"*	344
	Princess of Shoreditch	*"*	344
	Rivington Grill	*"*	333
	The Sign of The Don	*"*	244
	Paternoster Chop House	*British, Traditional*	332
	The Royal Exchange	*French*	224
	28-50	*"*	334
	Vivat Bacchus	*International*	222
	Taberna Etrusca	*Italian*	244
	José Pizarro	*Spanish*	443
	The Jones Family Project	*Steaks & grills*	243
	New Street Grill	*"*	233
	The Tramshed	*"*	223
	Cinnamon Kitchen	*Indian*	422
	Mint Leaf	*"*	332
	City Miyama	*Japanese*	342
£40+	Bodean's	*American*	223
	The Anthologist	*British, Modern*	223
	Bad Egg	*"*	433
	Café Below	*"*	334
	The Trading House	*"*	– – –
	George & Vulture	*British, Traditional*	225
	Fish Market	*Fish & seafood*	333
	Orpheus	*"*	431
	L'Anima Café	*Italian*	444
	Rucoletta	*"*	432
	Rocket Bishopgate	*Mediterranean*	333
	Camino Blackfriars	*Spanish*	333
	Relais de Venise L'Entrecôte	*Steaks & grills*	322
	Burger & Lobster	*Burgers, etc*	323
	Vintage Salt	*Fish & chips*	443
	Shoryu Ramen	*Japanese*	422
£35+	Simpson's Tavern	*British, Traditional*	245
	Restaurant de Paul	*French*	443

	Haché	*Burgers, etc*	334
	Caffé Vergnano	*Sandwiches, cakes, etc*	223
	Haz	*Turkish*	232
	Beer and Buns	*Japanese*	– – –
	K10, Appold Street	*"*	332
£30+	The Wine Library	*International*	144
	Hare & Tortoise	*Pan-Asian*	323
£25+	Hilliard	*British, Modern*	443
	Bibimbap	*Korean*	322
£20+	Patty and Bun	*Burgers, etc*	433
	Konditor & Cook	*Sandwiches, cakes, etc*	332
£15+	Street Kitchen (van)	*British, Modern*	33–
	Chilango	*Mexican/TexMex*	332
	City Càphê	*Vietnamese*	522
£10+	Coco Di Mama	*Italian*	342
	Nusa Kitchen	*Middle Eastern*	443
£5+	Pilpel	*Middle Eastern*	442

East End & Docklands (All E postcodes)

£80+	Galvin La Chapelle	*French*	445
	Typing Room	*International*	543
	Roka	*Japanese*	433
£70+	Plateau	*French*	233
£60+	Beach Blanket Babylon	*British, Modern*	113
	The Boundary	*"*	335
	Lyle's	*"*	553
	Tom's Kitchen	*"*	121
	Boisdale of Canary Wharf	*Scottish*	333
	Goodman	*Steaks & grills*	443
	Hawksmoor	*"*	333
£50+	Big Easy	*American*	223
	One Sixty Smokehouse	*"*	443
	The Gun	*British, Modern*	324
	Hoi Polloi	*"*	234
	Jones & Sons	*"*	444
	The Morgan Arms	*"*	433
	The Narrow	*"*	113
	One Canada Square	*"*	222

	The Richmond	"	4 3 3
	Rochelle Canteen	"	4 3 3
	Smith's Of Ongar	"	3 3 4
	Albion	*British, Traditional*	1 2 2
	Bumpkin	"	2 2 2
	The Marksman	"	– – –
	St John Bread & Wine	"	5 3 3
	Wright Brothers	*Fish & seafood*	4 4 3
	Brawn	*French*	5 4 4
	Blixen	*International*	3 2 3
	Mission	"	2 3 4
	Il Bordello	*Italian*	3 5 4
	Buen Ayre	*Argentinian*	5 3 3
	Ottolenghi	*Israeli*	4 2 2
	Café Spice Namaste	*Indian*	4 4 3
£40+	Balans	*British, Modern*	2 3 3
	Beagle	"	4 3 3
	Cafe Football	"	2 3 3
	The Culpepper	"	4 3 4
	The Empress	"	4 4 4
	Paradise Garage	"	– – –
	Resident Of Paradise Row	"	– – –
	Canteen	*British, Traditional*	2 2 1
	The Grapes	*Fish & seafood*	2 3 5
	Jago	*Fusion*	3 2 3
	Hungry Donkey	*Greek*	– – –
	Verden	*International*	4 4 4
	Lardo & Lardo Bebè	*Italian*	3 3 4
	Obicà	"	3 3 2
	Rotorino	"	3 3 3
	Verdi's	"	4 4 3
	Rocket Canary Wharf	*Mediterranean*	3 3 3
	Corner Room	*Portuguese*	3 4 4
	Taberna Do Mercado	"	4 3 3
	Bravas	*Spanish*	3 3 3
	Ibérica	"	3 3 4
	Cau	*Steaks & grills*	4 3 3
	Hill & Szrok	"	5 4 4
	Relais de Venise L'Entrecôte	"	3 2 2
	Ark Fish	*Fish & chips*	4 4 2
	Pizza East	*Pizza*	4 3 4
	Berber & Q	*Middle Eastern*	4 3 4
	Royal China	*Chinese*	4 1 2
	Sichuan Folk	"	4 4 2
	Yi-Ban	"	4 3 2
	Dishoom	*Indian*	4 3 4
	Sticks'n'Sushi	*Japanese*	3 3 3
	Viet Grill	*Vietnamese*	4 3 3
£35+	Eat 17	*British, Modern*	3 4 2
	Sager & Wilde	"	3 4 4

Price	Restaurant	Cuisine	Rating
	Provender	*French*	443
	Amaru	*Fusion*	— — —
	Eat 17	*International*	342
	Copita Del Mercado	*Spanish*	432
	Bird	*Chicken*	332
	Andina	*Peruvian*	344
	Haz	*Turkish*	232
	Shanghai	*Chinese*	323
	Little Georgia Café	*Georgian*	334
	Ippudo London	*Japanese*	232
	Rosa's Soho	*Thai*	432
	Som Saa	*"*	533
£30+	Luppolo	*Italian*	— — —
	Caboose	*Burgers, etc*	— — —
	Chick 'n' Sours	*Chicken*	424
	Chicken Shop & Dirty Burger	*"*	344
	DF Mexico	*Mexican/TexMex*	433
	Mangal 1	*Turkish*	544
	Tonkotsu East	*Japanese*	443
	Tayyabs	*Pakistani*	423
	Mien Tay	*Vietnamese*	311
	Sông Quê	*"*	212
£25+	Poppies	*Fish & chips*	434
	Gourmet San	*Chinese*	421
	Needoo	*Pakistani*	422
£20+	Shake Shack	*Burgers, etc*	322
	Lahore Kebab House	*Pakistani*	412
£15+	E Pellicci	*Italian*	345
	Bleecker Street Burger	*Burgers, etc*	432
	Chilango	*Mexican/TexMex*	332
£10+	Dirty Burger Shoreditch	*Burgers, etc*	322
	The Rib Man	*"*	53-
£5+	Brick Lane Beigel Bake	*Sandwiches, cakes, etc*	421
	Pilpel	*Middle Eastern*	442

MAPS

MAP 1 – LONDON OVERVIEW

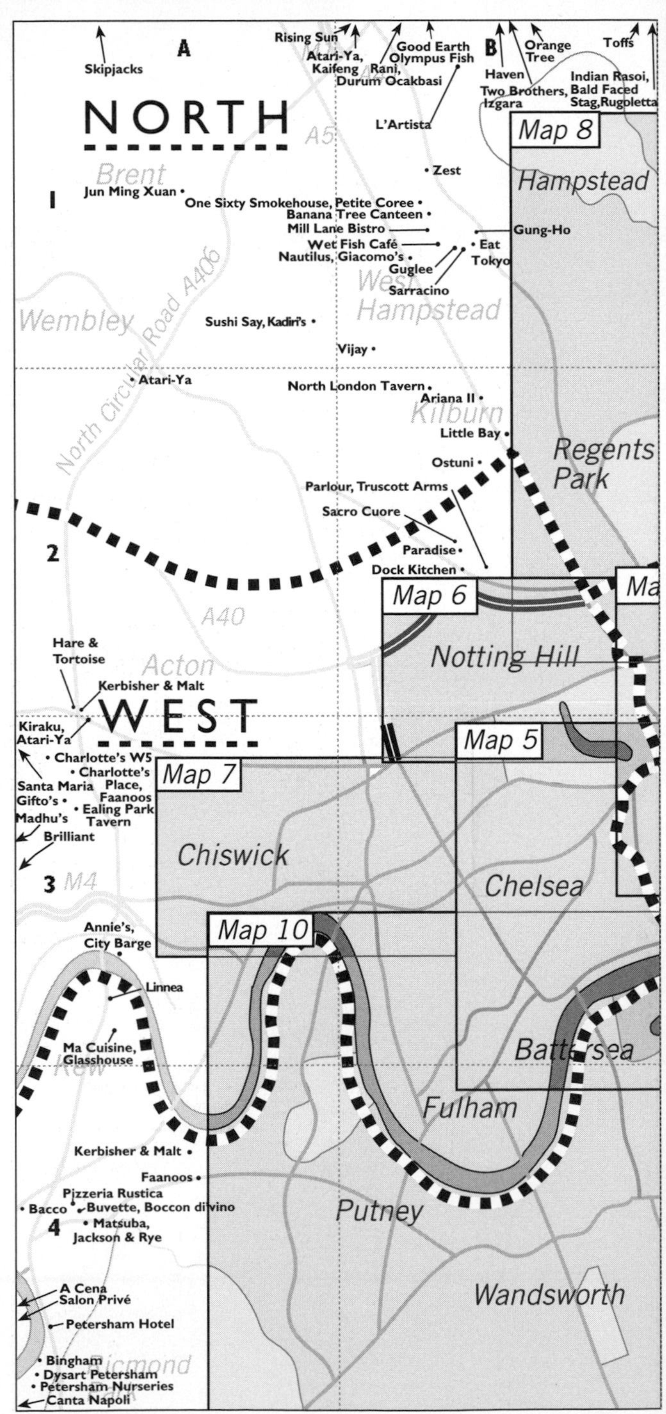

A
B
NORTH
WEST
1
2
3
4
Skipjacks
Rising Sun
Atari-Ya, Kaifeng
Rani, Durum Ocakbasi
Good Earth Olympus Fish
Haven
Orange Tree
Toffs
Two Brothers, Izgara
Indian Rasoi, Bald Faced Stag, Rugoletta
L'Artista
Map 8
Hampstead
Brent
Zest
Jun Ming Xuan
One Sixty Smokehouse, Petite Coree
Banana Tree Canteen
Mill Lane Bistro
Gung-Ho
Wet Fish Café
Eat Tokyo
Nautilus, Giacomo's
Guglee
Sarracino
West Hampstead
North Circular Road A406
Wembley
Sushi Say, Kadiri's
Vijay
Atari-Ya
North London Tavern
Ariana II
Kilburn
Little Bay
Regents Park
Ostuni
Parlour, Truscott Arms
Sacro Cuore
Paradise
Dock Kitchen
Map 6
A40
Notting Hill
Hare & Tortoise
Acton
Kerbisher & Malt
Kiraku, Atari-Ya
Map 5
Charlotte's W5
Charlotte's Place, Faanoos
Map 7
Santa Maria
Gifto's
Ealing Park Tavern
Madhu's
Brilliant
Chiswick
Chelsea
M4
Annie's, City Barge
Map 10
Linnea
Ma Cuisine, Glasshouse
Kew
Battersea
Fulham
Kerbisher & Malt
Faanoos
Pizzeria Rustica
Bacco
Buvette, Boccon di vino
Putney
Matsuba, Jackson & Rye
A Cena
Salon Privé
Wandsworth
Petersham Hotel
Bingham
Dysart Petersham
Petersham Nurseries
Canta Napoli
A5

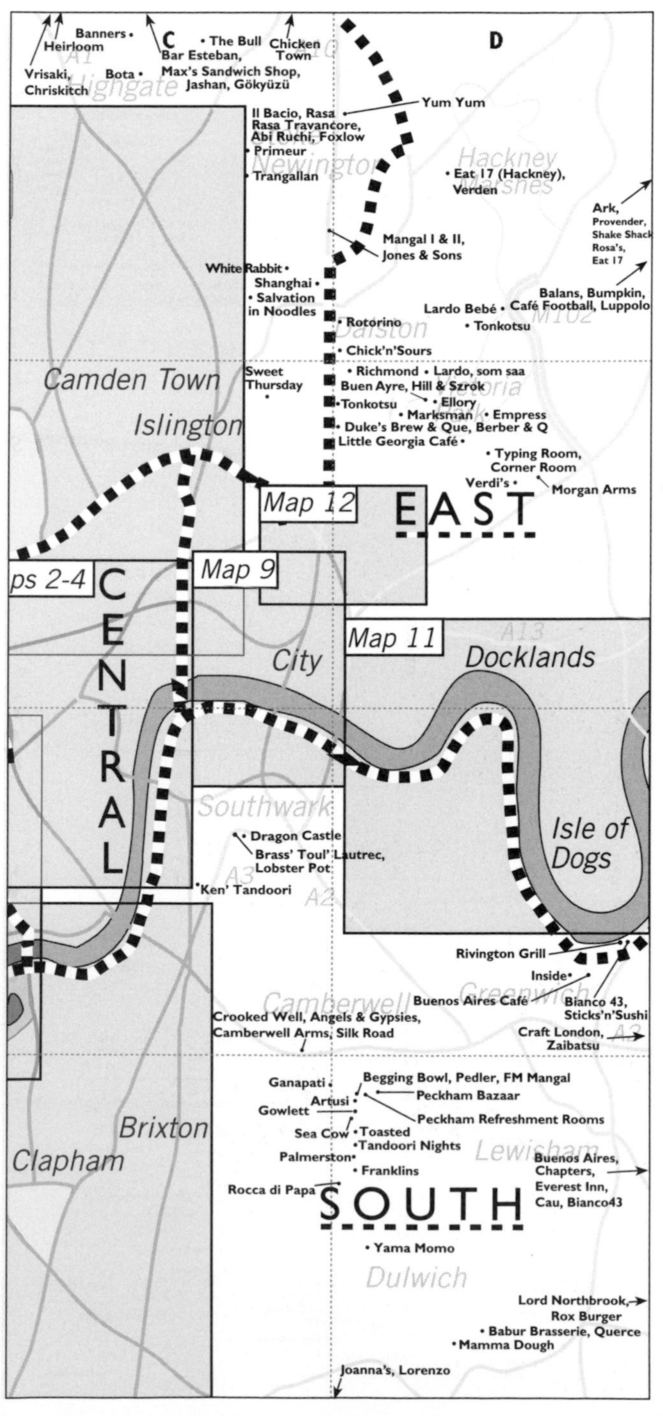
Banners
Heirloom
Vrisaki,
Chriskitch
Bota
C
The Bull
Bar Esteban,
Max's Sandwich Shop,
Jashan, Gökyüzü
Chicken
Town
D
Highgate
Yum Yum
Il Bacio, Rasa
Rasa Travancore,
Abi Ruchi, Foxlow
Primeur
Trangallan
Stoke Newington
Hackney Marshes
Eat 17 (Hackney),
Verden
Ark,
Provender,
Shake Shack
Rosa's,
Eat 17
Mangal I & II,
Jones & Sons
White Rabbit
Shanghai
Salvation
in Noodles
Balans, Bumpkin,
Café Football, Luppolo
Lardo Bebé
Rotorino
Dalston
Tonkotsu
Chick'n'Sours
Camden Town
Sweet
Thursday
Richmond
Lardo, som saa
Buen Ayre, Hill & Szrok
Victoria Park
Tonkotsu
Ellory
Marksman
Empress
Islington
Duke's Brew & Que, Berber & Q
Little Georgia Café
Typing Room,
Corner Room
Verdi's
Morgan Arms
Map 12
EAST
Map 9
ps 2-4
CENTRAL
Map 11
City
Docklands
Southwark
Dragon Castle
Brass' Toul' Lautrec,
Lobster Pot
Isle of
Dogs
Ken' Tandoori
Rivington Grill
Inside
Buenos Aires Café
Greenwich
Bianco 43,
Sticks'n'Sushi
Camberwell
Crooked Well, Angels & Gypsies,
Camberwell Arms, Silk Road
Craft London,
Zaibatsu
Ganapati
Begging Bowl, Pedler, FM Mangal
Peckham Bazaar
Artusi
Gowlett
Peckham Refreshment Rooms
Sea Cow
Toasted
Tandoori Nights
Brixton
Clapham
Palmerston
Lewisham
Franklins
Buenos Aires,
Chapters,
Everest Inn,
Cau, Bianco43
Rocca di Papa
SOUTH
Yama Momo
Dulwich
Lord Northbrook,
Rox Burger
Babur Brasserie, Querce
Mamma Dough
Joanna's, Lorenzo

MAP 2 – WEST END OVERVIEW

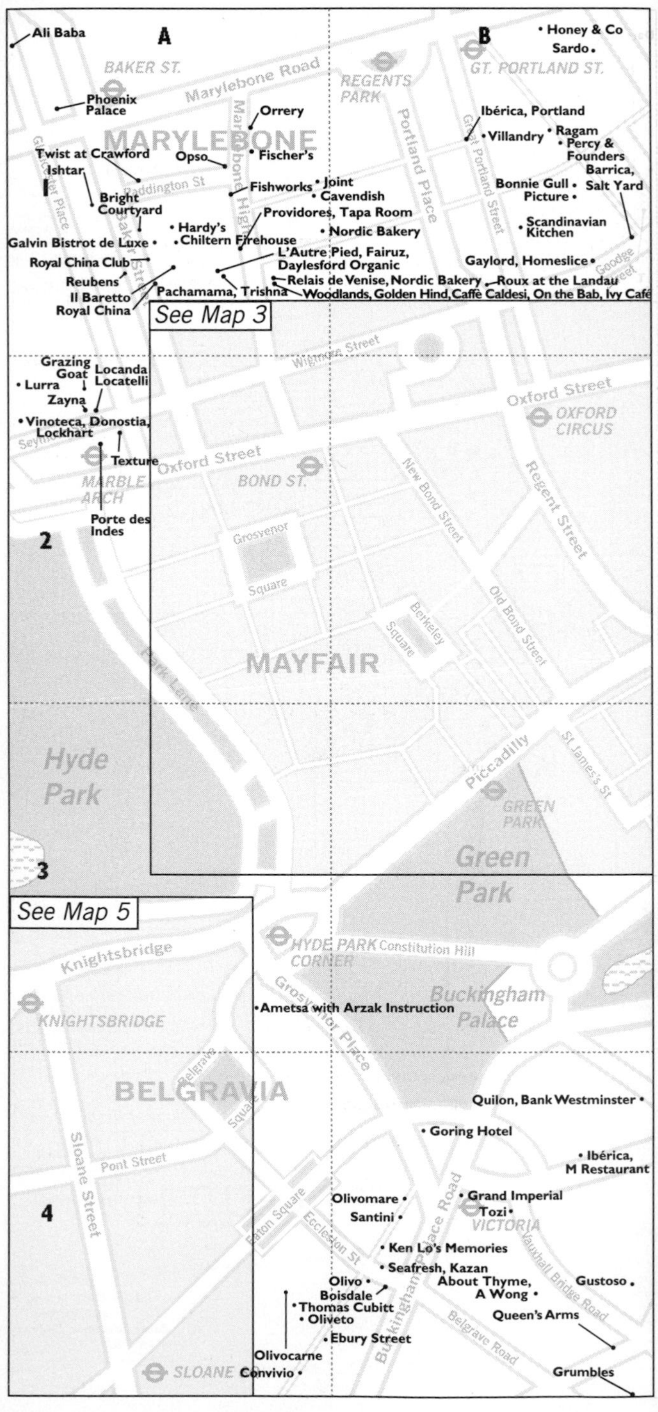

A
B
1
2
3
4
Ali Baba
Honey & Co
Sardo
BAKER ST.
Marylebone Road
REGENTS PARK
GT. PORTLAND ST.
Phoenix Palace
MARYLEBONE
Orrery
Ibérica, Portland
Villandry
Ragam
Percy & Founders
Twist at Crawford
Opso
Fischer's
Ishtar
Barrica, Salt Yard
Bonnie Gull
Picture
Fishworks
Joint
Cavendish
Bright Courtyard
Providores, Tapa Room
Portland Place
Great Portland Street
Scandinavian Kitchen
Hardy's
Chiltern Firehouse
Nordic Bakery
Galvin Bistrot de Luxe
L'Autre Pied, Fairuz, Daylesford Organic
Gaylord, Homeslice
Royal China Club
Reubens
Relais de Venise, Nordic Bakery
Roux at the Landau
Il Baretto
Pachamama, Trishna
Woodlands, Golden Hind, Caffè Caldesi, On the Bab, Ivy Café
Royal China
See Map 3
Grazing Goat
Locanda Locatelli
Lurra
Zayna
Vinoteca, Donostia, Lockhart
Texture
Wigmore Street
Oxford Street
OXFORD CIRCUS
BOND ST.
New Bond Street
Regent Street
MARBLE ARCH
Porte des Indes
Grosvenor Square
Berkeley Square
Old Bond Street
MAYFAIR
Park Lane
Hyde Park
Piccadilly
St James's St
GREEN PARK
Green Park
See Map 5
HYDE PARK CORNER
Constitution Hill
Knightsbridge
Buckingham Palace
Ametsa with Arzak Instruction
KNIGHTSBRIDGE
Grosvenor Place
BELGRAVIA
Belgrave Square
Quilon, Bank Westminster
Goring Hotel
Sloane Street
Pont Street
Ibérica, M Restaurant
Olivomare
Grand Imperial
Santini
Tozi
VICTORIA
Eaton Square
Eccleston St
Ken Lo's Memories
Seafresh, Kazan
Olivo
About Thyme, A Wong
Gustoso
Boisdale
Thomas Cubitt
Oliveto
Queen's Arms
Buckingham Palace Road
Vauxhall Bridge Road
Belgrave Road
Ebury Street
Olivocarne
SLOANE
Convivio
Grumbles

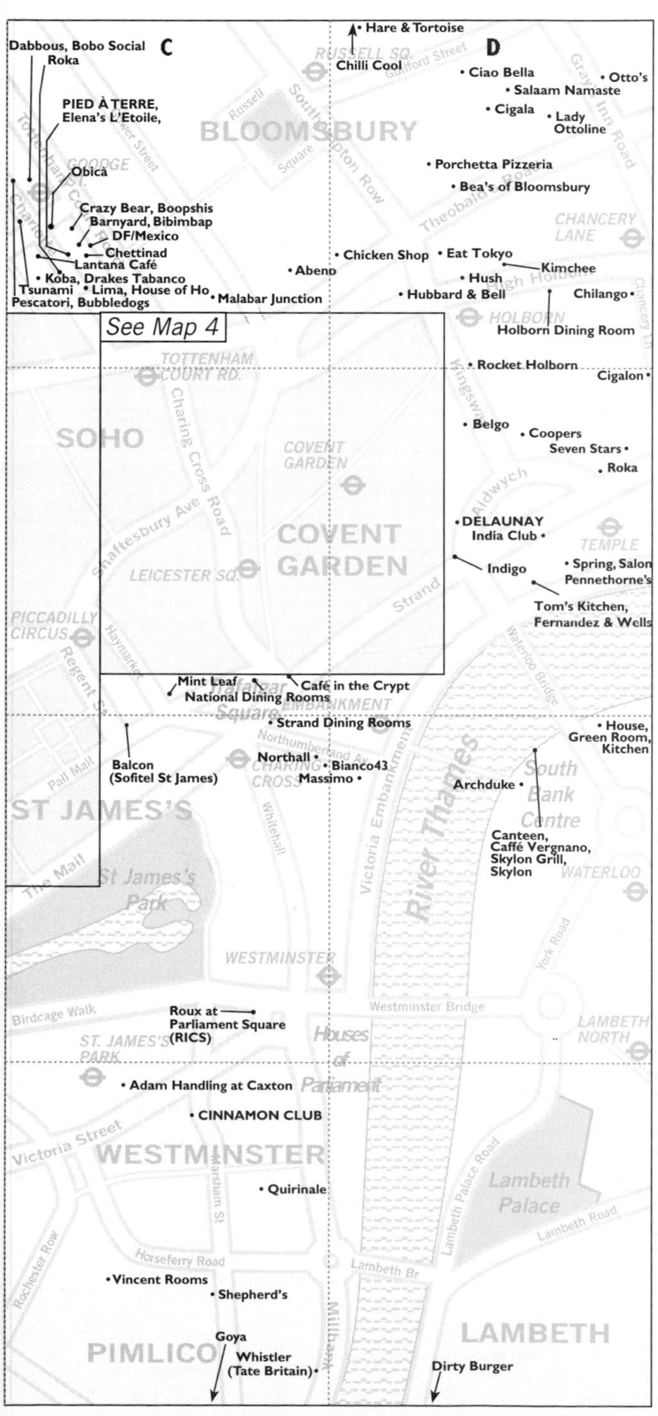

C
D
Hare & Tortoise
Dabbous, Bobo Social
Roka
Chilli Cool
Ciao Bella
Otto's
Salaam Namaste
PIED À TERRE, Elena's L'Etoile,
Cigala
Lady Ottoline
BLOOMSBURY
Obicà
Porchetta Pizzeria
Bea's of Bloomsbury
Crazy Bear, Boopshis
Barnyard, Bibimbap
DF/Mexico
Chettinad
Lantana Café
Koba, Drakes Tabanco
Tsunami
Lima, House of Ho
Pescatori, Bubbledogs
Malabar Junction
Chicken Shop
Eat Tokyo
Abeno
Kimchee
Hush
Hubbard & Bell
Chilango
Holborn Dining Room
See Map 4
Rocket Holborn
Cigalon
SOHO
Belgo
Coopers
Seven Stars
Roka
COVENT GARDEN
DELAUNAY
India Club
Indigo
Spring, Salon
Pennethorne's
Tom's Kitchen, Fernandez & Wells
Mint Leaf
National Dining Rooms
Café in the Crypt
Strand Dining Rooms
House, Green Room, Kitchen
Balcon (Sofitel St James)
Northall
Bianco43
Massimo
Archduke
ST JAMES'S
Canteen, Caffé Vergnano, Skylon Grill, Skylon
WESTMINSTER
Roux at Parliament Square (RICS)
Adam Handling at Caxton
CINNAMON CLUB
WESTMINSTER
Quirinale
Vincent Rooms
Shepherd's
Goya
Whistler (Tate Britain)
Dirty Burger
PIMLICO
LAMBETH

MAP 3 – MAYFAIR, ST JAMES'S & WEST SOHO

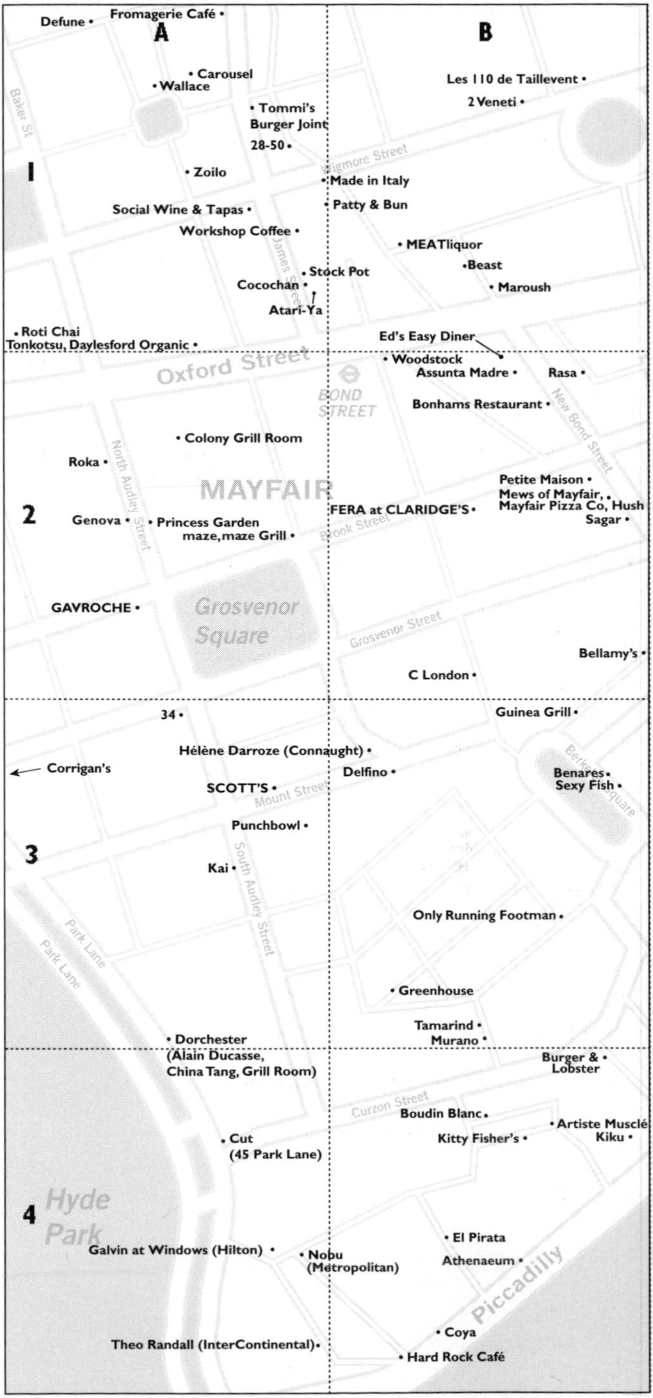

A
B
1
2
3
4

Defune •
Fromagerie Café •
• Carousel
• Wallace
Les 110 de Taillevent •
2 Veneti •
Baker St
• Tommi's Burger Joint
28-50 •
Wigmore Street
• Zoilo
• Made in Italy
• Patty & Bun
Social Wine & Tapas •
Workshop Coffee •
James Street
• MEATliquor
• Beast
• Stock Pot
Cocochan •
Atari-Ya
• Maroush
• Roti Chai
Tonkotsu, Daylesford Organic •
Ed's Easy Diner
Oxford Street
• Woodstock
Assunta Madre •
Rasa •
BOND STREET
Bonhams Restaurant •
New Bond Street
• Colony Grill Room
Roka •
North Audley Street
MAYFAIR
Petite Maison •
Mews of Mayfair, •
Mayfair Pizza Co, Hush
Sagar •
FERA at CLARIDGE'S •
Genova •
• Princess Garden
maze, maze Grill •
Brook Street
GAVROCHE •
Grosvenor Square
Grosvenor Street
Bellamy's •
C London •
34 •
Guinea Grill •
Hélène Darroze (Connaught) •
Corrigan's
Delfino •
Berkeley Square
Benares •
Sexy Fish •
SCOTT'S •
Mount Street
Punchbowl •
Kai •
South Audley Street
Only Running Footman •
Park Lane
Park Lane
• Greenhouse
Tamarind •
Murano •
• Dorchester
(Alain Ducasse, China Tang, Grill Room)
Burger & Lobster •
Curzon Street
Boudin Blanc •
• Artiste Musclé
Kiku •
• Cut
(45 Park Lane)
Kitty Fisher's •
Hyde Park
• El Pirata
Galvin at Windows (Hilton) •
• Nobu
(Metropolitan)
Athenaeum •
Piccadilly
• Coya
Theo Randall (InterContinental) •
• Hard Rock Café

MAP 3 – MAYFAIR, ST JAMES'S & WEST SOHO

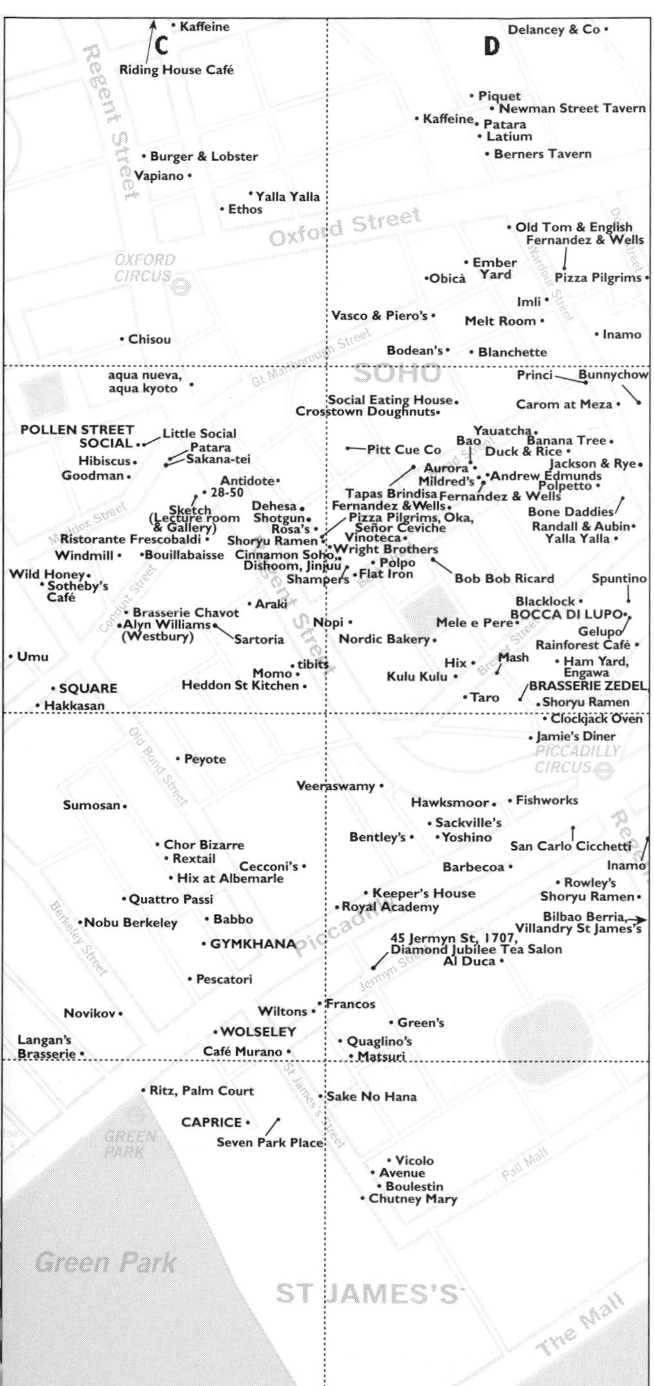

MAP 4 – EAST SOHO, CHINATOWN & COVENT GARDEN

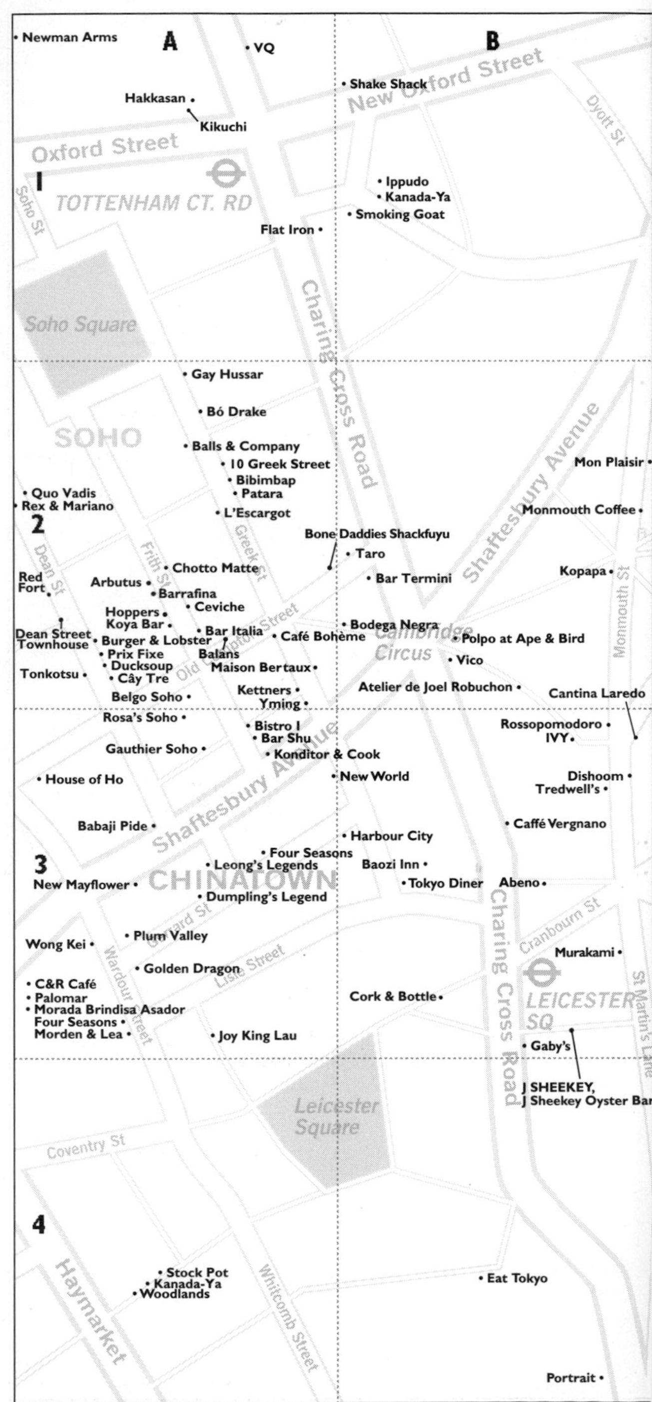
A
B
1
2
3
4
Newman Arms
VQ
Shake Shack
New Oxford Street
Dyott St
Hakkasan
Kikuchi
Oxford Street
TOTTENHAM CT. RD
Soho St
Ippudo
Kanada-Ya
Smoking Goat
Flat Iron
Charing Cross Road
Soho Square
Gay Hussar
Bó Drake
SOHO
Balls & Company
10 Greek Street
Bibimbap
Patara
Shaftesbury Avenue
Mon Plaisir
Quo Vadis
Rex & Mariano
L'Escargot
Monmouth Coffee
Bone Daddies Shackfuyu
Taro
Dean St
Frith St
Greek St
Red Fort
Chotto Matte
Arbutus
Barrafina
Bar Termini
Kopapa
Monmouth St
Ceviche
Hoppers
Koya Bar
Bar Italia
Old Compton Street
Café Bohème
Bodega Negra
Cambridge Circus
Polpo at Ape & Bird
Dean Street Townhouse
Burger & Lobster
Balans
Prix Fixe
Ducksoup
Cây Tre
Maison Bertaux
Vico
Tonkotsu
Belgo Soho
Kettners
Yming
Atelier de Joel Robuchon
Cantina Laredo
Rosa's Soho
Bistro I
Bar Shu
Rossopomodoro
IVY
Gauthier Soho
Konditor & Cook
House of Ho
New World
Dishoom
Tredwell's
Babaji Pide
Shaftesbury Avenue
Caffé Vergnano
Harbour City
Four Seasons
Leong's Legends
Baozi Inn
New Mayflower
CHINATOWN
Tokyo Diner
Abeno
Dumpling's Legend
Gerrard St
Cranbourn St
Wong Kei
Plum Valley
Murakami
Wardour Street
Golden Dragon
Lisle Street
C&R Café
Palomar
Morada Brindisa Asador
Four Seasons
Morden & Lea
Cork & Bottle
LEICESTER SQ
St Martin's Lane
Joy King Lau
Gaby's
J SHEEKEY,
J Sheekey Oyster Bar
Leicester Square
Coventry St
Haymarket
Stock Pot
Kanada-Ya
Woodlands
Whitcomb Street
Eat Tokyo
Portrait

MAP 4 – EAST SOHO, CHINATOWN & COVENT GARDEN

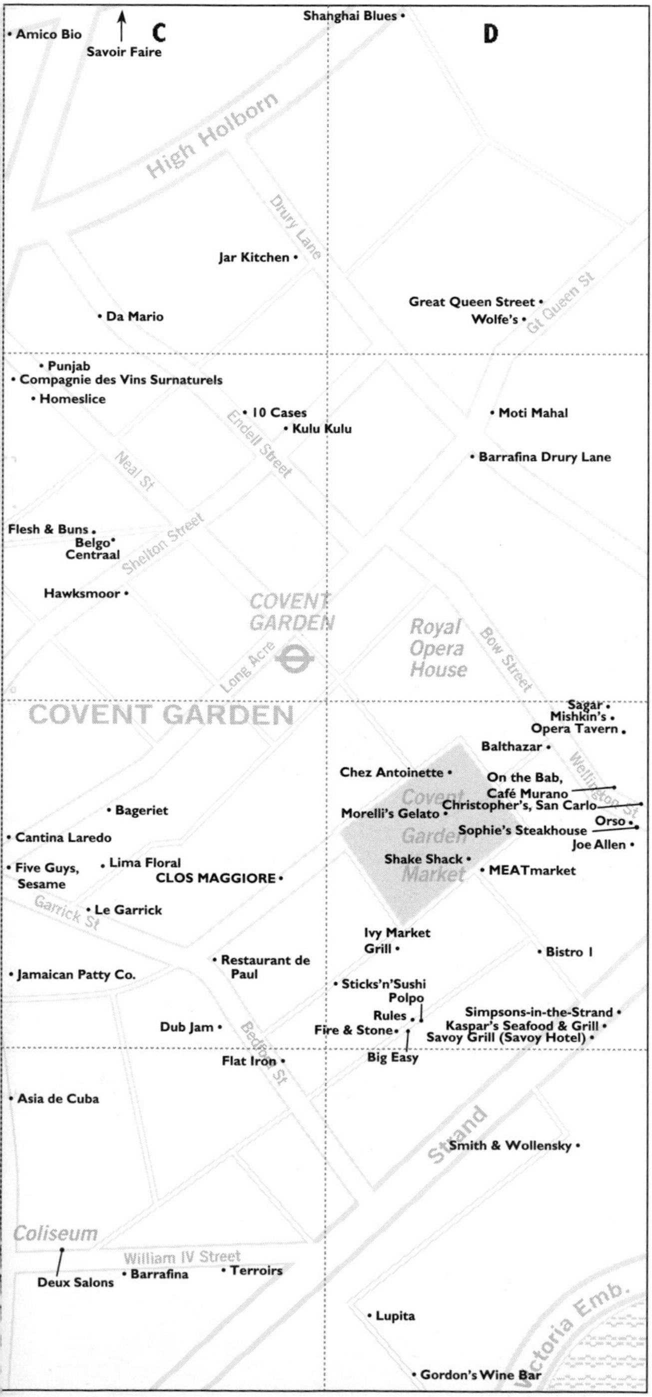

C
D
Amico Bio
Savoir Faire
Shanghai Blues
High Holborn
Drury Lane
Jar Kitchen
Da Mario
Great Queen Street
Wolfe's
Gt Queen St
Punjab
Compagnie des Vins Surnaturels
Homeslice
10 Cases
Kulu Kulu
Endell Street
Moti Mahal
Barrafina Drury Lane
Neal St
Flesh & Buns
Belgo Centraal
Shelton Street
Hawksmoor
COVENT GARDEN
Royal Opera House
Bow Street
Long Acre
COVENT GARDEN
Sagar
Mishkin's
Opera Tavern
Balthazar
Chez Antoinette
On the Bab,
Café Murano
Wellington St
Christopher's, San Carlo
Orso
Morelli's Gelato
Covent Garden Market
Sophie's Steakhouse
Joe Allen
Bageriet
Cantina Laredo
Five Guys, Sesame
Lima Floral
CLOS MAGGIORE
Shake Shack
MEATmarket
Garrick St
Le Garrick
Ivy Market Grill
Bistro 1
Jamaican Patty Co.
Restaurant de Paul
Sticks'n'Sushi
Polpo
Rules
Simpsons-in-the-Strand
Kaspar's Seafood & Grill
Savoy Grill (Savoy Hotel)
Dub Jam
Bedford St
Fire & Stone
Big Easy
Flat Iron
Asia de Cuba
Strand
Smith & Wollensky
Coliseum
William IV Street
Deux Salons
Barrafina
Terroirs
Lupita
Victoria Emb.
Gordon's Wine Bar

MAP 5 – KNIGHTSBRIDGE, CHELSEA & SOUTH KENSINGTON

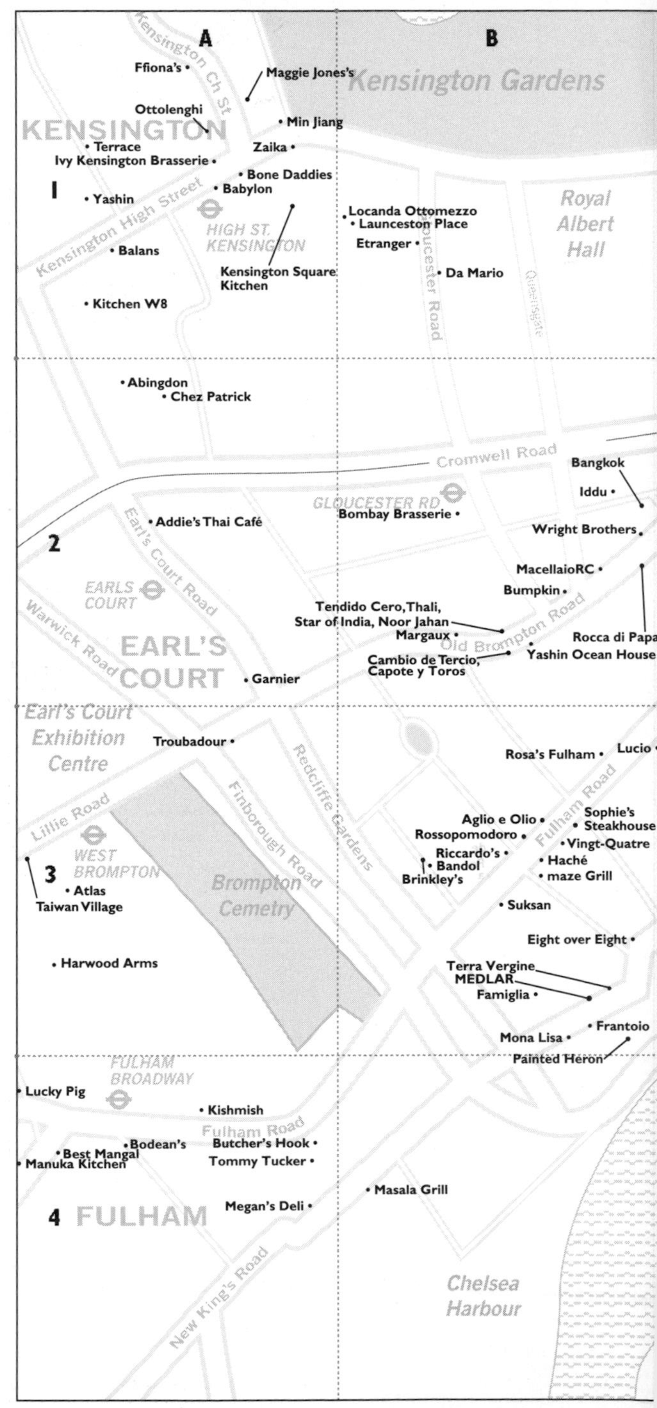

MAP 5 – KNIGHTSBRIDGE, CHELSEA & SOUTH KENSINGTON

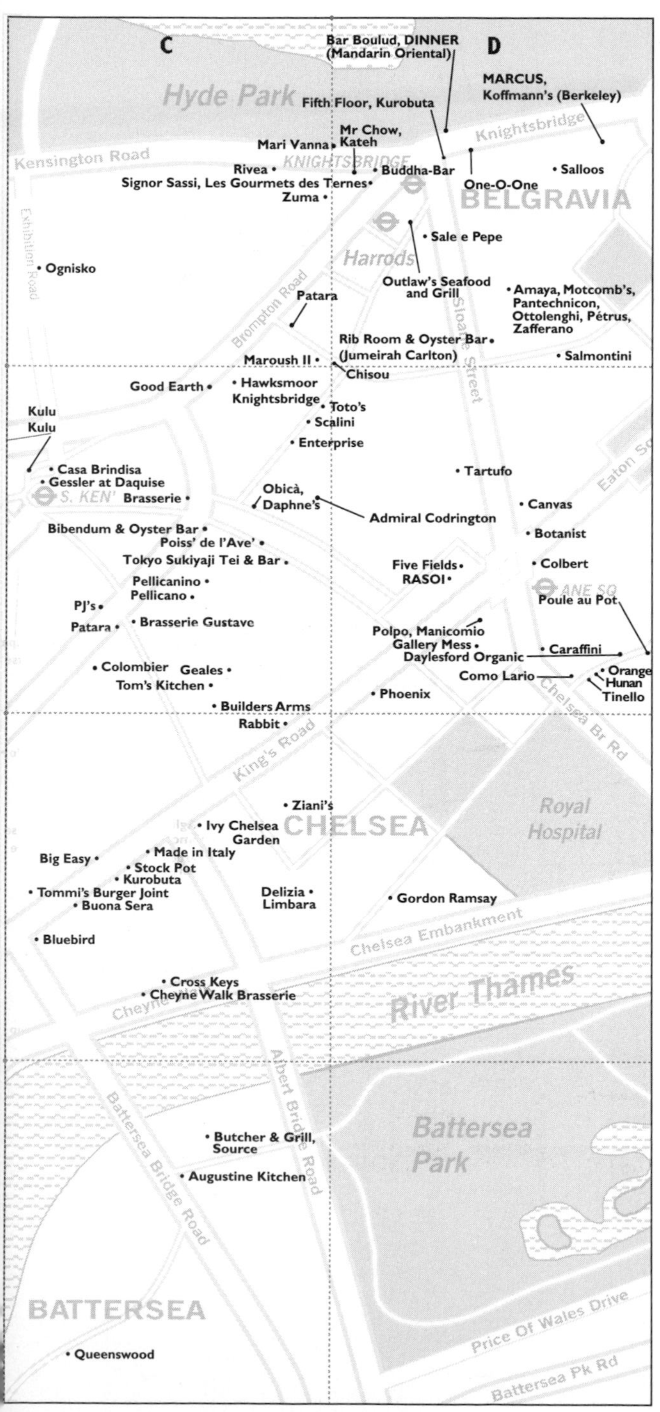

MAP 6 – NOTTING HILL & BAYSWATER

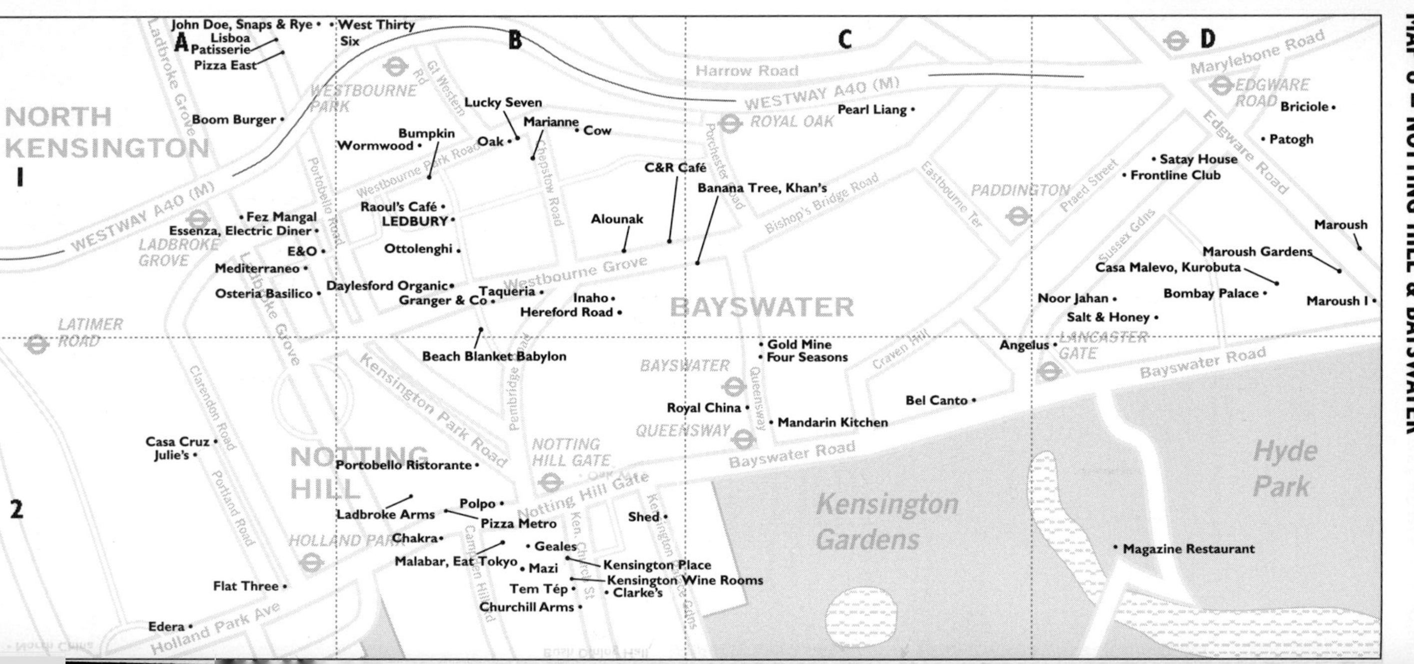

MAP 7 – HAMMERSMITH & CHISWICK

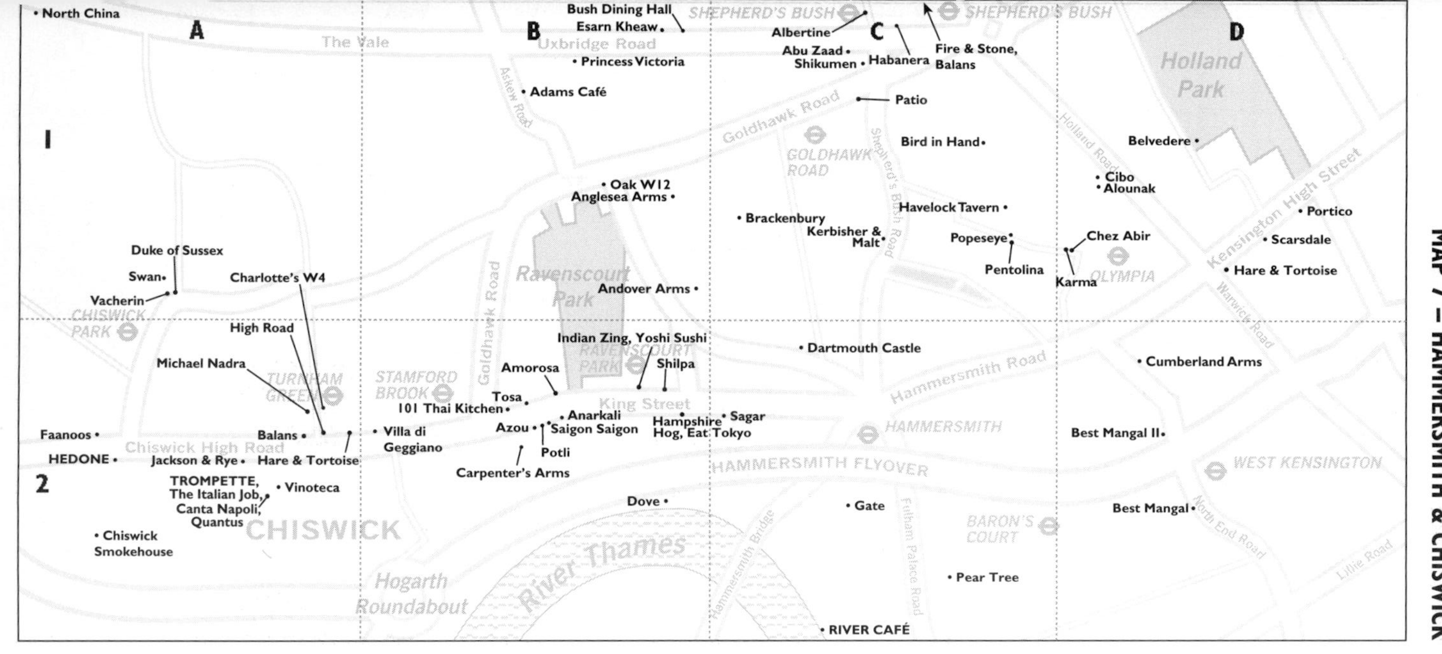

MAP 8 – HAMPSTEAD, CAMDEN TOWN & ISLINGTON

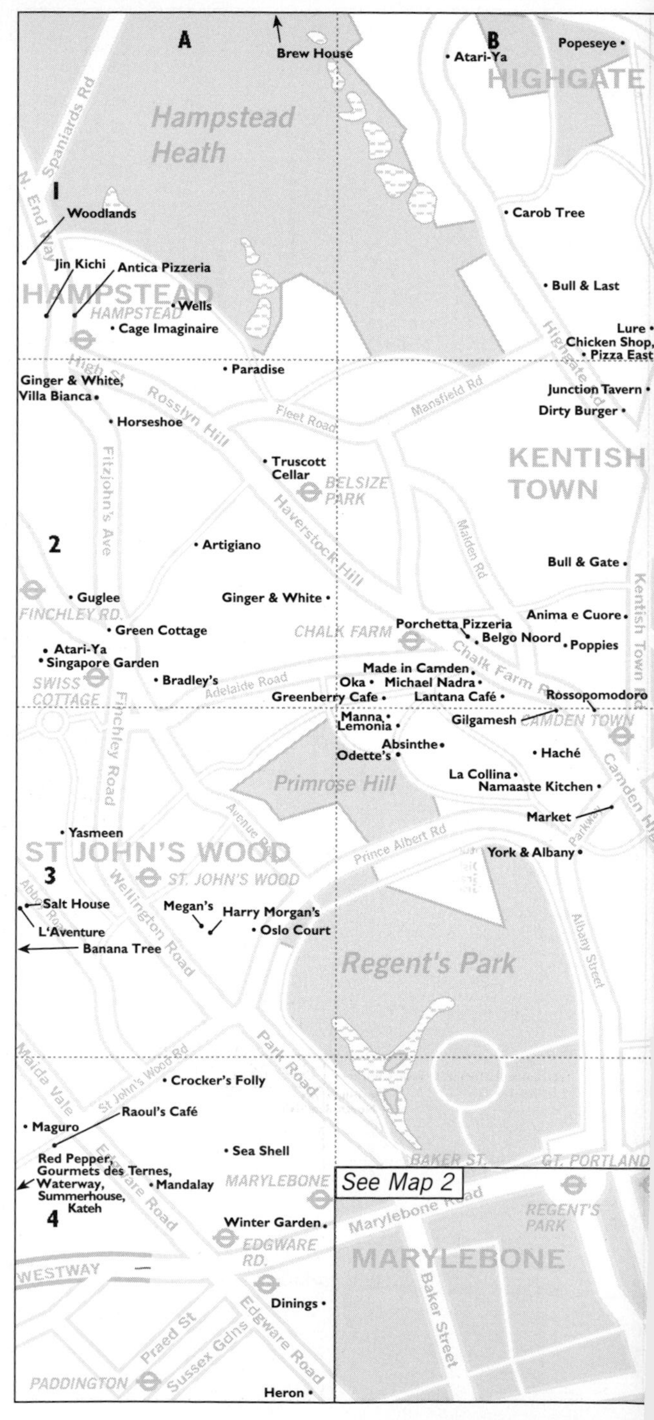

A
B
1
2
3
4
Brew House
Atari-Ya
Popeseye
HIGHGATE
Hampstead Heath
Spaniards Rd
N. End Way
Woodlands
Carob Tree
Jin Kichi
Antica Pizzeria
Bull & Last
HAMPSTEAD
Wells
Cage Imaginaire
Lure
Chicken Shop,
Pizza East
Highgate Rd
High St
Paradise
Ginger & White,
Villa Bianca
Mansfield Rd
Junction Tavern
Rosslyn Hill
Fleet Road
Dirty Burger
Horseshoe
KENTISH TOWN
Truscott Cellar
BELSIZE PARK
Fitzjohn's Ave
Haverstock Hill
Malden Rd
Artigiano
Bull & Gate
Kentish Town Rd
Guglee
Ginger & White
FINCHLEY RD.
Anima e Cuore
Porchetta Pizzeria
CHALK FARM
Green Cottage
Belgo Noord
Poppies
Atari-Ya
Chalk Farm Rd
Singapore Garden
Made in Camden
SWISS COTTAGE
Bradley's
Adelaide Road
Oka
Michael Nadra
Greenberry Cafe
Lantana Café
Rossopomodoro
Manna
Lemonia
Gilgamesh
CAMDEN TOWN
Finchley Road
Absinthe
Odette's
Haché
Primrose Hill
La Collina
Namaaste Kitchen
Camden High St
Market
Avenue Rd
Parkway
Yasmeen
Prince Albert Rd
York & Albany
ST JOHN'S WOOD
ST. JOHN'S WOOD
Wellington Road
Albany Street
Salt House
Megan's
Harry Morgan's
L'Aventure
Oslo Court
Banana Tree
Regent's Park
Park Road
Maida Vale
St John's Wood Rd
Crocker's Folly
Raoul's Café
Maguro
Sea Shell
Red Pepper,
Gourmets des Ternes,
Waterway,
Summerhouse,
Kateh
Mandalay
MARYLEBONE
BAKER ST.
GT. PORTLAND
See Map 2
Edgware Road
Marylebone Road
REGENT'S PARK
Winter Garden
EDGWARE RD.
MARYLEBONE
WESTWAY
Baker Street
Dinings
Praed St
Sussex Gdns
Edgware Road
PADDINGTON
Heron

MAP 8 – HAMPSTEAD, CAMDEN TOWN & ISLINGTON

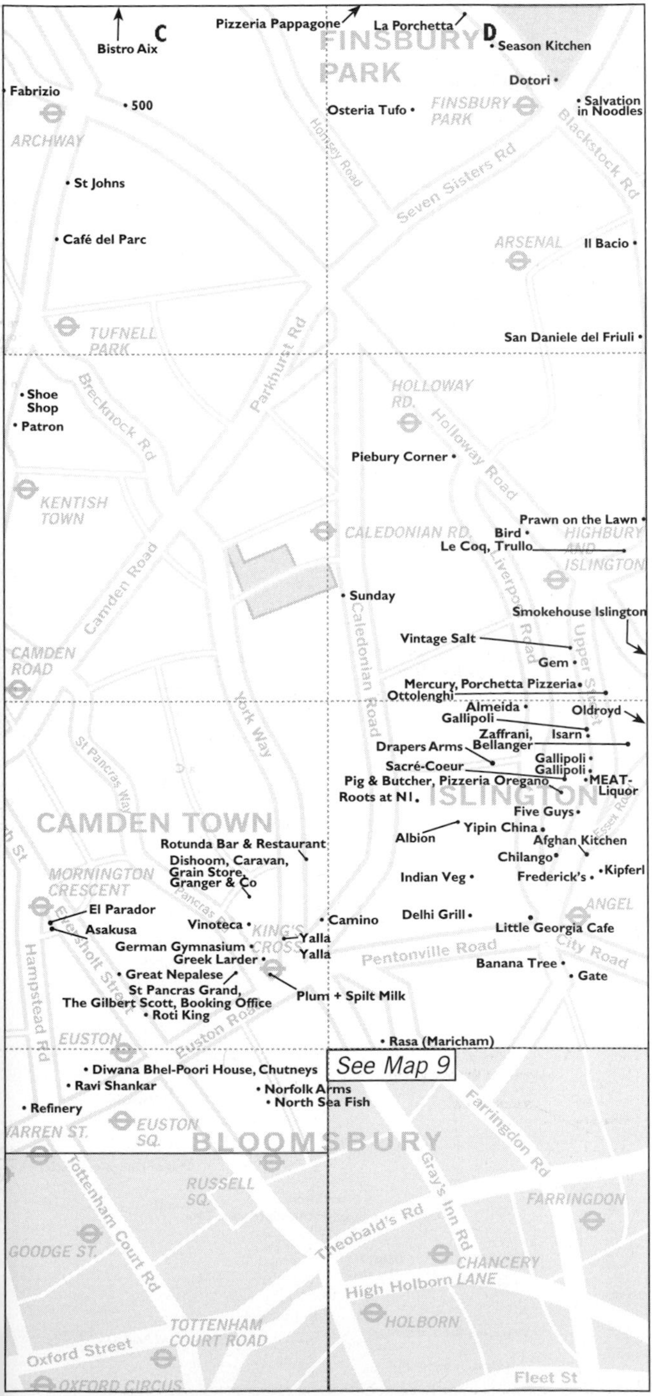

Bistro Aix
C
Pizzeria Pappagone
La Porchetta
D
FINSBURY PARK
Season Kitchen
Dotori
Fabrizio
500
Osteria Tufo
FINSBURY PARK
Salvation in Noodles
ARCHWAY
Hornsey Road
Blackstock Rd
Seven Sisters Rd
St Johns
Café del Parc
ARSENAL
Il Bacio
TUFNELL PARK
Parkhurst Rd
San Daniele del Friuli
Shoe Shop
Patron
Brecknock Rd
HOLLOWAY RD.
Holloway Road
Piebury Corner
KENTISH TOWN
Prawn on the Lawn
CALEDONIAN RD.
Bird
HIGHBURY AND ISLINGTON
Le Coq, Trullo
Camden Road
Liverpool Road
Sunday
Caledonian Road
Smokehouse Islington
Vintage Salt
Upper Street
CAMDEN ROAD
Gem
Mercury, Porchetta Pizzeria
Ottolenghi
Almeida
Oldroyd
Gallipoli
York Way
Zaffrani, Bellanger
Isarn
Drapers Arms
St Pancras Way
Gallipoli
Sacré-Coeur
Gallipoli
Pig & Butcher, Pizzeria Oregano
MEAT-Liquor
Roots at N1
ISLINGTON
Essex Rd
Five Guys
CAMDEN TOWN
Albion
Yipin China
Rotunda Bar & Restaurant
Afghan Kitchen
Dishoom, Caravan, Grain Store, Granger & Co
Chilango
MORNINGTON CRESCENT
Indian Veg
Frederick's
Kipferl
Pancras Rd
ANGEL
El Parador
Camino
Delhi Grill
Asakusa
Vinoteca
KING'S CROSS
Yalla
Little Georgia Cafe
German Gymnasium
Yalla
Pentonville Road
City Road
Greek Larder
Eversholt Street
Banana Tree
Great Nepalese
Gate
Hampstead Rd
St Pancras Grand, The Gilbert Scott, Booking Office
Plum + Spilt Milk
Roti King
Euston Road
EUSTON
Rasa (Maricham)
Diwana Bhel-Poori House, Chutneys
See Map 9
Ravi Shankar
Norfolk Arms
North Sea Fish
Farringdon Rd
Refinery
EUSTON SQ.
WARREN ST.
BLOOMSBURY
Gray's Inn Rd
RUSSELL SQ.
Tottenham Court Rd
FARRINGDON
Theobald's Rd
GOODGE ST.
CHANCERY LANE
High Holborn
HOLBORN
TOTTENHAM COURT ROAD
Oxford Street
OXFORD CIRCUS
Fleet St

MAP 9 – THE CITY

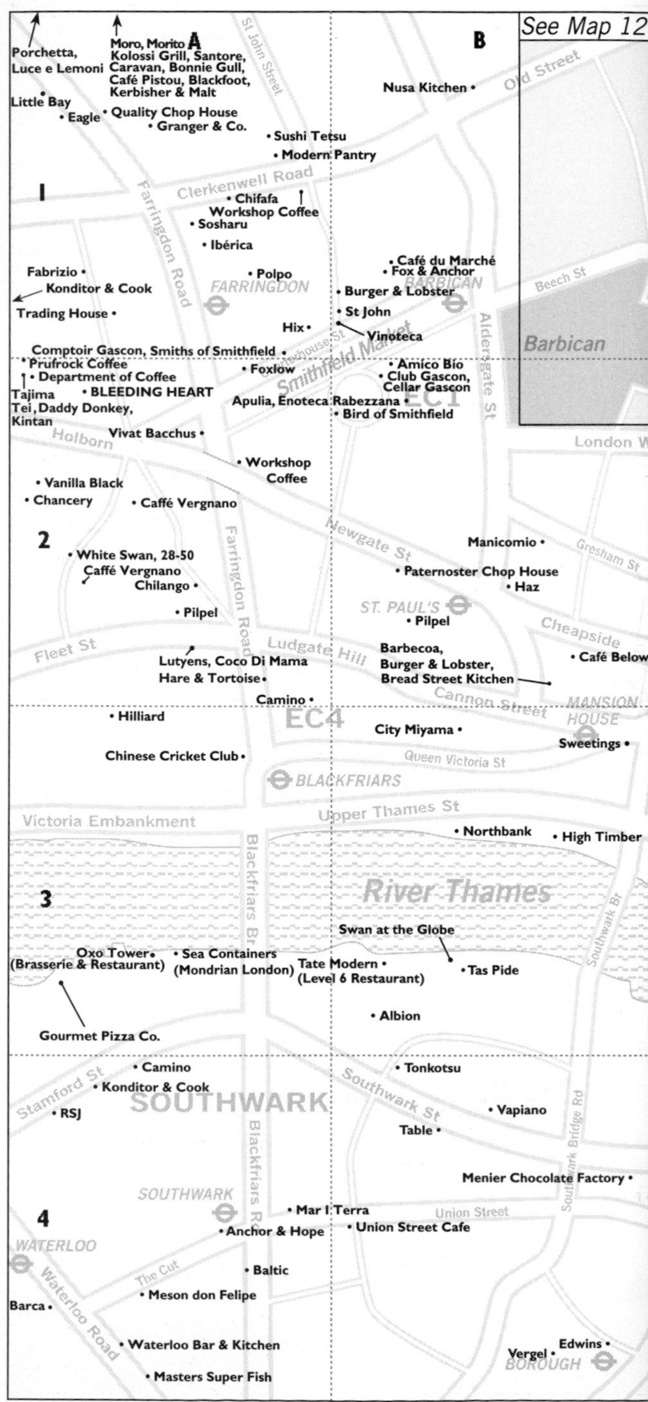

See Map 12
A
B
1
2
3
4
Porchetta,
Luce e Lemoni
Moro, Morito
Kolossi Grill, Santore,
Caravan, Bonnie Gull,
Café Pistou, Blackfoot,
Kerbisher & Malt
Little Bay
Eagle
Quality Chop House
Granger & Co.
Nusa Kitchen
Old Street
St John Street
Sushi Tetsu
Modern Pantry
Clerkenwell Road
Chifafa
Workshop Coffee
Sosharu
Ibérica
Farringdon Road
Café du Marché
Fox & Anchor
Fabrizio
Konditor & Cook
Polpo
FARRINGDON
BARBICAN
Beech St
Burger & Lobster
Trading House
St John
Hix
Vinoteca
Barbican
Comptoir Gascon, Smiths of Smithfield
Prufrock Coffee
Department of Coffee
Foxlow
Charterhouse St
Smithfield Market
Amico Bio
Club Gascon,
Cellar Gascon
Aldersgate St
Tajima
Tei, Daddy Donkey,
Kintan
BLEEDING HEART
Apulia, Enoteca Rabezzana
EC1
Bird of Smithfield
Holborn
Vivat Bacchus
London Wall
Workshop
Coffee
Vanilla Black
Chancery
Caffé Vergnano
Newgate St
Manicomio
Gresham St
White Swan, 28-50
Caffé Vergnano
Chilango
Paternoster Chop House
Haz
ST. PAUL'S
Pilpel
Pilpel
Cheapside
Fleet St
Ludgate Hill
Barbecoa,
Burger & Lobster,
Bread Street Kitchen
Café Below
Lutyens, Coco Di Mama
Hare & Tortoise
Camino
Cannon Street
MANSION
HOUSE
Hilliard
EC4
City Miyama
Sweetings
Chinese Cricket Club
Queen Victoria St
BLACKFRIARS
Upper Thames St
Victoria Embankment
Northbank
High Timber
Blackfriars Br
River Thames
Southwark Br
Swan at the Globe
Oxo Tower
(Brasserie & Restaurant)
Sea Containers
(Mondrian London)
Tate Modern
(Level 6 Restaurant)
Tas Pide
Albion
Gourmet Pizza Co.
Camino
Tonkotsu
Stamford St
Konditor & Cook
SOUTHWARK
Southwark St
RSJ
Vapiano
Table
Southwark Bridge Rd
Blackfriars Rd
Menier Chocolate Factory
SOUTHWARK
Mar I Terra
Union Street
Union Street Cafe
Anchor & Hope
WATERLOO
The Cut
Baltic
Waterloo Road
Meson don Felipe
Barca
Waterloo Bar & Kitchen
Edwins
Vergel
BOROUGH
Masters Super Fish

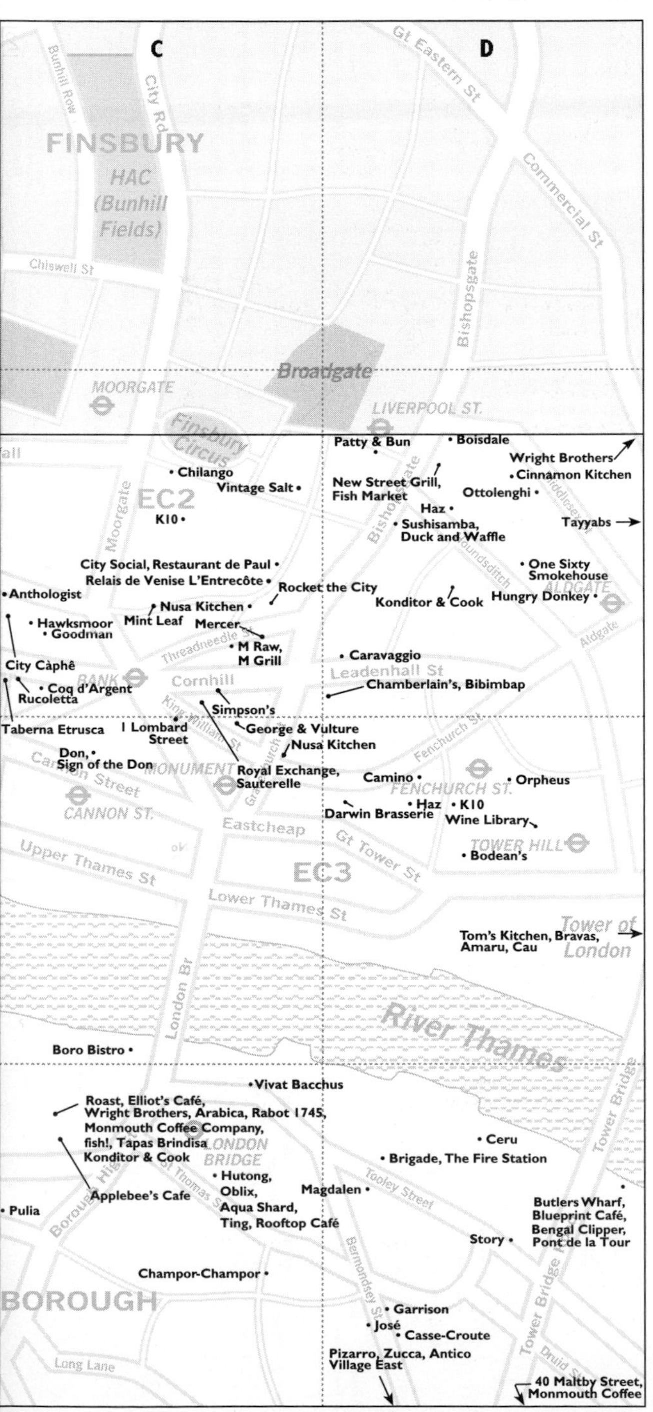
C
D
FINSBURY
HAC (Bunhill Fields)
Broadgate
MOORGATE
LIVERPOOL ST.
Patty & Bun
Boisdale
Wright Brothers
Cinnamon Kitchen
Chilango
Vintage Salt
New Street Grill, Fish Market
Ottolenghi
EC2
K10
Haz
Sushisamba, Duck and Waffle
Tayyabs
City Social, Restaurant de Paul
Relais de Venise L'Entrecôte
Rocket the City
One Sixty Smokehouse
Anthologist
Nusa Kitchen
Mint Leaf
Konditor & Cook
Hungry Donkey
ALDGATE
Hawksmoor
Goodman
Mercer
M Raw, M Grill
City Càphê
Caravaggio
BANK
Coq d'Argent
Rucoletta
Chamberlain's, Bibimbap
Simpson's
Taberna Etrusca
1 Lombard Street
George & Vulture
Nusa Kitchen
Don, Sign of the Don
MONUMENT
Royal Exchange, Sauterelle
Camino
Orpheus
CANNON ST.
FENCHURCH ST.
Haz
K10
Darwin Brasserie
Wine Library
TOWER HILL
Bodean's
EC3
Tom's Kitchen, Bravas, Amaru, Cau
Tower of London
River Thames
Boro Bistro
Vivat Bacchus
Roast, Elliot's Café, Wright Brothers, Arabica, Rabot 1745, Monmouth Coffee Company, fish!, Tapas Brindisa Konditor & Cook
LONDON BRIDGE
Ceru
Brigade, The Fire Station
Hutong, Oblix, Aqua Shard, Ting, Rooftop Café
Magdalen
Applebee's Cafe
Pulia
Butlers Wharf, Blueprint Café, Bengal Clipper, Pont de la Tour
Story
Champor-Champor
BOROUGH
Garrison
José
Casse-Croute
Pizarro, Zucca, Antico Village East
40 Maltby Street, Monmouth Coffee
Bunhill Row
City Rd
Gt Eastern St
Commercial St
Bishopsgate
Chiswell St
Finsbury Circus
Moorgate
Threadneedle St
Cornhill
Leadenhall St
King William St
Fenchurch St
Cannon Street
Eastcheap
Gt Tower St
Upper Thames St
Lower Thames St
London Br
Tooley Street
Borough High St
St Thomas St
Bermondsey St
Tower Bridge
Tower Bridge Rd
Long Lane

MAP 10 – SOUTH LONDON (& FULHAM)

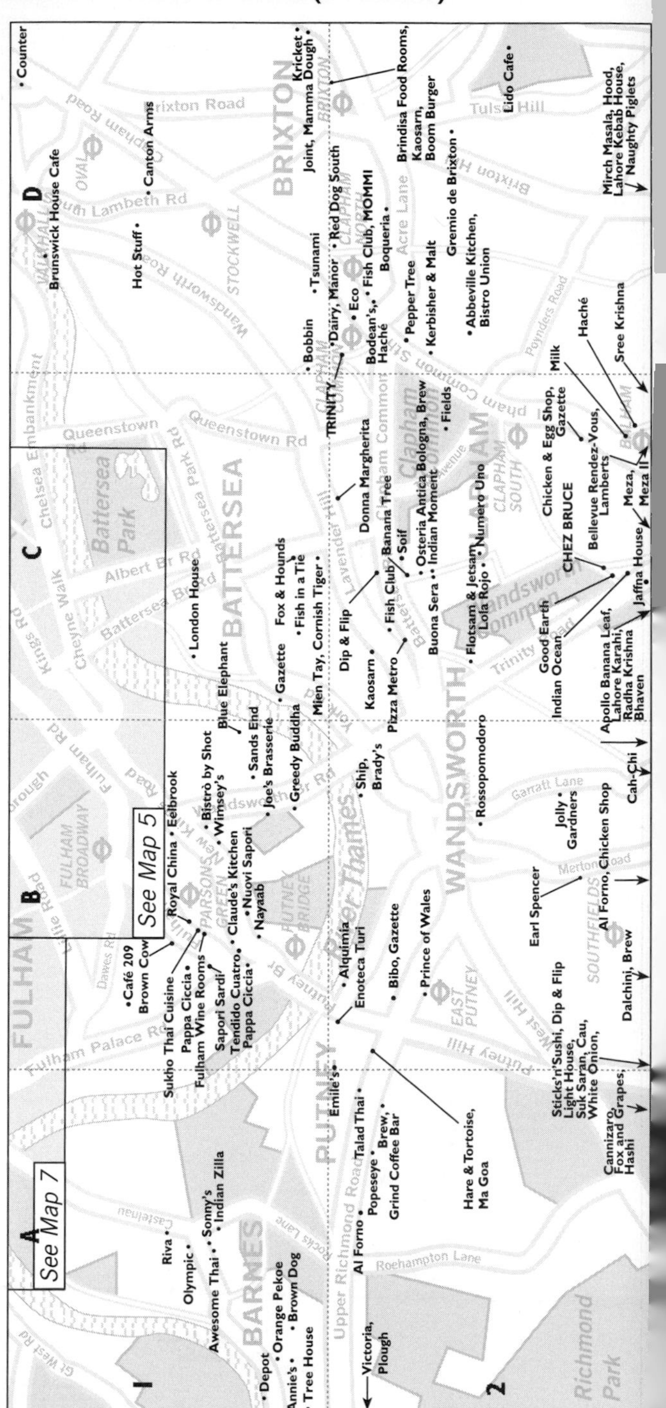

MAP 11 – EAST END & DOCKLANDS

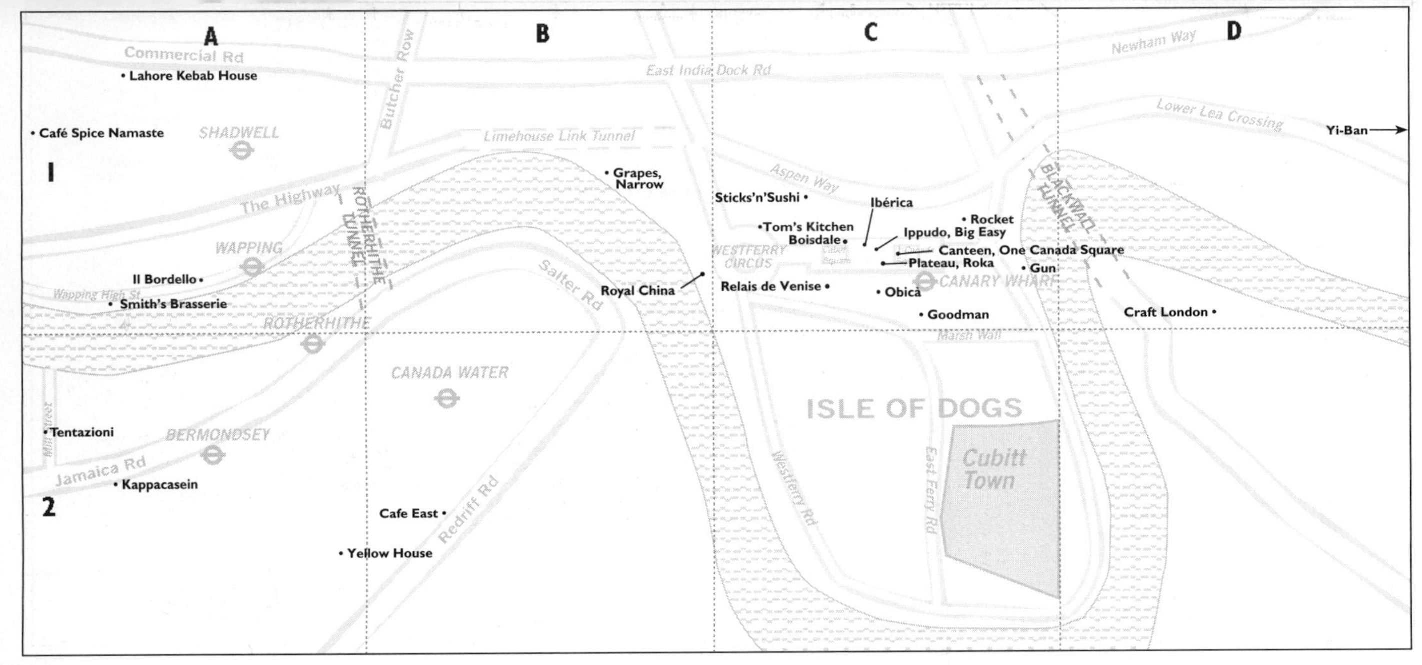

MAP 12 – SHOREDITCH & BETHNAL GREEN

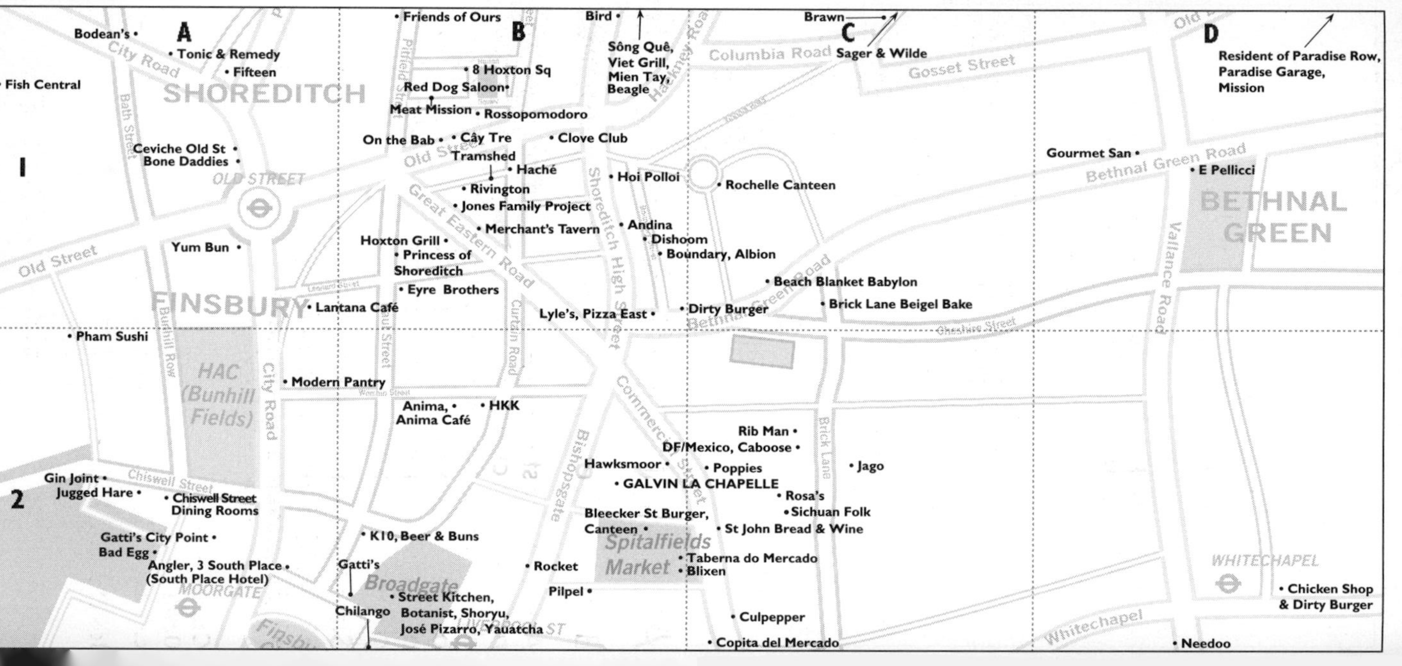
A
B
C
D
1
2
SHOREDITCH
FINSBURY
BETHNAL GREEN
WHITECHAPEL
OLD STREET
MOORGATE
Spitalfields Market
Broadgate
HAC (Bunhill Fields)
City Road
Bath Street
Old Street
Bunhill Row
Chiswell Street
Pitfield Street
Great Eastern Road
Curtain Road
Shoreditch High Street
Bishopsgate
Commercial Street
Brick Lane
Cheshire Street
Columbia Road
Hackney Road
Gosset Street
Bethnal Green Road
Vallance Road
Whitechapel
• Fish Central
Bodean's •
• Tonic & Remedy
• Fifteen
Ceviche Old St •
Bone Daddies •
Yum Bun •
• Pham Sushi
Gin Joint •
Jugged Hare •
• Chiswell Street Dining Rooms
Gatti's City Point •
Bad Egg •
Angler, 3 South Place •
(South Place Hotel)
• Friends of Ours
• 8 Hoxton Sq
Red Dog Saloon •
Meat Mission • Rossopomodoro
On the Bab • • Cây Tre
Tramshed
• Haché
• Clove Club
• Rivington
• Jones Family Project
• Merchant's Tavern
Hoxton Grill •
• Princess of Shoreditch
• Eyre Brothers
• Lantana Café
• Modern Pantry
Anima, • Anima Café
• HKK
• K10, Beer & Buns
Gatti's
• Street Kitchen, Botanist, Shoryu, José Pizarro, Yauatcha
Chilango
• Rocket
Pilpel •
Lyle's, Pizza East •
Bird •
Sông Quê, Viet Grill, Mien Tay, Beagle
• Hoi Polloi
• Andina
• Dishoom
• Boundary, Albion
• Dirty Burger
• Rochelle Canteen
• Beach Blanket Babylon
• Brick Lane Beigel Bake
Brawn
Sager & Wilde
• Jago
Rib Man •
DF/Mexico, Caboose •
Hawksmoor •
• Poppies
• GALVIN LA CHAPELLE
• Rosa's
• Sichuan Folk
Bleecker St Burger, Canteen •
• St John Bread & Wine
• Taberna do Mercado
• Blixen
• Culpepper
• Copita del Mercado
Gourmet San •
• E Pellicci
Resident of Paradise Row, Paradise Garage, Mission
• Chicken Shop & Dirty Burger
• Needoo

Take your love of food further

ACTION AGAINST HUNGER

Because those who love food, give food

Action Against Hunger works with hundreds of restaurants across the UK with one aim: to end child hunger worldwide. Be part of something bigger and take your love of food further. Find out why we are the food and drink industry's charity of choice.

Save lives whilst gaining:

- Positive PR and Marketing
- Employee engagement
- Customer satisfaction

Caroline Dyer
0208 293 6133
c.dyer@actionagainsthunger.org.uk

lovefoodgivefood.org

In association with:

Registered charity No. 1047501